D0198099

RELIGION TODAY: TRADITION, MODERNITY AND CHANGE

GLOBAL RELIGIOUS MOVEMENTS IN REGIONAL CONTEXT

WITHDRAWN FROM
THE LIBRARY

UNIVERSITY OF
WINCHESTER

KA 0263005 2

Religion Today: Tradition, Modernity and Change – an Open University/Ashgate series

The five textbooks and Reader that make up this series are:

- *From Sacred Text to Internet* edited by Gwilym Beckerlegge
- *Religion and Social Transformations* edited by David Herbert
- *Perspectives on Civil Religion* by Gerald Parsons
- *Global Religious Movements in Regional Context* edited by John Wolffe
- *Belief Beyond Boundaries* edited by Joanne Pearson
- *Religion Today: A Reader* edited by Susan Mumm

Each textbook includes:

- an introduction to the issues and controversies relevant to the topic under discussion
- a series of detailed case studies, which allow readers to see the theories and debates at work today in the experience of religious practitioners from various parts of the world
- extracts from other publications, which address the same issue from different perspectives (except *Perspectives on Civil Religion*)
- extensive references to other published material on the same topics
- supporting colour and black-and-white illustrations

The series offers an in-depth introduction to contemporary themes and challenges in religious studies. The contents highlight the central issues and ideas that are shaping religion today – and will continue to do so tomorrow. The textbooks contain plentiful contemporary case studies spanning many countries and religions, and integrate methods of analysis and theoretical perspectives. They work to ensure that readers will understand the relevance of methodologies to lived experience and gain the ability to transfer analytic skills and explanatory devices to the study of religion in context. The textbooks focus on the following key issues in contemporary religious studies: representation and interpretation; modernity and social change; civil religion; the impact of globalization on religion; and the growth of alternative religion.

The accompanying Reader presents primary and secondary source material structured around these core themes. It will serve as an invaluable resource book, whether used to accompany the textbooks in the series or not.

Cover. (clockwise from top left) A street scene in Dewsbury, Yorkshire, near the Markazi Mosque, headquarters of the Tablighi Jama'at in the UK. © Asadour Guzelian; The Taisekaji temple complex, at the foot of Mount Fujii, before its destruction. © 2000 by Daisanbunmei-sha, Inc.; The spectacular Crystal Cathedral in Garden Grove, California, led by Robert H. Schuller. © Steve McCurry/Magnum; An Evangelical banner in a São Paulo street proclaims a confident expectation of conquering the world for Jesus Christ. © Tony Morrison/South American Pictures; A Soka Gakkai *butsudan* containing the *gohonzon*. Courtesy of Soka Gakkai International-UK Publications Department; A Christian Coalition Faith and Freedom (anti-abortion/pro-life) rally at the Republican Convention in San Diego, California in 1996. Mark Peterson/Saba/ Network.

RELIGION TODAY: TRADITION, MODERNITY AND CHANGE

GLOBAL RELIGIOUS MOVEMENTS IN REGIONAL CONTEXT

EDITED BY JOHN WOLFFE

Ashgate

in association with

The Open
University

This publication forms part of an Open University course AD317 *Religion Today: Tradition, Modernity and Change*. Details of this and other Open University courses can be obtained from the Call Centre, PO Box 724, The Open University, Milton Keynes MK7 6ZS, United Kingdom: tel. +44 (0)1908 653231, e-mail ces-gen@open.ac.uk

Alternatively, you may visit the Open University web site at http://www.open.ac.uk where you can learn more about the wide range of courses and packs offered at all levels by the Open University.

To purchase this publication or other components of Open University courses, contact Open University Worldwide Ltd, The Berrill Building, Walton Hall, Milton Keynes MK7 6AA, United Kingdom: tel. +44 (0)1908 858785; fax +44 (0)1908 858787; e-mail ouwenq@open.ac.uk; web site http://www.ouw.co.uk

British Library Cataloguing in Publication Data

Global religious movements in regional context – (Religion today : tradition, modernity and change ; v. 4)
  1. Relgions
  I. Wolffe, John   II. Open University
  291

Library of Congress Control Number: 2001053653

The Open University
Walton Hall
Milton Keynes MK7 6AA

Ashgate Publishing Ltd
Gower House, Croft Road
Aldershot, Hants GU11 3HR

Ashgate Publishing Company
Burlington, VT 05401-5600
USA

Ashgate web site: http://www.ashgate.com

KING ALFRED'S COLLEGE
WINCHESTER

291
WOL   0263005?

First published 2002.

Copyright © 2002 The Open University

All rights reserved. No part of this publication may be reproduced, stored in a retrieval system, transmitted or utilized in any form or by any means, electronic, mechanical, photocopying, recording or otherwise, without written permission from the publisher or a licence from the Copyright Licensing Agency Ltd. Details of such licences (for reprographic reproduction) may be obtained from the Copyright Licensing Agency Ltd of 90 Tottenham Court Road, London W1P 0LP.

Edited, designed and typeset by The Open University.

Printed and bound in the United Kingdom by The Bath Press, Bath.

ISBN 0 7546 0747 X (hbk)
ISBN 0 7546 0819 0 (pbk)

Contents

Preface

Global Religious Movements in Regional Context is the fourth of a five-volume series entitled *Religion Today: Tradition, Modernity and Change*, published by Ashgate Publishing Ltd in association with The Open University. Like all the volumes in the series, *Global Religious Movements in Regional Context* has been compiled primarily with the needs of Open University undergraduate students in mind. However, it is hoped that the contents of the volume will also be of interest and value to other readers who would like to know more about the place of religion in the world today.

The authors have benefited greatly from the careful and constructive comments on the first drafts of their chapters by Professor Kim Knott of the University of Leeds (external assessor), Professor Ken Thompson of the Faculty of Social Sciences at The Open University (reader) and Dr Claire Disbrey (tutor consultant). Any inaccuracies or questionable judgements are the responsibilities of the authors alone. Thanks are also due to the writers and publishers who permitted the texts to be reprinted in Part Two of the volume.

The authors wish to acknowledge the contribution made to the production of this volume by: Adrian Roberts (course manager), Julie Bennett, Kate Clements and Peter Wright (editors), Paul Smith (picture researcher), Richard Hoyle (designer) and Pip Harris (compositor).

The authors of the three chapters in the volume are:

- John Wolffe Department of Religious Studies at The Open University
- Helen Waterhouse Department of Religious Studies at The Open University
- Sophie Gilliat-Ray Cardiff Research Fellow, Department of Religious and Theological Studies at Cardiff University

Introduction

From their very origins most religions have professed to teach truths and modes of living that are relevant to the whole of humankind. For some – notably Judaism, Sikhism and Hinduism – the impulse to a global coverage has been qualified by identification with particular ethnic groups or geographical territory, but even these traditions have in practice been widely spread across the world by the migrations of their adherents. Other traditions, however – notably Buddhism, Christianity and Islam, which form the particular subject of this book – while sharing in this diaspora of peoples, have also been purposeful in spreading their distinctive beliefs and practices, which are held to be applicable in all parts of the world, irrespective of location and ethnicity. Thus, in the early centuries of their existences, Buddhism spread from its north Indian origins into much of south, east and south-east Asia; Christianity from Palestine around the Mediterranean, into western Europe, south India and north-eastern Africa; and Islam from Arabia to much of west and south Asia and to eastern and southern Europe. In the last five centuries, Christianity has expanded around the globe, becoming predominant in the Americas, Australasia and the Philippines, and establishing a more or less influential presence in the other countries of Asia and sub-Saharan Africa (Freston, 2001). Buddhism and Islam have also significantly extended their geographical range, both traditions in Europe and North America, and Islam in Africa.

It is worth at the outset reminding the reader of these common-places of universal religious history because they provide an essential perspective for the consideration of global religious movements in the contemporary world. There is nothing new about the global aspirations and international spread of religions, and 'overall processes of globalization ... are at least as old as the rise of the so-called world religions two thousand and more years ago' (Robertson, 1992, pp.6–7). During the late nineteenth and the twentieth centuries, however, a much stronger secular sense of global identity has developed and has been reflected in the political, economic and cultural spheres. Physical movement around the globe has become ever easier, and communication is almost instantaneous. The associated phenomenon of globalization can be defined as 'both ... the compression of the world and the intensification of consciousness of the world as a whole' (Robertson, 1992, p.8). It is a complex process. It does not necessarily mean that the world is becoming uniform in character: indeed, its widespread corollary is a *growing* consciousness of local distinctiveness, reflected for example in nationalist movements among smaller ethnic groups. Moreover, globalization operates not only for 'modern' and secular movements, but also for 'traditional' and religious ones, even if they are themselves changed or even transformed in the process. It is with the profound implications of these processes for religion, as reflected particularly in the interplay between the global and the local, that this book is concerned.

Some of the issues can usefully be introduced by an example from each of the three religious traditions under discussion. In 1965, David Watson, a seemingly characteristic public-school and Cambridge-educated Anglican clergyman, took charge of St Cuthbert's, a run-down church with a tiny congregation beside the historic city walls of York, in northern England. (For details of Watson's life, see Saunders and Samson, 1992.) His beliefs in the objective truth of traditional Christian teaching regarding the incarnation, death and resurrection of Jesus Christ, and in the continuing authoritative status of the Bible as a basis for Christian life in the modern world, appeared to set him against the cultural and intellectual tide. Moreover, he was also increasingly an advocate of the expression of Charismatic gifts of the Spirit in the contemporary church. The Charismatic movement derived most immediately from an Episcopalian congregation at Van Nuys in California, and appeared to be very much at odds with rational modernity. Nevertheless, Watson's ministry in York flourished; by 1969, St Cuthbert's, which seated 200 people, was so overcrowded that two morning services became necessary, and in 1973, the congregation moved to the much larger building of St Michael-le-Belfrey, beside York Minster. During the ensuing decade, the 800-seat capacity of that building was also to be tested to the limits (Figure 1). Such success was very much against the trend of steeply declining church attendance in the UK as a whole, and attracted widespread interest.

By 1980, Watson's reputation had spread far outside the UK, and he was travelling widely to many parts of the world, including South Africa, Canada, Australia and New Zealand. Varied responses were indicative of differences of cultural context: for example, he was received with great enthusiasm at Fuller Seminary in California, but judged his mission in Durban, South Africa to have been 'frankly a disaster' (Saunders and Samson, 1992). His career, cut short by his premature death in 1984, thus reflects the growth of Evangelical Christianity in the later twentieth century. As John Wolffe shows in

Figure 1 David Watson with members of his congregation outside St Michael-le-Belfrey, York in 1982. © *Yorkshire Evening Press*, York.

Chapter 1 of this book, it has gathered momentum in the face of general Christian decline in the UK, has re-established itself as a major cultural, social and political force in the USA, and is growing rapidly in Latin America and other parts of the Third World. Its character varies across the world, formed by the interplay between local traditional religious and social structures, and rapid and extensive global interconnection.

In 1975, just as Watson was reaching the height of his influence in the Evangelical world, another apparently conventional Englishman, Richard Causton, an ex-army officer and businessman, became General Director of what was then Nichiren Shoshu UK. This was a branch of the international Soka Gakkai Buddhist movement, analysed by Helen Waterhouse in Chapter 2, which had originated in Japan in the 1940s, inspired by an ideology dating back to the thirteenth century. Over the next 20 years, Causton led the growth of the movement in the UK, which by the time of his death in 1995 had approximately 6500 adherents. Here, as in the USA and elsewhere, although starting from a base among Japanese expatriates, the Soka Gakkai successfully recruited from among the indigenous population. In all, it claims to be represented in 163 countries. Rooted as it is in centuries-old Japanese religious tradition, the Soka Gakkai might, like Watson's Evangelical Christianity, appear an unlikely candidate for widespread global acceptance in the contemporary world. Its focal mantra is chanted in ancient Japanese and its foundation doctrines have developed within the Buddhist world. Nevertheless, it too has spread impressively fast, having a presence in every continent and readily adapting to diverse cultural settings (Figure 2).

Adaptation, however, does not always occur, and when it does not the consequences can be explosive. Salman Rushdie's novel, *The Satanic Verses*, published in the UK in 1988, insightfully evokes the ways in which globalization and migration can be solvents of traditional religious and cultural identity. Paradoxically, though, the aftermath of the novel's publication dramatically illustrated the countervailing tendency for conservative religion to reassert itself in a globalized world. In February 1989, the Iranian political and spiritual leader Ayatollah Khomeini issued a *fatwa* (an authoritative interpretation of Islamic law) condemning the book as a blasphemy against Islam, and its British author as an apostate who was subject to the

Figure 2 A Soka Gakkai member chants in front of the *gohonzon*: a similar picture might have been taken anywhere in the world. Courtesy of Soka Gakkai International-UK Publications Department/*UK Express*.

death penalty. Khomeini's action needs to be understood in the specific context of his failing health (he died in June 1989) and his consequent anxiety to reinforce the imprint of his own uncompromising radicalism on the Iranian revolution. The aftermath, however, resounded around the world, stirring some Muslims to riot against the book, and western liberals to agonize over how best to tolerate Muslim minorities they perceived as intolerant (Figure 3).

In an earlier age, slow and fragmentary communication would have been likely to have taken much of the heat out of the affair. At the end of the twentieth century, the confrontation between two radically different religious and cultural systems was immediate and intense, and tended for a while to drown out more moderate voices on both sides. The affair also shows how media coverage of the actions of a particular individual – Khomeini – could make him for a time the apparently pre-eminent global representative of a religious tradition, despite the limitation of his direct authority to a particular sub-tradition and national context (cf. Beyer, 1994, pp.1–3).

The reality is that, as Sophie Gilliat-Ray demonstrates in Chapter 3, the range of interactions between Islam and the contemporary world, like those of Christianity and Buddhism, shows considerable variety. Contrary to western popular stereotypes – admittedly reinforced by extreme cases such as the Taliban in Afghanistan – Muslims are not

Figure 3 Burning of *The Satanic Verses* in Bradford. Copyright Asadour Guzelian.

called to the authoritarian imposition of their faith. Rather, Islam has been spread not so much by direct state action, as by a variety of governmental and non-governmental organizations, and through the settlement of Muslims in historically non-Muslim societies. The Muslim sense of belonging to a universal faith community, the *ummah*, gives Muslims a distinctive global vision, in tension with the practical need to establish a sense of local identity and integration with diverse social and political structures in various countries.

Two themes running through the material in this book merit further preliminary comment. First is the issue of adaptation and indigenization. The Soka Gakkai, Islamic movements and Evangelical Christianity show interesting differences in the way in which they handle the tension between, on the one hand, the maintenance of a consistent global identity and, on the other, the need to be responsive to local conditions. The Soka Gakkai is the only one of the three to have an explicit doctrine of 'adapting the precepts to the locality' (*zuiho bini*), although, as Gilliat-Ray shows, implicit in an authentically Islamic concept of *da'wah* (invitation) is a sensitivity to societal context and the views of non-Muslims. A similar tendency is evident in the practice of Evangelical and Pentecostal Christianity, albeit in tension (as in Islam) with a rhetoric that tends to emphasize the timelessness and universality of its teachings. Within the relatively small-scale framework of the Soka Gakkai, adaptations necessary for effective indigenization can be formally negotiated between local organizations and the Japanese leadership. In Islam and Evangelical Christianity, no such mechanisms exist, and the ongoing consequences are unresolved tensions and organizational fragmentation and instability. The balance of power between the global and the regional is, however, different in these two traditions. International Islamic organizations have, as Gilliat-Ray shows, widespread global support and an extensive influence. In Evangelical Christianity there is no equivalent to the convergence of one million Tablighi Jama'at preachers on Raiwind in Pakistan every autumn, nor indeed to the annual *hajj* to Mecca. Evangelicalism is a true child of Reformation Protestantism in respect of its suspicion of the authoritarian internationalist religious direction historically associated with the Roman Catholic Church. As Wolffe shows, Evangelicalism is strongly globalized insofar as widely separated geographical contexts can have a profound impact on each other, but the flows of this globalization are more polycentric than their Islamic counterparts and local manifestations are highly responsive to their surrounding culture. Herein may lie a key reason for the contemporary ability of Evangelical and Pentecostal Christianity to grow more strongly than

Islam in regions and among ethnic groups that lie beyond and outside its historic patterns of adherence.

Second, what are the implications of these movements for our understanding of the relationship between religion and modernization, and of the validity of the secularization hypothesis? Certainly, it is evident that religion can and does thrive in both modernizing and modernized societies. The latest technology is being used to promote the message of religion, even in otherwise backward parts of Africa and Latin America. Religious organizations are effective in advancing the kind of socialization that can facilitate economic advance and the building of civil society. Since the Second World War, the growth of the Soka Gakkai in Japan and the resurgence of Evangelicalism in the UK and the USA are important parallel examples of the ability of religious groups to regain ground in advanced industrial societies. In a globalized world, moreover, movements of religious growth and revival in one region or country are likely rapidly to have an impact elsewhere. It is true that in many countries functions such as education, health care and social welfare have moved outside religious control, limiting religion more to the private sphere, but it still retains considerable potential as a cultural resource (Beyer, 1994, p.97).[1]

In Chapter 1 of this book, these issues are explored in an extended case study of Evangelical and Pentecostal Christianity. Within the developed north Atlantic world, marked contrasts exist between the UK and the USA, thus illustrating alternative potentialities for religion in an environment of modernity. It is in the developing world, however, that Evangelicalism and Pentecostalism are growing most strongly: attention is focused on Latin America, but it is suggested that trends analysed there are also relevant to Africa and Asia. The case study illustrates the flexibility of the tradition and its capacity to be effective in widely varying locations. Indeed, the view from the southern hemisphere calls into question the conventional Anglo-American conception of Evangelicalism as carried outwards by missionaries from its original north Atlantic heartlands. The movement has established itself and spread in many and diverse ways, and its success in the Third World is founded on its ability to appear truly indigenous rather than as a western import.

The studies of Soka Gakkai Buddhism and of Islam in Chapters 2 and 3 establish perspectives from two other major world religions and from different parts of the world. Waterhouse's account of the

---

[1] Indeed, as David Herbert shows in his study of Islam in Egypt in *From Sacred Text to Internet* (Beckerlegge, 2001), Book 1 in this series, there remain contexts in which religion has considerable social significance.

Soka Gakkai adds depth by its focus on a specific organized movement within Buddhism; Gilliat-Ray's of Islam adds breadth through its overview of the tradition as a whole. These chapters also broaden the analysis in other significant respects, in particular by confirming the impression that global religious movements are largely independent of the dominant economic, political and technological forces that drive other forms of globalization. Islam, like Pentecostalism, has indeed spread as a kind of counter-establishment, carried around the globe by dispossessed migrants, and providing a source of identity, spiritual purpose and community solidarity in otherwise alien and anonymous surroundings. The Soka Gakkai, by contrast, appears to draw its support in the West disproportionately from more élite social groups, but in so doing demonstrates its own potential to modify the secular direction of the modernizing and globalizing trends to which its adherents are particularly exposed.

The chapters specially written for this volume are supported in Part Two by a series of texts taken from a variety of other publications. Andrew Walker explores the interaction in the UK between the Charismatic movement, modernity and post-modernity, while Christian Smith provides an analysis of the reasons for relative Evangelical success in the USA. David Martin locates the growth of Latin American Pentecostalism in a broad historical and theoretical framework. The global range of Waterhouse's and Gilliat-Ray's chapters is complemented by, respectively, Daniel Métraux's study of the Soka Gakkai in south-east Asia, which explores the operation of the movement in a particular regional context, and John King's account of Tablighi Jama'at in the UK, which investigates the national and global interconnections in a particular Islamic movement. Finally, Lamin Sanneh's overview of Christianity and Islam in Africa provides explicit comparison of the 'translatability' and indigenization of the two traditions in a geographical and cultural arena that is strongly contested between them.

Collectively the material in this book shows the importance of maintaining a creative balance between global and regional study of religion. Merely local and regional approaches can miss significant interconnections, and also the comparisons and contrasts that highlight the distinctive nature of religion in particular countries. On the other hand, an exclusive emphasis on the global would risk obscuring the very considerable specificities in regional circum-stances and hence the subtleties in the global picture itself.

References

Beckerlegge, G. (ed.) (2001) *From Sacred Text to Internet*, Aldershot: Ashgate/Milton Keynes: The Open University.

Beyer, P. (1994) *Religion and Globalization*, London: Sage.

Freston, P. (2001) *Evangelicals and Politics in Asia, Africa and Latin America*, Cambridge: Cambridge University Press.

Robertson, R. (1992) *Globalization: Social Theory and Global Culture*, London: Sage.

Saunders, T. and Samson, H. (1992) *David Watson: A Biography*, London: Hodder & Stoughton.

PART ONE

CHAPTER 1

Evangelicals and Pentecostals: indigenizing a global gospel

JOHN WOLFFE

Defining and locating Evangelicals and Pentecostals

At the outset, it will be helpful to locate Evangelicals within the wider framework of Christianity. For all Christians, a central and defining aspect of their religion is the question of how one obtains knowledge of God and his purposes and hence a basis for living a Christian life in this world and attaining salvation in the world to come. Three broad channels for the reception of God's revelation to humankind are recognized: the text of the Bible, the traditions of the institutional church, and the exercise of human intellect and reason. In practice, elements of more than one of these sources of authority are usually present in the outlook of particular churches and individuals. All Christian groups will at least reverence the Bible; nearly all respect some form of church structure; only a minority wholly deny the capacity of human reason to enhance knowledge of God; in addition, many recognize the **Holy Spirit** as present in some way in the life of the contemporary church. The relative priorities given to the three sources do, however, indicate the broad characteristics of the three major tendencies within contemporary Christianity:

1 *Catholic/Eastern Orthodox* communities believe that God reveals himself primarily through the teachings and life of the institutional church.

2   *Liberal Protestant* communities believe that God is revealed primarily through the use of human reason and culture.

3   *Evangelical Protestant* communities believe that God reveals himself primarily through the text of the Bible, which is held to be uniquely inspired and authoritative. In Pentecostal and Charismatic forms of Evangelicalism, such revelation is supplemented by the guidance and inspiration of the Holy Spirit held to be present with his people today and demonstrated in spiritual gifts, such as gifts of tongues and prophecy.

It should be noted that the distinction between liberal and Evangelical Protestants is as much one that operates *within* particular institutional churches as *between* them.

The above framework presents Pentecostalism as a form of Evangelicalism, whereas some scholars (for example, Bruce, 1984, pp.5–6) see Pentecostalism as constituting a fourth category whereby direct revelation of the Holy Spirit is the primary channel for knowledge of God. In practice, however, most Pentecostals have not seen the Bible as in any way superseded by their sense of direct empowering by the Holy Spirit. Rather, they have adopted an essentially Evangelical approach to the Bible alongside their emphasis on the **gifts of the Spirit**. Indeed, Pentecostals combine these two sources of authority through their view that the power of the Holy Spirit present in the New Testament church – described particularly in the Acts of the Apostles and I Corinthians – provides a model for contemporary Christians. Moreover, the long-term history of Evangelicalism is very much intertwined with ideas and religious experience associated with Pentecostalism, a point that will be developed below. This has become particularly apparent in recent decades, especially in the UK, as Evangelicals (such as **David Watson**) have adopted many Pentecostal beliefs and practices. A distinction can hence be made between Pentecostals, who have had an institutional identity since the early twentieth century, and Charismatics (or neo-Pentecostals), who share much of their outlook but remain members of other denominations.[1] The overlapping

---

[1] The word 'Charismatic' is here used with a capital 'C' to distinguish it from other applications, such as the concept of 'charisma' put forward by the sociologist Max Weber (1864–1920) and colloquial references to 'charismatic leadership' in secular as well as religious contexts. While the focus in what follows is on Evangelical Charismatics, it should be noted that there is a significant Charismatic movement in the Roman Catholic Church and also an affinity between some Charismatics and the Eastern Orthodox Churches. The latter connection is illustrated by the conversion to Orthodoxy in 1995 of Michael Harper, formerly an Evangelical Anglican and a prominent leader of the early Charismatic movement in England (Harper, 1997).

nature of these movements means that although more narrowly focused separate consideration of them has its place, more broadly based analysis of the kind that follows here is also essential if cross-connections and influences are to be properly appreciated.

The word 'Evangelical' has acquired a diversity of usages, and it is important to be clear about its specific application in this book. It derives from the original Greek root '*evangel-*', meaning gospel, but should not be confused with the related word 'evangelist'. An evangelist is someone who proclaims the Christian message, whether the original four gospel writers, Matthew, Mark, Luke and John, or later preachers who seek converts to *any* form of Christianity, including Roman Catholicism or liberal Protestantism. In common usage, the word (and its associated adjective, evangelistic) may also be extended to those who proclaim other ideologies and beliefs. An Evangelical, on the other hand, is someone who claims to adhere to a traditional Bible-based form of Christianity, which is located, as we shall see shortly, in a particular sequence of historical movements and influences. This is the sense in which the word (with a capital 'E' in the cause of further clarity and specificity) is applied in the survey and analysis that follow.[2]

Evangelical and Pentecostal tendencies can be discerned throughout the history of Christianity, but it was only in the sixteenth century that Protestantism as a whole split from Roman Catholicism and only in the eighteenth century that a definable Evangelical movement emerged within the Protestant churches. This chronology was by no means accidental, in that the onset of modernity in the forms of the **Enlightenment** and of industrialization posed a strategic dilemma for Protestant Christians. Should they reinterpret and reformulate their traditional beliefs in the light of new approaches to knowledge

---

[2] It is useful briefly to note three other applications of the word 'Evangelical' – variously with both a small 'e' and a capital 'E' – that are in current use. First, in a continental European (and especially German) context it has historically had a broader application to all non-Roman Catholic Christians. In fact, however, the German word used in this sense is *evangelisch*, and in recent decades an alternative word, *evangelikal*, has been introduced into German to provide a translation of the specific English 'evangelical' (Geldbach, 1998, pp.156–7). Second, there is a tendency to recognize affinities of influence and religious style between Evangelical Christians and other religious and quasi-religious groups, by writing, for example, of 'Evangelical Buddhists'. In terms of strict logic such a term is nonsensical, analogous to writing of, say, a 'Roman Catholic Muslim', if it is taken as meaning that individuals or movements so described simultaneously fully adhere to two mutually incompatible systems of religious belief and practice. It may, nevertheless, provide an indication of significant behavioural resemblances. Third, there is the theologically imprecise use – frequently encountered in the secular daily press – of the word 'evangelical' when the writer actually means 'evangelistic'.

and new modes of social organization (the liberal Protestant path)? Or should they affirm the nature of Christianity as a counter-culture, upholding the Bible as a timeless revelation of God, transcending and challenging prevalent contemporary forms of thought and action (the Evangelical Protestant path)? The divide should not be over-simplified: Evangelicals have extensively engaged with the wider culture as well as confronted it, and have turned modern social structures and technology to their own advantage. Meanwhile, most liberals held on to a conviction that Christianity still offered a distinctive revelation of God that transcended the limits of contemporary culture. The essential point, however, is that Evangelicals, by origin and definition, are the radical conservatives of the Protestant religious world, upholding their perception of traditional Christian teaching and adopting an approach to secular modernity that is usually critical and can sometimes be confrontational.

The formative phase of Evangelicalism occurred in the mid-eighteenth century and was a movement that extended from central Europe in the east to the American frontier in the west, with important developments occurring in the British Isles. It is variously labelled as 'the Evangelical Revival' or 'the Great Awakening'. The Moravian Brethren, led by Count Nikolaus von Zinzendorf, provided a link with the German pietist movement of the late seventeenth century, which anticipated some of the theological and devotional emphases of Evangelicals. Under Moravian influence, **John Wesley**, an **Anglican** clergyman (Figure 1.1), was 'converted' in 1738 to distinctively Evangelical religious views. Other key early leaders in Britain were George Whitefield, also an Anglican clergyman, and Howel Harris, a Welsh layman. All became energetic itinerant preachers of the Evangelical message. Meanwhile, at Northampton, Massachusetts in the 1740s, the ministry of Jonathan Edwards, a Congregational minister, provided a central stimulus to parallel development on the other side of the Atlantic.

Together with their stress on the divinely inspired and authoritative status of the Bible, a number of other characteristic Evangelical emphases emerged from the preaching of these early leaders. There was a call to **conversion**, meaning that the response to the Evangelical message required a radical turning-point in the life of the individual. The convert was expected decisively to reject the sinfulness and materialism of his or her past life, and acknowledge utter dependence on God in seeking to live a Christian life in the future. The experience of conversion was associated with a sense of personal spiritual encounter with Jesus Christ, and a conviction that it was his ultimate self-sacrifice through death on the Cross that had appeased the wrath of God against human sin. The Evangelical

Figure 1.1 John Wesley preaching in Cornwall in 1747. Although the image is a late Victorian reconstruction, the impression of the zeal and informality of early Evangelicalism rings true. Mary Evans Picture Library.

believer thus experienced a strong sense of divine forgiveness. It followed from these central experiences and convictions that Evangelicals were possessed of a powerful zeal to share their spiritual 'blessings' with others, and to seek to transform the world around them into an environment more consistent with their understanding of divine imperatives. (It follows, therefore, that *Evangelicals* are likely to be wish to be *evangelistic* about their beliefs, but the two words need to be clearly distinguished.) One influential definition of Evangelicalism has encapsulated these characteristics in the four words biblicism, conversionism, crucicentrism (emphasis on Christ's death as an atoning sacrifice for the sins of humankind) and activism (Bebbington, 1989, pp.1–19).

During the later eighteenth and early nineteenth centuries, Evangelicals became a strong presence in nearly all the Protestant denominations in the English-speaking world, notably Anglicans, Baptists, Congregationalists and Presbyterians. (The most significant exception was the Unitarians, whose emphasis on rational religious belief, and stress on the unity of God rather than the divinity of the three persons of the Trinity, located them firmly in the liberal Protestant camp.) Evangelicalism too led to the formation of an entirely new family of denominations, the **Methodists**, which resulted from the estrangement between John Wesley and the Anglican authorities and made it impossible for the movement he founded to remain within the Church of England.

It is noteworthy that Evangelicals established themselves as a major force in Protestant Christianity at just the time when the western world was experiencing those fundamental economic and social changes known as the 'industrial revolution'. Organizational energy and flexibility equipped Evangelicals to move quickly into new and rapidly growing centres of population, while the confident certainties of their teaching had a widespread appeal to people experiencing the insecurities of migration and dislocation of traditional patterns of work and social organization. The age was also one of extensive political changes, notably American independence in the 1770s, which was followed by a period of major Evangelical advance in the 1790s. There was also significant constitutional adjustment in Britain, such as important steps towards civil equality for non-Anglican Christians, including many Evangelicals. Moreover, although the more sceptical strands of Enlightenment thought were antipathetic to Evangelicals, in other significant respects the Evangelicals assimilated the Enlightenment as well as confronting it. Within the framework set by their own presuppositions, they cultivated rational and scientific modes of thought, notably in their approach to the interpretation and application of the Bible, while treating its authoritative and divinely inspired nature as axiomatic (Noll, 1994, pp.83–107). Thus, although Evangelical supernaturalism might appear 'pre-modern', its spread was bound up with various modernizing processes.

The spread of Evangelicalism was associated particularly with movements of mass conversion known as revivals. After the initial upsurge in the mid-eighteenth century, there were repeated cycles of revival, with notable peaks of activity occurring around 1800 and in the late 1850s. Revivals were intense experiences of collective emotion, to which individuals might respond in striking physical ways. For example, they might groan or collapse onto the floor, as they expressed their sense of sin and their subsequent feeling of forgiveness and release through an ecstatic encounter with the crucified and risen Christ. Leading revivalist preachers – such as Charles Grandison Finney in the mid-nineteenth century and Dwight L. Moody a generation later – traversed the Atlantic in a manner associated with Billy Graham in more recent decades.

During the first half of the nineteenth century, the Evangelical tide reached a high-water mark on both sides of the Atlantic. Evangelical influence was not limited to the institutional churches, but had much broader social, political and cultural implications. This occurred through the philanthropic reforming organizations the movement sponsored, and its formative impact on moral values, while its attitudes contributed to the domestic ideology of the Victorian family (Figure 1.2). Also in this period, the growth of the overseas missionary movement provided a channel for the export of Evangelical religion to the non-western world.

From the mid-nineteenth century onwards, however, Evangelical growth lost momentum. Sociologically, it would seem that the movement was at its strongest and most dynamic during the era of transition to an industrial, urban society, but once such 'modern' social structures began to stabilize and mature, there were fewer opportunities for further expansion. Meanwhile, an additional factor was intellectual and cultural change. The diffusion of critical biblical scholarship and of the Darwinian theory of evolution brought a new acuteness to the ongoing post-Enlightenment Protestant dilemma of whether and how to accommodate beliefs to new ideas. Among Evangelicals the trend was towards a divisive polarization between those (sometimes known as liberal Evangelicals) who sought to engage constructively with modern thought, and those who responded with a determined reassertion of traditional teachings, including the unique and infallible status of the Bible as divine revelation. The latter tendency was especially strong in the USA, where, following the publication, between 1910 and 1915, of a series of booklets called *The Fundamentals*, it became known as **fundamentalism**. In the 1920s in particular, fundamentalists assumed a crusading anti-modernist and anti-intellectual stance, symbolized in 1925 by their celebrated prosecution of John Scopes for teaching biological evolution to schoolchildren in Tennessee (Noll, 1992, pp.381–4; Noll, 1994, pp.109–45).

In England, actual numerical decline was becoming apparent by the time of the outbreak of the First World War in 1914.

Figure 1.2   A middle-class Victorian family kneels in prayer. Note the association between Evangelical devotion and the cosy domestic interior. Mary Evans Picture Library.

Evangelicalism proved rather more resilient in Scotland and Wales, where it gained a temporary boost from a revival in the principality in 1905. Above all, it strongly persisted in Northern Ireland, where it gained from being an important focus for Protestant identity in the face of the ongoing struggles over the constitutional status of the province. In the USA, the ideological retreat into a vigorous fundamentalist subculture secured an uncompromising adherence to full-blooded traditional teachings, but it was associated with divisions in denominations and declining numbers.

In the meantime, in 1906, events at the Apostolic Faith Gospel Mission in **Azusa Street**, Los Angeles had given birth to an important new movement. Under the ministry of a black preacher, William J. Seymour, members of the mixed-race congregation began to experience and express gifts of the Spirit, including speaking in tongues, prophecy, healings and outbursts of ecstatic worship. Pentecostalism rapidly gathered momentum not only in the USA, but also in other parts of the world, to which its message was carried by visitors to Azusa Street. In Britain, the movement drew upon the spiritual excitement stirred by the 1905 Welsh revival, while a leading role was taken by a Church of England clergyman, Alexander Boddy, vicar of All Saints', Sunderland. The distinctive emphasis of Pentecostalism that distinguished it from traditional Evangelicalism was its teaching of the need for Christians to be baptized in the Holy Spirit, as a second intense spiritual experience subsequent to conversion. This emphasis on the ecstatic and supernatural in worship and devotion was held alongside a conviction of the inspiration and infallibility of the Bible, which resembled that adopted by fundamentalists. Pentecostalism was particularly successful among the black and Hispanic communities in the USA, and from the 1950s onwards gained significant ground in the UK as a result of West Indian immigration. Several new Pentecostal denominations were formed, notably the Assemblies of God (AOG), the Elim Pentecostal Churches and, among West Indians, the New Testament Church of God (Hollenweger, 1972; Noll, 1992, pp.386–8).

Evangelicalism in the 1920s and 1930s seemed to be retreating into the subcultural and minority status represented by fundamentalism on the one hand and Pentecostalism on the other. In the event, however, the years following the end of the Second World War in 1945 were to see a significant recovery and broadening of appeal on both sides of the Atlantic. Then, in the 1960s, this resurgent Evangelicalism gained further dynamism and intensity from the emergence of the Charismatic movement, whereby teachings and practices initially associated with the Pentecostals gained acceptance in other denominations.

In the meantime, Protestantism in Latin America, hitherto a relatively marginal presence in predominantly Roman Catholic countries, began to expand substantially under the impact of Pentecostalism. This trend was evident in some places even in the earlier decades of the twentieth century: for example, in Chile the Iglesia Methodista Pentecostal (Methodist Pentecostal Church), which had broken away from the Methodist Church early in the century, grew from 54,000 members in 1930 to 425,000 in 1960 (Martin, 1990, p.51). Since the 1960s, however, this trend has both accelerated and been replicated, albeit to differing degrees, across most of the countries of Central and South America. One set of estimates of Pentecostal membership in South America tracks a nearly 20-fold increase from 1.16 million in 1960 to 7.36 million in 1980 and a projected 22.22 million in 2000 (Brierley, 1997, p.34).

The analysis in the following sections will be concerned with the contemporary situation as it has developed since the Second World War, and more particularly from the 1960s onwards, and will focus on three contrasting parts of the world; the UK, the USA and Latin America. In the UK, Evangelicals are a small minority in the population as a whole, but they are a dynamic and growing force within the otherwise generally declining institutional Christian churches. Trends in Evangelicalism in the UK will be introduced in some detail as a reference point for the analysis of the succeeding case studies. In the USA, the situation of Evangelicals within organized Christianity is a similar one, but in a context where active Christian adherence is both more stable and extends to a much larger proportion of the overall population. In 1999, 43 per cent of Americans attended church weekly and 70 per cent claimed to be church members (Anon., 2000a). Both the UK and the USA are advanced industrial modern societies in which Protestantism has been the historically dominant form of Christianity. Consideration of the Evangelical experience in these countries will provide insights into the dramatically different apparent fortunes of Christianity as a whole on the two sides of the north Atlantic. Latin America will then present the further contrast of a less economically and socially 'advanced' region of the world in which Roman Catholicism has historically been predominant, but in which Evangelicalism and Pentecostalism have recently been growing rapidly.

The United Kingdom

Evangelical numerical strength in the UK, as in other countries, cannot be precisely calculated, because the available figures relate to denominations, whose composition can be very mixed. Most **Protestant** denominations include liberal as well as Evangelical wings, and the Anglicans also include a significant Catholic element (known as **Anglo-Catholics**). A significant trend in the Church of England, albeit one that is supported anecdotally rather than statistically, has been for Evangelicals to increase as a proportion of active churchgoers at a time when overall numbers have been in steady decline. It is not clear, however, how far this merely means that Evangelicals have tended to hold their own more than liberal Anglicans or Anglo-Catholics have done, or how far Evangelicals have enjoyed an absolute increase in numbers. Similar points can be made about other 'mixed' denominations, notably the Church of Scotland.

Nevertheless, statistics do support the indications that there has been a strong upsurge in **Evangelicalism** in the UK during the second half of the twentieth century. Among long-established denominations, it is noteworthy that the Baptists, who are predominantly Evangelical, have declined much less than other churches. Between 1975 and 1994, for example, whereas Anglican membership fell by 23.4 per cent, the Baptists lost only 2.8 per cent of their 1975 numbers. Even more striking have been the substantial increases in the membership of other Evangelical denominations: during the same two decades **Pentecostal** membership almost doubled from 101,648 to 183,109, while the '**house**' or '**new**' **churches** increased exponentially from 12,060 in 1975 to 164,317 in 1994 (Brierley and Wraight, 1995, p.240). (Interestingly, the only other category of mainstream Christian churches to show significant increases in this period has been the Orthodox, a further indication that at a time when active Christian adherence as a whole has declined substantially, more conservative groups have been relatively resilient or have even bucked the trend.)

The resurgence in Evangelicalism in the UK since the Second World War occurred in two distinct phases. In the first period, between the 1940s and 1960s, it was founded in a recovery of what is termed conservative (or classical) Evangelicalism, implying a reference back to the standpoint adopted in the first century or so of the movement's history. This approach was characterized by a strong emphasis on the authoritative and divinely inspired status of the Bible, but a distancing from the literalistic and polemical extremes of inter-war American fundamentalism. In contrast with the fundamentalist tendency to mere anti-intellectual rejection of modern ideas, Evangelicals now sought to develop credible conservative alternatives to liberal critical scholarship. Their approach showed that post-Enlightenment rational modes of thought could be a tool in their own hands as well as in those of their liberal rivals. Prominent leaders included academics such as Norman Anderson and Donald Wiseman, and clergy such as **John Stott**, rector of All Souls, Langham Place (central London) (Figure 1.3), in the Church of England, and William Still, minister of Gilcomston South Church, Aberdeen, in the Church of Scotland. Both men began their long ministries in 1945.

Figure 1.3   John Stott, the most influential Evangelical in the Church of England in the second half of the twentieth century.   Courtesy of Hodder & Stoughton.

For some, notably two very influential writers and theologians, the Anglican James I. Packer and the **Nonconformist Martyn Lloyd-Jones**, significant inspiration was also derived from the teachings of the **Reformation** era and the Puritans of the seventeenth century. The influence of such men was diffused through numerous publications, and strategic preaching ministries in London and in university towns. Their work was complemented by important para-church organizations, such as the camps run by E.J.H. ('Bash') Nash for public-school boys and the Inter-Varsity Fellowship (later the **Universities and Colleges Christian Fellowship (UCCF)**), led by Douglas Johnson, which promoted conservative Evangelical teachings among students. The significance of such activity lay in the extent to which it strongly influenced an energetic minority among the educated middle-class British youth of the 1950s and 1960s, and thereby moulded a generation of leaders that was to remain influential throughout the remainder of the twentieth century. Herein lies a key factor, both in explaining the vigour of recent British Evangelicalism and in accounting for one of its obvious weaknesses, the predominance of a middle-class – even upper middle-class – ethos that has limited its capacity to integrate those from working-class and minority backgrounds (Ward, 1996, pp.11–12).

Meanwhile, in 1954, the American Evangelical **evangelist Billy Graham** made the first of his many visits to the UK, and drew very large audiences. For example, a total of 80,500 attended in the first week of his London crusade alone. Graham's approach was less cerebral than that of his British contemporaries, but it was consistent with their conservative theology, and it spread Evangelical influence among a somewhat broader social and educational constituency (Bebbington, 1989, pp.259–61; Barclay, 1997, pp.60–8). The Second World War had been followed by a general, if modest, recovery in organized religion, which was attributable, it would seem, to a shaking of confidence in purely humanistic and secular solutions to world problems. Evangelicals offered a clear message and a youthful vigour that equipped them effectively to respond to this mood and strengthen their own position.

The culmination of this phase of Evangelical growth came in 1967 with the National Evangelical Anglican Congress, held at the

University of Keele and led by John Stott. Although only Anglicans were directly involved, it was an important symbolic event for the movement as a whole (Bebbington, 1989, pp.249–50). It was indicative of a greatly increased confidence, and of aspirations to remould the Church of England, and indeed British Christianity, in an Evangelical image. It also presaged an engagement by Evangelicals in social issues, which was to become increasingly significant in the following years. At the same time, however, Keele congress pointed to growing tensions within the movement. The whole-hearted commitment of Anglican Evangelicals to working within their own church implied a divergence of strategy from some of their Nonconformist counterparts, who were uneasy about any association with liberal or Catholic traditions of Christianity. This difference had already been demonstrated in the previous year when, at a meeting intended to prepare the ground for an interdenominational National Evangelical Assembly, Lloyd-Jones and Stott had publicly disagreed on the extent to which Evangelicals should remain committed to their existing denominations. Stott dissociated himself from Lloyd-Jones's view that fellowship with other Evangelicals should always override other loyalties (Barclay, 1997, p.83). This clash was symptomatic of a wider variance of emphasis between those whose instincts were towards distinctiveness and 'purity' of witness, and those who felt that some involvement in non-Evangelical structures, whether religious or secular, could be used to extend their impact. This tension between accommodation and isolation in Evangelicalism is an issue that will be addressed further below in the subsection on acculturation.

The second phase of Evangelical resurgence, which began in the 1960s and was still continuing in the 1990s, occurred against a background of very rapid general social and cultural change, fully reflected in the wider British religious context. Between 1945 and the early 1960s, the advance in Evangelical fortunes can be seen as merely one manifestation of a modest recovery in traditional Christianity as a whole during the decade and a half following the Second World War (Parsons, 1993). In subsequent decades, on the other hand, almost all other traditional Christian groups were experiencing steep numerical decline. At the same time, British religion became strikingly more diverse, not only with the growth of large Hindu, Muslim and Sikh communities as a result of immigration, but also with the increasing appeal of 'eastern' and 'alternative' beliefs and practices to the indigenous British population. The apparent success of Evangelicals in maintaining and even expanding a traditional and conservative form of Christianity thus appears to run notably counter to other contemporary trends. How do we account for this success? What insights does it suggest into the possible reasons for the much greater strength of Evangelicalism in other parts of the contemporary world and for wider interactions between religion and social and cultural change?

The period since the 1960s was also marked off from the one that preceded it by the extent to which the movement rapidly lost its cohesive and homogeneous character and became multi-faceted and complex. To some extent this general observation provides an immediate broadbrush answer to the above questions. A diverse religious movement could naturally sustain more numerous points of effective contact with a diversifying and changing society than could a static and monochrome one. We need to probe more deeply and specifically, however, and to explore five trends in recent British Evangelicalism. These can be labelled as Charismaticization, reorganization, politicization, globalization and acculturation ((a) – (e) below). They have overlapped with each other, but can be distinguished for analytical purposes. None of these processes were total in their impact, and they hence led both to tensions and to pockets – sometimes large ones – of staunch resistance against change. In analysing these processes, we will gain tools both to understand the sometimes perplexing diversity of contemporary Evangelicalism and to explain its effectiveness as a form of religious expression for the modern and post-modern world.

(a) Charismaticization

During the first half of the twentieth century, **Pentecostalism** in Britain had appeared a marginal and somewhat exotic phenomenon. Although its early leaders had hoped to renew the existing churches, in practice they found themselves driven out into the small, distinctively Pentecostal denominations (Hollenweger, 1972, pp.207–8). In the late 1950s and early 1960s, however, there was a growing receptivity among Evangelicals in the larger churches to the gifts of the Spirit, a movement starting with particular pioneering individuals and congregations, but setting up ripples that rapidly spread outwards. Developments in the Church of England were especially noteworthy. In 1961, news reached the UK of widespread reception of spiritual gifts among the hitherto staid Episcopalian congregation at Van Nuys in California. Philip Hughes, an influential Evangelical Anglican, went to investigate, and in September 1962 published an approving editorial in the *Churchman* journal, judging the development to be 'a movement ... within the heart of the Church, not away from the Church' (Hocken, 1997, pp.110–11). By early 1963,

Charismatic phenomena were being experienced at a number of churches, including St John's, Burslem (Staffordshire) and St Mark's, Gillingham (Kent), where Watson had been a curate from 1959 to 1962 (Hocken, 1997, pp.65–9, 91–6). The flagship church of All Souls, Langham Place was rapidly drawn in: although Stott himself was cautious, two of his curates, Michael Harper and Martin Peppiatt, experienced **baptism in the Spirit** (Hocken, 1997, pp.70–8). Harper's subsequent formation and leadership of the Fountain Trust was to provide an important channel for the diffusion of Charismatic teachings and experience (Hocken, 1997, pp.115–22).

The period between 1965 and 1980 saw the widespread advance of the Charismatic tide, transforming the outlook of Evangelical churches in all denominations. Whereas an earlier generation of so-called 'classical' Pentecostals had been predominantly working class, the new Charismatics reflected the largely middle-class character of the larger Evangelical churches (Walker, 1997, pp.29–31). In the 1970s and 1980s, there was a so-called 'third wave' (the first two being those of the 1900s and 1960s), associated particularly with the impact in the UK of **John Wimber**, the Californian founder of the Association of **Vineyard** Churches (Figure 1.4) (Walker, 1997, p.33). Wimber laid particular stress on what he termed 'power evangelism', linking the proclamation of the Christian gospel to manifestations of the gifts of the Spirit. Especially striking has been his considerable impact on Evangelicals in the Church of England. Although traditional Anglicanism might seem to have little in common with the informal and anti-institutional ethos of the Vineyard, close personal contacts and networks have been established and parochial and diocesan structures have been flexible and accommodating (Hunt, 1995).

In the mid-1990s, the fires of Charismatic renewal were stoked yet again by the **Toronto Blessing**, an experience of spiritual ecstasy associated with the Airport Vineyard church in Toronto where it began in January 1994. It was rapidly disseminated in British churches across a range of denominations (Richter, 1995, pp.5, 11–12). The characteristic features of the Toronto Blessing – convulsive body movements, falling to the ground and uncontrollable laughter, weeping or physical activity – were not necessarily new in Charismatic and Pentecostal churches. What was distinctive about the phenomenon, however, was

Figure 1.4   John Wimber, founder of the Association of Vineyard Churches. Courtesy of Hodder & Stoughton.

its wide and rapid diffusion, to up to 3000 churches by October 1994. It influenced churches that had not hitherto appeared strongly Charismatic and individuals who had not hitherto shown signs of expressing and practising the gifts of the Spirit. The Blessing was not so much the monopoly of a spiritual élite, but more a collective experience shared by whole congregations, or substantial proportions of them (Richter, 1995, p.11). The consequences could be empowering, but also divisive and controversial.

As noted above, Charismatics can be distinguished from traditional Evangelicals by their emphasis on the powerful reality of the presence of the Holy Spirit with God's people today, providing the potential for experience and revelation of the divine that supplements (but does not contradict) the Bible. Their outlook has also shown significant differences of emphasis from classical Pentecostalism as it developed in the first half of the twentieth century. Charismatics did not adopt the Pentecostal view that the gifts of the Spirit were always received in a single, specific (and sometimes long-delayed) experience of baptism in the Spirit, demonstrated publicly by speaking in tongues. Rather, with a view to avoiding division within congregations where many still remained hesitant about full-blooded Charismatic experience, they adopted a less stereotyped model, which gave space for the acknowledgement that *all* Christians experience the presence of the Holy Spirit. However, some Charismatics appeared to be swept along by the excitement of new discovery. Pentecostals (whose denominational outlooks had been shaped by the American fundamentalism of the 1920s) became concerned that they were going too far in stressing testimony and experience at the expense of Bible teaching (Bebbington, 1989, pp.231–2). From a number of quarters Charismatics have been charged with ducking the necessary intellectual task of developing a clear-cut and consistent theology that can provide the necessary enduring framework for making sense of their experience (Craston *et al.*, 1981, p.39; Percy, 1997, pp.213–14; for an exploration of the potential for a Charismatic theology, see Smail *et al.*, 1995).

There are three particularly distinctive features of Charismatic experience and practice. First, speaking in tongues or glossolalia, whereby the believer under the claimed inspiration of the Holy Spirit utters sounds that appear to be gibberish, but are sometimes held to be words in a language unknown to the speaker, thus reliving the miracle of Pentecost, as recorded in Acts 2:5–13. Second, prophecy, in which a speaker, again claiming direct divine inspiration, offers guidance, encouragement or reproof to an individual, group or church. Sometimes such prophecies may profess to foretell future events. Third, healing, in which, usually accompanied with the laying on of hands, there is prayer for divine intervention to remove specific physical, mental or emotional maladies (Figure 1.5). This aspect has been particularly associated with the ministry of Wimber. (For fuller discussion of these and other features of Charismatic experience and practice, see Scotland, 1995, pp.28–34, 137–80.) Sceptics argue that speaking in tongues can be psychologically explained (Williams, 1984), that prophecy is either generalized or often proved inaccurate, and that objective verification of claims to miraculous healing independent of normal medical and biological processes is very rare if not non-existent. Adherents, though, would respond that the Holy Spirit works through natural processes as well as supernaturally, and that even when the admittedly illusory and the hysterical are discerned and discounted, a core of genuine and direct divine revelation and intervention remains.

When a Charismatic ethos became dominant or influential in a church, other consequences followed. Traditionally, in Evangelical churches, sung worship had taken relatively little time and the sermon had been the central focus of the service, constituting as it did the exposition of the divinely inspired text of the Bible. For Charismatics worship now assumed a greater importance, being comparable with or even more important than the sermon, as a perceived means of communication with God. The content of

Figure 1.5   Charismatics in a congregation meeting in a community centre at Ash Hill, Norfolk pray for a young man to be touched by the Holy Spirit. Mike Abrahams/Network.

worship also changed, with a decline in the use of hymns based on biblical texts or affirming particular doctrinal teachings, and an increased use of contemporary songs and choruses that emphasized the immediacy of personal spiritual experience.

There also sometimes followed from a belief in the contemporary reality of the power of the Holy Spirit a belief in the corresponding reality of 'evil' spiritual forces. The underlying challenge to the Christian church was thus perceived as coming not from the indifference and secularity of the contemporary world, but from the real spiritual power of Satan and his minions. There was accordingly a preoccupation with 'spiritual warfare', in which such hostile spiritual forces have to be confronted in prayer (Scotland, 1995, pp.115–35). Non-Christian religions, spiritualism, witches, Pagans and 'New Age' movements were viewed with particular alarm and paranoia. The consequent embattled mentality of some Charismatics has led to them being labelled by some observers as 'fundamentalist', but it is important to note that their outlook in fact differs significantly from the original fundamentalists of the earlier twentieth century. Their combativeness is based not so much on a literalistic understanding of the Bible as on a perception of cosmically polarized forces of light and darkness. Such beliefs have been crystallized by the works of two widely read American 'third wave' authors. Frank Peretti's *This Present Darkness*, published in 1986, is a novel concerned with the cosmic confrontation between angels and demonic powers, while the popular theological works of C. Peter Wagner describe the varieties of demonic forces that he believes to be at work in the world. These include 'territorial spirits', demons held to control particular geographical areas today (Cox, 1996, pp.281–5; Jamison, 2000). The growing impact of this outlook has been traced in the evolving content of the worship songs widely used in Evangelical churches. This shifted from a degree of constructive engagement with the world outside the church in *Youth Praise* (1966) to a sense in *Songs of Fellowship* (1981) of the people of God gathering together for refuge or marching out as an army to confront the powers of evil in the land (Ward, 1996, pp.107–42).

(b) Reorganization

The historic character of Evangelicalism as a form of Christianity that owes a lot to individual experience and sense of encounter with God, and relatively little to the structures and traditions of the institutional church, has always meant that organization has appeared comparatively fluid. There has been both fragmentation and regrouping. In the past, the impact of Evangelicalism has been a major contributory factor in the emergence of new denominations, above all the Methodists in the late eighteenth century, but also the Free Church of Scotland, which split from the Church of Scotland in 1843. Evangelicals certainly identified with particular denominations, but many also had a transdenominational consciousness, fostered by bodies such as the Bible Society, the **Evangelical Alliance (EA)** and the London City Mission, all with roots in the nineteenth century. The Keswick Convention, dating back to 1875, similarly cut across denominations and has had a continuous history as an annual gathering for holiday, fellowship and teaching in the Lake District. During the twentieth century, the Inter-Varsity Fellowship (later UCCF) had an important role in disseminating a conservative but non-denominational Evangelicalism among students.

In the period since the 1960s, these parallel centrifugal and centripetal tendencies have continued and have if anything become more pronounced. At one and the same, time Evangelicals have formed structures that seem to challenge existing denominations and invested considerable time and effort in transdenominational initiatives and activities.

The most obvious expression of the former tendency has been in the development of the 'house' or 'new' church movement. The term 'house church' reflects the small scale and informal origins of some of these groups in the 1960s and 1970s, but in reality they quickly outgrew the domestic setting and their characteristic meeting places are schools and public halls. Some such churches are genuinely independent, but there has been a tendency for them to coalesce into a number of networks and coalitions. The most significant of these are Covenant Ministries, led by Bryn Jones and centred on the east Midlands, and Terry Virgo's New Frontiers network, based in Brighton and strongest in the south, but establishing a growing presence across the country. Gerald Coates's Pioneer movement in Surrey and Roger Forster's Ichthus Fellowship in south London both have substantial but more localized presences (Wright, 1997, pp.66–72). All these groups are shaped by the Charismatic movement, and were initially inspired by a conviction that the pouring out of the Holy Spirit required the creation of new churches, rather than just an endeavour to transform the existing denominations. This outlook is known as 'Restorationism', signifying an aspiration to recover the perceived authentic experience of original New Testament Christianity, held to be obscured or at best distorted in the more longstanding churches (Wright, 1997, pp.61–3). The Restorationist impulse was at its height between the mid-1970s and the mid-1980s, but thereafter the movement became divided and the initial tendency of the new churches to offer a radical critique of existing denominations was more muted. Hence, by 1990, 'the charismatic scene had become not only a more co-operative movement, but also an increasingly integrated Christian market' (Walker, 1998, p.314).

The transdenominational dimension of contemporary Evangelicalism is represented above all by the EA. This organization dates back to 1846, but stagnated in the early and mid-twentieth century. It gradually revived from the 1960s onwards, and became much more prominent under the general directorship of Clive Calver from 1983. Calver's own background was in the Ichthus Fellowship and he was thus ideally placed to use the EA to bring the new churches into effective cooperation with more longstanding Evangelical groups. His energetic and visionary leadership, which emphasized a recovery of historic roots and a renewed focus on social action, brought striking results. Between 1989 and 1996, individual membership of the EA rose from 19,731 to 49,764. Over the same period, the number of affiliated churches rose from 1422 to 2690 (Edwards, 1996, pp.51, 53). By 2000, the number of personal members had dropped back slightly to 43,636, but affiliated churches had increased to 3085. There were also 715 affiliated organizations.[3] Such burgeoning support has enabled the EA to claim with increasing credibility to 'represent the widest cross section of evangelical Christians in the UK' and to establish a strong profile in the media (Anon., 2000b, p.20). During the same period, there was also a notable expansion in the work of the UCCF, which paralleled the growth in higher education: in 1968, the organization was employing 22 staff workers, but by 1995 the number had grown to 51, assisted by over 30 volunteers (Lewis, 1996, p.185). Such activity focused on educated young people at a particularly formative period of their lives had considerable strategic significance.

Alongside these organizations, which reflect the predominantly white and middle-class ethos of British Evangelicalism, there have been parallel movements among the substantial black minority (Figure 1.6). Several hundred thousand West Indians migrated to the UK in the 1950s and 1960s. Removed from the strong community base of Christianity in their original homelands and alienated by the initial racism of British churches, their religious observance was substantially lower than it had been in the Caribbean. It was still, however, appreciably higher than among whites, and largely Evangelical and Pentecostal in character.

The development of denominational networks in the 1960s and 1970s has been followed by the emergence of umbrella

---

[3] Figures supplied by the EA membership department, 13 October 2000.

Figure 1.6   Black Pentecostals worship at Kingsway Christian Centre in Hackney (north-east London) in September 1998. Carlos Reyes-Manzo/Andes Press Agency.

organizations, notably the Afro West Indian United Council of Churches in 1976 and the African Caribbean Evangelical Alliance (ACEA) in the 1980s (Parsons, 1993; Edwards, 1997). A significant recognition of the importance of the black contribution to British Evangelicalism came in the late 1990s with the appointment of Joel Edwards, formally leader of the ACEA, to succeed Calver as general director of the EA. At the same time, however, a considerable cultural and social gap remains between largely middle-class white Evangelicals and the more working-class black Pentecostal churches. For example, whereas the Mission to London **revivals** during the 1990s led by Morris Cerrullo attracted a numerous African-Caribbean constituency, they had a limited appeal to white Evangelicals (Schaefer, 1999).

Another important development has been the growth of Spring Harvest, Christian holiday camps held in April on the Butlins Family Entertainment Resorts sites at Minehead and Skegness, with an overall attendance that rose from 2700 in the late 1970s to around 80,000 in 1990 (Figure 1.7) before dropping back to 60,000 in 2001 (Walker, 1998, p.308; www.springharvest.org; accessed 3 August 2001). The holiday weeks offer an intense spiritual package of worship, Bible teaching and seminars, lightened by the availability

Figure 1.7   Spring Harvest 2001. © Spring Harvest 'The Main Event'.

of good leisure facilities. Like the EA, they provide a point of focus and contact for Evangelicals from a wide range of churches, denominations and social backgrounds, and a source of encouragement and renewal for those whose weekly church experience may well be much more mundane.

A summer gathering, New Wine, was started in 1989 by David Pytches, Vicar of St Andrew's, Chorleywood (north London) and a leading Anglican Wimberite. It has served as a further channel for the diffusion of Vineyard-style teaching and ministry. By 2000, it was attracting around 12,000 people to its conferences in Somerset (New Wine Conferences brochure, 2001). A further important focal point, especially for younger and more liberal-minded Evangelicals, has been the annual Greenbelt Christian music festival. The festival grew from small beginnings in 1973, but by 1983 was attracting nearly 30,000 people annually to the gatherings at Knebworth in Hertfordshire (Ward, 1996, p.101). At the turn of the millennium, attendance at the festival, now located at Cheltenham Race Course, had dropped back to around 10,000 (http://www.greenbelt.org.uk),[4]

[4] Unless otherwise indicated, all web sites subsequently cited in this chapter were most recently accessed on 28 June 2001.

but it continued to flourish and to exert a significant creative influence. Greenbelt has been important not only in promoting the development of a strong subculture of Christian youth music, but also in providing a stimulus to wider reflection about the interaction of Christianity and culture (Ward, 1996, p.100). Meanwhile, the Keswick Conventions continued, providing a similar service for the more conservative Evangelical constituency and attracting 8000–10,000 people annually (Lewis, 1996, p.186). In addition, the annual Marches for Jesus, started in 1989, and held in numerous towns and cities during the 1990s, provided a local focus for interdenominational Evangelicalism.

During the 1990s, the success of **Alpha courses** (Colour Plate 1) has been both yet another significant manifestation of transdenominational Evangelicalism and also an indication of the movement's continuing capacity to renew and extend its appeal. The Alpha course originated at the leading Anglican Evangelical church of Holy Trinity, Brompton (west London), where it was initially designed to provide basic instruction for new Christians. Under the leadership of Nicky Gumbel, however, it was transformed into a course at which enquirers who might otherwise be tempted to dismiss Christianity as 'boring, untrue and irrelevant' (Alpha publicity) were warmly welcomed. In contrast to the emphasis of traditional evangelistic preaching on immediate repentance and conversion, the Alpha course offers an introduction – with an Evangelical/Charismatic slant – to core Christian beliefs. It allows the uncommitted participant ample opportunity for questioning, discussion and dissent in a relaxed social context, enhanced by the provision of food at the beginning of meetings. From 1993 onwards, Alpha materials and methods began to be widely adopted in other churches, across the denominations. Early in 2000, it was claimed that more than 7000 churches were running Alpha courses (Anon., 2000c).

It is at least arguable that by 2000 such structures and events had become more important than traditional denominational loyalties in shaping the consciousness of Evangelicals. Anecdotal evidence suggests that, especially among those under 40 whose formative Christian experience occurred in the 1970s or later, the choice of what church to attend often owed relatively little to a sense of denominational affiliation. More significant in the decisions were likely to be such Evangelical/Charismatic criteria as 'Bible-believing', 'spirit-filled', 'lively worship' or 'good fellowship'. Conversely, similar patterns of worship and religious practice are apparent in Evangelical churches of a wide variety of denominations.

A further significant trend has been at least a reduction in the height of the barriers Evangelicals have historically interposed between themselves and other Christian groups. Whereas in the mid-twentieth century the feeling of Evangelicals that they were an embattled remnant meant that anti-Catholic and anti-liberal attitudes were seldom far below the surface, by the 1970s, under the solvent of the Charismatic movement, a change was under way. Watson was a representative and influential figure in this respect as in many others. He acknowledged that he had held strongly anti-Roman views in his youth, but encounters with Charismatic Catholics and first-hand experience of the consequences of sectarianism in Northern Ireland led to a radical change of attitude. In 1977, he was famously to say at the EA Conference in Nottingham that 'In many ways, the Reformation was one of the greatest tragedies that ever happened to the Church' (Saunders and Samson, 1992, pp.181–6). As subsequent criticism of Watson was to indicate, this was further than many were yet willing to go, but it was much more than a straw in the wind. Although, in 1990, the EA was to decide that it would be 'inappropriate' for it to join the Council of Churches for Britain and Ireland, attitudes at a less formal level were certainly changing. Moreover, not only were Evangelicals themselves prepared to find some common ground with other Christians, but also there are indications that Evangelical influences were increasingly present in non-Evangelical churches (Jones, 2000).

(c) Politicization

During its initial nineteenth-century heyday, British Evangelicalism had a substantial political impact, evident above all in the successful campaign for the abolition of colonial slavery and in the moral and social reforms promoted by the Earl of Shaftesbury. Non-Anglican Evangelicals were also stirred by their religion to engage in campaigns for civil equality, which resulted in the substantial liberalization of the British constitution and educational systems during the Victorian era. In the first half of the twentieth century, however, such Evangelical political activity largely vanished (Bebbington, 1995, pp.174–85).

From the 1960s, though, general Evangelical resurgence was associated with a recovery of political engagement. The initial emphasis was on moral issues, but there was a growing interest in social questions and attempts to develop wide-ranging political agendas. The 1964 'Clean Up TV' crusade developed into the National Viewers and Listeners Association, which was led by Mary

Whitehouse and had acquired 30,000 supporters by 1975. Then, in 1971, a 'Rally against Permissiveness' in Trafalgar Square, London led to the foundation of the National Festival of Light, which subsequently became Christian Action Research and Education (CARE). CARE has adopted a broad agenda, and developed sophisticated methods of lobbying and mobilization on moral and welfare issues. In the 1980s, legislation was secured to limit sexually explicit material in the media and to control the development of the sex industry (Thompson, 1997, pp.164–7). In recent years, CARE has maintained an active profile, campaigning on medical ethical issues, opposing abortion (although without the militant direct action of counterparts in the USA) and promoting the teaching of Christianity in schools. Together with the EA, it has resisted the repeal of the anti-homosexual Clause 28 of the 1986 Local Government Act (http://www.care.org.uk). Such moral campaigns feature prominently in the media image of Evangelicals.

Meanwhile, in 1968, the EA Relief Fund (TEAR Fund) was launched. It aims to support relief and development in Third World countries from an explicitly Evangelical standpoint, but without overt proselytism. It quickly became organizationally independent of the EA and by the mid-1990s its annual budget had grown to £21 million (Lewis, 1996, pp.181–2).

During the 1980s and 1990s, TEAR Fund was paralleled by the emergence of a growing range of organizations that promoted social engagement among Evangelicals at home. These included the Jubilee Trust, best known for its 'Keep Sunday Special' campaign against the legalization of Sunday trading, but, under the leadership of Michael Schluter, also a focus for creative thinking about realistic Christian-inspired community structures in the contemporary world. The industrialist and former MEP Sir Frederick Catherwood sought to develop Christian Action Networks in specific urban centres to provide coordination for local social engagement. The publication in 1984 of Stott's *Issues Facing Christians Today* served both as a crystallization of the steps that had already been taken and as a stimulus to further action (Calver, 1995, pp.201–5). A grass-roots dimension is also apparent, for example in the work of the Ichthus Fellowship in south London, where a successful ministry among the urban working class has been associated with a directly engaged social radicalism (Cotton, 1995, pp.52–7).

Such developments were political in the broad sense of the word without being party-political. Although on moral issues Evangelical standpoints might appear closer to the Conservatives than to other parties, especially when during the 1980s the Conservative Prime Minister Margaret Thatcher advocated a return to perceived 'Victorian values', such an affinity was a limited one. Even on the personal morality front it was qualified by the libertarian tendencies of the Tory Right, and on social and economic issues Evangelicals often appeared to adopt decidedly left-of-centre positions. Certainly, they lacked any automatic commitment to the virtues of the free market (Thompson, 1997, p.173). Thus, it was understandable that in 1989 Kenneth Clarke, a Cabinet minister and leading figure in the Conservative Party, felt it necessary to ask Calver 'What are you evangelicals, are you left-wing or right-wing?' (Calver, 1995, p.207). The perception of this leading politician that British Evangelicals cannot be slotted into convenient secular ideological pigeonholes has been supported by academic analysis, in which it is argued that religious beliefs and values must be regarded as a genuine and independent motivating force (Thompson, 1997, pp.168–9).

The Movement for Christian Democracy (MCD), formed in 1990, was itself a product of this non-partisan frame of mind. It called for 'Christians in all parties and those who feel unable to join any of the parties, to come together and bring Christian values back into political life' (MCD publicity leaflet, quoted in Wolffe, 1994, p.96). Although led by a Roman Catholic, David Alton, the organization received extensive support from Evangelicals (Thompson, 1997, p.174). The MCD developed as a pressure group and think-tank rather than as a political party in its own right, but by 2000 some of its members had concluded that the time was ripe for a fully fledged Christian political party. Following an unexpectedly successful showing in the London mayoral elections in May 2000, when their candidate, Ram Gidoomal, gained more support than any of the other minor parties, the Christian Peoples Alliance was launched as a national party at a rally in October 2000. At time of writing (Spring 2001), it is, of course, too early to tell how much momentum this initiative can gather, but it is certainly symptomatic of a growing political interest and self-confidence among British Evangelicals.

One important regionally specific example of Evangelical politicization requires distinct comment: the role of Ian Paisley (Figure 1.8) and his Free Presbyterian Church and Democratic Unionist Party (DUP) in the turbulent history of Northern Ireland in the decades after 1969. Paisley's background lay in an intensely conservative interwar Evangelicalism strongly influenced by contemporary American fundamentalism. In 1945, aged only nineteen, he became pastor of an independent Evangelical church in east Belfast. Following a profound religious experience in 1949, when he felt himself to have been 'filled with the Holy Spirit' (Bruce, 1986, p.35), he became active as an evangelist. In 1951, he became leader of the newly formed Free Presbyterian Church of Ulster (FPC), which

Figure 1.8 Ian Paisley in character-istic pose, addressing a rally. Homer Sykes/Network.

brought together congregations dissat-isfied with the Irish Presbyterian Church on account of its alleged theological liberalism and other factors. During the 1960s, the fiercely anti-Catholic and anti-liberal Paisley was a contentious critic of mainstream Unionism and Presbyterianism, and in 1966 he was imprisoned for public order offences. This perceived persecution inspired a considerable growth in the FPC, which continued in the 1970s. Meanwhile, Paisley was elected to the Stormont (Northern Ireland) Parliament in 1969 and to the Westminster Parliament in 1970. In 1971, the DUP was formed under his leadership and has since remained a political focus for those Protestants irreconcilably opposed to any compromise with nationalist and Roman Catholic aspirations. Paisley's political influ-ence was at its height in the 1980s and waned somewhat in the 1990s, but continued at the turn of the century to present a serious challenge to the implementation of the Good Friday Agreement of 1998. There was no straightforward equation between the FPC and the DUP, but there was considerable overlap of membership and a sense of common populist **Protestantism**, in which the Evangelical fervour of the FPC was respected even when DUP activists did not share it. (For detailed analysis of Paisley's career, the FPC and DUP, see Bruce, 1986.)

Paisley's remarkable career has to be understood in the specific context of Northern Ireland, where both cultural/political Protestantism and his distinctive brand of Evangelical religious fervour have a substantially greater popular appeal than on the mainland of the UK. Nevertheless, such radically conservative Evangelicalism is an important part of the wider picture, both because it parallels the resurgence of Evangelical political interest in the UK as a whole, and also because it points to alternative potentialities for an Evangelical politics that is high profile and confrontational rather than relatively inconspicuous and accommo-dating. Even though such tendencies have hitherto been dormant in the UK, they are, as we shall see, paralleled in other parts of the world.

(d) Globalization

The concept of globalization 'refers both to the compression of the world and the intensification of consciousness of the world as a whole' (Robertson, 1992, p.8). Evangelicalism has both been shaped by this process and been an agent of it. The movement has always had a vision and sense of identity that extended well beyond the shores of the British Isles. Wesley reputedly claimed the world as his parish, and Whitefield energetically ministered in North America as well as in Britain. In the 1790s, the foundation of missionary societies inspired by Evangelicalism, notably the Baptist Missionary Society, the Church Missionary Society (Anglican) and the London Missionary Society (Congregational), were expressive of an impulse to carry the gospel to all parts of the world. When the EA was formed in 1846, it initially aspired to a genuinely global coverage, and although such expectations were frustrated by the realities of mid-nineteenth-century religious and national politics, the vision remained (Wolffe, 1996).

A sometimes diffuse sense of global identity and ambition is not the same as fully fledged globalization. Nevertheless, impulses inherent to Evangelicalism have provided fertile ground for general globalizing trends. Billy Graham's rallies in the 1950s stood in a long tradition of visits by American evangelists, for example those of Dwight Moody and Ira Sankey in the later nineteenth century. They also, however, pointed the way forward to a world in which greatly accelerated and diversified communications ensured that developments in the USA and elsewhere were rapidly echoed in the UK. When Graham returned in 1984 to lead the 'Mission England' campaign, with his addresses relayed across the country by closed-circuit television, he was working in parallel with a Latin American evangelist, Luis Palau, who was the main speaker at rallies in London. Thus, the gospel message was delivered in a globalized rather than an indigenous British context. Wimber's impact was a further important example of the strengthening global connections of British Evangelicalism.

A further stage came with the emergence of the Toronto Blessing in Canada in 1994, at a time when e-mail and the Internet were becoming increasingly readily accessible, and electronic communication facilitated rapid dissemination of news of developments across the Atlantic and elsewhere. In its very origins, stemming from the influence on the Toronto Airport Vineyard church[5] of a South African

[5] The church subsequently parted company with the Association of Vineyard Churches, and was renamed Toronto Airport Christian Fellowship.

born international evangelist, Rodney Howard-Browne, it reflected global interconnections (Richter, 1995, p.11). Moreover, the ready physical accessibility of the Toronto church, close to a major international airport in an age of mass air travel, facilitated access from the UK and elsewhere, and encouraged large-scale Evangelical 'pilgrimage' to Toronto to experience the Blessing and to carry it back to churches in the UK. It has been estimated that, by as early as June 1995, 30,000 British pilgrims had made the journey to Toronto (Figure 1.9) (Richter, 1997, pp.104–5).

Hence, the Blessing was widely assimilated into the British Evangelical churches, almost simultaneously with its impact in North America. The precise forms that such assimilation took reflected conditions in particular churches and the personal circumstances of individuals. However, the intensity and rapidity with which the movement spread, apparently from a single epicentre, and brought the local into immediate encounter with the global, renders it the most striking example to date of the globalization of Evangelicalism.

It is important, however, not to confuse globalization with a one-way process of Americanization. For one thing, influences have been two way: British Evangelicalism has imported Billy Graham, Wimber and the Toronto Blessing, but it has exported the influence of its own leading figures, such as Stott and Packer, and the concept of the Alpha courses, which are rapidly spreading worldwide. In early 2001, there were 2900 courses registered in the USA, and Alpha was

Figure 1.9 Toronto Airport Christian Fellowship. Courtesy of the Toronto Airport Christian Fellowship.

described by the *New York Daily News* as a 'galloping global phenomenon' (http://www.alpha.org.uk). It is also evident that assimilation of external influences has been selective. In part this is a reflection of specific personal affinities, for example the links between Wimber, Watson and Pytches have led to the Vineyard having an influence in the UK that is disproportionate to its presence in the USA itself (Hunt, 1995, p.105). Similarly, Paisley has strong connections with American fundamentalist networks, including Bob Jones University, Greenville, South Carolina, which awarded him an honorary doctorate (Bruce, 1986, pp.168–9). Where such connections do not exist, however, British Evangelical religious culture has reflected an instinctive national caution towards things American. It is at least arguable that the Toronto Blessing would never have achieved the same instant appeal in the UK had it first emerged in the USA rather than Canada (Lyon, 1998, p.57). A further factor has been the important contribution of members of the Church of England to the wider Evangelical and Charismatic movements in England, which has given a distinctively Anglican dimension to developments here that is unusual in the context of global Evangelicalism. This point also, incidentally, suggests a significant contrast between the texture of Evangelicalism in England and that in Scotland and Wales, where Anglicanism as a whole is much weaker.

We shall return to discuss globalization further below in the broader context provided by the other regional case studies. For the present, however, it is useful also to introduce the related concept of glocalization, which:

> ... points up the interconnection between the local and the global. It punctures the inflated views of globalization as some mere macro-level socio-economic process involving 'world-systems' that either do not touch the everyday lives of ordinary people in local places, or, if they do, merely impose alien pressures upon them. Rather, the local and the global are mutually dependent.
>
> (Lyon, 1998, p.50)

Thus, movements may be global in their scope, and globalizing in their effect in that they strengthen a sense of connection between otherwise remote centres, while at the same time having a very distinctive local impact. This approach seems effectively to encapsulate the experience of British Evangelicalism as part of a wider international movement during the latter part of the twentieth century.

(e) Acculturation

There is a tendency among both the adherents and critics of Evangelicalism to see the movement as withdrawing from mainstream cultural trends to a distinctive subculture. For adherents, such a self-image reflects their sense of being set apart from 'the world' in virtue of their Christian commitment; for critics, this view readily allows them to dismiss Evangelicalism as eccentric and marginal. Like all caricatures, this one contains more than a grain of truth. There are, indeed, significant respects in which Evangelicals have differed from late-twentieth-century cultural and social norms, notably in a standard of morality in which premarital sex is strongly frowned upon. The efforts of UCCF to cultivate an intellectually robust Evangelicalism among university students and graduates had their counterpart in some church communities in an anti-intellectualism that led to a suspicion of higher education. There are also relatively small groups that have set their faces against many of the changes going on around them, for example the Free Church of Scotland ('Wee Frees') and the Free Presbyterian Church, or that have purposefully pursued a firmly 'alternative' lifestyle, for example the Jesus Fellowship.

It is in work with young people that the nature of the wider interactions between Evangelicals and the surrounding culture are most clearly delineated. Among teenagers and young adults, the peer pressure to conform to secular cultural values is greater than among their elders, while the longing of parents to keep their offspring in the fold – above all through finding an 'appropriate' marriage partner – is equally intense. There is a practical tension between aspirations to draw in hitherto unchurched young people while at the same time protecting the children of Evangelical parents from unsettling external influences. These pressures are partially resolved through the development of Evangelical youth subculture, with its own music, networks and magazines, aspiring to provide a 'safe' refuge from the ideological and sexual temptations of the outside world. This outlook is, however, unlikely to offer sufficient bridges to mainstream secular culture to win over the outsider, or to allow the insider opportunity to mature and experiment with new ideas and activities. Hence there is a tendency for young adults from Evangelical backgrounds either to appear trapped in a perpetual adolescence or to end up in wholesale rejection of their childhood and teenage experience (Ward, 1996, especially pp.214–15).

The reality is that in the UK (in contrast, as we shall see, to the USA) the great majority of Evangelicals cannot insulate themselves from the cultural and social forces experienced by the remainder of the population. Their development is better understood as assimilation with the surrounding culture rather than as resistance to it. Indeed, according to David Bebbington, one of the movement's leading historians, there is a continuing pattern here. Thus, Bebbington argues, in the Enlightenment era of the later eighteenth century, Evangelicals emphasized the rational character of their beliefs, supported by the empirical evidence of conversion and assurance of God's continuing providential care of the believer (Bebbington, 1989, pp.50–5). Subsequently, during the nineteenth century, Evangelicalism was also profoundly shaped by the cultural ascendancy of **Romanticism**, which led to a heightened sense of drama in religion and an 'intensified sense of the supernatural' (Bebbington, 1989, p.104), expressed particularly in an expectation of the imminent Second Coming of Christ. Then, during the early twentieth century, cultural preoccupation with the subjective and the subconscious increased, and there was also an emphasis on the virtues of self-expression in a manner that defied outward appearances. This cultural movement, known as Modernism, was associated with the philosopher Friedrich Nietzsche, novelists such as Franz Kafka and Virginia Woolf, and post-impressionism in art. According to Bebbington, the Charismatic movement, with its emphasis on direct personal experience of God, and on individual spiritual expression rather than assent to inherited doctrinal frameworks, constituted the delayed impact of Modernism on Evangelicalism (Bebbington, 1989, pp.231–48).

When Bebbington published his survey of Evangelical history in 1989, the concept of post-modernism, which has since loomed large in cultural and academic analysis, was not yet so generally current as it has since become. The reader may well be struck by the fact that the qualities of subjectivity and individual expression that Bebbington then labelled as 'Modernist' are now seen as characteristic of post-modernism. The confusion can be resolved, however, if we recognize that implicit in the use of the term 'post-modern' is a broad-brush conception of 'modernity' (articulated, for example, in Tomlinson, 1995, pp.64–5). In this view, modernity is seen as characterized by an Enlightenment view of an orderly and rational world interpreted by objective critical analysis and culturally dominant until the late twentieth century. Modern*ism* as a specific movement was at odds with modern*ity* in that broad sense, and needs to be understood as a precursor, rather than as the antithesis, of post-modernism.

Underlying the confusion of terminology is an important debate as to whether modern or post-modern tendencies are predominant in contemporary Evangelicalism. In other words, is the movement still locked in the cultural framework of the mid-twentieth century and before, or is it changing in tune with contemporary culture as a whole? In 1995, Dave Tomlinson, a former leader of Evangelical churches, published a wide-ranging critique of the movement. He argued that Evangelicalism was indeed in danger of being trapped in transient social and cultural moulds, in its association with family values and respectable middle-class behaviour, and in its dominant, controlling style of leadership. It also tended to define itself against a liberalism that was a product of passing Enlightenment intellectual assumptions. According to Tomlinson, effective Christian witness in a post-modern world needs to be 'post-Evangelical', implying a movement away from dogmatic conceptions of rigid doctrinal truth, a more critical approach to the Bible and a more positive engagement with a world in which spiritual searching is widespread but prepackaged frameworks of belief are unfashionable (Tomlinson, 1995). Tomlinson's sense of the need to move beyond the Evangelical tradition has, however, been seriously questioned, notably by Graham Cray, a leading Anglican supporter of Greenbelt and of the mode of constructive engagement with contemporary culture that the music festival represents. Although Cray acknowledged the importance of Tomlinson's contribution in stimulating Evangelicals to address the implications of post-modernism, he himself argued that Evangelicalism, while combining elements of the pre-modern, modern and post-modern, was in fact well equipped for 'post-modern mission'. Cray attributed this potential primarily to the impact of the Charismatic movement, which he characterized as a 'move from a rather rationalistic form of Scripture-centred Christianity to a more holistic form, equally Scripture-centred, but expecting encounters with God which engage the whole person, body, mind, emotions and spirit' (Cray *et al.*, 1997, p.14). He stopped short of arguing that the Charismatic movement was itself essentially post-modern, but clearly felt that such an argument should be taken seriously.

There are no easy resolutions to this debate, which is ongoing. It is apparent, however, that since the 1960s the tendency of the majority of Evangelicals to reflect rather than reject their wider cultural environment has become more pronounced. This is not to say that the Charismatic movement should be viewed *merely* as a projection of cultural post-modernism into the religious sphere. We need to take seriously the integrity of its own claims to divine origin and the extent to which it represents a recovery of dimensions of historic – and arguably *pre*-modern – Christianity that have been obscured in the more recent past. On the other hand, it has certainly been a powerful channel for an increased cultural responsiveness.

Indeed, one academic commentator has argued that the Charis-matic movement is now best characterized as 'hyper-modern', always seeking new experiences and forms of expression, and hence constituting a spiritual projection of the secular hedonism and consumerism of the turn-of-the-millennium UK. In his eyes, such extreme cultural sensitivity is not so much a basis for effective engagement with the secular environment as a prelude to disinte-gration (Walker, 1997). Only time will tell.

Estimates of the numbers of Evangelicals in the UK in 2000 range from 1.6 million to 3 million (Gledhill, 2000), the range reflecting varieties of measure and definition. This renders them a small minority, less than 5 per cent, of the total population, but a much more substantial proportion, up to 50 per cent, of active churchgoers. There are therefore grounds for arguing that, during recent decades, British Christianity has become increasingly Evangelicalized. This impression is confirmed by the extent to which some practices with Evangelical origins, such as new styles of worship and the Alpha course, have been adopted in non-Evangelical churches. In the light, however, of the operation of the five trends *within* Evangelicalism that we have discussed, it should be clear that this process is far from being a monolithic one. None of the five trends has had a uniform impact: there are Evangelical churches that resist Charismatic influences as heretical, others that continue strongly to identify with traditional denominational loyalties, and many that still see political and social action as a distraction from the essential Christian gospel. Some churches have a marked consciousness of global interconnections, but others have horizons largely limited to their local communities. Pre-modern, modern and post-modern worship styles and cultural outlooks are apparent in different churches, and even intermingled within the same Evangelical worship service or community of adherents.

In order to appreciate more tangibly the nature of Evangelical diversity as reflected in Sunday worship, a central point in the life of any church, it may be helpful to imagine an observer travelling around the UK at the dawn of the twenty-first century and attending a different Evangelical church every week.[6] Sometimes this individual would find himself or herself in historic Anglican churches of great

[6] The two paragraphs that follow are based on the author's own participant observation of a range of Evangelical churches during the last decade, and his assimilation of anecdotal and other evidence. They should be treated as well-informed speculation and hypothesis. There is a pressing need for properly rigorous research to substantiate and develop such impressions.

architectural merit, sometimes in more utilitarian modern buildings, sometimes in down-at-heel school halls hired for the occasion. Some churches would have congregations of many hundreds, others a few dozen or less. Sometimes, especially in the Church of England, the service would have some more or less traditional liturgical structure; often it would consist rather simply of a extended period of singing, followed by a sermon and a final period of prayer and 'ministry' (in this context, the exercise of Charismatic gifts, notably healing through the laying on of hands). Although sermon and sung worship would always be present in some form, our observer would be struck by the varying degrees of emphasis placed on the exposition of the Bible and on the cultivation of direct personal experience of God in worship, prayer and ministry. Sometimes the preaching would appear decidedly fundamentalist, with a literalistic acceptance of the Bible on matters such as human origins; elsewhere the Bible would still be taken very seriously but interpreted and applied with some subtlety and flexibility. The listener would sometimes encounter an uncompromising moral stance in relation to, for example, abortion, homosexuality and premarital sex. Gays and heterosexual cohabitees would be called on to repent of their sins and change their lifestyles before they could be accepted by God. Elsewhere, however, the observer would encounter an acknowledgement that such issues are 'difficult' for the twenty-first-century Christian, and that blanket condemnation of those who fall short of the Evangelical ideal of committed heterosexual marriage may be inappropriate. In some churches eighteenth- and nineteenth-century hymns would still predominate; in others any song written before 1995 would be perceived as old-fashioned and ripe for discarding. Sometimes the Holy Spirit would be directly invoked, with visible results such as speaking in tongues, prophecy, dancing in the aisles and prayer for healing; in other churches the whole atmosphere of the service would rigidly preclude such uncontrolled and ecstatic spontaneity. The notices, whether spoken or written, would give the observer an insight into each church's weekday and other activities and its relationship to wider networks. Mid-week small group meetings might variously tend to emphasize study of the Bible or 'fellowship' and prayer. Sometimes various practical socially engaged community activities would be prominent; elsewhere they might be entirely absent. On occasions, especially in larger churches, there would be little encouragement to pursue any wider networking. Elsewhere attention would be variously directed to denominational events and activities and to pan-Evangelical ones, such as a local mission initiative or the organization of a group from the church to attend Spring Harvest or New Wine.

Amidst all this diversity, however, some consistencies would be likely to be apparent. Except in the smallest and most conservative churches, our observer would be likely to note that the age distribution of congregations more closely mirrors that of the population as a whole than is the case in the majority of non-Evangelical churches, where the over-sixties are disproportionately in evidence. In many cases the predominant groups in the church would seem to be twenty- and thirty-somethings and their young children. In university towns strong student contingents would be noted. Most members of congregations would appear middle class and well educated, with many university graduates, but few really affluent people. A sprinkling of the skilled working class would, however, be present, and a few representatives of the underclasses of the long-term unemployed and drug and alcohol abusers might be receiving some kind of support from the congregation. Except, perhaps, in black Pentecostal churches, members of the mainstream employed working class would seldom be numerous. Women would be likely to be in the majority – some married women attending without their husbands – but would not have an overwhelming predominance. These broadly socially homogeneous congregations would be seen to be participating in a style of worship that emphasizes – albeit in different ways – liveliness and relevance rather than quiet reflection and detachment from everyday life (in contrast to, for example, Anglican choral Evensong or a Quaker meeting). The observer would be likely to note an elevation of the concept of the family: through advocacy of the moral values that sustain the nuclear family, through child-orientated 'family services' and through an idealized view of the congregation itself as a 'church family'. Running through it all, despite varying views of the Holy Spirit and of biblical interpretation, the observer would notice that there is always a profession to take the Bible very seriously as a source of religious authority. There would also probably be, everywhere in the British Evangelical world, some kind of call to conversion and personal commitment to Christ, directed both at waverers in the congregation itself and, through church members, at non-attenders with whom they come into contact in their daily lives.

Some commentators (for example, Wright, 1996; Smith, 1998) have attempted to produce typologies of the varieties of contemporary British Evangelicalism. This approach is useful up to a point, but has not been followed here because such categorization can confuse as well as illuminate, because it inevitably implies distinctions and solidarities that may not be meaningfully reflected at the grass roots. In concentrating, rather, on the trends that have had an impact on the whole Evangelical movement, although not in a consistent or uniform way, the above analysis has sought rather to provide tools for understanding diversity. If one's desired mental map is of a neat succession of pigeonholes into which various subdivisions of belief and practice can be neatly categorized, the attempt to understand Evangelicalism is likely to be a frustrating one. A more fruitful approach is to think of a kaleidoscope in which the pattern has a fixed centre and outer limits, and a finite number of different shapes and colours, but in which the permutations can appear almost infinitely varied.

Such acknowledgement of the kaleidoscopic nature of contemporary British Evangelicalism is not an admission of analytical defeat, but rather a key insight into its most essential and enduring characteristic. Superficially, such diversity may appear to be a reflection of weakness, of internal confusion of aims and strategies, and of too easy accommodation to a fragmented post-modern culture. There is, however, a substantially more positive reading founded on the recognition that internal diversity has always been inherent to Evangelicalism. The movement has always emphasized *individual* conversion and encounter with God, personal faith and action, and the right of everyone to study and interpret the authoritative Bible for themselves. It is therefore natural that in an increasingly complex and pluralist society, the movement should itself assume numerous different forms. Moreover, in its very ability to adapt and diversify, while still retaining a credible witness to a core of consistent teaching, may lie the secret of its relative success in standing out against the otherwise inexorable secularization of the later-twentieth-century UK.

Such an hypothesis provides a useful bridge to discussion in the two sections that follow of the Evangelical/Pentecostal presence in two contrasting contexts, which are both much more significant in global terms: the USA and Latin America. In both these regions, Evangelicalism has enjoyed much greater numerical success than in the UK. What are the reasons for that success, and what do the possible answers to this question tell us both about Evangelicalism itself and about the wider situation of religion in today's globalized world?

The United States of America

In the USA, as in the UK, it is difficult to establish a conclusive measure of Evangelical numbers. Approximately 19 per cent of the population of the USA define themselves as 'evangelical', 'pentecostalist', 'charismatic', 'fundamentalist' or some combination of these terms (Noll, 2001, pp.32–2). Alternative approaches, however, yield different figures. A Gallup poll indicated that, in 1976, 34 per cent of Americans identified themselves as 'born again', a proportion that rose to 40 per cent in 1984 and only declined marginally to 39 per cent in the 1990s. Stronger indications of Evangelical identification – a literal view of the Bible and activity in personal evangelism – were professed by 18 per cent in 1976 and 22 per cent in 1984 (Bebbington, 1994, p.377; Anonymous, 1998, p.2). In another survey in 1996, no less that 33.2 per cent of a sample indicated assent to four core Evangelical beliefs (Noll, 1998, p.14). Another alternative approach to counting Evangelicals is through the aggregate membership of predominantly Evangelical denominations. On this basis, Evangelicals amounted to 23.5 million or 11.3 per cent of the population in 1971, and 29.6 million or 11.9 per cent of the population in 1990 (Shibley, 1996, p.27). These latter figures may validly be regarded as something of a lower limit, insofar as they do not include some smaller churches or significant Evangelical minorities within some of the so-called **mainline Protestant** (i.e. non-Evangelical) denominations. The picture is further complicated by inconsistencies between the various measures: for example, by no means all members of Evangelical denominations profess to hold all the beliefs regarded as characteristically Evangelical. Even a minority of self-defined Evangelicals do not profess to hold all these beliefs (Noll, 2001, pp.34–6). Whatever precise interpretations are put on the data, however, it is clear that in the USA not only are Evangelicals at least ten times more numerous than in the UK, but also they make up a much more substantial proportion of the overall population. Moreover, as in the UK, Evangelicals in the USA are becoming a larger proportion of active Christians. In the same two decades from 1971 to 1990 in which numbers in Evangelical denominations rose by 6.1 million, mainline Protestant numbers declined by 2.6 million, so that by 1990 the mainline Protestants (with a total of 28 million) had been overtaken by the Evangelicals (Shibley, 1996, p.27).

The distribution of Evangelicals across the country is very uneven. In 1990, adherents of Evangelical denominations amounted to 22.8 per cent of the population in the south, but only 9.9 per cent in the Midwest, 6.3 per cent in the west and a mere 1.8 per cent in the north-east (Shibley, 1996, p.30). On an alternative measure, in 1996, the south had 35 per cent of the total population, but 44 per cent of those professing core Evangelical convictions, whereas the north-east had 20 per cent of the total population, but only 14 per cent of those professing core Evangelical convictions (Noll, 1998, p.14). It is thus noteworthy that in New England, the region of the country with the strongest historic cultural and religious links with the UK, the numerical situation of Evangelicalism is closest to that in the UK itself.

In the USA, as in the UK, the continuing Evangelical resurgence can be traced back to developments in the 1940s and the 1950s. The symbolic point of departure was in 1942 when, led by Harold Ockenga and J. Elwin Wright, the National Association of Evangelicals (NAE) was formed in St Louis. This organization was intended to establish a new direction away from the defensive fundamentalism of the inter-war years. The outlook it represented has recently been summarized as follows:

> The vision and program these young, restless reformers began to develop ... can best be described as 'engaged orthodoxy.' In keeping with their nineteenth-century Protestant heritage, they were fully committed to maintaining and promoting confidently traditional, orthodox Protestant theology and belief, *while at the same time* becoming confidently and proactively engaged in the intellectual, cultural, social, and political life of the nation. Their commitment to orthodoxy and engagement, respectively, distinguished these incipient 'neo-evangelicals' – as they began to call themselves – from their liberal Protestant cousins, on the one hand, and from their fundamentalist siblings, on the other.
>
> (Smith, C., 1998, pp.10–11)

Initially, the leaders of the NAE had hoped to steer fundamentalism as a whole onto a new track, but in reality what they were to achieve during the next fifteen years was the growth of a robust Evangelicalism, which located itself between fundamentalism and mainline Protestantism, drawing support from both, but superseding neither. Key developments were the foundation in 1947 of Fuller Theological Seminary in Pasadena, California to serve as an educational focus for the movement, and the establishment of a journalistic flagship, *Christianity Today*, in 1956. By that time, Billy Graham, who took a leading role in setting up *Christianity Today*, had emerged as the movement's pre-eminent public representative. Graham's readiness in 1957 to cooperate with liberal Protestants on a crusade in New York led to a final breach with the fundamentalists (Figure 1.10) (Smith, C., 1998, pp.11–15).

The separation between Evangelicals and fundamentalists is not always recognized by scholars. For example, one recent study (Shibley, 1996) treats them both under the heading of 'Evangelicalism', while recognizing significant variations of emphasis and outlook. On the other hand, for Christian Smith (1998), the distinction between self-identified Evangelicals and fundamentalists

Figure 1.10　Billy Graham in 1953. Archives of the Billy Graham Center, Wheaton, Illinois/Billy Graham Evangelistic Association.

is a key starting-point for analysis. Shibley's approach is probably correct to the extent that institutional and theological differences at a national level may well be blurred for local churches and individual believers. Smith's data, though, point to significant demographic and sociological differences between the two groups. In general, Evangelicals have more formal education and somewhat higher incomes than fundamentalists. Sixty-five per cent of Evangelicals are women, but only 57 per cent of fundamentalists (a possible consequence of greater fundamentalist conservatism on gender roles); 13 and 19 per cent, respectively, are non-white. Fundamentalists are stronger in the south, Evangelicals in the north. Differences in religious outlook are also interesting. In some ways Evangelicals are more conservative than fundamentalists. Although 61 per cent of fundamentalists compared with 52 per cent of Evangelicals believe the Bible to be literally true, 75 per cent of Evangelicals, but only 65 per cent of fundamentalists, believe in the existence of moral absolutes. Evangelicals are also more active in practising their faith: 80 per cent of them compared with 61 per cent of fundamentalists attend church at least once a week, and significantly higher proportions of Evangelicals have publicly demonstrated their commitment to their beliefs (Smith, C., 1998, pp.22–40). Such statistics indicate that the contrast between Evangelicals and fundamentalists may well be best seen as one of religious culture as much as of theology, with Evangelicals tending to be more activist and critically engaged with the secular world, while fundamentalists are liable to be more defensive, polemical and inward looking. The extensive survival of fundamentalism in the USA contrasts with its almost complete eclipse in the UK.

A related and distinctive feature of the beliefs of many American Evangelicals is what is technically termed 'dispensational premillennialism'. This framework for interpreting the Bible, and applying its teachings regarding the Second Coming of Christ and the end of the world, was initially developed by the English founder of the Plymouth Brethren, John Nelson Darby, in the mid-nineteenth century. Darby believed that human history could be divided into seven periods or dispensations, during each of which God modified his covenant with humankind. The sixth and current dispensation had been initiated with the coming of the Holy Spirit at Pentecost. The seventh and final one would start with the Second Coming of Christ, which Darby believed to be imminent, and would consist of Christ's rule on earth for 1000 years, as predicted in Revelation 20. Although Darby's ideas attracted a limited following in the UK and have influenced some Charismatics in recent years, their impact in the USA has been much greater. The expectation of imminent dramatic divine intervention in human history was consistent with the increasingly insecure temper of Evangelicalism in the decades following the Civil War in the 1860s, and with the sense of stark confrontation between worldliness and Christianity that was engendered by early-twentieth-century fundamentalism. The scheme of thought was very widely disseminated through the Scofield Reference Bible (Figure 1.11), first published in 1909 but still very influential today. Notes giving a dispensationalist reading appear alongside the scriptural text, and are implicitly allowed to assume an authoritative status in the minds of fundamentalists (see Balmer, 1993, pp.32–7).

Moreover, there is a strong strain of apocalyptic interest in American popular culture, which extends well outside specifically Evangelical circles. Fifty per cent of college graduates (and it appears an even higher proportion of less well-educated groups) expect the Second Coming of Christ (Boyer, 1992, pp.14–15). Hal Lindsey's popularization of premillennialism, *Late Great Planet Earth*, was the best selling non-fiction book in the USA in the 1970s and had sold 28 million copies by 1990. Many other books on prophecy have attracted at least six-figure sales (Boyer, 1992, pp.5–6). Widespread interest in such subjects is further stimulated by films and novels,

7 3] REVELATION [7 17

a loud voice to the four angels, to whom it was given to hurt the earth and the sea,

3 Saying, [a]Hurt not the earth, neither the sea, nor the trees, till we have sealed the servants of our God in their foreheads.

(1) *The remnant out of Israel sealed.*

4 And I heard the number of them which were sealed: [b]and there were sealed an hundred *and* forty *and* four thousand [c]of all the tribes of the children of Israel.

5 Of the tribe of Juda *were* sealed twelve thousand. Of the tribe of Reuben *were* sealed twelve thousand. Of the tribe of Gad *were* sealed twelve thousand.

6 Of the tribe of Aser *were* sealed twelve thousand. Of the tribe of Nepthalim *were* sealed twelve thousand. Of the tribe of Manasses *were* sealed twelve thousand.

7 Of the tribe of Simeon *were* sealed twelve thousand. Of the tribe of Levi *were* sealed twelve thousand. Of the tribe of Issachar *were* sealed twelve thousand.

8 Of the tribe of Zabulon *were* sealed twelve thousand. Of the tribe of Joseph *were* sealed twelve thousand. Of the tribe of Benjamin *were* sealed twelve thousand.

(2) *Vision of the Gentiles who are to be saved during the great tribulation.*

9 After this I beheld, and, lo, [d]a great multitude, which no man could number, of all nations, and kindreds, and people, and tongues, stood before the throne, and before the Lamb, clothed with white robes, and palms in their hands;

10 And cried with a loud voice, saying, [e]Salvation to our God which sitteth upon the throne, and unto the Lamb.

11 And all the [f]angels stood round about the throne, and *about* the elders and the four [g]beasts, and fell before the throne on their faces, and worshipped God,

12 Saying, Amen: Blessing, and glory, and wisdom, and thanksgiving, and honour, and power, and might, *be* unto our God for ever and ever. Amen.

13 And one of the [h]elders answered, saying unto me, [i]What are these which are arrayed in white robes? and whence came they?

14 And I said unto him, [j]Sir, thou knowest. And he said to me, [k]These are they which came out of [l]great [1]tribulation, and have washed their robes, and made them [m]white in the blood of the Lamb.

15 Therefore are they [n]before the throne of God, and serve him day and night in his temple: and he that sitteth on the throne shall dwell among them.

16 They shall hunger no more, neither thirst any more; neither shall the sun [o]light on them, nor any [p]heat.

17 For the [q]Lamb which is in the midst of the throne shall feed them, and shall lead them unto [r]liv-

Marginal notes:

[a] Cf. 2 Thes. 2. 7.
[b] Israel (prophecies). Rev. 21. 12. (Gen. 12. 2, 3; Rom. 11. 26.)
[c] Gen. 49. 3, 27; cf. Deut. 33. 6-25; cf. Ezk. 48. 1-7, 23-28.
[d] Cf. Rom. 11. 25; cf. Isa. 60. 5.
[e] Rom. 1. 16, note.
[f] Heb. 1. 4, note.
[g] living creatures.
[h] Elders. vs. 11, 13, 14; Rev. 11. 16. (Acts 11. 30; Tit. 1. 5-9.)
[i] who.
[j] My Lord.
[k] Remnant. vs. 4-8, 12, 17; Rev. 12. 17. (Isa. 1. 9; Rom. 11. 5.)
[l] Tribulation (the great). vs. 13, 14. (Psa. 2. 5.)
[m] 1 John 1. 7; cf. Zech. 3. 3-5.
[n] v. 9.
[o] strike upon.
[p] burning heat.
[q] Shepherd. Ezk. 34. 23.
[r] fountains of waters of life.

[1]The great tribulation is the period of unexampled trouble predicted in the passages cited under that head from Psa. ii. 5 to Rev. vii. 14 and described in Rev. xi.-xviii. Involving in a measure the whole earth (Rev. iii. 10), it is yet distinctively "the time of Jacob's trouble" (Jer. xxx. 7), and its vortex Jerusalem and the Holy Land. It involves the people of God who will have returned to Palestine in unbelief. Its duration is three and a half years, or the last half of the seventieth week of Daniel (Dan. ix. 25-27, *note*; Rev. xi. 2, 3). The *elements* of the tribulation are: (1) The cruel reign of the "beast out of the sea" (Rev. xiii. 1), who, at the beginning of the three and a half years, will break his covenant with the Jews (by virtue of which they will have re-established the temple worship, Dan. ix. 27), and show himself in the temple, demanding that he be worshipped as God (Mt. xxiv. 15; 2 Thes. ii. 4). (2) The active interposition of Satan "having great wrath" (Rev. xii. 12), who gives his power to the Beast (Rev. xiii. 4, 5). (3) The unprecedented activity of demons (Rev. ix. 2, 11); and (4) the terrible "bowl" judgments of Rev. xvi.

The great tribulation will be, however, a period of salvation. An election out of Israel is seen as sealed for God (Rev. vii. 4-8), and, with an innumerable multitude of Gentiles (Rev. vii. 9), are said to have come "out of the great tribulation" (Rev. vii. 14). They are not of the priesthood, the church, to which they seem to stand somewhat in the relation of the Levites to the priests under the Mosaic Covenant. The great tribulation is immediately followed by the return of Christ in glory, and the events associated therewith (Mt. xxiv. 29, 30). See "Remnant" (Isa. i. 9; Rom. xi. 5, *note*); "Beast" (Dan. vii. 8; Rev. xix. 20, *note*); "Armageddon" (Rev. xvi. 14; xix. 11, *note*).

1337

Figure 1.11   A page from the annotated text of the Book of Revelation in the Scofield Reference Bible shows a characteristically dispensationalist interpretation. By permission of the British Library (shelf mark 03051.l.4).

sustained by an underlying sense that the USA has a special place in the divine purposes, and reinforced by fears of nuclear war and cosmic or ecological catastrophe (Boyer, 1992). The extensive presence of such ideas in American popular culture constitutes a noteworthy contrast with the UK and may well be a significant factor in explaining the more widespread appeal of Evangelical ideas in the USA.

In other respects, however, we can see many of the trends analysed in relation to British Evangelicalism replicated and extended across the Atlantic. The Charismatic movement has had a widespread impact, both in shifting theological assumptions and changing styles of worship within the existing denominations, and in prompting the emergence of new, independent Charismatic churches (Hocken, 1994; 1996). As in the UK, the third wave of the 1970s and 1980s has been associated with the advance of ideas of 'spiritual warfare' disseminated by the books of Peretti, Wagner and others (Cox, 1996, pp.281–5).

In 1979, 19 per cent of Americans reportedly identified themselves as Pentecostal or Charismatic (Bebbington, 1994, p.371). A more sophisticated survey carried out in 1992 enabled a distinction to be drawn between those (12.1 per cent) who explicitly identified themselves as Pentecostal or Charismatic, and those (23 per cent) who showed some affinity with these groups in at least one of four ways (self-identification, speaking in tongues, membership of an appropriate denomination or a sense of proximity to such an outlook). The distribution of Pentecostals and Charismatics among different traditions (that is, the percentage of the total number of Pentecostals and Charismatics who identify with each group) was as follows:

Pentecostal denominations 15.5%
Independent Charismatic churches 6.0%
Other Evangelical denominations 25.8%
Mainline Protestants 12.7%
Black Protestants[7] 11.5%
Roman Catholics 22.1%
Others 2.6%

Secular 3.6%

(Smidt *et al.*, 1999, pp.120–2)

---

[7] The category 'black Protestant' relates to non-Pentecostal denominations the membership of which has historically been predominantly or exclusively black. Black people are, of course, also present in the other categories.

These figures are interesting in showing the wide permeation of Charismatic influence across the American religious scene, including numerous Roman Catholics, and even, it would appear, a small element among those not otherwise considering themselves religious. They do, however, point to a particular affinity between Evangelical and Charismatic religious outlooks. A case study of the American Baptist Convention and the Southern Baptist Convention (SBC) shows how both these denominations fairly readily assimilated a significant Charismatic presence during the late 1960s and 1970s. Some tensions were apparent, especially in the more conservative SBC, but these did not become seriously divisive (Schenkel, 1999).

There has also been even more extensive *organizational* change and development in the USA, with numerous denominational splits and regroupings, and the formation of many new local churches. The law and material circumstances are all more conducive to such development than in the UK: building land remains relatively plentiful, planning restrictions are less onerous, and donors of funds are likely to be more numerous and better resourced. There is less cultural attachment to long-standing institutions and structures, and a greater readiness decisively to draw a line under the past and to take vigorous new initiatives. The para-church, educational and literary dimensions of neo-Evangelicalism have also developed apace (see Bebbington, 1994, pp.370–2, 377–8; Smith, C., 1998, pp.12–13). Especially under the influence of the Charismatic movement, with its tendency to break down old boundaries and stir new visions, the trend has been for core denominational structures to become less important relative to interdenominational special-purpose groups and specialist agencies within denominations, such as those specifically promoting Charismatic renewal. Loyalties within congregations can become divided, as some continue to identify primarily with the denomination while others give more weight to other agencies and networks. Each congregation needs to find its own way of resolving such tensions. Hence local diversity within denominations increases, and, in extreme cases, congregations can secede from (leave) their existing denominations in the knowledge that alternative wider networks will remain open to them. The resulting tendency to flexibility and decentralization can be characterized as a distinctively post-modern form of religious organization when contrasted with the bureaucratized and centralized denominational organizations characteristic of modernity (Eisland, 1999, pp.177–85).

In terms of *politicization*, too, British trends can be seen magnified in the USA. By the 1980s, in contrast to the 1950s and 1960s, Evangelicals were the religious group in the USA that was most likely to become politically involved (Hunter, 1987, p.126). Specific moral concerns, above all concerning abortion and homosexuality, loom particularly large, and for some entirely obscure any other agendas (Balmer, 1993, pp.147–75).[8] Moral causes have been vigorously advocated in the 1980s and 1990s by James Dobson's Focus on the Family (founded in 1977), Jerry Falwell's Moral Majority (1979) and Pat Robertson's Christian Coalition of America (1989). These organizations have derived much of their influence from the association of their political campaigns with radio or television ministries, and are large-scale operations. Focus on the Family has nearly 1300 employees and receives up to 55,000 letters a week. Dobson's daily radio broadcasts are carried by 3000 stations in the USA and a further 3000 in 95 other countries (http://www.fotf.org). The Christian Coalition of America claims a membership of 'well over a million', including Roman Catholics and 'other people of faith' as well as Evangelicals, and '1,500 local chapters in all 50 states' (http://www.cc.org). There is a plethora of other organizations and pressure groups, with a total of up to four million active supporters in the late 1980s, although the figures are debatable (Hunter, 1987, pp.125–6).

This 'new Christian Right' has become an important source of support for the Republican Party, even if the sector's particular preoccupations – on abortion above all – have also at times been an embarrassment to the party (Colour Plate 2). The new Christian Right was a substantial factor in popular support for the presidency of Ronald Reagan between 1980 and 1988, and in campaigns for the Republican nomination by Pat Robertson in 1988 and Patrick Buchanan in 1992 and 1996. In the 1996 presidential election, an exit poll suggested that 17 per cent of voters identified with the new Christian Right: of these, 26 per cent supported the incumbent Democratic President, Bill Clinton, and 65 per cent voted for his Republican challenger, Bob Dole (Diamond, 1998, p.4).

As these voting figures indicate, the affinity between Evangelicals and the Republicans, although predominant, was not exclusive. Among black Protestants, who share many Evangelical character-istics, Democratic loyalties are, by contrast, almost universal (Noll, 2001, pp.187–8). Even among whites the picture is much more variegated than it might initially appear. The first and most

---

[8] A personal anecdote seems germane here. In April 1992, while waiting for a flight, I attended worship in the chapel at O'Hare International Airport in Chicago. In subsequent extended conversation with the minister, I made a general remark about the desperate social needs apparent within a few miles of that very airport. I had in mind the deprivation and crime then endemic in parts of west and south Chicago, but my comment was interpreted as a reference to the large numbers of abortions carried out in local hospitals.

authentically 'born again' President of the later twentieth century was a Democrat, Jimmy Carter (1976–80), and it was his election that first led to a sense that Evangelical influence had become a significant political force. Under Bill Clinton (1992–2000), the main source of Evangelical inspiration and guidance in the White House was Tony Campolo, whose high-profile ministry in inner-city Philadelphia is linked to a socially engaged agenda for the renewal of urban community. Campolo's Evangelical Association for the Promotion of Education, founded in 1972, seeks to promote a revolution of the spirit on the streets of the USA 'that reflects the coming Kingdom of God as individuals and entire communities are transformed by God's love' (http://www.tonycampolo.com). The emphasis, in contrast to the stress on moral and family values that characterizes the new Christian Right, is on offering educational opportunities to vulnerable young people in the USA and the Caribbean (http://www.tonycampolo.com). In other churches, at the grass roots, a more liberal and social reformist approach can be found, accompanied by a tendency to treat anti-abortion and anti-gay beliefs as matters of private conviction rather than imperatives for public agitation (Shibley, 1996, pp.101–7). Moreover, two important studies of Evangelical opinion, based on data collected in the mid-1980s (Hunter, 1987) and mid-1990s (Smith, 2000) both point to considerable varieties of outlook. In James Davison Hunter's survey of Evangelical college students in the mid-1980s, nearly as many (30 per cent) were classified as 'liberal' or 'very liberal' as those (36 per cent) who were 'conservative' or 'very conservative'. The majority expressed a commitment to principles of toleration and civility and 76 per cent were either neutral towards or disapproving of the goals of the Moral Majority (Hunter, 1987, pp.136, 146–7). Smith's more recent data point in a similar direction, showing indeed that there was significant opposition to new Christian Right groups among ordinary Evangelicals, and a particular distaste for attempts to force unbelievers to act as if they were Christians. Smith points out the fallacy of assuming that certain high-profile individuals necessarily reflect the views of the rank and file, and concludes:

> When we penetrate with open ears beyond the standard and sometimes hysterical depictions of evangelical politics, we find in evangelicalism instead an enormous amount of diversity, complexity, ambivalence, and disagreement. This has important political consequences, for it generates a multidimensional field of complex clusters of views about faith and politics. In fact, only a minority of evangelicals represent anything like the political threat that evangelicals' antagonists fear. Instead, when it comes to politics, the millions of

ordinary evangelicals look not like a disciplined, charging army, but something more like a divided and hesitant extended family.

(Smith, 2000, p.128)

It is important, therefore, that the high profile of the new Christian Right does not lead to its automatic equation with Evangelicalism as a whole. Indeed, although its cultural and ideological inspiration owes much to Evangelicalism, it has also been shaped by the impulses of civil religion, insofar as the endeavour to create or maintain a 'Christian America' reflects an aspiration to relate the nation as a whole to a sense of purpose and absolute meaning. In 1990, Dobson notably linked the new Christian Right agenda to a formative era in American civil religion by calling on Christians to 'serve as foot soldiers' in what he described as 'a new Civil War of values' (Diamond, 1998, p.2). It may well be that for some supporters of the new Christian Right the appeal of Evangelicalism lies not so much in assent to its core theological and spiritual teachings, as in the sense that it provides a bastion of legitimacy for a crusade against perceived moral decline that seems to threaten traditional American values and identity. The Christian Coalition of America web site (http://www.cc.org) conspicuously displays national symbols, such as the Lincoln and Mount Rushmore monuments, and appears to equate the promotion of 'Christian values in government' almost exclusively with the 'pro-family agenda'.[9]

If, even when the above qualifications are taken into account, the politicization of Evangelicalism is more obvious in the USA than in the UK, its *globalization* is rather less in evidence. It is true that some British ideas and individuals had a wide influence in the USA, and that American Evangelicalism's pre-eminent figure, Billy Graham, developed a genuinely worldwide ministry that can be seen as having a significant globalizing effect. Within the USA itself, however, the sheer size and diversity of the country means that many, perhaps most, Evangelicals continue to have little sense of direct contact with parts of the world beyond its borders. Their consciousness of their religion is that it is something distinctively 'American' rather than being an expression of a global Christian identity that transcends nationality (cf. Balmer, 1993, pp.279–80; Bebbington, 1994, p.280).

[9] On civil religion in the USA, see Parsons (2001), Book 3 in this series. The new Christian Right, however, professes to seek a specifically 'Christian America' rather than the deistical 'one nation under God' of the civil religion derived originally from the founding fathers of the republic. Mark Noll points out that 'The founders' guidelines for religion and society came out of a situation that was much more theistic than some modern liberals admit, but also out of a situation that was much less explicitly Christian than modern evangelicals wish it had been' (Noll, 2001, p.200).

On the other hand, *acculturation* is strongly apparent in American Evangelicalism. One immediately obvious manifestation of this process has been, as in the UK, the changing styles of worship. Political fashion and correctness have led to new hymn texts – including the revision of William Cowper's 'O for a closer walk with God' because of its perceived offensiveness for the disabled (Hamilton, 1999, p.31). More radically, there has been a greatly increased use of songs that have been shaped by contemporary musical and cultural idioms, forms that are increasingly global rather than indigenous in their sources of inspiration. These are a significant exception to the prevailing insularity of American Evangelicalism noted above. Musical trends, moreover, had an impact on the wider culture of Evangelicalism in two notable respects. First, for the baby-boomer generation, whose teenage and young adult experience was moulded in the 1960s, music itself has become 'the primary carrier of its symbols and values', and hence musical preferences may be a defining feature of congregations and a source of dissension and schism within them (Hamilton, 1999, p.30). Second, the growth since the 1970s of commercially produced recordings of Christian music has meant that, especially for young adults, devotional and inspirational music is no longer limited primarily to the immediate context of collective Sunday worship, and the experience of it is as much individualistic as corporate. At the same time, the Christian music industry has increasingly been driven by the search for commercial success, which has encouraged the 'popularization and dilution of the evangelical message necessary to build a large mass market' and an accommodation to the styles of secular popular music (Romanowski, 2000).

In other ways too American Evangelicals are divided by their varying levels of accommodation to contemporary culture. Some happily reconcile a secular yuppie lifestyle with their core convictions, whereas others see themselves at odds with a decadent modern world. In general, churches that espouse the former position are the more successful (Shibley, 1996, pp.83–92). An extreme but revealing example is provided by Willow Creek Community Church near Chicago, where the whole context and style of worship has been developed with a view to enabling previously unchurched 'seekers' to feel immediately at home (Figure 1.12). Having surveyed its target audience of younger middle-class adults, Willow Creek adopted a marketing strategy redolent of secular commercialism. The physical appearance of the church resembles a corporate headquarters and a place of secular entertainment far more than a conventional place of worship. Services are rigorously planned and rehearsed to ensure professional standards in components such as drama and music. The

Figure 1.12   The food court at Willow Creek Church illustrates its policy of reproducing mainstream American material culture so as to make 'seekers' feel at home. Fred Mayer/Magnum.

preaching, led by Bill Hybels, the church's founder and senior pastor, is inclusive and non-threatening. It is designed to lead people to Christian faith gradually, through teaching that engages with their current felt needs, rather than through the calls to immediate radical conversion characteristic of traditional Evangelicalism. Hybels's approach has been notably successful, as measured by the tens of thousands of people drawn to the church, but has been criticized by fellow Evangelicals for a tendency to compromise the perceived essence of the gospel and to accept a shallow Christianity (Pritchard, 1996).

At the same time, more traditional approaches to evangelism continued. For example, the ageing Billy Graham was still preaching at mass evangelistic rallies in the late 1990s. He showed himself very adaptable to cultural and technological change, espousing both contemporary Christian music and the Internet as media for his message, but his essential approach and challenge to repentance and decision remained what it had been half a century before. It still brought impressive results, with many thousands of conversions claimed at his crusades in Tampa, Florida in October 1998 and in St Louis in October 1999 (Gillespie, 1998, p.30; Paulson, 1999, pp.6–10).

If, as I have argued, kaleidoscopic diversity characterizes contemporary British Evangelicalism, this quality is found in greatly magnified and multidimensional form on the other side of the Atlantic. In the late 1980s and early 1990s, Randall Balmer, a leading scholar of American religion, travelled widely around the USA observing various expressions of Evangelicalism. His account provides one of many possible cross-sections of Evangelical activity in the USA (Balmer, 1993). At Calvary Chapel, Santa Ana, California, a so-called megachurch whose activities involve up to 25,000 people a week, he found a literalistic approach to the Bible. (For an illustration of another megachurch, see Colour Plate 3.) This might prompt application of the 'fundamentalist' label, but the worship has a non-confrontational style and shows an effective engagement with contemporary culture that attracts many young people.

At Dallas Theological Seminary in Texas, however, a major centre for the dissemination of a fundamentalist view of an **inerrant** Bible, cultural and social attitudes (notably regarding the status of women) were much more conservative. A similar conservatism was apparent at Multnomah School of the Bible in Portland, Oregon. This provides a degree curriculum dominated by study of the Bible, conservative theology and morality, and has a subculture seemingly insulated from much of contemporary America. A professor who went to jazz festivals was regarded as 'avant garde'.

Charismatic and Pentecostal influences have had a variegated impact. In Phoenix, Arizona, Balmer encountered Neal Frisby, a Pentecostal revivalist leading his own ambitious movement and claiming prophetic revelations and healing powers, but in reality ministering to a dwindling band of followers at his so-called Capstone Cathedral. Frisby's faltering religious showmanship can be contrasted with the blend of tradition and spirit-led innovation evident at the Church of the King, a Charismatic Episcopalian Church in Valdosta, Georgia. This congregation originated when the pastor of an Assemblies of God (AOG) Pentecostal church was removed as a result of his ecumenical and liturgical inclinations. Members of the congregation left with him, formed a new congregation, and subsequently decided to affiliate to the Episcopal Church.

A range of other activities and enterprises help to sustain the Evangelical subculture. Balmer visited Donald Thompson, a director of films with an Evangelical message, at work on location in Iowa, and explored the exhibition hall of the Christian Booksellers Association annual convention, at which numerous Bibles, books on Christian lifestyle and assorted ephemera were on sale. At a youth camp on Word of Life Island on Schroon Lake in upstate New York, teenagers shared a week of outdoor pursuits and fundamentalist bible teaching, and were called to conversion or rededication to Christ. At 'Camp Freedom' in Florida, the camp meeting tradition of early-nineteenth-century revivalism continues to inspire an older generation, who meet for twelve days of 'old time gospel preaching and singing'. In Central Park, New York, Billy Graham reiterated his well-tried formula for 'getting right with God' (Balmer, 1993).

Political and social engagements are various. Evangelical Republican activists campaigning for Pat Robertson in the 1988 Iowa caucuses, with opposition to abortion uppermost on their agenda, were certainly representative of much Evangelical opinion. A rounded picture, however, needs to take into account organizations such as Voice of Calvary Ministries working among underprivileged black people in Mississippi, promoting community development and social justice focused on multi-racial church fellowship. At the end of his explorations, Balmer somewhat wearily concluded that 'Discerning any single pattern in American evangelicalism is difficult at best' (Balmer, 1993, p.278).

It may well be, however, that the multifarious nature of American Evangelicalism is actually its greatest strength. It offers, beneath the capacious umbrella of belief in the need for conversion and the authoritative status of the Bible, such numerous forms of religious and cultural expression that it has proved to be adaptable to almost any context. Mark Noll, a leading American Evangelical historian, has recently described his tradition as 'the premier example of "culturally adaptive biblical experientialism" in the whole history of Christianity' (Noll, 2001, p.287). Thus, in the USA, Evangelicalism can be viewed as a 'popular' religion, with mass support to an extent remote from the British experience. Especially in the south, Evangelicalism attracts substantial lower- as well as middle-class participation. Of course, individual churches and organizations can and do falter – as in the case of Frisby, who had evidently seen better days at the time Balmer visited him (Balmer, 1993, p.86). At the same time, however, others closer to short-term cultural currents can be gaining ground substantially. Thus, in a 'midsize California city' studied by Mark Shibley, both Hope Baptist Church, affiliated to the SBC, and New Life Christian Assembly, linked to the AOG, were struggling, while local Vineyard and Calvary Chapel congregations were flourishing. The latter churches, Shibley argues, were much better attuned to the secular culture and lifestyles of the 1980s and 1990s (Shibley, 1996, pp.45–92).

Meanwhile, the tens of millions of believers who make up the Evangelical subculture in the USA are numerically strong enough to sustain a breadth and range of activity that limits potentially corrosive encounters with secular American life. Childhood friendships can be centred on the church as much as on school, and young people seeking higher education have a range of Bible institutes and

Christian liberal arts colleges from which to choose. Hence, unlike their British counterparts, even firm conservatives have little reason to fear that their children's acquisition of a degree will corrode the purity of their faith. Adult social networks can similarly be largely church-based, while Evangelical mindsets are sustained by a wide range of books, magazines, films, music and other media. One commentator observes that Evangelicals create:

> ... a nearly total 'Christian' environment within the American culture, with an evangelical clone of nearly every secular organization, service, or product. It has resulted in, among possible examples, 'Christian' versions of the Scouts like AWANA (Approved Workmen Are Not Ashamed), tour packages to the Holy Land on the Lord's Airline, and the high kitsch of 'Jesus Junque': the Jesus frisbees, bumper stickers, posters, pencils, plaques, tea bags, and T-shirts that are often prominently displayed in evangelical bookstores. To quote an evangelical bumper sticker of the 1970s, the prevailing sentiment seems to be that 'Things Go Better With Jesus,' whether it be in having a family doctor who belongs to the Christian Medical Association or insisting that it be a 'Jesus frisbee' one throws to the family dog.
>
> (Eskridge, 1989, pp.131–2)

While some such resources are increasingly available in the UK, scope for living entirely within the subculture is much more limited.

Broadcasting is a particularly prominent characteristic of the American Evangelical subculture, and serves further to maintain and extend its impact. By contrast, in the UK, with its history of close regulation of the airwaves and domination of religious broadcasting by the establishment ethos of the BBC, there has until very recent years been little scope for any kind of sustained Evangelical presence on radio and television. In the USA, however, broadcast Evangelical ministries have a history almost as long as the medium of radio itself, beginning in the 1920s with pioneers such as Aimee Semple McPherson and continuing in the 1930s and 1940s with programmes such as Charles E. Fuller's 'Old Fashioned Revival Hour'. In the mid-1950s, Evangelicals were buying more than $10 million worth of radio air time annually, and some pioneers, such as Oral Roberts (Colour Plate 4), to be followed shortly by Jerry Falwell and Pat Robertson, were already beginning to experiment with television.

Robertson's Christian Broadcasting Network first went on the air in October 1961, serving a merely local audience in Portsmouth, Virginia (http://www.cbn.com). It expanded rapidly, however, and by the 1980s had an annual budget of $110 million from contributions, and cable access to 20 million homes. Like other Evangelical television stations, it offered evangelistic and teaching programmes alongside a substantial element of 'wholesome' secular entertainment. Such broadcasting serves both to reinforce the commitment of the faithful and to facilitate outreach to wider audiences: on the basis of one survey, it appears that approximately 34 million American households watched at least one religious programme during February 1985. Religious broadcasting also serves as a prominent and significant illustration of the ambivalent relationship of Evangelicals to modernity. In the 'electric church' as it has been termed, there is enthusiastic exploitation of high technology and contemporary entrepreneurialism in order to disseminate a message that at times seems very much at odds with the dominant values of secular culture (Eskridge, 1989, pp.128–35; Frankl, 1987, pp.149–55; Ostling, 1984, p.52).

How, at a more theoretical level, can we attempt to explain the strength of Evangelicalism in contemporary America, flying as it apparently does in the face of the religious decline that secularization theorists would hold to be characteristic of modernized societies? A significant attempt to engage with this question was made by the sociologist James Davison Hunter in the 1980s. Hunter argued that the predominant trend among contemporary Evangelicals was an accommodation to the secular world. They tended to adapt and rationalize their spirituality to conform to modernity, acquiring a civility – as Hunter put it – that led them to downplay the potentially more offensive aspects of their beliefs, such as divine judgement on human sinfulness. They were also increasingly prone to emphasize the subjective dimensions of their beliefs, as a means to self-fulfilment. At the same time, Hunter acknowledged, the growing politicization of Evangelicals in an attempt to confront the perceived moral decline of American public life was a sign of their resistance to modernity. His prognosis for their future was pessimistic, because he judged that although they were gradually being assimilated to secular mores, they were most successful among social and cultural groups that were relatively insulated from the modern world (Hunter, 1983), whose support would consequently fall away.

The latest and most convincing attempt to answer the question posed above has been through a detailed survey and series of personal interviews with Evangelicals and others, led by Christian Smith and conducted at the University of North Carolina in the mid-1990s. Smith judges that Hunter's approach is not supported by the data. In his view, Evangelicals are neither insulated from the modern world nor ready to capitulate to it (Smith, C., 1998, pp.75–82). His material also leads him to question an alternative suggestion that Evangelical religious activism has been stirred by a consciousness of threatened social status. Evangelicals might worry that the USA as a whole was in peril of decline because it was turning from God's ways, but these national concerns did not translate into fears for their individual situations (Smith, C., 1998, pp.83–4). Another possibility, advanced by Dean Kelley in the 1970s and Laurence Iannaccone in the 1990s, is that it is 'strict' religious groups, which demand intense commitment from their adherents, that thrive best in the modern world. Again, Smith is sceptical, on the grounds that 'strictness' is a quality more readily associated with fundamentalists than Evangelicals, whereas it is the latter, with their general readiness to be open and undemanding towards the enquirer, who are more evidently flourishing (Smith, C., 1998, pp.84–5). Further support for Smith's argument here is provided by Shibley's work on Californian churches, which shows the more rigid fundamentalist churches to be in decline, while those that are less inflexible, at least in terms of explicit lifestyle demands, are flourishing (Shibley, 1996).

A more promising approach, according to Smith, is provided by the 'competitive marketing' theory advanced by Roger Finke and Rodney Stark. These two scholars have argued that Evangelicalism has succeeded in contemporary America because it has in effect adopted many of the cultural characteristics of secular free market capitalism. In the UK and other European countries, Finke and Stark argue, a history of state churches and government regulation of religion has been productive of religious lethargy. In the USA, however, the absence of such constraints has allowed a free rein for religious 'entrepreneurs', who have been able successfully to 'market' their spiritual 'products'. Although individual churches and movements may decline because they are insufficiently attuned to the market, the wide variety of religious options available ensures that overall there is an expanding ability to attract more consumers. In American Evangelicalism, as in secular American entrepreneurialism and consumerism, the diversity and fluidity that permits a widespread popular appeal is very much more of a strength than a weakness (Smith, C., 1998, pp.73–4, 85–7).

Smith proceeds to develop Finke and Stark's arguments, advancing the wider proposition that Evangelicalism thrives in a context of cultural pluralism by providing a distinctive subcultural identity that is consistent with modernity rather than at odds with it. He sees it as exemplifying his theory that in general:

> Religion survives and can thrive in pluralistic, modern society by embedding itself in subcultures that offer satisfying morally orienting collective identities which provide adherents meaning and belonging.
>
> ...

> In a pluralistic society, those religious groups will be relatively stronger which better possess and employ the cultural tools needed to create both clear distinction from and significant engagement and tension with other relevant outgroups, short of becoming genuinely countercultural.
>
> (Smith, C., 1998, pp.118–19)

Evangelicals, Smith argues, have a strong sense of their distinctiveness, both from the contemporary secular world and from other forms of Christianity. They believe themselves to be possessed of ultimate truth, practical moral superiority and a distinctive lifestyle. At the same time, they do not turn their backs on the rest of society, but engage with it in pursuing evangelistic and social mission, and in seeking to call back to God a nation that they perceive as morally and spiritually degenerate. The consequent sense of tension and conflict further strengthens Evangelical identity and solidarity (Smith, C., 1998, pp.120–44).

It is important to note that Smith's approach is predicated on an initial clear distinction between Evangelicals and fundamentalists. In relation to fundamentalism, it would seem that some of the arguments he rejects have a continuing validity, notably the indications that a somewhat lower educational and social status provides some insulation from modernizing trends, and that 'strictly' held beliefs can retain a large following. Nevertheless, such a recognition supports rather than weakens the underlying argument that American Evangelicalism's strength lies precisely in the diversity of approaches and strategies that it offers to its adherents as they maintain conservative Christian convictions in the face of modernity.

In concluding this section, we need finally to engage with the claim made by Balmer and others that 'Evangelicalism itself ... is quintessentially American' (Balmer, 1993, p.280; Hunter, 1983, p.7). Stated thus baldly, the assertion appears a problematic one, in the light of an awareness that the historic origins of Evangelicalism were as much European as American, and that its contemporary presence is apparent in many parts of the globe. Balmer goes on to explain that the absence of a state church in America has led to a free market and populist style of religious observance to which Evangelicalism has proved itself particularly well suited. This, however, does not make Evangelicalism 'quintessentially American', although it certainly has assumed distinctive American forms and has enjoyed a degree of success in the USA that is unparalleled elsewhere in the developed world. As we have noted, although the much smaller British Evangelical movement has been exposed to numerous influences from the USA and has developed in many parallel ways, it still has distinctive characteristics that stem from specific circumstances indigenous to the UK. In particular, in a manner that would seem directly at odds with Balmer's linking of Evangelical success to the absence of a state church, Evangelicals and Charismatics have become increasingly influential in the Church of England.

Nevertheless, although it hardly makes sense to regard the global Evangelical movement as 'quintessentially American', in view of the economic, cultural and political power of the USA, American expressions of Evangelicalism are likely to be particularly influential in other parts of the world. The case of Latin America, to which we now turn, provides an important context in which the scale and extent of their impact can be explored.

Latin America

The previous sections have emphasized the kaleidoscopic quality of Evangelicalism as a shifting and diverse religious movement that defies neat categorization and whose relationships to processes of modernization, secularization and cultural change in the north Atlantic world are complex and ambiguous. Moreover, not only is the pattern a variegated and constantly changing one, but its overall shape appears very different depending on the geographical and cultural perspective of the observer. From the standpoint of the more secular kind of British journalism or academic analysis, the Evangelical and Charismatic movements are apt to appear as a relatively marginal subcultural aberration in a process of seemingly inexorable secularization. Even in the UK, though, the view from the inside, for example from the EA, or in the context of particular localities (above all, Northern Ireland) or social groups (notably university students) would give these movements much greater significance. In the USA, the sheer scale of these movements, and of at least diffuse sympathy for their tenets, makes it impossible for even their critics to see them as merely marginal. It is still possible for secular commentators, at least in the relatively non-Evangelical metropolises of the east coast, to play down the depth of their impact, but the reality of their role in contributing to a widespread religious reference in modern American life cannot easily be denied.

Despite these obvious differences, however, the American and British cases are both located within the framework of advanced industrial societies that have historically been predominantly Protestant. In both countries, the key analytical issues thus relate, as we have seen, to varieties of confrontation, resistance or accommodation between Evangelicalism, modernity and secularity. The Latin American perspective, to which we now turn, immediately raises a radically different set of questions. Here the central issue is not why Evangelicalism/Pentecostalism has flourished, or at least held its own, in a secular modern society. Rather, it is why Evangelicalism/ Protestantism has in recent decades so dramatically expanded in cultures whose historic religious allegiances have combined official Roman Catholicism with a strong vein of traditional popular belief. This expansion, moreover, has occurred primarily in lower-class social groups, a noticeable difference of emphasis from American Evangelicalism and an almost complete contrast with the more socially élite character of British Evangelicalism. A further striking contrast is that in Latin America, unlike the UK or the USA, Pentecostalism is the overwhelmingly predominant manifestation of Evangelicalism, rather than being merely a prominent strand within a diverse whole. Why is it that the Latin American poor have been drawn to Pentecostalism in such substantial numbers? In the light particularly of similarly rapid Pentecostal growth in other regions, such as sub-Saharan Africa and east Asia, what can this process tell us about the wider situation of religion in the contemporary world?

Before addressing these questions directly, it will first be helpful to give some greater specificity to the broad figures for Pentecostal expansion in Latin America. The estimate of increase in membership in South America from 1.16 million to 22.22 million during the last four decades of the twentieth century noted above is indicative of the exponential nature of the growth that has occurred, but the actual figures need to be treated with caution. A parallel estimate of 'probably 30–35 million' (Freston, 1998c, p.337) for the whole of Latin America (including Central America) in the mid-1990s does, however, appear consistent. Pentecostals amount to about two-thirds of a total Evangelical/Protestant[10] population of about 45 million, which is itself about 10 per cent of the overall population of the region. With the figures thus stated, Pentecostals might appear to be a relatively small minority in a population in which nominal Roman Catholicism is still overwhelmingly dominant. The scale and dynamism of their recent expansion, however, gives some substance to the proposition that Latin America may be 'turning Protestant' (Colour Plate 5). It has been estimated that 'perhaps less than 20 per cent' (Martin, 1990, p.58) of the population are actively Catholic, in the sense of attending mass on a regular basis. Even though not all professed Protestants are

[10] In Latin America, the words *protestante* and *evangélico* are synonymous (Freston, 1998c, p.38).

regularly committed to the practice of their religion, the proportion of activists appears to be significantly larger, barely below a half even on a pessimistic estimate (Cleary and Sepúlveda, 1997, p.110). Accordingly, the balance between committed Pentecostal and Catholic religious practitioners may be less radically unequal than would appear at first sight.

Moreover, the overall figures obscure considerable national and social variation in the Pentecostal presence (Figure 1.13). The Evangelicals, of whom over 60 per cent are Pentecostal, are disproportionately numerous in Brazil, the largest country in the continent, where their numbers amounted to as much as 15 per cent of the population by 1998 (Freston, 1998a, p.337). In the mid-1980s, the number of full-time Protestant pastors in the country already exceeded the number of Roman Catholic priests. In Chile, between 15 and 20 per cent of the population are Protestant (Martin, 1990, pp.50–1). Recent decades have seen particularly rapid Pentecostal growth in the smaller countries of Central America: up to 30 per cent of the population of Guatemala are now Protestant, and three-quarters of these Protestants are Pentecostals, while Costa Rica, El Salvador and Nicaragua all have a Protestant presence in the 15–20 per cent range. Other countries, including Argentina, Columbia (which has traditionally had particularly strong Catholic loyalties) and Mexico, have shown slower rates of growth. Even in Mexico, however, although the proportion of Protestants, at 6–7 per cent of population, appears relatively modest, this still represents a substantial presence of up to 5 million people. Bolivia is now 11 per cent Protestant, although there – as in Peru (2–3 per cent Protestant) – within Protestantism **Adventist** groups have predominated over Pentecostals. Significantly, the stoniest ground for Pentecostal advance has been in the two most developed and secularized countries of Latin America, Uruguay and Venezuela (Freston, 1998c, pp.337–8; Martin, 1990, pp.51–2).

In seeking to explain the appeal of Pentecostalism in Latin America, we can usefully begin by quoting an evocative passage from the (1990) survey of the phenomenon by a leading British sociologist of religion, David Martin. He is writing specifically about Columbia, but his account can be applied to impoverished urban areas across the continent.

> The difficulties of the present time of transition are so dramatically illustrated in Bogota (as in São Paulo, Rio, Lima, Guatemala City, Mexico City) that they need brief enumeration. People in the *barrios* [shanty towns] of Bogota live in conditions of total frustration bordered by unattainable hope. In the near distance are vast insurance blocks; in the immediate vicinity there are women leading donkeys

Figure 1.13   Political map of South America. From *Philip's Atlas of the World*, Comprehensive Edition (1998). George Philip Ltd.

carrying firewood and homeless urchins importuning passers-by or squabbling in murderous gangs. Unemployment is chronic and over-employment in terms of hours worked for money received severe. ... The Columbian city-dweller is familiar with the desertion of wives by husbands, and the short duration of a fractured childhood. Desperate women have recourse to prostitution. The city-dweller suffers from sleeplessness and irritability and even from poor hearing, all brought on by noise and confusion and the tremors of continuous uncertainty. The nightmare breeds a mal-aise, dis-ease, and dis-tress, in which the physical and the psychical are intermingled.

Into this transitional zone of pullulating [expanding/sprouting] city life, emerging within the context of rapid and warped economic development, comes the new message proferred [*sic*] by the Pentecostals. The Pentecostals speak the language of the people, either through vast campaigns or through the intimate invitations of relatives, friends and evangelists. They propose a restoration of scarred and fractured relationships, a repudiation of corruption, a discipline of life, an affirmation of personal worth, a cancellation of guilt, a chance to speak and to participate, sisterhoods and brother-hoods of mutual support in sickness and in health, and a way to attain *Sanidad Divina* [divine healing]. The *Sanidad Divina* deals precisely in the psychical and physical viewed as intimately bound up together. Pentecostalism offers the old fiesta in the form of lively worship, the old trances in the form of spiritual ecstasy, and the old networks in the form of the brotherhood. Perhaps ... it is the autonomy, the self-support, the liveliness, and the chance of release and participation which count for most in the Pentecostal appeal, plus a sense of having something which nobody else has. So far as the Pentecostals themselves are concerned their conversion is a matter of being literally 'shaken' by a total reorientation of the heart and the will in order to join the ultimate fiesta: 'Estamos de fiesta con Jesus; al cielo yo quiero ir ...' [We are at fiesta with Jesus; I seek to go to heaven ...].

(Martin, 1990, p.83)

This passage powerfully conveys a sense of the interaction of spiritual and more material factors (Colour Plate 6) in first drawing people to Pentecostalism and then sustaining their involvement. Although distinct analytical categories are foreign to lived human experience, it is nevertheless helpful to draw out some of the threads in these processes, in suggesting reasons for the spiritual appeal of Pentecostalism and in pointing up the social and cultural forces with which it is interwoven.

It is apparent above all that Pentecostalism provides many of the Latin American poor with intense spiritual and psychical experience that serves as a genuine source of meaning and comfort in otherwise depressing and marginalized lives (Colour Plate 7). Its effectiveness rests to a considerable extent on its congruence with a primarily oral and popular culture, in which both the authoritarian religious structures of the Roman Catholic Church and the intellectual and textual ethos of non-Pentecostal Protestantism are alienating to many. For illiterate and semi-literate people, the Pentecostal sense of direct empowering encounter with God, supported through the oral narratives of those who have already experienced conversion and baptism in the Spirit, can be compellingly attractive. Such accounts draw others by their palpable expressions of joy and peace and the attainment of a sense of inner wholeness and purpose. The mood is sustained by shared worship, as in a congregation meeting in a courtyard in a run-down neighbourhood of Rio de Janeiro, where almost all the worshippers are brown and black:

> They belt out joyful choruses, clap their hands, and raise their arms toward the stars, dimmed but not defeated by Rio's mantle of smog. The lyrics proclaim that God is here, that rivers of blessings are flowing, that Jesus loves us. Sometimes the mood changes and the people sing a muted, almost mournful melody about the sorrow and heartbreak of life, but underneath a *cantus firmus* [steady chant] about the love and nurturance of God continues to pulsate.
>
> (Cox, 1996, p.162)

Moreover, among Pentecostal communities, experiences of perceived miraculous physical healings are widespread, even to the extent of apparent raisings of the dead. The outsider may well be sceptical, but can still acknowledge the power of linkages of body, mind and spirit that are beyond current medical understanding. To the insider, however, such events serve to confirm conviction and spiritual excitement and offer a dramatic testimony to further potential converts. According to one recent study, initial attendance at a Pentecostal church often arises from illness or personal troubles and 'for Pentecostal Churches and their members the healing experience is indissolubly linked to their conversion, which in turn is the core religious experience' (Lehmann, 1996, p.145).

In this respect, contemporary Latin American popular culture provides receptive soil for Pentecostal claims and experience in a manner reminiscent of the world of the New Testament or of the north Atlantic world in the seventeenth and eighteenth centuries. This is a world in which many continue to acknowledge the reality and immediacy of non-material forces. Some scholars interpret the growth of Pentecostalism as founded in a folk Catholicism, in which popular shrines, charms and miracles had always been widespread. For people reared in such a tradition, Pentecostalism offers a similar access to the supernatural, but one relatively free from the sometimes tiresome obligations of ritual and pilgrimage, and with its own all-encompassing sacred object, the Holy Bible (Cox, 1996, pp.174, 178). A further significant affinity is with Afro-Brazilian religions. These movements, notably Umbanda and Candomblé, draw on transplanted African primal religiosity and emphasize the exorcism of evil spirits and propitiatory sacrifices to deities. They originated among the black population, but have increasingly spread to all classes and ethnic groups, with a particular appeal to urban dwellers. Although only 1.5 per cent of the Brazilian population are active adherents of these religions, they have a widespread cultural influence (Pierucci and Prandi, 2000, pp.233–4). Despite the ideological antagonism of Pentecostals to these 'possession cults', there is an obvious affinity in the endeavour to harness spiritual forces, seek healing and expel devils. The difference lies in the Pentecostal stress on human free will, on the church rather than a medium as mediator with the spirit world, and on the single transforming presence of the Holy Spirit rather than on the encounter with numerous individual spirits. For Pentecostals, exorcism has a once and for all quality; for the cults, it is an endless ongoing process of negotiation (Lehmann, 1996, pp.145–52). Thus, Pentecostalism can relate to a spiritual culture derived from the cults while offering more radical and lasting solutions to the perceived cosmic struggle with the powers of evil. Meanwhile, as Martin points out, Pentecostalism offers a spiritualization of the fiesta, with all its central importance in Latin American popular culture. Such preconditions do not fully explain why particular individuals and not others are drawn to Pentecostalism, as much is dependent on the contingencies of individual personality and circumstance, but they do provide a good indication of why this particular form of Christianity has found much fertile soil in Latin America (Martin, 1990, pp.68–70, 169–71, 185–97, 203 onwards; Schulze, 1994; Wilson, 1994, pp.98–103).

At the same time, Pentecostalism offers significant material advantages to its adherents. In a society where personal association and connection is of crucial importance in securing employment and basic social support, it offers a framework of committed community to dwellers in the otherwise socially fragmented slums. Evidence on whether Pentecostalism provides a channel to social and economic advance for its adherents is hitherto inconclusive, but it certainly offers a degree of security against lapse into the destitute underclass, and for its pastors and other leaders an important source of status and influence in the community.

It also makes a significant contribution to bettering the situation of women, who predominate in Pentecostal congregations. For them, it provides a source of human dignity and spiritual purpose in the face of often degrading circumstances, and the potential for forms of activity and even leadership denied to them in other spheres. Where their menfolk are also drawn into Pentecostalism, the ethos of the movement can serve to check the destructive dimensions of cultural *machismo* (whereby men assert their virility in flamboyant, violent and promiscuous ways), and to induce a new commitment to sobriety, sexual fidelity and domestic duties that significantly improves the circumstances of their partners and families (Martin, 1990, pp.181–3, 205–32; Smilde, 1994). Granted that the underlying ideology of Pentecostalism remains deeply patriarchal, its assertion of the spiritual equality of the sexes can still serve to empower women in the domestic sphere, and the patriarchalism of the pastor can exercise a check on that of the husband. Although in this respect the impact of Pentecostalism is as yet largely confined to private and family life, it still suggests a long-term potential for prompting more wide-ranging improvements in the role of women in Latin American society (Drogus, 1997). There is an interesting parallel to be drawn here with the paradoxical role of Evangelicalism in nineteenth-century Britain, in prompting an expansion of women's dignity and social roles even as it asserted an ideology that appeared to maintain their subordination to men (Davidoff and Hall, 1987).

Martin locates his analysis of the spectacular growth of Pentecostalism in Latin America in an historical and theoretical framework that relates it more widely to the similarly impressive growth of **Methodism** in Britain and the USA in the eighteenth and early nineteenth centuries. In all three contexts, according to Martin, one observes the growth of a new voluntarist counterculture breaking up the traditional religious and cultural unities that had been Anglican in the north Atlantic world, Roman Catholic in Latin America (Martin, 1990). These changes appear to be fuelled by urbanization and other rapid social change associated with modernization, although it is important to note that in contemporary Latin America – as in Britain and the USA in the past – Protestant religious revivalism has been very much in evidence in rural as well as urban settings. The breakdown of a religious monopoly and an upsurge in pluralism can be seen as providing long-term preconditions for secularization, but in the medium term, in Latin America as in the USA, it appears to be a source of religious innovation and vitality. Such an interpretation inevitably glosses over historical and geographical specificities, notably the differences between historically Anglican and Roman Catholic cultures, but it offers much broad coherence and plausibility.

Evangelicalism and Pentecostalism in Latin America have grown out of a complex and controversial interaction between external and indigenous influences. The origins of Protestantism in the region lay in an era of missions and of Bible distribution and translation in the nineteenth century. This was followed by a period in which liberal governments encouraged immigration by Europeans and North Americans as a means of promoting economic and social advance. In Guatemala at least, under Liberal rule from 1873, an expanded Protestant presence was encouraged as a means of checking the power of the Roman Catholic Church in the education system and in the rural social order (Steigenga, 1994, pp.146–8). In more recent times, American influences have remained significant. Billy Graham has visited on a number of occasions, addressing total audiences of well over half a million in Rio de Janeiro in 1974. In 1991, his crusade in Buenos Aires was beamed to 850 satellite locations in 20 countries across South and Central America, and drew total audiences of around 5 million (Billy Graham Center Museum, information sheets). American televangelism has also had a considerable impact, with Jimmy Swaggert enjoying great popularity in Latin America until his ministry was destroyed by scandals in the late 1980s (Greenway, 1994, p.192).

Some commentators have continued to dwell on the extent to which Latin American Protestantism constitutes an export of the 'American gospel' (for example, Brouwer *et al.*, 1996, pp.51–73), but there has been an increasing readiness to acknowledge that, almost from the outset, the movement has also had a strongly indigenous character. For example, the origins of Chilean Pentecostalism have been presented as independent of the Azusa Street revival (1906) in Los Angeles. The enforced secession in 1910 of the Chilean revivalists from the Methodist Episcopal Mission Board:

> ... converted the young Chilean Pentecostalism into becoming one of the earlier self-supporting, self-governing and self-propagating Latin American Protestant churches. Since then, a complex relation of continuity and discontinuity between the new movement and its surrounding popular culture developed. Chilean pentecostal identity (or identities) can be seen as a result of this dynamic of continuity and discontinuity. As the process of selection and/or substitution implied in this dynamic has been made from within instead of from without the local culture, Pentecostalism has effectively succeeded in incarnating the gospel into the *mestizo* [mixed Spanish and native] culture of Chilean peasantry and lower class urban population. Chilean pentecostal identity is, then, the fruit of a process of syncretization between the Protestant (Methodist) legacy and the religious culture of the *mestizo* lower classes of Chilean society.
>
> (Sepúlveda, 1999, pp.131–2)

A similar process has been apparent in Guatemala, albeit originating at a later period – the early 1960s – when splits between indigenous Protestants and American missionaries resulted in the emergence of a new generation of indigenous leaders. The new leaders developed churches with a much stronger affinity with local culture, and these proceeded to grow rapidly. At the same period, disruption of traditional patterns of agriculture, the general modernization of Guatemalan rural society and extensive political violence stirred insecurities that provided receptive soil for Pentecostalism. Guatemala, geographically much closer to the USA than is Chile, has continued to be exposed to strong American involvement in its religious life, but the spectacular growth of Pentecostalism in recent decades is only explicable when it is recognized that the movement has also become extensively indigenized (Steigenga, 1994; Wilson, 1997). Significantly, one scholar, who began his research on Latin American Protestantism with the assumption that its expansion was primarily a factor of influences and money from the USA, eventually concluded that 'Latin Protestants explode in growth because they are an autochthonous [indigenous] movement, coming primarily from the poor' (quoted in Núñez and Taylor, 1996, p.457).

Although the core appeal of Pentecostalism has been to the urban poor, the movement has increasingly established itself in a wide variety of cultural and social settings, an adaptability that is a product of its own internal diversity. In a study of Brazil, which has much the most substantial Pentecostal community in the continent, three waves of advance during the course of the twentieth century have been identified (Freston, 1995). The first wave followed the initial emergence of Pentecostalism as an international movement in the first two decades of the century. This was reflected in Brazil in the formation of two major churches, the Christian Congregation (1910) and the AOG (1911). The former originated among Italian immigrants; the latter was founded by Swedish missionaries and maintains formal contact with the AOG in the USA. Both, however, are now thoroughly indigenized. In the mid-1990s, the Christian Congregation had between 1 and 2 million members, concentrated in the state of São Paulo; the AOG had between 7 and 8 million members and a presence across the country. Initially, though, these churches had grown slowly. Indeed, Pentecostalism as a whole appeared relatively marginal in Brazil until the second wave of the 1950s and 1960s saw the formation of the Church of the Four-Square Gospel (1951), Brazil for Christ (1955) and God is Love (1962). The Church of the Four-Square Gospel was initially an American import, having originated in Los Angeles in the 1920s, although the Brazilian branch achieved full independence in 1988. It appealed to 'the top social rung of the

Pentecostal world' (Freston, 1995, p.126). Brazil for Christ, however, was founded by a Brazilian, Manoel de Mello. Both these churches sought to move beyond the traditional church-based activity characteristic of the first wave, using tents and secular buildings such as cinemas and stadiums, and beginning to experiment with broadcasting. Together with God is Love, which has a particular appeal to the very poorest, they responded effectively to rapid urbanization and the rise of mass society, above all in the São Paulo region. The third wave of the 1970s and 1980s is represented by the Universal Church of the Kingdom of God (1977) and the International Church of the Grace of God (1980). In the form of the Universal Church, Pentecostalism offered a 'prosperity theology', in which material and business success is portrayed as a divine blessing and reward for spiritual commitment, and which catered for the growing yuppie element in Brazilian society. At the same time, notably through an emphasis on exorcism, it maintained contact with popular religious tradition.

Evangelicalism and Pentecostalism have had a significant appeal to indigenous ('Indian') peoples. Among the Airo-Pai, a small group of Amazonian people on the borders of Peru, Ecuador and Columbia, a particular factor in the movement's appeal has been the manner in which it has served to prevent alcoholism and drug abuse. At a deeper level, moreover, the Airo-Pai have not so much converted to Evangelicalism as incorporated it into their prior framework of belief. They see it as a means of maintaining their cultural value of 'living well', and eventually of avoiding death, an aspiration deeply seated in their culture but not a prospect offered by their traditional shamanism on its own. For the Airo-Pai, the Evangelical promise of 'eternal life' is to be taken literally (Belaunde, 2000). Assessments of the general impact of Protestantism on indigenous communities vary widely: to some observers it is seen as a primary source of negative disruption of traditional social and cultural structures, but to others as a means of restoring community ties that have already been fractured by other influences (Freston, 2001, pp.207–8). To the Maya of central America, Pentecostalism provides a social structure that resembles the traditional, but increasingly fragile, native village organization, combining a 'sharing community with authoritarian or patriarchal leadership' (Cook, 1997, p.89). There is also an affinity between Pentecostalism and the ecstatic and millennial dimensions of traditional religion. As one pastor put it, 'We Pentecostals are very suspicious of anything that smells of the ancient cult. We consider it paganism; but we would like to think that Pentecostals are closest to the ancient Maya religiosity of any Protestant movement' (Cook, 1997, p.90).

The extent of the assimilation between Pentecostalism and the various cultural and social contexts in which it has expanded in Latin America helps to explain the rapidity of its growth, but also means that converts are by no means always retained. A 1989 survey in Costa Rica suggested that 8.1 per cent of the population had been Protestant at one time, but were so no longer. Of the sample group, 62 per cent had become Roman Catholics, 31 per cent had stopped professing religion at all, 6 per cent were Mormons or Jehovah's Witnesses and 1 per cent had converted to Judaism (Greenway, 1994, p.199). In 1990, in Chile, only 48 per cent of a sample of self-identified Evangelicals (predominantly Pentecostals) attended church weekly and 38 per cent very seldom or never attended (Cleary and Sepúlveda, 1997, p.110). The inference that can be drawn from figures of this kind is that many of those drawn to Pentecostalism in some moment of personal or spiritual crisis subsequently move to other religious traditions or even to secularity. This is perhaps because of a reluctance to accommodate themselves to the heavy financial and moral demands of long-term wholehearted commitment to the Pentecostal community. The lack of theological sophistication of many Pentecostal pastors may well be a further factor, as they prove unable sufficiently to nourish the faith they have stimulated or to respond adequately to educational advance among their congregations (Greenway, 1994, p.201). There are, conversely, indications that some second-generation Pentecostal churches have tended to move with their members into more middle-class lifestyles and modes of worship, adopting a colder and more formal ethos and relaxing norms of moral and social conduct (Corten, 1999, p.141). Such adaptation may enable them to retain their existing congregations, but at the price of the loss of the radical transforming spiritual appeal that enabled them to attract converts in the first place.

If, however, there are some channels where the flow of Latin American Pentecostalism can run into the sand, its expansion also needs to be seen in the context of a general renewal and reorganization of Christianity in the continent, which has begun to affect the Roman Catholic Church too. To the extent that Pentecostals have tended to recruit most successfully in the poorer urban areas where Catholicism is institutionally at its weakest (Prokopy and Smith, 1999, p.9), the majority of Pentecostal adherents are likely hitherto to have been nominal rather than committed Catholics. On the other hand, during the pontificate of John Paul II, the Roman Catholic Church in Latin America has been stirred by the challenge to its prior religious monopoly position into extensive reorganization, which is likely to enhance its effectiveness at the grass roots. Although there are still insufficient clergy, recruitment of priests has expanded markedly in recent decades. A Charismatic presence in the Catholic Church itself and the formation of *comunidades eclesiales de base* (base Christian communities) as a focus for socially engaged local pastoral activity have give further stimulus to renewal (Gill, 1999; Cleary, 1999, p.135). From this perspective, the 're-conversion' of ex-Pentecostals to Catholicism may be regarded as indicative not of failure but of more far-reaching success. Indeed, one recent analyst has been moved to conclude that 'with the Catholic Church learning to live in an environment of increased religious pluralism, Latin America will be likely to undergo a spiritual renewal the likes of which it has never seen before' (Gill, 1999, p.36).

As a means of further developing analysis of the Latin American situation and of pinpointing its similarities and contrasts with the north Atlantic one, it is instructive to assess the nature and extent of the five trends previously discussed in relation to Evangelicalism in the UK and the USA.

The scale of the advance of the Pentecostal churches in Latin America among lower-class groups sets the region apart from the UK and the USA, but since the 1960s there has also been a *Charismaticization* of Evangelicalism within the other Protestant churches that is reminiscent of developments elsewhere. As in other parts of the world, Charismatics are distinguished from Pentecostals by their lesser emphasis on speaking in tongues as a sign of baptism in the Spirit, and by the fact that they do not join distinctively Pentecostal denominations. They are also primarily middle class in social background, in contrast to the predominantly working-class Pentecostals, a distinction that is especially significant and pronounced in the context of the prevalent extreme social inequality of Latin America (Freston, 1997, pp.187–8). In the relatively large Protestant churches of Brazil, a pattern resembling the UK and the USA has been followed, with initial resistance to Charismatic renewal giving way to more accommodating attitudes, but continuing diversity of response. In the meantime, as elsewhere, Charismatics have formed independent churches, notably the Comunidades Evangélicas (Evangelical Communities), which by the mid-1990s had over 100 congregations, and Renascer in Christo (Reborn in Christ), which in 1995 had about 40 churches in Brazil. A Brazilian version of the Full Gospel Businessmen's Fellowship International has been in operation since 1975 and has become a channel of converts to Charismatic churches among the prosperous middle class (Freston, 1997, pp.188–96). In Peru, where the Protestant churches are, however, much smaller than in Brazil, Charismatics have become the dominant influence (Freston, 1997, p.198).

One can also observe considerable *organizational* dynamism in Latin American Evangelicalism and Pentecostalism. The most obvious expression of this has been, as elsewhere, in the formation of new churches and denominations, as noted above. At the same time, there has been a growing consciousness of a common identity and interest among Evangelicals, both within particular countries, such as Argentina, Brazil and Peru (Freston, 1997, pp.197–8), and on a continent-wide basis. A Congress on Evangelization in Bogotá in 1969 was followed by the formation in 1970 of the Latin American Theological Fraternity (FTL). This body not only promoted academic discussion, but also involved a range of professional people and gave a much-needed stimulus to practical action as well as theological reflection. It was complemented in 1982 by the foundation of the Confraternity of Evangelicals of Latin America (CONELA) and in 1984 by the establishment of the Congress of Ibero-American Missions (COMIBAN). The extent of commitment to international cooperation and vision within the continent was symbolized by further Latin American Congresses on Evangelization: a second in Lima in 1970 and a third in Quito in 1992, which was attended by over 1000 delegates (Cook, 1994, pp.135–6; Núñez and Taylor, 1996, pp.172–3, 414, 466). A fourth conference in September 2000, again in Quito, drew 1300 participants. It provided an opportunity for particular reflection on the need to draw Pentecostals and non-Pentecostal Evangelicals into closer cooperation, through a balanced understanding of the respective roles of the Holy Spirit and the Word of God in the Bible, in the Christian revelation of God (MacHarg, 2000; report at http://www.ocms.ac.uk/news/20001009_clade.shtml).

As Latin American Pentecostalism has grown in numerical and institutional strength, it has acquired an increasingly *politicized* dimension. As elsewhere, an impression of an affinity with the political Right has some validity, but needs to be carefully qualified.

Those who wish to stress the authoritarian political potential of Pentecostalism can cite the dictatorship of General Efraín Ríos Montt in Guatemala from March 1982 to August 1983 (Figure 1.14). Ríos Montt, who led a military junta, was a committed member of a Pentecostal group, the Church of the Word. The American televangelist Pat Robertson gave him very public support and raised money to assist his regime (Brouwer *et al.*, 1996, p.56). Ríos Montt appointed religious associates to government positions and sought to use the Protestant churches as allies in counterinsurgency measures. He appeared on national television every Sunday 'to preach on issues from personal morality to public duty' (Steigenga, 1994, pp.160–4). Relations between Pentecostals and the military rapidly became strained, however, and Ríos Montt was eventually overthrown by

Figure 1.14   General Efraín Ríos Montt, flanked by fellow members of the junta, announces the formation of his military government at a press conference in Guatemala City on 23 March 1982. Associated Press.

another general, who denounced his predecessor and his advisors as a 'fanatical and aggressive religious group' (Steigenga, 1994, p.164). Ríos Montt has, though, remained a significant force in Guatemalan politics and Jorge Serrano Elias, a former leading member of his government and a fellow Evangelical, was himself president from 1990 to 1993. Nevertheless, whatever the personal beliefs and affiliations of Ríos Montt and Serrano Elias, there is little indication that the policies of their governments assumed a distinctively Evangelical cast (Freston, 2001, pp.268–80).

In Chile, some Protestant church leaders, notably Javier Vásquez, pastor of the flagship Jotabeche 'cathedral' of the Iglesia Methodista Pentecostal, gave public support to the dictatorship of Augusto Pinochet in the 1970s and 1980s. The Consejo de Pastores (Council of Pastors) was formed in 1975 to represent Protestant interests to the government. These links, however, never commanded general Pentecostal enthusiasm, and did not prove to be enduring. Support for Pinochet stemmed primarily from the hope that the military government could be persuaded to introduce full religious equality in this historically Roman Catholic country, rather than from any developed ideological affinity with the regime. By the early 1980s, there was increasing criticism of the government and its perceived Protestant collaborators from within the Pentecostal community itself. From 1986, Pentecostal churches were among those openly campaigning for democracy (Cleary and Sepúlveda, 1997, pp.104–5; Freston, 2001, pp.220–3).

Thus, Pentecostal links with the political Right appear more opportunistic than committed and the overall picture is a complex and variegated one. It is important to recall the predominantly lower-class and poorly educated composition of many of the Pentecostal churches. To a considerable extent their theology of personal redemption and ecstatic experience of conversion and the Holy Spirit inclines many to an apolitical position. It is true that they can be influenced by the language of 'spiritual warfare', which can inspire a sense of the need actively to confront perceived demonic evils in society and to believe in the divine right of their religious leaders to govern in the cause of building a 'Christian nation'. Thus, they may be vulnerable to manipulation by right-wing politicians, who can articulate an affinity with their religious beliefs. For example, during his 1990 presidential campaign in Guatemala, Serrano Elias was also supporting a proclamation that 'Jesus is Lord of Guatemala', with a view to exorcising the country from a curse believed to relate to pre-Christian religion (Freston, 2001, pp.16, 274, 280). Among grass-roots congregations, however, passivity and naïvety is by no means the same thing as active support. On the contrary, the predominant social location of Pentecostalism can stir a sympathy for more progressive causes. As one observer notes:

> It has become very difficult for conservative Protestants to ignore the social ills of their countries. Christian compassion, enlightened self-interest, and pastoral expertise combine to mobilize Evangelicals socio-politically. And Pentecostals, who are closer to the masses of poor than any other Protestant movement, are uniquely situated to respond creatively.

> (Cook, 1994, p.133)

The language of spiritual warfare can also be turned to support the cause of the Left: in Rio de Janiero, in 1989, an Evangelical committee supporting the left-wing presidential candidate, Lula, asserted:

> Demons must be expelled from social life in the name of the vote, justice, organisation and democracy by power of the name of Jesus ... We desire a Brazil free from spiritual oppression such as hunger, misery, unemployment, inflation, corruption, organised crime ... No demon can resist our faith.

> (Freston, 2001, p.40)

There is thus no automatic equation between conservative theology and conservative politics, and there are – especially in Brazil – significant instances of Pentecostal commitment to a pro-labour

KING ALFRED'S COLLEGE
LIBRARY

stance. For example, Benedita da Silva, a Pentecostal and a member of the Workers Party, has had a notable political career, being elected to the Rio Town Council in 1982 and to the Brazilian Federal Congress in 1986. In 1994, she topped the poll for the Brazilian Senate, being the first black woman ever to be elected to that body. She is an influential advocate of human rights, with a particular interest in issues relating to women, children and ethnic minorities (Freston, 1998b, p.42; Cook, 1994, p.134; http://www.senado.gov.br/web/senador/bene). In the lower house of the Brazilian Congress, in 2000, there were 54 Evangelical deputies, 10.3 per cent of the total. Although their party allegiances tended somewhat more to the Right than those of non-Evangelicals, they still showed a spread across the political spectrum (Freston, 2001, p.51).

Recent overviews (Cleary and Stewart-Gambino, 1997, pp.232–8; Freston, 1998b, 2001) of Evangelical political involvement in Latin America have therefore tended to avoid the inappropriate application of secular ideological categories and to stress the primacy of religious motivations. These stir Evangelicals to take up conservative positions on moral questions, but also to show a progressive social engagement at the local level, a pattern broadly reminiscent of that operative in a very different context in the UK. Where Pentecostals have been elected to political office, they are more likely to see themselves as representatives of the interests of their particular religious group than as participants in broader alignments, an outlook that reflects the characteristic corporatism of Latin American politics. In the countries of Spanish-speaking Latin America, a total of more than 20 professedly Evangelical political parties have been formed in recent years, while in Brazil, the Universal Church exercises a significant political influence and effectively controls two small parties in Congress (Freston, 2001, pp.51, 195). Various other Evangelical agencies have interested themselves in politics: for example, the FTL held consultations on the theology and practice of power in 1983 and on political involvement in 1991 (Cook, 1994, p.137). Although the balance of Evangelical political involvement is weighted more to the Right than to the Left, the movement's capacity to nurture leadership skills in a context of internal institutional diversity and ideological pluralism can be regarded as a positive force in promoting the democratization of Latin America (Freston, 1998b, pp.42–3).

Latin America provides ample evidence both of the *globalization* of Evangelicalism and Pentecostalism and of the local and regional circumstances that give a distinctive colour to global movements. For some critics of these movements, globalization in the Latin American context really means Americanization. There is a conspiracy theory of recent history whereby the religious Right in the USA has promoted an 'invasion of the sects' to subvert traditional Catholic allegiances and provide a channel for American political influence in the region. Such an interpretation gains some credibility from the declared intentions and activities of elements in the American religious Right, notably Pat Robertson, who during the 1980s supported the Contras[11] in Nicaragua as well as the Ríos Montt regime in Guatemala. American-based missionary and relief organizations, such as World Vision and the Wycliffe Bible Translators/Summer Institute of Linguistics, have had hidden political agendas attributed to them (Stoll, 1990, pp.xiv–xix). Certainly, one can identify specific religious enterprises and groups in Latin America that are sustained by American personnel and resources, for example the Agua Viva (Living Water) missionary centre in the western highlands of Guatemala. Among activists there 'Americanism and Christianity are interchangeable in their thinking and indispensable for people who must be rescued from a life of laziness and sin' (Brouwer *et al.*, 1996, pp.68–71).

Nevertheless, as was emphasized above, the spectacular growth of Pentecostalism in Latin America in recent decades can only be explained on the basis of its effective indigenization. Links with the USA certainly exist, but these do not mean control from the USA: churches are primarily financed locally and their pastors and ministers are predominantly Latin American nationals. Indeed, in some countries, the Roman Catholic Church employs many more foreign clergy than the Pentecostals do. When the AOG in the USA makes much of its association with its Brazilian counterpart, it is not so much asserting control as seeking to bask in the reflected glory brought by the apparent scale and effectiveness of activity in Brazil (Stewart-Gambino and Wilson, 1997, pp.228–31). As one sociologist observes, to the extent that Pentecostalism has been exported from the USA to Latin America, this has been primarily not a consequence of manipulation by powerful missionary élites, but rather a movement of the 'underside':

> Born among the poor, blacks and women, it was exported at virtually no cost, often by non-Americans, by-passing the usual channels (religious and otherwise) of American wealth and power. It is precisely this counter-establishment Western Christianity that has become the most globalized. It is not the abstract and elitist 'cosmic Christ' but the Jesus of the gospels and the charismatic outpourings of the Acts of the Apostles which, despite (or perhaps because of) their cultural rootedness, seem able to found a global theology.
>
> (Freston, 1998a, p.74)

---

[11] Insurgents who opposed the left-wing Nicaraguan government.

External influences, moreover, have come not only from the USA but also from Europe, especially Italy and Sweden (Stewart-Gambino and Wilson, 1997, pp.229–30) and Africa. One analyst judges that 'it is fruitless today to weigh what is part of Anglo-Saxon religious emotion and what is part of African emotion' (Corten, 1999, p.34). In the last two decades, influences stemming from Latin America have themselves begun to be globalized. The COMIBAN Congress in São Paulo in 1987 concluded that 'Christ was leading them to assume responsibility for the unreached peoples within their region and beyond, and to move from being a mission field area to being a sending force for mission everywhere' (Greenway, 1994, p.198). In the meantime, the Argentinian Luis Palau has developed an international ministry as an evangelist that is second only to Billy Graham's in its geographical range and impact (Figure 1.15). The Brazilian-based Universal Church of the Kingdom of God has begun to establish itself in 60 other countries (Freston, 1998c, p.81), including the UK and the USA.

The increased visibility of Latin American Pentecostalism is beginning to colour the self-image and public perception of Evangelicalism throughout the world. The Latin American Pentecostal experience shows that the globalization of Evangelicalism and Pentecostalism flows in many different channels and directions.

Finally, the acculturation of Latin American Evangelicalism has been implicit in much of the above analysis. This process, however, has a significantly different starting-point from its counterparts in the UK and the USA. Whereas in the north Atlantic world the adaptation of Evangelicalism to the modern and post-modern world can be regarded primarily as merely another phase in a history that now stretches back over more than two centuries, in Latin America the relatively recent establishment of the tradition and the scale of its recent expansion points to a qualitatively different process. Latin American Pentecostals are not merely adapting to the secular cultural background of their adherents, but are engaged in a creative reshaping of their outlooks in a manner that remains culturally accessible but has a distinctive radical appeal. In that respect, to recall Martin's analysis, they are reminiscent more of eighteenth-century Methodists or the revivalists of American camp meetings in the early decades of independence than of the majority of their British and American contemporaries at the turn of the twenty-first century. It would be a

Figure 1.15   Luis Palau preaching in Bolivia in November 1995. AP/Wide World Photos/Luis Palau Evangelistic Association/Gary S. Chapman.

serious mistake, however, to interpret the Pentecostal advance in Latin America as a kind of reflection of the continent's religious and cultural backwardness and to assume it will eventually decline in a manner analogous to British Methodism in the twentieth century. In other respects, such as the use of television and other media, its place in globalizing networks, and the emergence of 'prosperity theology' to legitimate the materially successful lifestyles of a growing Pentecostal and Charismatic middle class, this is entirely a contemporary phenomenon. Certainly, Latin American conditions, above all the extent of the material deprivation and spiritual responsiveness of the urban poor, have created particularly fertile ground for these movements. At the same time, however, the success of Pentecostalism in this continent is perhaps indicative of still unrealized potentialities elsewhere.

The global and the local

The three preceding case studies have exemplified the contrasting characteristics of Evangelicalism and Pentecostalism in different parts of the world but have also pointed to significant threads of consistency and connection. The purpose of this final section is to set this material in a broader worldwide scope, while briefly referring to some other national and regional contexts, particularly that of South Africa. In doing so, we will revisit three key issues: the definition and conceptualization of Evangelicalism and Pentecostalism; globalization and its implications for local manifestations of religion; and the significance of these movements for a wider understanding of the situation of religion in the modern and postmodern world.

The total world population of Evangelicals has recently been estimated at 638 million (Barrett, 1998). Of these, more than half are Charismatics or Pentecostals (Hutchinson, 1988, p.46). This calculation comes from an academically reputable source, albeit one sympathetic to Evangelicals and using a relatively expansive definition. It should therefore be regarded as something of an upper limit, but if it is accepted as broadly accurate it points to Evangelicals as making up one-third of the world's Christians and one-tenth of total world population, a substantial presence by any standards. Moreover, recent decades have seen strong numerical growth in Africa and Asia as well as in Latin America, while the kind of modest resurgence apparent in the UK is observable in other developed countries, such as Australia and Sweden, and in eastern Europe.

South Korea has seen some of the most dramatic Evangelical growth of recent decades. In this historically Confucian country, Protestant numbers tripled between 1940 and 1961, doubled again between 1961 and 1971, and tripled yet again in the 1970s. In the early 1980s, Protestants already made up 20 per cent of the total population. By 2000, there were 12.2 million, constituting more than a quarter of the population of 47.41 million. In 1999, there were 36,832 churches in the country, including the largest single church in the world, the Yoido Full Gospel Church in Seoul (Figure 1.16), founded in 1958, which in 2001 had an estimated total Sunday attendance of 230,000 (Hong, 2001, p.2).

Such spectacular and speedy success can be attributed to a combination of vibrant Pentecostal worship, dynamic leadership and the appeal of churches (and small cell groups within them) as a basis for community and personal support in a rapidly urbanizing society (Martin, 1990, p.143; Ma, 1999, pp.195–6). Martin perceives a literal 'spiritual enterprise culture' in which 'The chief pastor/executive combines many secular roles, as, indeed, he does in Brazil. He is a social worker and employment exchange official, a kind of store manager and a broker, an educator and a fixer' (Martin, 1990, pp.143–4). Although the rapidity and extent of Evangelical success in Korea is remarkable, similar trends are apparent elsewhere in Asia,

Figure 1.16   Yoido Full Gospel Church in Seoul, Korea. Abbas/Magnum.

notably in mainland China. Here, however, there can be no reliable statistics.

There has also been strong growth in Africa, where the number of Evangelicals has been estimated at 3.13 million in 1900 and 108.5 million in 1998, making up 13 per cent of the population of the continent (Barrett, 1998). This growth is apparent in most regions south of the Sahara, although, as in Asia and Latin America, analysis has to take careful account of varying national and local conditions. There is no space here to undertake an overall survey, but some brief account of the situation in South Africa will serve to exemplify wider trends and issues in African Evangelicalism. Although South Africa, with its large (18 per cent) white minority, relative economic prosperity and distinctive recent political history, differs in some important respects from the rest of Africa, for those very reasons it provides a particularly instructive point of comparison with the other regions discussed above.

A significant Evangelical presence can be identified in many of the historic Protestant churches in South Africa, but the dominant numerical force in Christianity in the country consists of Pentecostals and African Initiated Churches (AICs). These latter have a Pentecostal-type style of religious culture and worship, which causes one leading scholar to regard them as constituting 'the African expression of the worldwide pentecostal movement' (Cox, 1996, p.246), but they have an entirely black membership and independent local organization. The two groups amount to about 10 million people out of the total South African population of 32 million. More than 10 per cent of the overall population of the country are Pentecostals, while AICs account for more than 40 per cent of the black population (Anderson and Pillay, 1997, pp.227, 233).

The AICs are, by definition, a distinctive feature of the Christian scene in South Africa, as in other African countries. However, they provide a further illustration of the tendency of Evangelical and Pentecostal spiritual inspirations to be reflected in wholly indigenous churches alongside international denominations and networks. Elsewhere in the world, such nationally and regionally specific manifestations of the broader movement can also be found, for example the Iglesia Methodista Pentecostal in Chile (which seceded from the Methodist Church in 1910), Brazil for Christ and God is Love, also in Brazil. The comparison might be extended to Charismatic new churches in the UK, such as Pioneer and New Frontiers. The AICs, however, constitute a particularly rich indigenous expression of Christianity, which it is important to understand on its own terms, and which some analysts perceive as having little connection with wider global Evangelical and Pentecostal networks.

Certainly, their history is a relatively long one, dating back to the beginning of the twentieth century and owing little to the supposed North American inspiration of international Pentecostalism spreading out from the Azusa Street revival of 1906. Two broad categories have been identified. So-called 'Ethiopian' churches originated in black secessions from white-dominated mission churches, the earliest of which occurred on the Witwatersrand in 1892 and specifically called itself 'The Ethiopian Church'. Other such groups have retained an identification with their parent denomination, by calling themselves, for example, 'African Congregational' or 'African Methodist'. A secession from the Dutch Reformed Church in Zimbabwe called itself the African Reformed Church. The significance of the 'Ethiopian' label lies in its implied claim that the true origins of African Christianity lay not in recent western missions, but in the ancient church of Ethiopia, traditionally derived from the eunuch converted by Philip on the road to Gaza (Acts 8:26–40). Ethiopia was believed to be the land of Cush, grandson of Noah (Genesis 10) and precursor of all black Africans. Other Old Testament references, such as the visit of the Queen of Sheba to King Solomon (I Kings 10), are also used to point to the perceived independent place of Africa in the divine purposes. The emphasis of the 'Ethiopian' churches on the legitimating force of such African biblical mythologies as well as elements of continuity from their original non-Pentecostal denominations distinguish them from the wider Pentecostal movement (Kiernan, 1995, pp.118–21; Daneel, 1999).

In some respects, the other main category of AICs, the 'Zionist' churches, appear closer to Pentecostalism, insofar as they draw their legitimacy and power from a sense of direct encounter with the Holy Spirit, as catalysed by particular leaders claiming prophetic inspiration. They engage in characteristically Pentecostal practices, such as speaking in tongues, exorcism and healing (Anderson and Pillay, 1997, pp.230–3). Such movements have developed particularly among migrant workers in urban settings of impoverishment, alienation and insecurity. There is thus an obvious parallel with the circumstances in which Pentecostalism has flourished in Latin America (as indeed in Korea) in recent decades. Zionist AICs, however, are distinguished by a conscious readiness to assimilate aspects of traditional African religion, in a manner that sets them apart from Pentecostals among whom any such pre-Christian affinities are generally unconscious and unintended. Healing practices are especially significant in this regard: they are a more consistently central part of worship than in western Pentecostal churches, and superficially they owe much to African traditional religion. There is a fundamental difference, however, in that traditional healers seek to placate the evil spirits believed to cause illness or discord, whereas in the AICs the superior beneficent power of the Holy Spirit is invoked in order to drive out evil by means of good (Figure 1.17) (Cox, 1996, pp.254–6). (We noted above the same distinction between Pentecostal and Afro-Brazilian approaches to healing.)

Zionism manifests 'bewildering variety' within itself, with differing proportions of Christian and African elements. The result, moreover, is not a mere variant of Pentecostalism: 'It will not do ... simply to think of Zionism as a combination, as if each of the components, African and Christian, was merely grafted onto the other. Their fusion has produced a true synthesis, and the result is the creation of something new' (Kiernan, 1995, p.122).

Alongside the AICs are churches that have a more clear-cut association with Pentecostalism: the AOG, the Apostolic Faith Mission (AFM) and the Full Gospel Church of God (FGC). All of these originated in the early twentieth century, in the case of the AOG and the FGC initially through the work of missionaries from Europe and North America. They are interracial in contrast to the exclusively black composition of the AICs. Under the apartheid regime, they were controlled by whites, and the AFM in particular was increasingly subservient to the government. During the early 1990s, however, blacks asserted themselves. In the meantime, as elsewhere, the Charismatic upsurge from the 1960s led to the formation of new

Figure 1.17   An exorcism to drive evil spirits out of a woman at a Zionist service in a park in Johannesburg, South Africa. Abbas/Magnum.

churches – notably Rhema Bible Church in Johannesburg, Grace Bible Church in Soweto and Hatfield Christian Church in Pretoria – which were brought under the umbrella of the International Fellowship of Christian Churches (IFCC), founded in 1985. Although the Charismatic movement has tended to appeal more to whites than to blacks, IFCC as a whole is multiracial, as are some of its constituent churches, such as Rhema Bible Church (Anderson and Pillay, 1997, pp.233–8).

The Pentecostal/Charismatic churches with significant white involvement are liable to be perceived as channels for external, and particularly American, influences in South Africa. They are charged with importing both a right-wing politics that was in the past at best uncritical of apartheid, and a prosperity theology that legitimates the extreme material inequalities of South African society. Elsewhere in Africa, economic collapse in the 1980s led local churches to seek support from the USA. Extensive American influence has been mediated through evangelistic crusades, conferences, Bible schools, Christian broadcasting and imported literature (Hexham and Poewe, 1994, p.59; Brouwer *et al.*, 1996, pp.150–78). The perception of significant external influence has some validity, in respect particularly of the influence of American megachurches on South African church leaders. The social and religious ethos of Rhema in Johannesburg can be seen as having some similarities with that of Willow Creek in Chicago, or more immediately with Rhema Church in Tulsa, Oklahoma (Anderson and Pillay, 1997, p.237). But the case should not be pressed too far. In Africa, as in Latin America, evidence of American *influence* must not be construed as constituting American *domination*, and American models have been distinctively adapted to South African conditions. Even those who argue for the 'overriding influence' of the USA on African Christianity concede that 'African experience and needs are a huge force in forging the Christianity emerging on the continent' (Brouwer *et al.*, 1996, p.178). Moreover, the networks centred on a figure such as Ray McCauley, founder of Rhema, are genuinely global rather than narrowly centred on the USA, including links with other parts of Africa, Europe and Australia (Hexham and Poewe, 1994, pp.63–4).

There is some substance to the charge that Evangelicals and Pentecostals acquiesced too readily in apartheid. Not only did the Afrikaaner-led Dutch Reformed Church give theological legitimacy to the regime, but in 1985 the Zion Christian Church, largest of the AICs, welcomed President Botha to its headquarters (Freston, 2001, pp.167–8, 172–3). Like some Chilean Pentecostals under Pinochet, a narrow conception of their specifically religious interests led them to give tacit support to an oppressive government. On the other hand, from the late 1980s onwards, Evangelicals, in common with other Christian leaders, were a significant force in establishing the preconditions for political transformation. A document drawn up by a group of black Evangelicals from Soweto in 1986 established a stance critical of apartheid. This was developed in 1988 by a statement entitled 'The Relevant Pentecostal Witness'. Frank Chikane, an active Pentecostal and a former general secretary of the South African Council of Churches, has been a leading anti-apartheid activist (Anderson, 1999a, pp.104–5; Freston, 2001, p.171). White Evangelicals were initially more equivocal, but McCauley of Rhema Church was a member of the important Rustenburg Committee associated with the consultation of church leaders held in the eponymous Transvaal town in November 1990 (Hexham and Poewe, 1994, p.64; Freston, 2001, pp.169–72). The Rustenburg Declaration, supported by representatives of 97 denominations, stated that apartheid was a sin, proposed an ethical agenda for the new South Africa and suggested measures to bring an end to the ongoing violence (Hofmeyr and Pillay, 1994, pp.294–8; Freston, 2001, p.172). Such activity fits the pattern of growing Evangelical political involvement, and of variegated and shifting secular ideological orientations, already noted in other parts of the world.

This brief discussion of South Africa serves to emphasize points already evident in other case studies. It well illustrates the need for sensitivity in the application of concepts like 'Evangelical', 'fundamentalist', 'Pentecostal' and 'Charismatic'. Judgements as to whether these words can be applied to groups such as the AICs are ultimately likely to be as much political as intellectual, depending on whether the observer wishes to emphasize the AICs' commonalties with 'western' white Christianity or rather to accentuate their distinctive black character. A more useful approach is to recognize that there are no firm limits to religious movements and that churches may well be strongly influenced by particular forms of belief and practice without being totally identified with them. Local and national specificities remain very important. Further, models and histories derived from particular national circumstances or from the 'western' world in general should not be hastily imposed on non-western societies. An assumption of diffusion of Pentecostal influence from Azusa Street, Los Angeles makes little sense of the South African experience in the twentieth century. Some analysts (for example, Dayton, 1991), even when limiting themselves to a relatively narrow geographical range, have gone so far as to question the very usefulness of the term 'Evangelical' on the grounds of its slippery and diverse applications. A similar view might be taken of the word 'Pentecostal' once one moves outside the relatively well-defined and institutionally clear-cut contexts in which it is applied in the north Atlantic world. The reader may well have some sympathy with such scepticism, but before giving way to it should ask what terminology could viably be substituted, and how else one could do justice to significant elements in the self-understanding of the religious groups under consideration. It may well be better, however, to think of such terms as signposting tendencies rather than delineating precise categories.

These terms are, moreover, a necessary label for identifying and tracing the global networks, which, as we have seen, are an important aspect of the overall picture. It is essential to emphasize the indigenization and cultural specificity of Evangelicalism in particular contexts, but such identities exist in varying degrees of creative tension with a sense of much wider connections and mission. Evangelicals, after all, see themselves as commanded by the reported words of Jesus at the end of Matthew's gospel to 'Go therefore and make disciples of all nations' (Wolffe, 1998, pp.100–4). The implementation of this 'Great Commission' has historically become implicated in the enterprise of British and, more recently, American imperialism, and the USA remains an important centre of worldwide Evangelical influence. For example, the so-called 'Faith movement' within Pentecostalism, which emphasizes material prosperity, health and wealth as divine blessings given to the believer, originated in the USA, and has found wide acceptance in other parts of the world. Nevertheless, it has taken diverse forms in various local contexts, some of which may owe little to the American original (Hunt, 2000).

The USA is, though, not the only centre of Evangelical influence, and globalizing connections can flow from São Paulo, Johannesburg or Seoul as well as from Chicago or Los Angeles. More particularly, one can identify particular nodes and points of focus of activity that may be anywhere in the world, but are most probably in major cities with good international air links. Examples include the Toronto Airport Christian Fellowship, Holy Trinity, Brompton (west London), the Rhema Bible Church in Johannesburg, the Jotabeche 'cathedral' in Santiago and the Word of Life Bible Centre in Uppsala (Sweden). A recent study (Coleman, 1998) of this last example has shown how it succeeds in cultivating both a 'cosmopolitan spirituality' and a sense of rootedness in its particular Swedish national context. Globalizing links are also sustained by the itinerant ministries of particular individuals, who, as the instances of Palau and McCauley illustrate, come from diverse parts of the world. Nor should less prominent figures be discounted. The plethora of nationalities and locales involved in the following personal story may be exceptional, but it illustrates strands of global connection and interchange that owe relatively little to the supposed north Atlantic historic and economic heartland of Evangelicalism. Mario Lindstrum, a musician, was the son of a Swedish immigrant in Brazil and was converted through the agency of Japanese Christians. An Armenian woman prophesied that he should go to Asia by way of Australia in the company of Luigi Schilró, a powerful preacher. Lindstrum and Schilró arrived in Sydney in 1975 and encountered an American-born pastor who took them to both a Slavic Pentecostal Church and his own Italian immigrant church. Their ministry stirred a strong revival, leading eventually to the formation of a Portuguese church in Sydney and the sending of missionaries to Spain, Portugal and Latin America (Hutchinson, 1998, pp.46–7). Personal contacts are supplemented by the easy global dissemination of literature, videos and tapes, by television ministries and, increasingly, by the Internet. Globalization of this kind does not mean homogenization to an imposed American blueprint – and as we have noted, American Evangelicalism is itself extremely diverse – but rather an immensely variegated picture that is continually shifting in response to both changing local circumstances and external global influences.

To a significant extent, indeed, the globalization of Pentecostalism has been achieved through an inversion of normally dominant world economic and cultural power structures. Pentecostalism's adherents are disproportionately non-white and tend to have limited education and material resources. Among AICs and black Pentecostals, whether in Africa or the USA, independent religious organization has been an important source of resistance to white racism and oppression, even when explicit political agendas are muted or absent (Kunnie, 1994). It has been argued, moreover, that authentic Pentecostalism is rooted in the experience of the African diaspora and sustained by a powerful engagement with the Holy Spirit, which is expressed in the bodily responsiveness and strong community life that is characteristic of black people. Among whites, who are prone to be both more inhibited and more individualistic, its expressions tend to be more constrained (Gerloff, 1995). It is also noteworthy that women have been much more prominent in the global spread and ongoing practice of Pentecostalism than is the case in most other religious traditions: in terms of gender, as of race, this is a movement that challenges conventional authority and assumptions (Cox, 1996, p.121).

Finally, how does this analysis of global Evangelicalism and Pentecostalism illuminate questions about the interaction of religion, modernity and post-modernity, and the general situation of religion in the contemporary world? It shows above all the dangers of generalization from a particular national or regional situation: with due respect to Walker (1997, p.34), the categorization of the

Charismatic movement as 'hyper-modern' may well be valid in a limited British context but does not relate well to the situation in Africa or Latin America. Nor, with respect to Balmer (1993, p.280), does it make sense to describe Evangelicalism itself as 'quintessentially American', even though it certainly has distinctive manifestations in the particular cultural and social contexts of the USA. It follows, with respect to Brouwer *et al.* (1996), that over-emphasis on the export of 'the American gospel' leads to only a partial understanding of complex and diverse patterns of assimilation and indigenization.

Nor is it satisfactory to see the success of Evangelicalism in the contemporary world as merely a reflection of traditional subcultural resistance to secularization (in the West) or of cultural 'backwardness' (in the developing world). In fact, while its expansion in recent decades may draw on longstanding traditions – that is, both the mediated teachings and experience of New Testament Christianity and the pre-existing religious cultures of particular localities – the specific forms that it takes are generally innovative. The modest but significant resurgence of Evangelicalism in the UK, its continuing large-scale presence in the USA, its extensive utilization of globalized media resources, and its symbiotic relationship with processes of social change and economic development in Latin America, Asia and Africa, are all indicative of an altogether more constructive and complex interaction with modernity. At the same time, in its more fragmented and polycentric manifestations it would be easy to characterize Evangelicalism as a distinctively post-modern religious phenomenon.

On the political front, the record of Evangelicals and Pentecostals is also a variegated one. Sometimes they are linked to the support of right-wing groups, which are apt to be seen as the best guarantors of their specific moral and religious agendas, but they also can be inspired to espouse much more progressive and radical causes. A recent survey of their political impact in 27 Asian, African and Latin American countries can only be 'cautious and open-ended' about the overall relationship between Evangelicals and democratization, but demonstrates extensive significant interconnections (Freston, 2001, p.310).

The broad conclusion to be drawn, therefore, is that the success of Evangelicalism – especially in its Pentecostal and Charismatic forms – in today's world lies precisely in its chameleon-like capacity effectively to adapt to changing cultural and social environments. At times it can even itself serve as an agent of change: 'Pentecostalism's inherent flexibility means that it is more easily able to adjust to any context, even when that context is a rapidly changing one, as is the case in many of the cities of the Third World' (Anderson, 1999b, p.29).

In comparison with many other forms of religion – Christian and non-Christian – this is a form of belief that does not identify strongly with specific traditions and so is well equipped to make such transitions relatively painlessly. It may appear marginal in the UK, but it has a much greater prominence in other parts of the world. Accordingly, is it the UK, with its lingering adherence to traditional religious forms, rather than Evangelicalism, in all its creative adaptability, that is on the fringes of the mainstream of contemporary religious development?

Harvey Cox, a leading American scholar of religion, indeed argues that Pentecostalism represents an especially effective religious response to the contemporary world, which potentially points the way forward to forms of human spirituality and religious practice that will become increasingly influential in the twenty-first century. According to Cox, its success rests particularly on the scope it gives to express the 'language of the heart' in the face of consumer society and to give 'shape and expression' to chaotic emotions without suppressing them. Moreover, it provides 'despondent people with an alternative metaphor, a life vision at variance from the image of the "good life" the culture had dangled before them' (Cox, 1996, pp.120–1). Cox, however, portrays Pentecostalism as a key 'battle-ground' in an ongoing struggle between 'fundamentalist' and 'experiential' tendencies in contemporary religion, the former emphasizing the maintenance of 'non-negotiable bedrock beliefs', the latter the personal lived expression of the religious tradition in the lives of individual people. Cox's own sympathies are definitely with the experientialists, whom he sees as offering an 'alternative to the authoritarianism and anxious closemindedness of the fundamentalist temptation'. Nevertheless he recognizes that their ascendancy cannot be confidently assumed (Cox, 1996, pp.302–5, 310). What Cox argues of Pentecostalism can be applied more broadly to global Evangelicalism, increasingly leavened as it is by Pentecostal and Charismatic currents, diversified by competing forms of authority, old and new, and by the spontaneity of personal religious experience and action. Certainly, the Evangelical movement as a whole demonstrates the continuing potentialities of reshaped forms of traditional Christianity not merely to survive, but to thrive in a modernized and globalized world.

Glossary

Adventist/ism a form of **Protestantism**, common in the USA and Latin America, in which belief in the Second Coming of Christ is particularly emphasized.

Alpha courses courses in basic Christian doctrine pioneered at Holy Trinity, Brompton (west London) in the early 1990s and since adopted in many thousands of other churches around the world.

Anglican relating to the Church of England or its sister Episcopal churches in other countries.

Anglo-Catholics members of the wing of the Church of England that holds an essentially Catholic view of the Church.

Azusa Street the Los Angeles Street in which **Pentecostalism** is conventionally considered to have originated in 1906.

baptism in the Spirit for **Pentecostals**, a specific intense occasion on which they receive the **gifts of the Spirit**. **Charismatics** maintain that the gifts can be received in a more gradual manner.

Charismatic see the first section of the chapter, 'Defining and locating Evangelicals and Pentecostals'.

conversion the formative spiritual experience in the life of an **Evangelical**, involving an acknowledgement of sin, an encounter with Christ and a commitment of future life to him.

Enlightenment movement of European thought in the eighteenth century that emphasized rational thought and scientific enquiry.

Evangelical/ism see the first section of the chapter, 'Defining and locating Evangelicals and Pentecostals'.

Evangelical Alliance (EA) umbrella organization for British **Evangelicals**.

evangelist see the first section of the chapter, 'Defining and locating Evangelicals and Pentecostals'.

fundamentalism initially a specific movement within American **Evangelicalism** in the early twentieth century, which emphasized the inerrancy (see **inerrant**) of the Bible. The word is often more loosely (and sometimes polemically) applied to a broader segment of **Evangelicals** and other conservative religious believers.

gifts of the Spirit abilities bestowed on the Christian believer as a result of his or her empowering by the **Holy Spirit**. Some gifts, such as those of tongues, healing and prophecy, are regarded as directly supernatural; others, such as those of wisdom and teaching, constitute a development of natural gifts. The seminal New Testament account of the bestowal of gifts is in I Corinthians 12–14.

Graham, Billy (1918–) international **evangelist**, and a formative influence on neo-**Evangelicalism** in the USA.

Holy Spirit the third person of the Christian Trinity, whose power is believed to have been poured out on the Church at Pentecost (Acts 2), and held by **Charismatics** and **Pentecostals** to be a living reality in the life of the present-day Church.

house churches see **new churches**.

inerrant adjective derived from 'inerrancy', the belief, associated with **fundamentalism**, that the Bible is throughout literally and factually true.

Lloyd-Jones, **Martyn** (1899–1981) minister of Westminster Chapel and a leading figure in English **Nonconformist Evangelicalism**.

mainline Protestants non-**Evangelical Protestants** in the USA.

Methodists/ism initially members of a society within the Church of England, the Methodists developed in the period after the death of their founder **John Wesley** in 1791 into an independent denomination, Methodism.

new churches independent congregations in the UK, initially known as 'house churches', which developed from the 1960s onwards as a result of the inspiration of the **Charismatic** movement.

Nonconformist/ism term applied to **Protestant** religious denominations in England other than the Church of England. Also known as Free Churches.

Pentecostal/ism see the first section of the chapter, 'Defining and locating Evangelicals and Pentecostals'.

Protestant/ism see the first section of the chapter, 'Defining and locating Evangelicals and Pentecostals'.

Reformation a sixteenth-century religious movement, originating as a reform movement within late medieval Catholicism, which ended with the formation of a variety of Reformed (or **Protestant**) denominations in Europe.

revivals see the first section of the chapter, 'Defining and locating Evangelicals and Pentecostals'.

Romanticism movement in European culture in the late eighteenth and early nineteenth centuries that stressed intense emotion, history, mythology and the supernatural.

Stott, John (1921–) rector of All Souls, Langham Place (central London), the leading **Anglican Evangelical** of his generation.

Toronto Blessing physical manifestations of ecstatic experience of the **Holy Spirit** originating in January 1994 at the Toronto Airport **Vineyard** church.

Universities and Colleges Christian Fellowship (UCCF) Evangelical movement among British higher education students.

Vineyard network of churches founded by **John Wimber** characterized by intense **Charismatic** experience and informal worship styles.

Watson, David (1933–1984) vicar of St Cuthbert's and St-Michael-le-Belfrey, York, and a key leader of the **Charismatic** movement in England and elsewhere.

Wesley, John (1703–91) founder of **Methodism** and a seminal influence on **Evangelicalism**.

Wimber, John (1934–97) founder of the Association of **Vineyard** Churches, exponent of 'power **evangelism**', and the catalyst for the third wave of **Pentecostal/Charismatic** renewal in the UK and North America in the 1970s and 1980s.

References

Anderson, A.H. (1999a) 'Dangerous memories for South African Pentecostals', in A.H. Anderson and W.J. Hollenweger (eds), pp.89–107.

Anderson, A.H. (1999b) 'Introduction: world Pentecostalism at a crossroads', in A.H. Anderson and W.J. Hollenweger (eds), pp.19–30.

Anderson, A.H. and Hollenweger, W.J. (eds) (1999) *Pentecostals after a Century: Global Perspectives on a Movement in Transition*, Sheffield: Sheffield Academic Press.

Anderson, A.H. and Pillay, G.J. (1997) 'The segregated spirit: the Pentecostals', in R. Elphick and R. Davenport (eds) *Christianity in South Africa: A Political, Social and Cultural History*, Claremont: David Philip, pp.227–41.

Anonymous (1998) 'Massive sampling reveals major differences in denominational beliefs and behaviour', *Emerging Trends*, vol.20, no.9, November, pp.1–2.

Anonymous (2000a) '43% attended church in a typical week of 1999', *Emerging Trends*, vol.22, no.3, March, pp.1–2.

Anonymous (2000b) 'Building bridges: Evangelical Alliance Annual Review 1999–2000', *Idea*, September/October, pp.19–22.

Anonymous (2000c) 'Inviting the UK to supper!', *Alpha News*, March–June (www.alpha.org.uk/news/00-02/index.htm; accessed 4 September 2001).

Balmer, R. (1993) *Mine Eyes Have Seen the Glory: A Journey into the Evangelical Subculture in America*, New York: Oxford University Press.

Barclay, O. (1997) *Evangelicalism in Britain 1935–1995*, Leicester: Inter-Varsity Press.

Barrett, D.B. (1998) 'A century of growth', *Christianity Today*, 16 November, pp.50–1.

Bebbington, D.W. (1989) *Evangelicalism in Modern Britain: A History from the 1730s to the 1980s*, London: Routledge.

Bebbington, D.W. (1994) 'Evangelicalism in its settings: the British and American movements since 1940', in M.A. Noll, D.W. Bebbington and G. Rawlyk (eds) *Evangelicalism: Comparative Studies of Popular Protestantism in North America, the British Isles, and Beyond, 1700–1990*, New York: Oxford University Press, pp.365–88.

Bebbington, D.W. (1995) 'The decline and resurgence of Evangelical social concern 1918–80', in J. Wolffe (ed.), pp.175–97.

Belaunde, L.E. (2000) 'Epidemics, psycho-actives and Evangelical conversion among the Airo-Pai of Amazonian Peru', *Journal of Contemporary Religion*, vol.15, no.3, pp.349–59.

Blumhofer, E.L., Spittler, R.P. and Wacker, G.A. (eds) (1999) *Pentecostal Currents in American Protestantism*, Urbana and Chicago: University of Illinois Press.

Boyer, P.S. (1992) *When Time Shall Be No More: Prophecy Belief in Modern American Culture*, Cambridge, Mass.: Belknap Press.

Brady, S. and Rowdon, H. (1996) *For Such a Time as This: Perspectives on Evangelicalism, Past, Present and Future*, Bletchley and London: Evangelical Alliance and Scripture Union.

Brierley, P. (ed.) (1997) *World Churches Handbook*, London: Christian Research.

Brierley, P. and Wraight, H. (1995) *UK Christian Handbook 1996/97 Edition*, London: Christian Research.

Brouwer, S., Gifford, P. and Rose, S.D. (1996) *Exporting the American Gospel: Global Christian Fundamentalism*, New York and London: Routledge.

Bruce, S. (1984) *Firm in the Faith*, Aldershot: Gower.

Bruce, S. (1986), *God Save Ulster! The Religion and Politics of Paisleyism*, Oxford: Oxford University Press.

Calver, C. (1995) 'Afterword: hope for the future?', in J. Wolffe (ed.), pp.198–201.

Cleary, E.L. (1999) 'Latin American Pentecostalism', in M. Dempster *et al.* (eds), pp.131–50.

Cleary, E.L. and Sepúlveda, J. (1997) 'Chilean Pentecostalism: coming of age', in E.L. Cleary and H.W. Stewart-Gambino (eds), pp.97–121.

Cleary, E.L. and Stewart-Gambino, H.W. (1997) *Power, Politics and Pentecostals in Latin America*, Boulder and Oxford: Westview Press.

Coleman, S. (1998) 'Charismatic Christianity and the dilemmas of globalization', *Religion*, vol.28, no.3, pp.245–56.

Cook, G. (1994) 'Protestant presence and social change in Latin America: contrasting visions', in D.R. Miller (ed.), pp.119–41.

Cook, G. (1997) 'Interchurch relations: exclusion, ecumenism, and the poor', in E.L. Cleary and H.W. Stewart-Gambino (eds), pp.77–96.

Corten, A. (1999) *Pentecostalism in Brazil: Emotion of the Poor and Theological Romanticism*, Basingstoke: Macmillan.

Cotton, I. (1995) *The Hallelujah Revolution: The Rise of the New Christians*, London: Little Brown.

Cox, H. (1996) *Fire from Heaven: The Rise of Pentecostal Spirituality and the Reshaping of Religion in the Twenty-first Century*, London: Cassell.

Craston, C., Buchanan, C., Gregg, D., Gunstone, J., Howard, C. and Pattinson, D. (1981) *The Charismatic Movement in the Church of England*, London: COI.

Cray, G., Dawn, M., Mercer, N., Saward, W., Ward, P. and Wright, N. (1997) *The Post-Evangelical Debate*, London: Triangle.

Daneel, M.L. (1999) 'African Initiated Churches in southern Africa: protest movements or mission churches?', unpublished paper for Currents in World Christianity Project.

Davidoff, L. and Hall, C. (1987) *Family Fortunes: Men and Women of the English Middle Class, 1780–1850*, London: Hutchinson.

Dayton, D.W. (1991) 'Some doubts about the usefulness of the category "Evangelical"', in D.W. Dayton and R.K. Johnston (eds) *The Variety of American Evangelicalism*, Knoxville: University of Tennessee Press, pp.245–51.

Dempster, M., Klaus, B.D. and Petersen, D. (1999) *The Globalization of Pentecostalism: A Religion Made To Travel*, Oxford: Regnum.

Diamond, S. (1998) *Not by Politics Alone: The Enduring Influence of the Christian Right*, New York: Guilford Press.

Drogus, C.A. (1997) 'Private power or public power: Pentecostalism, base communities, and gender', in E.L. Cleary and H.W. Stewart-Gambino (eds), pp.55–75.

Edwards, J. (1996) 'The Evangelical Alliance: a national phenomenon', in S. Brady and H. Rowdon (eds), pp.49–59.

Edwards, J. (1997) 'Afro-Caribbean Pentecostalism in Britain', *EPTA Bulletin: Journal of the European Pentecostal Theological Association*, vol.17, pp.36–48.

Eisland, N.L. (1999) 'Irreconcilable differences: conflict, schism and religious restructuring in a United Methodist church', in E.L. Blumhofer *et al.* (eds), pp.168–87.

Eskridge, L.K. (1989) 'Evangelical broadcasting: its meaning for Evangelicals', in M.L. Bradbury and J.B. Gilbert (eds) *Transforming Faith: The Sacred and Secular in Modern American History*, Westport, Connecticut: Greenwood, pp.127–39.

Frankl, R. (1987) *Televangelism: The Marketing of Popular Religion*, Carbondale: Southern Illinois University Press.

Freston, P. (1995) 'Pentecostalism in Brazil: a brief history', *Religion*, vol.25, pp.119–33.

Freston, P. (1997) 'Charismatic Evangelicals in Latin America: mission and politics on the frontiers of Protestant growth', in S. Hunt *et al.* (eds), pp.184–204.

Freston, P. (1998a) 'Evangelicalism and globalization: general observations and some Latin American dimensions', in M. Hutchinson and O. Kalu (eds), pp.69–88.

Freston, P. (1998b) 'Evangelicals and politics: a comparison between Africa and Latin America', *Journal of Contemporary Religion*, vol.13, no.1, pp.37–49.

Freston, P. (1998c) 'Pentecostalism in Latin America: characteristics and controversies', *Social Compass*, vol.43, no.3, pp.335–58.

Freston, P. (2001) *Evangelicals and Politics in Asia, Africa and Latin America*, Cambridge, Cambridge University Press.

Geldbach, E. (1998) '"Evangelisch", "Evangelikal" and pietism: some remarks on early Evangelicalism and globalization from a German perspective', in M. Hutchinson and O. Kalu (eds), pp.156–80.

Gerloff, R. (1995) 'The Holy Spirit and the African diaspora: spiritual, cultural and social roots of black Pentecostal churches', *EPTA Bulletin: Journal of the European Pentecostal Theological Association*, vol.14, pp.85–100.

Gill, A. (1999) 'The struggle to be soul provider: Catholic responses to Protestant growth in Latin America', in J. Prokopy and C. Smith (eds), pp.17–42.

Gillespie, N.N. (1998) 'Graham journeys to cyberspace', *Christianity Today*, 7 December, p.30.

Gledhill, R. (2000) 'Is the Bible Belt here?', *The Times*, 19 April.

Greenway, R.S. (1994) 'Protestant mission activity in Latin America', in D.R. Miller (ed.), pp.175–204.

Hamilton, M.S. (1999) 'The triumph of the praise songs', *Christianity Today*, 12 July, pp.29–35.

Harper, M. (1997) *The True Light: An Evangelical Journey to Orthodoxy*, London: Hodder & Stoughton.

Hexham, I. and Poewe, K. (1994) 'Charismatic churches in South Africa: a critique of criticisms and problems of bias', in K. Poewe (ed.) *Charismatic Christianity as a Global Culture*, Columbia: University of South Carolina Press.

Hocken, P. (1994) 'The Charismatic movement in the United States', *PNEUMA: The Journal of the Society for Pentecostal Studies*, vol.16, no.2, pp.191–213.

Hocken, P. (1996) 'A survey of independent Charismatic churches', *PNEUMA: The Journal of the Society for Pentecostal Studies*, vol.18, no.1, pp.93–105.

Hocken, P. (1997) *Streams of Renewal: The Origins and Early Development of the Charismatic Movement in Great Britain*, Carlisle: Paternoster.

Hofmeyr, J.W. and Pillay, G. (eds) (1994) *A History of Christianity in South Africa*, Pretoria: HAUM.

Hollenweger, W.J. (1972) *The Pentecostals*, London: SCM.

Hong, Y-G. (2001) 'Encounter with modernity: the McDonaldization and Charismatization of Korean mega-churches', unpublished paper presented to the 'Currents in World Christianity' Conference, University of Pretoria.

Hunt, S. (1995) 'The Anglican Wimberites', *PNEUMA: The Journal of the Society for Pentecostal Studies*, vol.17, no.1, pp.105–18.

Hunt, S. (2000) '"Winning ways": globalization and the impact of the health and wealth gospel', *Journal of Contemporary Religion,* vol.15, no.3, pp.331–47.

Hunt, S., Hamilton, M. and Walter, T. (eds) (1997) *Charismatic Christianity: Sociological Perspectives*, Basingstoke: Macmillan.

Hunter, J.D. (1983) *American Evangelicalism: Conservative Religion and the Quandary of Modernity*, New Brunswick: Rutgers University Press.

Hunter, J.D. (1987) *Evangelicalism: The Coming Generation*, Chicago: University of Chicago Press.

Hutchinson, M. (1998) 'It's a small church after all', *Christianity Today,* 16 November, pp.45–9.

Hutchinson, M. and Kalu, O. (eds) (1998) *A Global Faith: Essays on Evangelicalism and Globalization,* Sydney: Centre for the Study of Australian Christianity.

Jamison, I. (2000) 'War in heaven: spiritual warfare in a Plymouth community church', unpublished paper.

Jones, I. (2000) 'The "mainstream" churches in Birmingham, c.1945–1998, the local churches and generational change', unpublished PhD thesis, University of Birmingham.

Kiernan, J. (1995) 'The African independent churches', in M. Prozesky and J. de Gruchy (eds) *Living Faiths in South Africa*, New York: St Martin's Press, pp.116–28.

Kunnie, J.E. (1994) 'Black churches in the United States and South Africa: similarities and differences', in G.C. Oosthuizen, M.C. Kitshoff and S.W.D. Dube (eds) *Afro-Christianity at the Crossroads: Its Dynamics and Strategies*, Leiden: E.J. Brill, pp.80–94.

Lehmann, D. (1996) *Struggle for the Spirit: Religious Transformation and Popular Culture in Brazil and Latin America*, Cambridge: Polity Press.

Lewis, P. (1996) 'Renewal, recovery and growth: 1966 onwards', in S. Brady and H. Rowdon (eds), pp.178–91.

Lyon, D. (1998) 'Wheels within wheels: glocalization and contemporary religion', in M. Hutchinson and O. Kalu (eds), pp.47–68.

Ma, J. (1999) 'Pentecostal challenges in east and south-east Asia', in M. Dempster *et al.* (eds), pp.183–202.

MacHarg, K. (2000) 'Word and Spirit together', *Christianity Today*, 23 October.

Martin, D. (1990) *Tongues of Fire: The Explosion of Protestantism in Latin America*, Oxford: Basil Blackwell.

Miller, D.R. (ed.) (1994) *Coming of Age: Protestantism in Contemporary Latin America*, Lanham: University Press of America.

Noll, M.A. (1992) *A History of Christianity in the United States and Canada*, Grand Rapids: Eerdmans.

Noll, M.A. (1994) *The Scandal of the Evangelical Mind*, Grand Rapids: Eerdmans.

Noll, M.A. (1998) 'Religion in Canada and the United States: comparisons from an important survey featuring the place of Evangelical Christianity', *Crux*, vol.38, no.4, pp.13–25.

Noll, M.A. (2001) *American Evangelical Christianity: An Introduction*, Oxford: Blackwell.

Núñez, E.A. and Taylor, W.D. (1996) *Crisis and Hope in Latin America: An Evangelical Perspective*, Pasadena: William Carey Library.

Ostling, R.H. (1984) 'Evangelical publishing and broadcasting', in G. Marsden (ed.) *Evangelicalism and Modern America*, Grand Rapids: Eerdmans.

Parsons, G. (1993) 'Filling a void? Afro-Caribbean identity and religion', in G. Parsons (ed.) *The Growth of Religious Diversity: Britain from 1945. I Traditions*, London: Routledge/The Open University.

Parsons, G. (2001) *Perspectives on Civil Religion*, Aldershot: Ashgate/Milton Keynes: The Open University.

Paulson, B. (1999) 'The Greater St Louis Billy Graham Crusade: the beginning is here', *Decision*, December, pp.6–10.

Percy, M. (1997) 'The city on a beach: future prospects for Charismatic movements at the end of the twentieth century', in S. Hunt *et al.* (eds), pp.205–28.

Pierucci, A.F. and Prandi, R. (2000) 'Religious diversity in Brazil: numbers and perspectives in a sociological evaluation', *International Sociology*, vol.15, no.4, pp.629–39.

Pritchard, G.A. (1996) *Willow Creek Seeker Services: Evaluating a New Way of Doing Church*, Grand Rapids: Baker Books.

Prokopy, J. and Smith, C. (eds) (1999) *Latin American Religion in Motion*, New York and London: Routledge.

Richter, P. (1995) '"God is not a gentleman!" The sociology of the Toronto Blessing', in S.E. Porter and P.J. Richter (eds) *The Toronto Blessing – Or Is It?*, London: Darton, Langman & Todd, pp.5–37.

Richter, P. (1997) 'The Toronto Blessing: Charismatic Evangelical global warming', in S. Hunt *et al.* (eds), pp.97–119.

Robertson, R. (1992) *Globalization: Social Theory and Global Culture*, London: Sage.

Romanowski, W.D. (2000) 'Evangelicals and popular music', in B.D. Forbes and J.H. Mahan (eds) *Religion and Popular Culture in America*, Berkeley: University of California Press.

Saunders, T. and Samson, H. (1992) *David Watson A Biography*, London: Hodder & Stoughton.

Schaefer, N.A. (1999) '"Some will see miracles": the reception of Morris Cerullo world Evangelism in Britain', *Journal of Contemporary Religion*, vol.14, no.1, pp.111–26.

Schenkel, A.F. (1999) 'New wine and Baptist wineskins: American and southern Baptist denominational responses to the Charismatic renewal, 1960–80', in E.L. Blumhofer *et al.* (eds), pp.152–67.

Schulze, Q.J. (1994) 'Orality and power in Latin American Protestantism', in D.R. Miller (ed.), pp.65–88.

Scotland, N. (1995) *Charismatics and the Next Millennium*, London: Hodder & Stoughton.

Sepúlveda, J. (1999) 'Indigenous Pentecostalism and the Chilean experience', in A.H. Anderson and W.J. Hollenweger (eds), pp.111–34.

Shibley, M.A. (1996) *Resurgent Evangelicalism in the United States: Mapping Cultural Change since 1970*, Columbia: University of South Carolina Press.

Smail, T., Walker, A. and Wright, N. (1995) *Charismatic Renewal: The Search for a Theology*, London: SPCK.

Smidt, C.E., Kellstedt, L.A., Green, J.C. and Guth, J.L. (1999) 'The spirit-filled movements in contemporary America: a survey perspective', in E.L. Blumhofer *et al.* (eds), pp.111–30.

Smilde, D.A. (1994) 'Gender relations and social change in Latin American Evangelicalism', in D.R. Miller (ed.), pp.39–64.

Smith, C. (1998) *American Evangelicalism Embattled and Thriving*, Chicago: University of Chicago Press.

Smith, C. (2000) *Christian America? What Evangelicals Really Want*, Berkeley: University of California Press.

Smith, D.W. (1998) *Transforming the World? The Social Impact of British Evangelicalism*, Carlisle: Paternoster.

Steigenga, T.J. (1994) 'Protestantism, the state and society in Guatemala', in D.R. Miller (ed.), pp.143–72.

Stewart-Gambino, H.W. and Wilson, E. (1997) 'Latin American Pentecostals: old stereotypes and new challenges', in E.L. Cleary and H.W. Stewart-Gambino (eds), pp.227–46.

Stoll, D. (1990) *Is Latin America Turning Protestant?*, Berkeley: University of California Press.

Thompson, W. (1997) 'Charismatic politics: the social and political impact of renewal', in S. Hunt *et al.* (eds), pp.160–83.

Tomlinson, D. (1995) *The Post-Evangelical*, London: Triangle.

Walker, A. (1997) 'Thoroughly modern: sociological reflections on the Charismatic movement from the end of the twentieth century', in S. Hunt *et al.* (eds), pp.17–42.

Walker, A. (1998) *Restoring the Kingdom: The Radical Christianity of the House Church Movement*, Guildford: Eagle.

Ward, P. (1996) *Growing up Evangelical: Youthwork and the Making of a Subculture*, London: SPCK.

Williams, C.G. (1984) 'Speaking in tongues', in D. Martin and P. Mullen, *Strange Gifts? A Guide to Charismatic Renewal*, Oxford: Basil Blackwell, pp.72–83.

Wilson, E.A. (1994) 'The dynamics of Latin American Pentecostalism', in D.R. Miller (ed.), pp.89–116.

Wilson E. (1997) 'Guatemalan Pentecostals: something of their own', in E.L. Cleary and H.W. Stewart-Gambino (eds), pp.139–62.

Wolffe, J. (1994) '"And there's another country ...": religion, the state and British identities', in G. Parsons (ed.) *The Growth of Religious Diversity: Britain from 1945. II Issues*, London: Routledge/Milton Keynes: The Open University, pp.85–121.

Wolffe, J. (ed.) (1995) *Evangelical Faith and Public Zeal: Evangelicals and Society in Britain 1780–1980*, London: SPCK.

Wolffe, J. (1996) 'Unity in diversity? North Atlantic Evangelical thought in the mid-nineteenth century', in R.N. Swanson (ed.) *Unity and Diversity in the Church: Studies in Church History 32*, Oxford, Basil Blackwell/Ecclesiastical History Society, pp.363–75.

Wolffe, J. (1998) 'Historical method and Christian vision in the study of Evangelical history', in M. Hutchinson and O. Kalu (eds), pp.89–107.

Wright, N. (1996) *The Radical Evangelical: Seeking a Place to Stand*, London: SPCK.

Wright, N. (1997) 'The nature and variety of restorationism and the "house church" movement', in S. Hunt *et al.* (eds), pp.60–76.

Web sites

Alpha courses (http://www.alpha.org.uk)

Christian Action Research and Education (CARE) (http://www.care.org.uk)

Christian Broadcasting Network (http://www.cbn.com)

Christian Coalition of America (http://www.cc.org)

Focus on the Family (http://www.fotf.org)

Greenbelt Christian annual music festival (http://www.greenbelt.org.uk)

Tony Campolo (http://www.tonycampolo.com)

CHAPTER 2

Soka Gakkai Buddhism as a global religious movement

HELEN WATERHOUSE

> There is no true happiness for human beings other than chanting *Nam-myoho-renge-kyo*.
>
> (Nichiren, 1276)

Introduction

This chapter turns its attention to an evangelistic movement that offers both similarities to, and contrasts with, the mainly Christian focus of this volume. The Soka Gakkai is a modern religious lay movement based on an ancient form of Japanese Buddhism. The movement became established in Japan in the second half of the twentieth century, but it is founded on the teachings of a thirteenth-century Buddhist prophet/monk, Nichiren (1222–82). Nichiren is known to his followers as Nichiren Daishonin, meaning Nichiren the great sage or saint. The Soka Gakkai presents a highly portable, simple, although not necessarily easy, practice, which is now thoroughly global, reputedly being established in 163 countries.[1]

Versions of many of the analytical questions asked in this volume about Evangelical/Pentecostal/Charismatic Christianity are relevant to the study of the Soka Gakkai. Among these are: what has been the impact of dynamic individuals in the process of establishing the Soka Gakkai in Japan and elsewhere? How has a Japanese religious movement based on a highly controversial thirteenth-century Buddhist monk managed to appeal to twentieth- and twenty-first-century lay people, living in contrasting cultural environments? How

[1] According to Kazuo Fujii, Vice General Director of Soka Gakkai International-UK (SGI-UK).

do people understand their involvement with the movement? To what extent is the Soka Gakkai a genuinely global movement and to what extent do national contexts affect Soka Gakkai organization and practice?

The composite term 'glocalization', which developed in Japan (Robertson, 1992, p.173), refers to the relationship between globalization and localization: that is, the interaction between macro, global forces and micro, local concerns. Examples of glocalization are the way in which an American traveller abroad may demand the same kinds of facilities he or she might expect at home, or the overriding concern for local connections in items of world news. News on television in the UK, for example, will usually mention whether or not British people have been involved in an airline accident that has taken place on the other side of the world. In a similar way, when religions that are presented as universal in scope (which the Soka Gakkai is) travel from one culture to another, there is an inevitable process of adaptation, as they become embedded in their new situations and local demands encounter religious thinking with contrasting cultural assumptions. What we will consider here is whether the Soka Gakkai is one global religion or whether, as it has spread, it has assumed local identities that override its global characteristics.

In order to provide a foundation on which to base analysis of these questions, it will be necessary to describe elements of the history, practices and institutions of the Soka Gakkai. This volume, like the others in this series, is about religion in the modern world, but, in common with many contemporary religions, the Soka Gakkai traces its roots back several centuries, and it makes little sense without its historical context. The central chanting practice of the movement was established in the thirteenth century. Its ancient lineage forms part of the Soka Gakkai's claim to authenticity; although distant in terms of the passing of centuries, Nichiren is present in his writings and in the practice he advocated. Like many Buddhist groups that have achieved global success, however, contemporary practitioners within this school of Buddhism are interested in their ancient past and in their immediate organizational history, but not in the intervening centuries (Waterhouse, 1997, p.205). For this reason, this account jumps, rather sharply, from the thirteenth to the twentieth centuries with little in between.

There are other forms of Buddhism that have enjoyed global success over the last decades of the twentieth century. The same questions could be asked, for example, of Zen Buddhism, of Tibetan forms of Buddhism or of forms of 'insight meditation' emanating from south and south-east Asia. All these Buddhist forms have an increasingly global presence and it would be possible to examine their spread as examples of global Buddhism. However, like Evangelical Christianity, Buddhist movements exist through contrasting lineages of teachers and have no single central organization. In addition, internal diversity within Buddhism is significantly more marked than that found in Christianity. This chapter therefore has as its focus just one form of Buddhism, which provides a case study through which to examine global processes within the broad category of Buddhism. The case study serves as a parallel with, for example, the Billy Graham ministries within Evangelical Christianity. It provides a particularly relevant contrasting case study to the chapters on Christianity in this volume for several reasons. First, the Soka Gakkai has a clear evangelistic strategy.[2] Other schools of Buddhism have engaged in periods of recruitment. In particular, during the last three or four decades they have set up centres in entirely new areas, such as Europe and the USA. These centres succeed in attracting new converts, but those who run such centres and engage in more or less subtle forms of recruitment often lack a coherent articulation of their strategy. They simply demonstrate the desire to spread what they regard as access to the truth and the practices that lead to this, in keeping with the Buddha's admonition to his followers to spread the truth that he taught. The Soka Gakkai is not in this position. It has a clearly articulated recruitment strategy based on the writings of Nichiren, its thirteenth-century patriarch. This strategy has developed and mellowed during the lifetime of the movement but remains central to its activities.

Another reason why the Soka Gakkai provides a relevant contrasting case study is that it is a lay movement that, in 1991, split in rather public fashion from a priestly hierarchy. As a result, some scholars have suggested that the movement has protestant tendencies (Bocking, 1993; 1994; Hurst, 1998, p.93; 2000, pp.82–6; Wilson and Dobbelaere, 1994, p.232). A major characteristic of protestantism is its questioning of traditional authority, with, in particular, a move away from reliance on priestly intermediaries and towards individual interpretation and responsibility. The term 'protestant' as applied to the Soka Gakkai (or to any other form of non-Christian religion) is controversial because it has a specific meaning in relation to Christianity. However, the Soka Gakkai has to some

---

[2] Daniel Métraux (1996, p.365) calls this an 'evangelical stance'. Jan Nattier (1998, pp.189–90) and others specifically refer to the Soka Gakkai as Evangelical Buddhism. The use of the term 'evangelical' in relation to Buddhism is, of course, as John Wolffe indicates on page 15 footnote 2, problematic. It nonetheless illustrates how words that have a specific meaning within one context are sometimes adopted and adapted for use within another.

extent encouraged the use of the term at times in its literature, where it draws parallels between its own stance *vis-à-vis* priestly authority and that of Protestant Christian reformers (see, for example, the words of the current President of the Soka Gakkai, Einosuke Akiya, quoted in Wilson and Dobbelaere, 1994, p.242). Part of the Soka Gakkai's new 'priestless' identity is the idea that no intermediary is required between members of the movement and the truth that it promotes. Instead, it holds that members can go straight to the writings of the founder, or to the object of worship that he provided (described below), in ways that resonate with the Protestant Evangelical Christian position. Evangelical Christianity and the evangelistic Soka Gakkai Buddhism are poles apart in terms of doctrine and forms of practice, but they have in common their global impact.

The Soka Gakkai is often classified as one of the new religions that emerged in Japan during the twentieth century. It will be referred to as such in this chapter. Most of these religions were based on a new revelation or had as their focus a charismatic leader who claimed personal religious authority. Like some other so-called 'new religions', however, the Soka Gakkai does not regard itself as new.[3] Instead, in its own view, it teaches well-established Buddhist doctrines and practices and continues the mission of Nichiren, who founded the only truly 'home-grown' Japanese variety of Buddhism.[4] The Soka Gakkai is not the only movement to claim direct descent from Nichiren. There are other contemporary forms of Nichiren Buddhism, both priestly and lay in character, which trace their lineage back to Nichiren and his immediate disciples and which act in some sense as competitors to the Soka Gakkai. This is not unusual within Buddhism. Many contrasting schools of Buddhism claim direct descent from the Buddha of fifth- and fourth-century BCE India (who is known to Nichiren Buddhists as Shakyamuni, the wise one of the Shakya clan) or from other great Buddhist teachers. The only Nichiren-derived movement, apart from the Soka Gakkai, that is relevant for our purposes here, however, is the priestly Nichiren Shoshu sect to which the Soka Gakkai aligned itself early in its development. Nichiren Shoshu means 'the orthodox Nichiren school' and it is one of the most radical (Tamaru, 2000, p.27) and 'rigorously purist' (Stone, 1994, p.252) of the Nichiren sects. For many years, the Soka Gakkai was bound up in a complex relationship with Nichiren

[3] We might draw a parellel here with the Restorationist strand of Charismatic Christianity: see pages 31–2.

[4] Other forms of Buddhism that are numerically strong in Japan, for example Zen, Pure Land and Shingon Buddhism, were imported there from China.

Shoshu and part of this chapter examines this relationship and its eventual disintegration.

Significant tensions developed between the priestly sect and its claims and the activities of the lay movement. These tensions are indicative of the tensions that exist within the Soka Gakkai between tradition and modernity, between Japan and the West and, more generally, between global and local needs. The tensions are rooted, to a degree, in the fact that the Soka Gakkai recognizes two founding eras. These are, first, that of the thirteenth-century Buddhist monk Nichiren, who founded the practices that Soka Gakkai Buddhists carry out. These practices are broadly common to the priestly Nichiren Shoshu sect and the Soka Gakkai and we might take them as representing tradition. Second, the lay movement recognizes a twentieth-century lineage of presidents, the most significant of whom have been the first three: Tsunesaburo Makiguchi (1871–1944), Josei Toda (1900–58) and Daisaku Ikeda (1928–). The Soka Gakkai has changed and developed under each of these leaders, but we can regard its contemporary status as representing modernity. The following account begins with Nichiren and the practices he promoted. It goes on to discuss the modern lay movement and its proselytizing methods, the global spread of the Soka Gakkai and the split with the priestly sect. Finally, it gives some examples of the way the Soka Gakkai operates throughout the world.

The traditional practice

Shakyamuni Buddha, who figures with differing degrees of prominence in all schools of Buddhism, is overshadowed within the Soka Gakkai by Nichiren. Nichiren first promoted the chanting practice that is central in the activities of all the groups that acknowledge his innovations, of which the Soka Gakkai is now the largest. According to his own account, Nichiren was born to a humble fishing family in eastern Japan. Nichiren stressed these humble origins in his writings, and contemporary followers make much of the idea that what he achieved is made all the more remarkable by his inauspicious start in life. Kiyoaki Murata, a Japanese journalist who wrote a substantial English-language account of the Soka Gakkai, suggests that by stressing Nichiren's humble birth the monk and his followers set up a contrast with Shakyamuni Buddha, who was born into a wealthy and influential family (Murata, 1969, p.29). This stress helps to emphasize the fact that the practices taught by Nichiren are equally available to all, regardless of their background.

When he was twelve, Nichiren entered a temple in his home town. The temple and its priests belonged to the Tendai sect of Buddhism, which combines textual study with esoteric, or secret, ritual and ascetic practices. It also classifies the texts thought to have been preached by Shakyamuni Buddha in accordance with the audience to which they were addressed and the period of the Buddha's life in which they were preached. The Tendai sect considers the *Lotus Sutra* to be the final, perfect ***sutra*** (teaching text). Nichiren became a priest in the temple at the age of fifteen or sixteen. At his home monastery and on his later travels, he studied the texts held to be authoritative by the Tendai sect and also those revered by other Buddhist sects, including Zen, Shingon and Pure Land Buddhism. Nichiren gained a prodigious knowledge of Buddhist canonical writings and the ways in which they were interpreted by the popular sects of his day. His familiarity with the Buddhist canon and with these sects is evident in his own writings, which are extensive.

Many Buddhists of this time, including Nichiren, believed that Japan had entered a degenerate phase in which traditional Buddhist teachings were no longer powerful and were unable to change either individual lives or the environment in which people lived. This period, known in Japanese as ***mappo***, and usually translated within the Soka Gakkai as the 'Latter Day of the Law', was predicted by Shakyamuni Buddha. In the earliest of Nichiren's major writings, translated as *Establishment of the Legitimate Teaching for the Protection of the Country*, he claimed that Buddhists from all schools 'exhaust themselves in vain' (Yampolsky, 1990, pp.13–14) because the Buddhist practices they undertook no longer had an impact. He described the degenerate age in the following terms:

> In recent years, there are unusual disturbances in the heavens, strange occurrences on earth, famine and pestilence, all affecting every corner of the empire and spreading throughout the land. Oxen and horses lie dead in the streets, the bones of the stricken crowd the highways. Over half the population has already been carried off by death, and in every family someone grieves.
>
> (Yampolsky, 1990, p.13)

Nichiren's travels and studies were directed at discovering which Buddhist teaching was sufficiently powerful to effect three outcomes: to ensure that Buddhist enlightenment remained possible, to contend with the natural disasters of the degenerate age and to give Japan its rightful status. He came to believe that the solution he was looking for was sole reliance on the saving power of the *Lotus Sutra*, the text favoured by the Tendai sect. The quintessence of the truth of Buddhism, he believed, was to be found in repeating homage to the *Lotus Sutra* (*Myoho-renge-kyo*). Thus, *Nam-myoho-renge-kyo*,[5] became the mantra or chant of all Nichiren Buddhism, a practice known as **daimoku**. Nichiren inscribed traditional symbols of the Buddhist universe with this mantra, written down the centre of the page and surrounded by the names of various buddhas, *bodhisattvas* (Buddhas to be) and *kami* (Japanese indigenous gods). Nichiren's symbolic representation or *mandala* became known as the **gohonzon** and is the object of worship for Nichiren Buddhists, in front of which the chanting practice is carried out. Nichiren inscribed many *gohonzon*s, perhaps as many as 700. Figure 3.1 shows a *gohonzon* inscribed by Nichiren. This is not precisely the same as the *gohonzon* used by the Soka Gakkai but very similar to it.[6] The remainder of Nichiren's life was dedicated to advocating the practice of chanting the mantra in front of the *gohonzon*. His writings were often directed to individual disciples to encourage them in their practice but also to the government in Japan. Indeed, the Buddhist practice that Nichiren advocated was directed as much to socio-religious reform at national level as it was to individual salvation. For this reason, Nichiren is often regarded as a nationalist. There is little doubt, however, that he viewed the practice he advocated as appropriate for all people and not just for Japan. The practice is universalistic and, according to Nichiren and his followers, it is the key to bringing about fundamental changes to the way in which the world operates. It is the only hope for a degenerate age and has the power to radically reverse decline and bring about a peaceful era.

Nichiren not only advocated the chanting practice for all people but also condemned all other Buddhist practices. For example, he described Zen Buddhism as 'a false doctrine' and Shingon, another school of Buddhism, as 'a major form of heresy'. He was uncompromising in his condemnation and in this way alienated Japan's rulers, many of whom followed the very practices that he

[5] *Nam* or *namu* means 'homage to'. The movement supplies a further detailed explanation of the chant, which expounds Soka Gakkai (and therefore Nichiren Shoshu) doctrine.

[6] Nichiren Shoshu and the Soka Gakkai do not permit or approve the reproduction of their *gohonzon*s outside their own religious practice. Photographic representations or filming are therefore not allowed. This is because they believe the *gohonzon* should always be treated with respect and they cannot be sure that reproductions will always be treated in this way. It is, however, possible to view a copy of a Nichiren Shoshu *gohonzon* in the frontispiece to Resplica Rodd (1980). The Nichiren Shoshu *gohonzon* includes a warning in the top right-hand corner that people who criticize the *gohonzon* will have their heads broken into seven pieces (Bocking, 1994, p.131 n.14), although I have never heard a Soka Gakkai member refer to this.

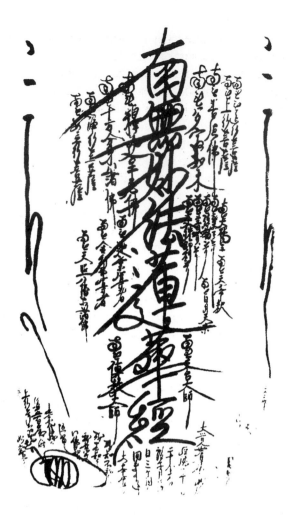

Figure 3.1   An example of a *gohonzon* inscribed by Nichiren and used as the object of worship in Nichiren Buddhism. The centre characters read '*Nam-myoho-renge-kyo*' (homage to the *Lotus Sutra*). Reproduced with permission from Heinz Bechert and Richard Gombrich (eds) *The World of Buddhism*, London: Thames & Hudson, 1983, p.226. Photo: Rod Leach.

condemned. Consequently, Nichiren spent many years in exile and suffered for his beliefs, at one point only narrowly escaping from the implementation of a death sentence. This served to confirm him in his work. According to the *Lotus Sutra*, in the degenerate age true devotees of the *sutra* suffer persecution at the hands of ignorant men, including forest-dwelling monks, of 'twisted wisdom, their hearts sycophantic and crooked' (Hurvitz, 1976, p.205). Nichiren claimed that Shakyamuni Buddha, 'was cursed by all the followers of non-Buddhist teachings and labelled as a man of great evil' and that other prominent teachers experienced equal difficulty (Yampolsky, 1990, p.147). To suffer for the sake of the *Lotus Sutra* is therefore proof of being an authentic follower of the truth.

This belief leads to a paradox that operates at the heart of Buddhism as practised by those who claim to be the true descendants of Nichiren. The practice aims to be successful and to transform Japan; if it is powerful and effective then its effects ought to prove its power. And yet, at the same time, if it becomes too popular or mainstream it does not attract the kind of persecution, outlined in the *Lotus Sutra*, which proves its authenticity. Because of this paradox, unpopular priests have been able to rely on their unpopularity as proof that they are the true followers of the *Lotus Sutra*, and lay followers denounced by the priests have made the same claim.

Nichiren believed that as a result of directly slandering the *Lotus Sutra* or ignoring it in favour of other practices, the people of Japan were bringing trouble on themselves in the form of earthquakes and epidemics. To preach the message about the *Lotus Sutra* was therefore an act of compassion. It followed that it was incumbent on him to engage in evangelistic practices to convince people that he was right and why.

Nichiren made a distinction in his writings between two proselytizing methods.[7] He based this distinction on his reading of Buddhist **Mahayana** texts. The first method, **shakubuku**, meaning literally 'to break and subdue', entails propagating Buddhism by forceful methods, in particular refuting others' (false) views by careful and detailed argument. As a scholar of Buddhist texts, Nichiren was well placed to engage in this activity. The Nichiren scholar Jacqueline Stone points out that, '*shakubuku* as employed by Nichiren required considerable mastery of doctrine, since his criticism of other sects rested on detailed arguments based on the *sūtras* and commentaries' (Stone, 1994, p.233). Without such detailed knowledge, Nichiren could not have engaged in the finer points of the debate nor explained his precise position. The second method of proselytizing, **shoju**, meaning literally 'to embrace and accept', is a gentler method of propagation, which involves teaching by example without the forceful refutation of views. This is the method of proselytizing appropriate for people who do not slander the *Lotus Sutra*, because they have no knowledge of it, but who nonetheless ignore it at their peril. These days, although this has not always been the case, *shoju* is usually taken to be the most appropriate evangelistic method for use

---

[7] Nichiren was not the only Buddhist teacher to regard these two methods as traditional Buddhist practices (Murata, 1969, p.102; Stone, 1994, p.233), although other contemporary Buddhist groups do not articulate the need to spread Buddhist teachings in these terms.

outside Buddhist countries. In such areas, people are ignorant of the true Law of the *Lotus Sutra*, since it is not part of their cultural heritage. In his own time, Nichiren taught that these two proselytizing methods are both necessary. In 1272, for example, in the second of his five major works, translated as *The Opening of the Eyes*, he wrote:

> These two methods of spreading the Law, *shōju* and *shakubuku*, are like water and fire. Fire hates water, water detests fire. The practitioner of *shōju* laughs with scorn at *shakubuku*. The practitioner of *shakubuku* despairs at the thought of *shōju*. When the country is full of ignorant or evil persons, then *shōju* is the primary method to be applied ... But at a time when there are many persons of perverse views who slander the Law, then *shakubuku* should come first ...

> In the Latter Day of the Law, however, both *shōju* and *shakubuku* are to be used. This is because there are two kinds of countries, the country that is passively evil, and the kind that actively seeks to destroy the Law. We must consider carefully to which category Japan at the present time belongs.

(Yampolsky, 1990, pp.143–4)

Nichiren's conclusion later in this text was that in the thirteenth century Japan, as a nation, actively opposed the Law of the *Lotus Sutra*. Unlike non-Buddhist countries, it had knowledge of the *sutra* but chose not to honour it in the way that the *sutra* itself advocated. Consequently, the *shakubuku* method was appropriate to Japan at that time. There is more to be said, later in this chapter, about these two methods of proselytizing in relation to the twentieth-century spread of Nichiren's Buddhism. A related concept is **kosen-rufu**, meaning 'to widely declare and spread'. Nichiren engaged in *kosen-rufu* in order to spread what he regarded as the teachings of the *Lotus Sutra*, as do his modern-day followers. Nichiren advocated the exclusive use of practices based on the mantra *Nam-myoho-renge-kyo*. According to him, mixing the *daimoku* chant with other religious practices was like mixing 'grain with excrement' (Nichiren's letter to Akimoto, cited in Stone, 1994, p.232). It was Nichiren's uncompromising stance – his emphasis on proselytizing and his exclusive approach to Buddhist practice – that won him enemies.

After much trouble and conflict, Nichiren eventually settled in a secluded part of Japan. Here he continued to write letters of encouragement to his followers. These letters, called **gosho**, many of which are preserved, still provide inspiration and encouragement to contemporary Nichiren Buddhists. Extracts are regularly reproduced in Soka Gakkai publications and Soka Gakkai Buddhists have their personal favourites. Although he was an uncompromising figure, Nichiren's compassion is evident in these letters, in his concern for the welfare of his followers and in his gratitude for their material support. Nichiren died in 1282. It has been estimated that he had just 260 followers, 65 of them priests, at the time of his death (Murata, 1969, p.40). After Nichiren's death, the tradition that he had founded splintered into a number of priestly lineages or sects, each of which took forward different interpretations of his teachings, and each of which naturally regarded its own teachings as perfectly continuous with those of its master. Nichiren Shoshu developed from Nikko, one of Nichiren's senior priests, who, its own orthodoxy holds, was Nichiren's closest disciple and had received from him certain proofs of that, including the *dai* (great) *gohonzon*, the focus of worship inscribed by him.

In 1939, nearly 700 years after Nichiren's death, the Japanese Ministry of Education conducted a survey which showed that there were almost 5000 Nichiren temples in Japan, 4500 Nichiren priests and well over three million adherents of Nichiren's Buddhism. Of the Nichiren sects at that time, the Nichiren Shoshu – the priestly sect in which we have an interest here – was one of the smallest and least significant. It had just 75 temples and fewer than 100,000 adherents (Murata, 1969, pp.70–1). This was to change.

Figure 3.2 Tsunesaburo Makiguchi. Courtesy of Soka Gakkai International-UK Publications Department/*UK Express*.

The modern movement

Makiguchi and the Soka Kyoiku Gakkai

In 1937, an educational society by the name of Soka Kyoiku Gakkai (the Value-creating Educational Society) began its activities (Tamaru, 2000, p.31). The society was opposed to the educational theories then prevalent in Japan and promoted creative education for all. It was the outcome of several years during which the society's founder, Tsunesaburo Makiguchi (Figure 3.2), building on his experience as a primary school teacher and school principal, had been developing a theory of education that emphasized value and the importance of nurturing children.[8]

Makiguchi had been connected to Nichiren Buddhism (although not to the Nichiren Shoshu sect) through his family all his life but had never shown any interest in it. An encounter with a Nichiren Shoshu adherent in 1928, shortly before Makiguchi retired from an unsatisfactory and turbulent teaching career, stirred his interest and a formal link was later made between the educational society, which was mainly supported by teachers, and the small priestly sect.

The early years of the link between the two organizations coincided with the Second World War. During this time, in an attempt to unite the country, the Japanese government promoted 'State Shinto'. It demanded that all Japanese families pray to the sun goddess (*Amaterasu*) and that a tablet, or talisman, from her temple at Ise in southern Japan be installed in every **butsudan** (the household Buddhist altar where the spirits of ancestors are enshrined and where, in Nichiren's Buddhism, the family copy of the *gohonzon* is installed). In the tradition of Nichiren this demand was unacceptable. To combine the *daimoku* chant before the *gohonzon* with other religious practices, such as worship of the sun goddess, would be, according to Nichiren, like 'mixing grain with excrement'. Equally, if not more, problematic was the requirement that all Nichiren sects unite under a government-controlled umbrella organization. This was also unacceptable, given the history of the Nichiren sects and the insistence of each that it alone was Nichiren's legitimate heir. But times were hard, and the majority of Nichiren Buddhists, including the Nichiren Shoshu priests, bowed to the government decree, joined the organization and accepted the Ise talisman. However, Makiguchi, his chief follower Josei Toda (Figure 3.3) and 19 other members of the Soka Kyoiku Gakkai would not comply and were imprisoned for their stance. The majority of these 21 stalwarts subsequently renounced their faith and were released from prison, but Makiguchi, Toda and two others refused to compromise. Makiguchi died in prison in November 1944.

---

[8] Makiguchi's educational theory (which is described in detail in Bethel, 1989) is pragmatic in nature. It distinguishes between truth – which Makiguchi argued does not change and therefore has no relation to human beings – and value – which is relative from person to person and from age to age.

Figure 3.3 Josei Toda and the young Daisaku Ikeda at a Japanese Youth event. Courtesy of Soka Gakkai International-UK Publications Department/*UK Express*.

Toda and the Soka Gakkai

Toda had worked under his master Makiguchi and was fully behind Makiguchi's educational theories. Like Makiguchi, he had made his own way in life through hard work, having been born into a poor family unable to afford to educate him in the conventional way. Toda converted to the Nichiren Shoshu sect after having tried both Christianity and other schools of Buddhism (Murata, 1969, p.88). In early 1944, while he was still in prison, Toda resolved to chant the *daimoku* 10,000 times every day. After two million repetitions he claimed to have had an ecstatic experience, which served to affirm his faith in the *Lotus Sutra*. After his release from prison, in 1945, and without his master Makiguchi, who had died there, Toda set about rebuilding the successful business empire he had left behind him at the time of his imprisonment. He also reformulated the Soka Kyoiku Gakkai, which had been disbanded. Under Toda, the society changed its name from Soka Kyoiku Gakkai (the Value-creating Educational Society) to Soka Gakkai (the Value-creating Society), thus dropping the explicit link to education. Toda's business enterprises boomed and waned under the immediate post-war speculative Japanese economy. Early membership of the Soka

Gakkai tended to reflect Toda's business success, or lack of it, but proselytizing campaigns were vigorous and membership grew overall.

Recitation of the *daimoku* was never intended to achieve inner or spiritual benefit alone. According to Nichiren Shoshu and Soka Gakkai orthodoxy, correct religious practice brings material success as well as less measurable gains. The practice is therefore expected to prove itself. The potential to judge the success of the practice against specified goals has been instrumental in attracting and keeping recruits who are encouraged right from the outset to chant for specific benefits, so that the practice can prove its power. In keeping with a train of thought prevalent in certain forms of Mahayana Buddhism, Nichiren taught that 'Earthly Desires are Enlightenment' (Yampolsky, 1990, p.343), in other words, the state of enlightenment is not to be found outside human experience. Equally, in Nichiren's theology, the mind and body are considered to be inseparable, such that 'whatever affects the mind will affect the body and vice versa' (Causton, 1995, p.106). The movement reasons that unhappiness represents an undesirable state by any measure. Unhappiness, caused by poverty, ill-health or other disappointment, is the result of negative actions in past lives, which are experienced as negative results in the present life through the outworking of **karma**. One of the aims of Soka Gakkai practice is to reverse negative *karma* so that unhappiness – whatever its cause – can no longer taint the experience of this life and future lives. Nichiren taught that faith in the *Lotus Sutra* can change *karma* no matter how firmly imprinted it is. Since good actions lead to benefits such as wealth or good relationships, which engender happiness, those things are regarded as benefits. There is no intrinsic value in being poor or ill and therefore no reason why one of the results of chanting *Nam-myoho-renge-kyo* should not be material or physical gain. While Japanese and, indeed, other Buddhist cultures see no contradiction in this general principle (Reader and Tanabe, 1998),[9] those who have been raised in Protestant Christian cultures often find the idea difficult to accept. It is an aspect of Japanese religion that can draw criticism from religious groups and the media operating outside Asia. In addition, within Japan, many 'new religions', including the Soka Gakkai, are criticized for having too sharp a focus on material gain (Reader and Tanabe, 1998, pp.2–3). In a similar way, some Christians are wary of prosperity theology (see Chapter 1).

---

[9] There is a Japanese term (*genze riyaku*) that means benefits in this lifetime. The scope of such benefits within Japanese religious ideology is very wide indeed.

The Soka Gakkai promises that chanting *Nam-myoho-renge-kyo* will bring benefits. If benefits elude practitioners, then they are likely to stop practising. If, on the other hand, benefits are experienced, then practitioners' faith is likely to increase, leading them to continue with the chanting and, according to the movement, to even greater tangible and non-tangible benefits. This life-affirming stance is undoubtedly attractive to many members. It promises the members an element of control not only over this life and but also over the results of actions in past lives and therefore over lives to come. 'As long as he chants he need not be a victim, and must not perceive himself as such' (Wilson and Dobbelaere, 1994, p.221). Soka Gakkai Buddhists are not much interested in the idea of a life beyond this world.

Ikeda and the present day

Toda died in 1958, leaving behind him a successful movement which had developed powerful political connections. In 1955, for example, three members of the Soka Gakkai had been elected to Japan's political Upper House and the Prime Minister of Japan, Shinsuke Kishi, participated in Toda's funeral (Dumoulin, 1976, p.255). There were initial doubts about whether a successor could be found to take over the society, maintain its cohesiveness and lead it on. Daisaku Ikeda (1928–), who was not yet quite 30, but who had joined the movement in 1947, aged 19, and become close to Toda through working for him, took on much of his master's work. Two years later, in 1960, Ikeda became the third President of the Soka Gakkai.

Ikeda was brought up in Tokyo. By all accounts he was a sickly child from a poor family. His avid interest in philosophy, however, led him to accept an invitation to attend a meeting in the home of a friend, at which Toda gave a lecture on one of Nichiren's major writings, the *Establishment of the Legitimate Teaching for the Protection of the Country* (Murata, 1969, p.121). Shortly afterwards, on 24 August 1947, Ikeda joined the Soka Gakkai, and soon became an employee and associate of Toda in a close master–disciple relationship. Ikeda has spoken of Toda as follows: 'Mr Toda's easy-going voice had penetrated the gloom of my heart and, for some inexplicable reason, filled me with joy.' He often refers to Toda as his 'master in life' (see, for example, Anon., 1993, p.33). The movement's growth under President Ikeda was meteoric. When Toda died in 1958, membership of the Soka Gakkai stood at 1,050,000. By the end of 1959, before Ikeda had been formally recognized as the new leader, it had risen to 1,300,000 and by May 1969, when he was fully established, it had multiplied to 6,240,000 (Murata, 1969, p.124). Even accounting for some elevation in the figures common in the accounts of Japanese religious movements, this still represents an enormous success. In 1964, a political party called the Komeito (the Clean Government Party) was founded to promote world peace through globalism, egalitarianism and democratic government. The political party, which enjoyed considerable success for two decades (before becoming part of a coalition called the New Frontier Party in 1995), was closely affiliated to the Soka Gakkai, although legally separate from the movement. In Ikeda the society had found its third successful leader.

The organization of the Soka Gakkai

A large organization needs structures in order to function. The Soka Gakkai in Japan has effective structures in place which allocate convert families to progressively smaller units in order to provide both personal support and a means by which to disseminate information. The top leaders of the organization oversee head-quarters, below which is a hierarchy of chapters, districts, groups and then units. A unit is a small collective of members linked together through what is known as a *shakubuku* relationship: a relationship based on what can be an aggressive form of proselytizing. People introduced to the movement by the *shakubuku* effort of an existing member are thought to be joined to that member by a bond that is stronger even than family ties. In addition to their attachment to a unit, each individual member belongs to a division of people in similar circumstances. There are Men's, Women's, Young Men's and Young Women's divisions, a Youth division and so on. Each division supplies leaders for the different levels in the hierarchical structure. In this way, members are included in the organization via a compre-hensive network. A further strand of the network is that of special interest groups in which, for example, lawyers, teachers or other professionals meet together to discuss their common interests and the ways in which Soka Gakkai practice may be relevant to these.

Soka Gakkai practices

We have already noted that the central practice advocated by Nichiren and continued by the priestly sects of which he is regarded as the founder is *daimoku*. In addition to chanting *daimoku*, Soka Gakkai members recite two specified chapters from the *Lotus Sutra* and offer prayers. This ritual practice, called **gongyo**, takes place every morning and evening in front of the *gohonzon*. It is usually accompanied by burning candles and incense. Colour Plate 9 shows a

Soka Gakkai *butsudan*, the shrine in which the *gohonzon* is hung. Members also hold in their hands prayer beads, which they periodically rub together to aid concentration. Experienced members know the words and order of *gongyo* by heart but those who are newer to the practice follow the instructions in a small *gongyo* book (Figure 3.4). *Gongyo*, once learnt, takes about half an hour to perform; this time can be extended indefinitely by periods of *daimoku* practice (Figure 3.5). *Gongyo* practice can be problematic for modern Japanese followers to begin with because it is spoken in classical Japanese, however members soon learn to pronounce the words and become speedy and proficient.

In addition to *gongyo*, members are also expected to engage in the study of Nichiren's writings. It is possible to take examinations on Soka Gakkai doctrine and to gain certain prestige in the organization through examination success (Murata, 1969, p.144). All members are also expected to attend discussion meetings, where they can take part in efforts to teach others about the doctrine and practices that the movement promotes and share their experiences of doing the practice.

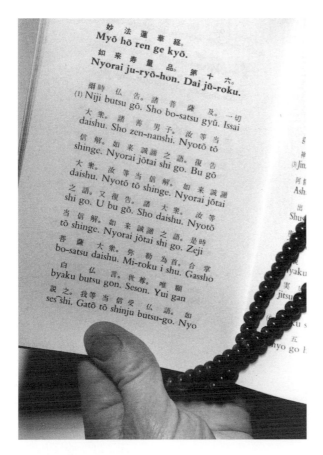

Figure 3.4 A sample page from a Soka Gakkai *gongyo* book. Courtesy of Soka Gakkai International-UK Publications Department/*UK Express*. Photo: Rod Leach.

Figure 3.5   A Soka Gakkai member chanting in front of the *gohonzon*. She is holding prayer beads and a *gongyo* book. Courtesy of Soka Gakkai International-UK Publications Department/*UK Express*.

Why has the Soka Gakkai been so successful?

Exact statistics are not available, but the Soka Gakkai today claims several million followers in contemporary Japan (Tamaru, 2000, p.28).[10] It has headquarters in Tokyo, with other centres all over the country. True to its original link with education it runs a number of schools and a highly successful university near to Tokyo which, although without the prestige of Japan's top universities, nonetheless attracts good teachers and motivated students (Métraux, 1996, p.382).

Brian Bocking, a British scholar of Japanese religions, has observed that the reasons why people join the Soka Gakkai within Japan do not need 'explaining away' by sociological or psychological analysis (Bocking, 1980, p.38). While explanations are interesting, we should not be surprised that, in a country that has been Buddhist for fourteen centuries, a form of Buddhism 'home grown' in Japan has been strikingly successful. Whether or not the movement has correctly interpreted Nichiren's teachings (which other Nichiren

[10] In 1984, Shupe (1984, p.239) cited a figure of 10–15 million individual members. It is likely that this figure represents an exaggeration. Métraux (1996, p.365) suggests 8–10 million which, although more modest, still represents 6–8 per cent of the population of Japan.

sects argue it has not), and whether or not Nichiren correctly interpreted the Buddha's teachings (which other Buddhist schools and indeed some western scholars[11] argue he did not), is not at issue; continuity and hermeneutics are problematic in any religious tradition[12] and Buddhism is no exception. Regardless of this, the resolution of continuity and authenticity issues that the Soka Gakkai offers is, according to the movement's own figures, convincing for upwards of about 6 per cent of the population of Japan. These people regard themselves as 'true' Buddhists, who follow the path that they believe the Buddha and, more especially, Nichiren taught.

More specific explanations for the movement's success have, however, been offered. These include: the promise of worldly benefits; opportunities for advancement through the organizational structure of the Soka Gakkai (which may be attractive to practitioners of low social status); and the centrality of the doctrine of *shakubuku* in the movement's early years (Stone, 1994, p.253). It is also the case that the early development of the Soka Gakkai took place during the post-war decades in Japan in a period of rapid urbanization and heightened mobility of population (Tamaru, 2000, p.28).

The secret of the Soka Gakkai's success, according to the scholar of Buddhism Heinrich Dumoulin, is its 'belief in itself as absolute' (Dumoulin, 1976, p.251): the movement offers certainty to its members. Nichiren claimed the exclusivity of the ultimate Law of the *Lotus Sutra*. He also taught a simple practice that anyone, male or female, young or old, rich or poor, intellectually gifted or not, can carry out. The combination of a simple practice and the promise of certainty is attractive because it makes the ultimate accessible. Susumu Shimazono, a Japanese scholar, argues that the movement presents a 'straightforward magical practice' which has the potential to be universally attractive (Shimazono, 1991, p.119). The magical practice to which he refers is, of course, the chanting of the mantra, which is presented as intrinsically powerful regardless of whether it is understood by the practitioner in intellectual terms.

We have already seen that part of the practice as taught by Nichiren – a part that is prominent in Soka Gakkai teaching – is its emphasis on *shakubuku*. Nichiren offered a clear doctrinal basis for this proselytizing method and was persuaded that such activity is motivated by compassion for individuals and for the world. No religious tradition will become popular unless potential converts

---

[11] See Stone, 1994, pp.231–2 for examples of critiques by scholars. Stone argues that criticisms on the part of modern scholars 'tell us more about modern scholarly presuppositions than they do about the Nichiren tradition' (p.232).

[12] Hermeneutics is introduced in Herbert, 2001, Book 2 in this series, chapter 3.

come to know of its existence. Unlike other Nichiren sects who retained the rhetoric of *shakubuku* but were unwilling to practice it, Soka Gakkai members engaged in confrontational *shakubuku* campaigns within Japan, which brought considerable success. As we have seen, ideally *shakubuku* requires detailed doctrinal knowledge in order that others' views can be effectively refuted. Members were therefore supplied with handbooks containing quotations from Nichiren's writings and explanations of the *Lotus Sutra*'s teachings. These handbooks also contained sample arguments that members could use to counter objections to Nichiren's perspective that were commonly put forward by potential converts (Stone, 1994, p.252).

Shakubuku campaigns also had a less savoury side, before President Ikeda put a stop to certain techniques in the early 1960s. For example, young Soka Gakkai women would take jobs in Tokyo bars in order to attract American military personnel and thereby persuade them to attend Nichiren Shoshu temples. This technique was exposed in *Time* magazine and subsequently discontinued (Dator, 1969, pp.55–6). Some enthusiastic young practitioners would smash the *butsudans* in their parents' homes on the grounds that they represented ancestor worship and were heretical. President Ikeda responded by directing members to 'cease their contempt of other religions' (Shupe, 1984, p.241) and decreeing that while members must not worship ancestors they could honour and respect them. Others would target and pursue individuals who they thought represented likely converts. The result of these techniques was that even the tolerant League of Japanese New Religious Movements condemned the movement. Even now, Japanese people, when asked about the Soka Gakkai, may associate the movement with such techniques.

Whether as a result of these techniques or due to less aggressive tactics, potential converts were persuaded to attend neighbourhood discussion meetings, where they would hear members speak of the benefits they had gained from undertaking *daimoku* and *gongyo* practice. As we have already seen, because chanting *Nam-myoho-renge-kyo* is said to bring both tangible and non-tangible benefits, the practice that the movement promotes constantly proves itself to members, to their own satisfaction, as they achieve the goals they chant for. Members of the Soka Gakkai readily affirm at discussion meetings that this is the case. Whereas Evangelical Christians are often keen to give their testimony about the ways in which their lives have been changed by Jesus Christ, Soka Gakkai Buddhists readily retell their experiences of the benefits they have gained from doing the practice. While members frequently report, for example, an upturn in their business or financial fortunes, or an improvement in their personal relationships, they also report that their focus soon changes from chanting solely for worldly, personal benefits to chanting for more altruistic reasons. If the desired material benefits are not forthcoming, then members can cope with this by arguing that they have gained instead the things they really needed rather than the things they thought they wanted. In this way, members with faith in the practice can rationalize why it is that specific, tangible benefits may elude them for a period.

Just as Nichiren was concerned with thirteenth-century Japan's national fortunes, so Soka Gakkai Buddhists today are concerned about the state of the world. This concern and the activities that accompany it are popular among Soka Gakkai Buddhists, who believe they are having a positive impact on the world and not merely on their own lives. Ikeda consistently emphasizes the role that the Soka Gakkai can play in bringing about peace and harmony between nations. The emphasis on the promotion of peace strikes a very particular chord in Japan, following the Second World War and the atom bomb. Like other Japanese leaders of religious movements, Ikeda meets with world leaders (although not Buddhist leaders) (Figures 3.6 and 3.7), suggesting cordial relationships, and he emphasizes, for example, ecological awareness and concern for the planet. There is no doubt that while the movement promotes

Figure 3.6 President Ikeda with Mikhail Gorbachev. Courtesy of Soka Gakkai International-UK Publications Department/*UK Express*.

Figure 3.7   President Ikeda with Nelson Mandela. Courtesy of Soka Gakkai International-UK Publications Department/*UK Express.*

individual welfare and benefits and community activity (Colour Plate 8), it is also concerned with global issues. The English-language publication *SGI Quarterly* is subtitled *Buddhist Perspectives on Peace, Culture and Education*, and regularly contains articles on human rights, 'corporate citizenship' and world health issues. The key to the achievement of such global goals, according to the movement, is direct, charitable action and involvement in global initiatives, such as the United Nations (UN) and the United Nations Educational, Scientific, and Cultural Organization (UNESCO). However, primarily the movement sees the resolution of global problems in faithful chanting of the mantra, which, it believes, has the power to change the world.

One of the movement's major goals is 'human revolution'. This term, which was initially coined by Toda, refers to the idea that when, as a result of chanting *Nam-myoho-renge-kyo*, an individual changes his or her view of life and society, that personal change also impacts on the nation and ultimately on humankind as a whole. President Ikeda has expressed this as follows: 'the vibration of each individual human life affects all other types of life, and even alters the undercurrents of a people's consciousness' (Anon., 1997a, p.20). Early in their association with the Soka Gakkai, individuals are encouraged to chant for superficial, tangible benefits to prove to themselves the efficacy of the practice and strengthen their faith. As they develop, according to the movement's own understanding, they will change so that the short-term, superficial view is no longer focal. The satisfaction brought by the achievement of short-term goals is replaced by a more long-term view and more altruistic goals. This change, it is said, benefits not just these individuals but also the society of which they are a part. This ideology is attractive in a world where individuals often feel powerless in the face of impersonal global forces.

Going global

Much has been written of Nichiren's patriotism and of his Japan-focused concerns. Nichiren's self-styled representatives in the twentieth century, the Soka Gakkai, however, have much wider concerns and have turned their attention, under the leadership of Ikeda, to the entire world. The Soka Gakkai is not the only Japanese 'new religion' to widen its horizons in this way. Many of the large movements have expanded, often initially via Japanese nationals who settled outside Japan as a result of Japan's economic and industrial success,[13] but the Soka Gakkai has been the most successful of these movements (Bocking, 1994, p.118; Shupe, 1984, p.239). According to its own accounts, it is now represented in 163 countries, over five continents. This figure contradicts the findings of the scholar of Japanese new religions Peter Clarke, who writes that Japanese new religions overall are present in over 80 countries (Clarke, 2000a, p.272). The mismatch is almost certainly due to differences of opinion about whether a religion is present in a country if there are just one or two members practising there. The Soka Gakkai would probably claim that it is, while Clarke might need more convincing of the presence of a religion as opposed to the presence of practitioners of a religion in a given location.

There are a reported 30,000 Soka Gakkai members in Europe (Causton, 1994, p.9). Of the European countries where the Soka Gakkai has a presence, only five are estimated to have more than 500 members: Italy, which has proved to be the most receptive country within Europe, with around 20,000 members (Macioti, 2000, p.14); the UK where there are between 5000 and 7000 members;[14] Germany, where there are 2000 members (Ionescu, 2000, p.188); France; and Spain. Figures given for membership within the USA vary

[13] For example, Rissho Koseikai, Tenrikyo, Seicho No Ie.

[14] Interview with the current General Director of SGI-UK, 19 October 2000.

significantly. According to the US organization's Internet pages, there are 330,000 Soka Gakkai practitioners in the USA (www.sgi-usa.org/aboutsgi-usa, accessed 18 January 2000).[15] A Soka Gakkai administrator, however, estimates that there are a more modest, but nonetheless significant, 110,000–120,000 members, approximately half of whom live in California (Clarke, 2000c, p.279).

There are populations of Soka Gakkai Buddhists in South and Central America, including Venezuela, Uruguay and Mexico (Okubo, 1991, p.195). The movement has been especially successful in Brazil, where there are a reputed 150,000 members (Shimazono, 1991, p.107; Clarke, 2000c, p.286; Clarke, 2000a, p.326).[16] There are also a reputed 800,000–900,000 Soka Gakkai Buddhists in Asia, including Hong Kong, Malaysia, Korea and Taiwan (Métraux, 2000, p.404), with an estimated 2000 members in India (Sinha, 1994, p.36), the birthplace of Buddhism.[17] Daniel Métraux's account of the Soka Gakkai in south-east Asia can be found in Part Two. Australia's 1991 Census indicated that there were nearly 143,000 Buddhists living there (Adam and Hughes, 1996, p.41), but fewer than ten of these gave the Soka Gakkai as their religion (Bouma *et al.*, 2000, p.76).[18] In 1995, the Australian District of the Soka Gakkai could list 1350 members, of whom two-thirds were Asian (Bouma *et al.*, 2000, p.76). In Africa, there are active members practising in 32 countries out of 53 (Anon., 1997b, p.18). On 28 December 1997, the first *gohonzon* was taken to the island of Mauritius in the Indian Ocean, where there were reputed to be a total of 92 Soka Gakkai members.

The reasons why the Soka Gakkai has become so successful outside Japan are not entirely different from the reasons why it is successful inside Japan. The 'straightforward magical practice' (Shimazono, 1991, p.119) that it offers is appealing to some people

[15] Philip Hammond and David Machacek, who have carried out a sociological survey of the Soka Gakkai in the USA, claim that estimates of this order are 'greatly inflated' (1999, p.37). The figure for Germany, on the other hand, is said to be deflated in order not to be seen to be posing a threat to the German government (Ionescu, 2000, p.196 n.1).

[16] It is interesting that these figure do not show any change between 1991 and 2000. This may indicate a plateauing of growth in Brazil or, alternatively, a change in the way in which members are counted.

[17] While this figure is so small as to be virtually insignificant as a proportion of India's population, it is nonetheless significant that this form of Buddhism is present within the land of Buddhism's birth.

[18] This contradicts the findings of Robert Humphreys and R. Ward, who record that as early as 1980 there were more than 400 Soka Gakkai members in Australia, mainly in New South Wales (Adam, 1995, p.36).

in other parts of the globe, just as it is in Japan. The simplicity of the practice and the fact that there is no need for the central practices of *gongyo* and *daimoku* to be translated out of their classical Japanese format mean that anyone in the world can begin chanting at any time. This is also a unifying factor. Any member can practise alongside any other member in any part of the world and expect a welcome at Soka Gakkai homes in any continent. This pull towards unity can have precise and practical consequences. For example, when war broke out between the UK and Argentina over the sovereignty of the Falkland Islands, in keeping with the movement's anti-war stance the UK General Director immediately contacted Soka Gakkai members in Argentina and organized *daimoku* meetings to chant for an end to the conflict (Samuel, 1995, p.22). It is increasingly the case that the Soka Gakkai is presented as a movement for peace as well as a religious path. For example, publicity fliers for a public meeting in Somerset, England in November 2000 advertised the Soka Gakkai as 'a registered charity affiliated to the United Nations'.

The next section considers how the Soka Gakkai, which is generally known as Soka Gakkai International (SGI) outside Japan, has adapted to new and diverse cultural settings. Just as the Soka Gakkai has a doctrine to explain its proselytizing methods, it also has a doctrine on which it can draw to justify the adaptations made when the practice transfers to new cultural settings. This doctrine is known as *zuiho bini* ('adapting the precepts to the locality'). This concept, originally based on changes to monastic discipline, is used to explain how, while central practices must stay the same, the detail of the ways in which practice is carried out can change in accordance with local or even individual needs. The section also considers the more specific reasons offered to account for why national groups affiliated to SGI have been successful. Before we turn to this, however, we consider the role of the Nichiren Shoshu priesthood, to which Makiguchi affiliated the movement in its early days but which has not featured in this account so far.

The split with the priesthood: protestant tendencies?

In the story so far we have all but lost sight of what happened to the Nichiren Shoshu priestly sect – which represents tradition – while the Soka Gakkai went from strength to strength, or, indeed, of what the sect thought about the rise of the lay movement. In 1976, Dumoulin described the relationship between Nichiren Shoshu and the Soka Gakkai as a 'unique bond' and as 'one of the most remarkable phenomena within the modern history of religions' (Dumoulin, 1976, p.257). The close relationship between the small, centuries-old priestly hierarchy and the large, modern, dynamic lay movement did not last, however. Even as early as 1952, under the leadership of President Toda, there were hints of what might be to come, when one of the Nichiren Shoshu priests was forced by the lay movement to sign a confession admitting that he had suppressed the Soka Gakkai during the war and been responsible for Makiguchi's death (Dumoulin, 1976, p.258). At the outset of the Second World War, at the decree of the state, the Nichiren Shoshu priests accepted the Ise tablet into their altars and joined the government-controlled umbrella organization, whereas, as we have seen, the leaders of Soka Kyoiku Gakkai did not. With hindsight, it seems that even then the society may have been both flexing its muscles and taking what it saw as the orthodox doctrinal high ground over the priesthood. From his 1970s perspective, Dumoulin could not have foreseen the possible significance of this early quarrel or the troubled relationship that lay ahead.

The relationship between the two institutions (which have always formed separate legal entities) has never been easy. They share the common goal of promoting the growth of Nichiren Shoshu Buddhism,[19] but the broad tensions that exist in the modern world between 'traditionalism and modernism, hierarchy and egalitarianism, objective knowledge traditions and subjective understanding, mysticism and rationalism, collective authority and individualism, sacredness and secularism, faith and scepticism' (Bocking, 1994, p.119) have been played out in their relationship and subsequently within the internal workings of the Soka Gakkai.

In 1979, under pressure from Nichiren Shoshu, Ikeda resigned as president of the Soka Gakkai. He did not resign all power; officially, he took a side step to became the President of the international arm of the movement, Soka Gakkai International, which started to become successful after this date. It is likely that Ikeda continued to have the same degree of influence over the lay movement unofficially, in spite of the official change in his status. The new President of the Soka Gakkai, Einosuke Akiya, does not command the same degree of charismatic authority as his predecessor and it is Ikeda's picture that is prominently displayed on the walls of Soka Gakkai offices in Japan and worldwide (Hammond and Machacek, 1999, p.19). The cause of Ikeda's resignation was directly related to the ongoing power

---

[19] The Soka Gakkai has another primary aim not shared by the priesthood, which is to 'create value'.

struggle between Nichiren Shoshu and the Soka Gakkai. The former claims to hold the authentic authority of Nichiren through the line of High Priests, while the latter claims a true understanding of Nichiren's teachings and the capacity to ensure the spread of those teachings in contemporary ways that speak to contemporary people:

> The Nichiren priesthood is essentially locked into an ancient ritualistic and quasi-monastic system, concerned to preserve its authority and jealous of its monopoly of certain sacred teachings, places, and objects ... The priesthood has distrusted the very modernity of Sōka Gakkai, has looked somewhat askance at the cultural mass events which that movement has promoted, and the social and political concerns it has espoused.
>
> (Wilson and Dobbelaere, 1994, p.243)

Understood in these terms it is no surprise that there were tensions. Until Makiguchi affiliated his Value-creating Educational Society to it, Nichiren Shoshu was a minor, virtually unknown sect within Japan, one of the smallest of the Nichiren sects. When the membership of the Soka Gakkai grew under Presidents Toda and Ikeda, Nichiren Shoshu also grew in prestige and importance, but it was financially dependent on the Soka Gakkai.

The Soka Gakkai generated and managed the financial backing for both organizations and therefore could justifiably claim to have had a decisive influence on the growth of Nichiren Shoshu. However, unresolved tensions existed. The immediate problems at the time of Ikeda's resignation, from the Nichiren Shoshu perspective, were the following: claims that Ikeda had pretensions to be declared the 'True Buddha' of the age;[20] that he had initiated innovations that ran counter to orthodoxy; that the Soka Gakkai building programme was threatening the economic stability of Nichiren Shoshu; and that in keeping with its controversial position in Japanese society, the Soka Gakkai was embroiled in a number of lawsuits (Bocking, 1980). The Soka Gakkai made comparable claims against the priesthood, which, it indicated, was not operating within the spirit of Nichiren's teachings. Specifically, the Soka Gakkai objected to what it regarded as the High Priest's claim to infallibility. Furthermore, the early leaders of the Soka Gakkai had resisted compromise with the state and been imprisoned for their stance, while the priesthood had capitulated to state demands, thus, according to the Soka Gakkai, compromising Nichiren's example and providing the Soka Gakkai with a degree of moral advantage. The disputes, which reached a degree of resolution in 1979 with the formal resignation of the

---

[20] Ikeda denied this claim.

powerful Ikeda, were arguably about traditional versus more modern forms of authority. On the one hand was the authority of the Nichiren Shoshu priesthood, based on a hierarchical lineage traced back to Nichiren, via his immediate follower Nikko, and on the other was what we might see as the power of the lay movement, as a result of its success in spreading the 'true' teachings of Nichiren.

Both organizations had something to gain from their relationship. As well as providing financial support to the Nichiren Shoshu priesthood, the Soka Gakkai relieved it of much of the responsibility and trouble of the campaign to increase membership (Métraux, 1993, p.327). According to the Soka Gakkai, the lay movement could provide a proselytizing strategy more suited to the modern age:

> The priesthood's leadership methods and ways of conducting religious affairs in the past will probably be insufficient to bring the True Law to the ordinary people of today and tomorrow. Furthermore, the clergy is too limited in number to provide leadership for large numbers of believers. To compensate for these weaknesses, a large lay organization is essential.
>
> (Quoted in Métraux, 1993, p.327)

The Soka Gakkai never regarded itself – as the priests would like it to have done and as it formally was – as a subsidiary organization working on behalf of Nichiren Shoshu. Instead, it saw itself as a separate institution, drawing its authority not from the priests but from the master, Nichiren himself, and from his writings and ritual instruction.

In return for the financial support and influence of the lay movement, the Nichiren Shoshu priesthood provided the Soka Gakkai with a legitimacy that it would have had difficulty operating without, at least at the outset. Buddhist priests in Japan are ritual specialists concerned principally with funeral rites. They carry out rites that install ancestral spirits in the *butsudan*, the household altar (Colour Plate 9), and rites to commemorate or, indeed, to pacify dead ancestors. Such practices are thought to be essential, not just for the welfare of the deceased, but also for the welfare of the living. According to the Japanese world-view, the ancestors, if not properly regarded, are apt to make trouble for living members of their families, in the form of sickness or ill-fortune. Helen Hardacre, a specialist in Japanese religion, has written that:

> ... many [Japanese] new religions find it difficult to overcome the attachment to established Buddhist funeral and ancestral rites, producing the incongruous situation of religions able to provide doctrine, ritual and an organization perfectly adequate for a human

life span but forced at death to return their believers to Buddhist temples for final disposition.

(Quoted in Bocking, 1994, p.129)

Through the Nichiren Shoshu priests, the Soka Gakkai was able to provide death rites for its members, as well as to promote a life-affirming doctrine and practice. Since this was the case, the relationship of the Soka Gakkai lay movement with the Nichiren Shoshu priestly sect, including its temples and priests, provided both traditional legitimacy and essential priestly services for Soka Gakkai members. In addition, and just as importantly, the priests acted as initiators in the distribution of the *gohonzon*. A lay organization would have been unable to operate without this service. The great *gohonzon*, the *dai gohonzon*, transmitted through Nichiren's disciple Nikko and held by the Nichiren Shoshu priests at their head temple, is transcribed by each High Priest. It is photographic copies of this transcribed *gohonzon* that lay members receive. A *gohonzon*, such as the one reproduced in Figure 3.1, is not thought to be fully powerful unless it has been passed to the recipient according to certain ritual requirements, which act as formal initiation into the movement. According to traditional precedent, only the High Priest could perform this initiatory function either directly or through his designated priestly representatives.[21] A copy of a *gohonzon* without the transfer of priestly initiation is thought to be unauthorized and therefore in some sense incomplete.

In the early 1990s, the relationship between the priestly sect and the lay organization hit a new low. Amidst accusation and counter-accusation, some of which involved legal proceedings, the Soka Gakkai was excommunicated *en masse* by the current High Priest of Nichiren Shoshu, Nikken. The vast head temple at Taiseki-ji underneath Mount Fujii, used by priests and lay members from all over the world but financed by the Soka Gakkai, has been torn down by Nichiren Shoshu. Colour Plates 10 and 11 show the temple complex before and after its destruction. This is the situation that pertains at the beginning of the twenty-first century: the relationship between the priesthood and the Soka Gakkai has completely broken down.

The rhetoric of the Soka Gakkai subsequent to the split has tended towards militarism. A 1994 newsletter article headed 'Victory to the Soka Gakkai', for example, talks of winning 'a total victory' and 'defeating the Nichiren Shoshu Priesthood' (Anon., 1994, p.10). The High Priest and his representatives no longer distribute *gohonzon* to

---

[21] Although Soka Gakkai representatives now argue that this practice was not laid down by Nichiren.

members or perform any other rites on their behalf, including funerals (Astley, 1992, p.173). Fortunately for the lay movement, however, just as some lay followers left the Soka Gakkai and remain loyal to the priests, a number of priests left Nichiren Shoshu and remain loyal to the Soka Gakkai. These few have been able to maintain the priestly services needed by lay members within Japan, and in particular they have been able to procure for the international movement's use a copy of the *dai gohonzon* transcribed by the twenty-sixth High Priest, Nichikan, who is untainted by the accusations made against the current priesthood. It is a copy of this *gohonzon* that is now photographically reproduced and used for distribution to all lay members.

For the Soka Gakkai outside Japan, it has been comparatively straightforward for the movement to stress the direct relationship between members and the *gohonzon* and between members and Nichiren's writings, *without the need for intermediaries*. Indeed, based on Nichiren's writings, the international movement has emphasized the internal nature of the *gohonzon* as well as its external form:

> Never seek this Gohonzon outside yourself. The Gohonzon exists only within the mortal flesh of us ordinary people who embrace the Lotus Sutra and chant Nam-myoho-renge-kyo ... The Gohonzon is found in faith alone. As the sutra states, 'Only with faith can one enter Buddhahood.'

> (Nichiren, Gosho Translation Committee, 1979, p.213)

The altered stress on the nature of the *gohonzon* as being found as much within as in its external form was necessitated by the transition period between the excommunication of the lay movement from Nichiren Shoshu and the availability of the Nichikan *gohonzon*. During this transition period, new members could not be issued with a *gohonzon* and were forced to practise without it. Up until that time, the importance of the *gohonzon* for *gongyo* practice was emphasized regularly and it was comparatively easy for new members to obtain a copy. But during the period in which new copies of the *gohonzon* were unavailable, it was necessary for the movement to explain that, according to Nichiren's writings, the *gohonzon* has an internal aspect as well as an external form. By placing a new emphasis on the internal aspect, the movement showed that practice could continue without the external object of worship.

The majority of international members, who have never valued the priests as fully as their Japanese co-religionists do because they see no need for Japanese-style funerary rituals, have been troubled much less by the excommunication than those inside Japan (Hurst, 1998, p.93; Waterhouse, 1997, pp.131–2).[22] Some international members have, however, been disturbed about the way in which the schism was managed by SGI (Hammond and Machacek, 1999, p.84). Their concerns focus on the campaign undertaken by President Ikeda and SGI to discredit the High Priest Nikken. For example, much of the rhetoric that emerged from the lay organization around the time of the split claimed that Nikken is an evil person. A significant emphasis in SGI practice is on the negative results of 'slandering' others. The anti-Nikken campaign was seen by some as falling into the category of slander and therefore as against much of what SGI stands for and inconsistent with Nichiren's teachings. In addition, the Nichiren Shoshu priests were able to rely on the idea embedded in Nichiren's teachings that those who follow the true Law are destined for trouble and persecution.

Questions remain about whether it is legitimate to claim that SGI has protestant tendencies and, if it does, whether these tendencies owe more to personalities and particular circumstances than to anything intrinsic within the practices the movement promotes. These questions are not straightforward to answer. The split with the priesthood and the new emphasis on the direct relationship between the practitioner and the *gohonzon* certainly resonate with elements within Protestant Christianity. These developments owe something to modern times and to the geographical spread of the movement, but also something to Makiguchi's original vision. They run broadly counter to Nichiren's Buddhism in its traditional forms. SGI now functions fully without its original source of priestly legitimacy (although it can still offer priestly functions due to the fact that some priests remained loyal to the lay movement). Indeed, the split with the traditional priesthood coincided with a phase in which SGI was modernizing and adapting according to local conditions. The split may therefore have come at a significant, if not optimum, moment in the development of the movement's international arm. So established has the Soka Gakkai become that it now represents tradition in its own right, in particular for non-Japanese members of the international movement for whom the Nichiren Shoshu priests have had little significance. In some locations, it is the Soka Gakkai itself, its systems and its structures that have become the traditional establishment against which some members of the modern international movement kick.

---

[22] In some Catholic countries, for example Italy, where the role of priests is perhaps better understood, the split may have been more 'deeply felt' (Macioti, 2000, p.14).

Local contexts

In this section brief accounts are provided of Soka Gakkai practice in the USA, the UK and Brazil.

United States of America

The Soka Gakkai in the USA – now known as SGI-USA – was imported there largely as a result of the entry into the USA of Japanese nationality wives of American servicemen returning from the Korean War. Such women would meet in each other's homes for discussion meetings. In 1960, President Ikeda visited the country and marked it out for what he believed was a significant future role. Subsequent to that visit, the Japanese women members organized 'street *shakubuku*', in which passers-by were invited to attend their meetings, but it was not until 1963 that the first English-language meeting was held in the USA. SGI-USA is currently led by George Williams, who, although born in Korea, is of Japanese descent. Williams changed his name (from Masayasu Sadanaga) as a symbol of his desire to be seen as a citizen of the USA. SGI-USA is no longer a religion of immigrants, but nonetheless an estimated 23 per cent of members are Japanese speakers (Hammond and Machacek, 1999, p.43). This figure (which compares with just 9 per cent of members of Japanese descent in the UK (Wilson and Dobbelaere, 1994, p.41)), when added to estimates of the percentage of Hispanic and Afro-American members[23] in SGI-USA, indicates the multi-ethnic nature of SGI there.

Hammond and Machacek regard proselytizing effort among both the American Japanese and non-Japanese populations as instrumental in shaping the current identity of SGI-USA:

> SGI-USA has gone to some lengths to reformulate its identity from a religion of Japanese immigrants into an American religion. It has done so not only through proactive assimilation of Japanese members as the organization itself adjusted to American culture, but also through competitive recruitment of non-Japanese Americans. By and large, it has been successful in this strategy.
>
> (Hammond and Machacek, 1999, p.42)

---

[23] Jane Hurst (1998, p.89) estimates that between 25 and 30 per cent of American members are of Hispanic or Afro-American origin. Hammond and Machacek (1999, p.43) estimate that there are a total of 36 per cent non-white, non-Japanese SGI-USA members.

The 1960s *shakubuku* campaign continued until 1978, when it was officially dropped in favour of the less overt *shoju*. Although the campaign drew significant numbers into contact with SGI, it had only limited long-term success. As Hammond and Machacek have observed, the promise of happiness and worldly success was probably the major draw for many:

> This technique was ... associated with high rates of recruitment, but also with low rates of conversion. Most of the people introduced to Soka Gakkai through this means stayed long enough to satisfy whatever curiosity they may have had about a religion that advertises itself as a means to happiness and success in this world – but then left.
>
> (Hammond and Machacek, 1999, p.103)

In promising these benefits, the Soka Gakkai resonates with the ethos of American culture, including contemporary liberal views on morality. There are no ascetic practices associated with SGI Buddhist practice. Those who choose to join could therefore be said to be enriching their lives rather than altering them in radical ways. It is straightforward to engage fully in American life while practising Soka Gakkai Buddhism. To carry out Soka Gakkai practices assiduously simply means altering life patterns and daily routines to incorporate periods of chanting and *gongyo* practice and attendance at meetings. In terms of the movement's philosophy, these practices open members to the possibility of radical life changes – this is one of the future benefits the practice promises. But at the outset there is no need for practitioners to alter their values to coincide with any that the movement promotes.

A BBC television documentary, broadcast in October 1995, was concerned less with aggressive recruitment tactics than it was with SGI-USA's methods of raising money to support the movement's activities in the USA. (It also challenged SGI's financial status and political role in Japan.) Ex-SGI-USA members reported that the movement used pressure tactics to extract money from members. These ploys, the ex-members claimed, were based on the organization's assertion that benefits to the individual would arise from the good of the movement as a whole. SGI in Japan is often accused of putting pressure on members to give money to fund its activities, including *kosen-rufu* proselytizing activities. This is one aspect of religious activity that the media in particular like to focus on, in attempts to cast doubt on the authenticity of religious movements both new and old. However, all religious organizations need money in order to survive. Attempts to raise money are generally accepted by the majority, who are happy to support their chosen religious organization, but they may be offensive to some. Discontent about this aspect of religious movements is sufficiently specific to make good news copy.

It is possible that it is in the USA that SGI's status as a UN Non-governmental Organization has had most significance. Indeed, Hammond and Machacek point out that SGI in the USA could have been presented as a peace movement or as a 'Value-creating Society' rather than as a religion (Hammond and Machacek, 1999, p.106). The final goal of the Soka Gakkai is genuine world peace, where war has disappeared and individuals and societies live alongside each other in harmonious ways, but there is no suggestion that this goal can be attained without the religious practices that the movement promotes. The fact that SGI was not presented in the USA as a peace movement alone, but that the religious practices it promotes remain central, confirms that, while many of President Ikeda's activities and teachings are now directed towards peace issues (Métraux, 1996, p.372), the Soka Gakkai is not primarily a peace movement. World peace is a pressing concern, but the Soka Gakkai's approach to its attainment is primarily a religious one. The movement promises world peace and the creation of value through religious practice not simply through dialogue and practical action, important as these aspects might be.

United Kingdom

One of the most significant features of the Soka Gakkai in the UK (SGI-UK) is that it has been led, almost from the outset, by a UK national rather than by a leader of Japanese descent. The first Soka Gakkai Buddhists in the UK, in the early 1960s, were the wives of Japanese businessmen accompanying their working husbands. In 1974, however, they were joined by Richard Causton (1920–95), an ex-Army officer whose business interests had taken him to Japan, where he encountered Nichiren Shoshu and the Soka Gakkai. In 1975, Causton became the General Director of what was then called (before the split between Nichiren Shoshu and the Soka Gakkai) Nichiren Shoshu UK. Three years later, he gave up his business to lead the movement full time. At the time of writing, in early 2000, there are only about 20 General Directors, from 160 located all around the world, who are not Japanese nationals.[24] As early as 1975, Causton fulfilled this role and was, furthermore, a Vice President of SGI worldwide, operating directly under President Ikeda. According to contemporary members and leaders of the Soka Gakkai in the UK, Causton was respected by the Japanese parent organization for his

---

[24] Interview with the current General Director of SGI-UK, 19 October 2000.

wisdom and life experience. There is little doubt that Causton rates as a remarkable individual, who was instrumental in establishing the UK organization. He led the growth of a unified movement which, at his death in 1995, numbered approximately 6500, of whom 3000–4000 were described as active in the organization (Waterhouse, 1997, p.92).

In 1994, the findings of a major sociological survey of the Soka Gakkai in the UK, carried out by the prominent sociologists of religion Bryan Wilson and Karel Dobbelaere, were published. Based on extensive questionnaires sent to 1000 members[25] and 30 interviews, Wilson and Dobbelaere built up a sociological picture of the movement at that time. Among their findings was the fact that UK members are equivocal about elements of the Japanese pattern for the organizational structure. These elements included the role of the master–disciple relationship within the movement. The UK movement is structured after the pattern of the Soka Gakkai in Japan, in progressively smaller structural units and on divisions based on age and gender, all overseen by a UK Central Committee. In theory, leaders within the different layers of the organization are there to offer guidance to those in their charge, both through discussion meetings and through personal counselling. However, according to Wilson and Dobbelaere's survey, it is common for members to report that they have little respect for local leaders, indeed they are often critical of them.[26] The general equivocation about leaders identified by Wilson and Dobbelaere increased after Causton's death, so that members began to question whether the leadership structure of SGI-UK, based as it was on the Japanese model, was best fitted for the UK.

In late 1995, a reassessment group was set up to act as a point of co-ordination for discussions, which took place throughout the organization. Much of the discussion was carried out in focus groups established around members with common interests. The General Director of SGI-UK, Ricky Baynes, who took over from Causton, describes a period during which there existed tensions between what he has referred to as the traditionalists and the modernists within the movement.[27] The traditionalists were reluctant to see change, while the modernists were all for forging ahead with a new structure broadly based on team-working rather than on identified leaders within the existing stratified hierarchy. Baynes's use of the terms

[25] Returned completed by 619 members (Wilson and Dobbelaere, 1994, p.41).

[26] Although they point out that admiration was frequently expressed for Causton and the more distant President Ikeda (Wilson and Dobbelaere, 1994, pp.224–5).

[27] Interview with the current General Director of SGI-UK, 19 October 2000.

'traditionalist' and 'modernist' is a reminder that for SGI in the UK, as elsewhere outside Japan, tradition is represented by the patterns established by the modern Japanese lay movement not by the centuries-old priestly hierarchy. While all members are content to continue with the Japanese chanting and the Buddhist philosophy that underpins the movement, many members are not content to continue with a Soka Gakkai leadership structure that they regard as a Japanese invention, peripheral to Buddhist practice and not necessarily appropriate for the UK cultural context. Other members, the traditionalists in Baynes's terms, prefer to keep with familiar patterns. The doctrine of *zuiho bini*, as we have seen, allows adaptations to be made, but the adaptation process is not always straightforward.

In order to resolve these tensions, Baynes and his leadership team consulted with the Japanese parent organization and met intensively with them and with other representatives from Europe. The result of these discussions has effectively been that the traditionalists have won out. Only minor changes have been made to the organizational structure, and leaders continue to hold positions of responsibility within each stratum. One of the justifications offered for this is that identified leaders commit to their responsibilities, while team work can easily degenerate so that tasks are either not completed at all or fall to one or two overworked individuals. Baynes and the Vice General Director for the UK, Kazuo Fujii, claim that few members now complain about the way in which these structural problems have been resolved. But other members within the organization report that they are less positive that a long-term resolution has been found. They also point out that, as a result of the decision to maintain the status quo, certain energetic members have left the organization altogether. While we might see these tensions in terms of the tensions between traditional and modern forms of authority and organizational structure, for members of SGI in the UK the issues are more pragmatic. They are focused on whether there are enough people to carry out leadership tasks and whether leaders are people whom members can respect. While the more liberal viewpoint did not win out this time, there is every reason to suppose that the debates have not ended altogether. It is significant, however, that the differences are not focused on the central religious practices of the movement, which are not negotiable, but on organizational structure.

Another of Wilson and Dobbelaere's findings about SGI in the UK is that its members are drawn disproportionally from those employed in the mass media, the entertainment industries or the arts. It is to be expected that such members, who 'espouse the expansive values of the permissive society' (Wilson and Dobbelaere, 1994, p.221) should be attracted to a movement that endorses a search for personal happiness and acknowledges, in its emphasis on personal fulfilment, the secular ethos of the post-Christian UK. This trend is not reflected in the USA, where members are most likely to be employed in 'competitive professional and corporate occupations' (Hammond and Machacek, 1999, p.138). Other related attractions of the movement are the fact that individuals are encouraged to take responsibility for themselves within the context of their relationship with the *gohonzon*. They are not bound by rules and regulations as priests would be, nor by the guilt that accompanies any failure to live up to external moral or organizational standards.

While the membership profile in the UK is very similar to that in the USA, a difference that may be significant for the future is that the average age of UK members is somewhat younger than that of US members, with 6 per cent of UK members still in full-time education. The figure for the USA is just 3 per cent.

Brazil

The initial presence of the Soka Gakkai in Brazil, like its presence in many other locations outside Japan, can be attributed to the high numbers of Japanese who emigrated there in the first four decades of the twentieth century. In 1941, there were an estimated 234,000 Japanese immigrants in Brazil (Clarke, 2000c, p.273) and there are now thought to be 1,300,000 Brazilian citizens of Japanese descent or origin (Clarke, 2000c, p.273). Of the estimated 150,000 SGI members now living in Brazil,[28] 80 per cent are of non-Japanese origin (Clarke 2000a, p.326), whereas in 1967 all the Soka Gakkai members were of Japanese descent (Shimazono, 1991). This indicates the extent to which SGI in Brazil (BSGI), although established within the Japanese population there, has shifted significantly to become attractive to the non-Japanese population also.

In spite of the success of some Protestant groups and the impact of new religious ideologies, Brazil remains a predominantly Catholic culture. Catholic practices and beliefs, including, in particular, those focused on Mary the Mother of Jesus, are successfully syncretized with Amerindian, African Brazilian, Spiritist and Spiritualist beliefs. When these contrasting beliefs and rituals have each merged with Catholicism they have been reconciled with it to form unified

---

[28] Although there is a high rate of adherence to the Soka Gakkai in Brazil, it is not the largest Japanese-derived new religion operating there. For example, Seicho no Ie and Sekai Kyusei Kyo have been more popular (Clarke, 2000a, p.327).

systems.[29] The degree of success that BSGI has achieved among the non-Japanese population is, however, surprising, since its ideology is not easily reconciled with Catholic beliefs and its ritual practices are not comparable. Other Japanese new religious movements have recognized that 'there can be no religion in Brazil without Jesus and Mary' (Clarke, 2000b, p.328) and responded to that by, for example, including images of Mary alongside those of Japanese figures.

It is much more difficult for BSGI with its exclusivist heritage to accommodate Catholic practices, although it has found a creative solution to the Brazilian need for a concept of an all-powerful God: a concept that the Soka Gakkai does not supply. Clarke reports that some of the problems have been resolved by the introduction of the idea of a Buddhist form of God:

> The usual practice of a BSGI evangelist ... is to stress that there are many ways of thinking about God, and that clear similarities exist between saying that God is *Nam-myoho-renge-kyo* and the Catholic notion of God as Creator of the Universe. Moreover, members of religions, including those of the African Brazilian religion of Candomblé, who understand God as Nature are said to be 'close to the Buddhist idea of God.'
>
> (Clarke, 2000a, pp.346–7)

This particular problem, and its creative solution, would not have arisen in locations such as the USA or the UK, where positions that challenge belief in God are familiar and may be attractive. It therefore represents another instance of a religious movement that, while developing a global identity, has found it necessary to adapt to local conditions. Like many syncretic positions, however, as a solution to the problem of the mismatch between Brazilian Catholicism and the Soka Gakkai, it is only partially successful. Members in Brazil, as elsewhere, regard Buddhist teaching about *karma* and the idea of a personal Father God as entirely incompatible (Clarke, 2000a, pp.346–7).

BSGI has as its aim the conversion of one-third of the Brazilian population (Clarke, 2000a, p.348). The aim is modest in its own highly ambitious terms and reflects the difficulty that it recognizes in reconciling Brazilian cultural assumptions with Soka Gakkai teachings. Steady growth so far, however, indicates that the possibility of some further growth is not unlikely.

---

[29] For a discussion of syncretism, see Pearson (2002), Book 5 in this series, chapter 3.

Conclusion

In the introduction to this chapter, I suggested that it is both legitimate and relevant to ask questions of the Soka Gakkai similar to those asked of Protestant Evangelical Christianity elsewhere in this volume. I also suggested that, while the Soka Gakkai is based on a form of Buddhism founded in thirteenth-century Japan and, like most Buddhist forms, is doctrinally opposed to much of Christianity, it nonetheless shares in common with Protestant Evangelicalism a proselytizing attitude and a tendency to protest against priestly functions and status. In this conclusion, the four questions introduced in the introduction will be reviewed in the light of the account of the movement given here.

Dynamic individuals

The history of the Soka Gakkai in Japan and throughout the world is characterized by its reliance on radical individuals, charismatic in terms of their ability to reinterpret old religious truths and apply them in meaningful ways to the age in which they live. According to the movement's orthodoxy, these individuals operate following a pattern established by the controversial thirteenth-century Buddhist monk Nichiren. The Presidents of the Soka Gakkai have interpreted Nichiren's writings to coincide with Tsunesaburo Makiguchi's educational ideas and, in the case of Daisaku Ikeda, to be of value to late twentieth- and early twenty-first-century people throughout the world, not just in Japan. In the locations to which the Soka Gakkai spread, there are also instances of dynamic leaders who have had the vision to establish a thoroughly Japanese religious ideology among disparate cultures. These dynamic individuals have undoubtedly shaped the way in which the Soka Gakkai operates today. While the majority of SGI General Directors are of Japanese nationality or descent, there are exceptions, of whom Richard Causton, the General Director of SGI-UK, was one. In this case, the death of this significant individual coincided with other changes within the movement, especially in the aftermath of the schism with the Nichiren Shoshu priesthood.

The Soka Gakkai's appeal

Throughout this account, explanations have been offered for the appeal of the Soka Gakkai, and its growth as a result of that appeal. In summary, we might say that both a 'push' and a 'pull' operate in the process of establishing SGI in new cultural settings. The religious practice is supplied by SGI through its proselytizing efforts – this is the 'push' – but what SGI promises, that is, the possibility of material as well as non-material benefits, is attractive to those who take up the practice of chanting *Nam-myoho-renge-kyo* – and this provides the 'pull'.

SGI has made the practice available all over the world. Arguably, in spite of the accounts of proselytizing presented here, the movement does not engage in *shakubuku* outside Japan and probably never has done in the terms in which Nichiren described the activity. The focus of *shakubuku* is the refutation of other's views based on Buddhist teachings, in particular the teachings contained in the *Lotus Sutra.* There are very few Soka Gakkai members with sufficient familiarity with Buddhist canonical texts to engage in the kinds of argumentation that Nichiren himself promoted. Equally, most of those who are proselytized on behalf of the movement outside Japan base their existing religious or spiritual views on very different cultural assumptions from those that pertain in Japan. Many of these views would not require the proselytizer to have detailed knowledge of any religious texts in order to refute them, and certainly a knowledge of Buddhist texts would influence only very few. While members know that the emphasis within the movement is now on *shoju* – proselytizing by example – rather than on *shakubuku*, it is the latter term that persists. This is in spite of the fact that there has otherwise been an effort to move away from Japanese terminology, and in spite of the fact that *shakubuku* is unpopular as a term with many members, implying, as it does, a degree of militancy and compulsion. Somewhat anachronistically, members, at least those in the UK, still speak in terms of 'who *shakubuku*'d whom' when they discuss introductions to SGI and its practices. The ideology of *shakubuku* is barely consistent with the contemporary movement, which otherwise goes out of its way to accommodate liberal cultural values and hesitates to condemn the views of others. Many SGI members are reluctant to present the movement and the practice it promotes as the only truth, although they are often aware of the problems this creates in terms of Nichiren's own exclusive claims. One member expressed this as follows:

> I think we are all moving in a similar direction but I do think that Buddhism has got the right message, particularly SGI Buddhism, but it's a dilemma that I'm tackling at the present moment. Are we unique? I'm hopefully on the fence. I'm uncomfortable with holding that flag up. I think in Nichiren's time he probably had to. He had a lot of ammunition and a lot of targets but I wonder these days if we need to be so special.

(Waterhouse, 1997, p.102)

This extract, taken from an interview with an SGI-UK member, is couched in a militaristic idiom. Although it should not be taken as an official SGI position, the quotation does clearly indicate the dilemma felt by many members: Nichiren taught that his was an exclusive path, the only effective path for the degenerate age of *mappo*, but this approach is difficult to uphold in the liberal context in which the majority of members operate. While it is acceptable to chant an ancient Japanese mantra, it seems that it is not acceptable to promote exclusivity. Sociological studies in the UK and the USA have shown that the majority of members have been recruited through friends and family contacts and not through the aggressive *shakubuku* campaigns that helped to establish the movement in Japan (Wilson and Dobbelaere, 1994, p.52; Hammond and Machacek, 1999, p.60). Without the desire to spread the teachings – the push – however, the Soka Gakkai would not have left Japan.

The pull in societies where the Soka Gakkai is successful lies in many factors. The practice is simple to learn and therefore highly portable, offering an accessible religious path which anyone can begin, regardless of cultural or educational background. This has clearly been instrumental in establishing the Soka Gakkai as a global movement. The ideology of the movement promises immediate as well as future benefits, benefits that are wide-ranging in nature and can encompass contrasting personal and communal priorities for this life and life beyond death. This gives the movement and the practice it promotes a broad appeal. It promises the satisfaction of individual, communal and global desires. Indeed, it promises that by changing their personal lives for the better, practitioners have a beneficial impact on the entire world, just as Nichiren taught that ignoring the *Lotus Sutra* had material consequences such as hunger, epidemics and earthquakes.

The practice is life-affirming and does not require an ascetic attitude to the world. It is also optimistic, upbeat and potentially joyful. These characteristics are self-evidently appealing. The practice promises members control over their present and future lives through the transformation of *karma*. Whether or not members see tangible benefits in their own lives, the ideology teaches them that they are changing their future, at least, for the better. Through global and national initiatives, the organization offers a complete and rewarding lifestyle and a sense of community and identity. And finally, the practice and the results it promises are consistent with, or presented as consistent with, the cultural ethos of each area to which the movement has spread.

Individuals and their involvement

The hierarchy for the movement inherited from Japan, although not universally popular, has provided an effective organizational structure through which individuals have become involved with SGI practice and the lifestyle that can accompany it. Dedicated individuals spend a large part of their leisure time at Soka Gakkai meetings, so that the Soka Gakkai is at the core of their social lives. Individuals affirm that they have received benefits from the chanting practice, and they have strategies to account for why the benefits they seek do not always come in the anticipated ways. In promoting long-, medium- and short-term goals, the movement allows its members to understand all achievements as the result of chanting. While sceptics might argue that what they achieve may have other causes, SGI members have faith that the practice enriches their lives. Those who remain with the movement enjoy their religion. This is evident at SGI meetings, where one is likely to encounter a positive attitude and a capacity among members to enjoy life.

Global or local?

Is SGI a global or a local religious movement? The short answer to this question is that, like other religious initiatives, it incorporates both local and global characteristics. Institutional connections maintain a cohesive religious movement which, although it continues to be co-ordinated from Japan, also allows for local innovation. The movement promotes a traditional religious practice, which is remarkably stable across cultures. Members all over the globe, whatever their mother tongue, repeat a centuries-old text and the mantra initiated by their thirteenth-century founder. No attempt has been made to translate the recitation into the vernacular and the fact that practice is identical the world over is a cohesive factor. It is not at all uncommon to find members of several nationalities together in one small local meeting. Unlike other forms of Buddhism in the West, the Soka Gakkai is not élitist, in fact it has been characterized in the USA as socially inclusive (Chappell, 2000, pp.324–5). Although the lives they lead may be very different, members from contrasting backgrounds share a practice that is identical.

The movement also promotes global social initiatives through such bodies as the UN and UNESCO. For example, it has organized collections for humanitarian aid efforts and members are mobilized to care for refugees or earthquake victims. The movement is also much concerned with environmental issues and in 1992 organized a well-attended conference prior to the UN World Summit in Rio de Janeiro.

Colour Plate 1 Worship at a large gathering of the Alpha course, introducing participants to basic Christian teaching, in the UK in 2000. Gideon Mendel/Network.

Colour Plate 2 A Christian Coalition Faith and Freedom (anti-abortion/ pro-life) rally at the Republican Convention in San Diego, California in 1996. A woman raises her hands in worship. Mark Peterson/Saba/Network.

Colour Plate 10 The Taisekaji temple complex, at the foot of Mount Fuji, Japan before its destruction. © 2000 by Daisanbunmei-sha, Inc.

Colour Plate 11 The Taisekaji temple complex, at the foot of Mount Fujii, Japan after its destruction. © 2000 by Daisanbunmei-sha, Inc.

Colour Plate 12 The early-seventeenth-century Blue Mosque (Sultanahmet Camii) in Istanbul is a striking visual symbol of the spread of Islam into south-east Europe. Robert Harding Picture Library.

Colour Plate 13 A street scene in Dewsbury, Yorkshire, near the Markazi Mosque, headquarters of the Tablighi Jama'at in the UK. © Asadour Guzelian.

Colour Plate 14 Girls in Islamic dress take part in a chemistry lesson at Feversham College in Bradford. © Asadour Guzelian.

It organizes travelling exhibitions to promote human rights. Such exhibitions have gained the promotional support of the UN and of national governments. The movement also promotes dialogue and co-operative effort through the founding of research centres in Japan and elsewhere.

At the same time, wherever SGI spreads, certain adaptations are made in order to make the practices it promotes accessible for its members. These adaptations range from practical details to significant ideological reinterpretations, from allowing practitioners to sit on a chair rather than on the floor to chant, to enabling them to retain the concept of God; in each locality the demands for adaptation vary. The Soka Gakkai has so far been skilled in making these adaptations and in the process of listening to the needs of its members. The resolution of grassroots demands is not always straightforward, but is an ongoing process. There remains a tension between the exclusive roots of the movement and the desire to extend its appeal into new cultures. It is this tension that is often brought into play when, as in Brazil, potential converts cannot leave behind their cultural heritage or, as in the UK, certain liberalizing adaptations may seem to some to be a step too far.

Glossary

butsudan in Japan, the household Buddhist altar in which the spirits of ancestors are enshrined. The altar may also contain tablets or amulets from Shinto or Buddhist shrines. Where Soka Gakkai Buddhism is practised, the *butsudan* ideally contains only the family copy of the object of worship, the **gohonzon**.

daimoku the chanting of *Nam-myoho-renge-kyo*, which is the central practice for all Nichiren Buddhists.

gohonzon the focus of practice within the Soka Gakkai. The *gohonzon* takes the form of a calligraphic symbol of the Buddhist universe. The mantra *Nam-myoho-renge-kyo* is written down the centre of the page with the names of Buddhas, Buddhas-to-be and Japanese indigenous gods around the sides. The *gohonzon* is said to represent buddhahood. As well as being represented in physical form, the *gohonzon* is said to be present within.

gongyo literally, 'assiduous practice'. The ritual repetition of two chapters from the *Lotus Sutra* with extended *daimoku* chanting and formulated prayers. According to Soka Gakkai orthodoxy, *gongyo* is ideally carried out twice per day, morning and evening, the precise form for each being slightly different.

gosho literally, 'honourable writings'. Nichiren's individual and collected writings. *Sho* means writings; *go* is an honorific prefix, as in **gohonzon**.

karma literally, 'action'. In Buddhism, *karma* is action with intention, which produces automatic results that may be experienced in the same life or a future life. Karmically fruitful, good actions lead to benefits while bad actions lead to disadvantage.

kosen-rufu literally, 'to widely declare and spread' Buddhism in the world.

Mahayana the 'great way' of Buddhism, which entails practice for one's self and for others.

mappo (*mappō*) the third of three periods predicted by the Buddha of India, during which the practices that he taught would no longer be powerful. The term is translated within the Soka Gakkai as the 'Latter Day of the Law'.

sutra (*sūtra*) a Buddhist text containing the teaching of the Buddha or of one of his enlightened disciples.

shakubuku literally, 'to break and subdue'. An assertive proselytizing method, which involves refuting heretical views and leading people to correct Buddhist teachings.

shoju (*shōju*) literally, 'to embrace and accept'. A proselytizing method that involves showing by example rather than by assertion.

References

Adam, E. (1995) *Buddhism in Western Australia*, published by the author.

Adam, E. and Hughes, P. (1996) *The Buddhists in Australia*, Canberra: Australian Government Publishing Service.

Anonymous (1993) *The Art of Living*, special issue of *UK Express*, Taplow: SGI-UK.

Anonymous (1994) 'Victory to the Soka Gakkai', *SGI-UK Bulletin*, no.138, July, p.10.

Anonymous (1997a) 'Human revolution', *UK Express*, no. 310, April, p.20.

Anonymous (1997b) 'A new chapter in Mauritius', *SGI Quarterly*, no.8, April, p.18.

Astley, T. (1992) 'Nichiren Shōshu and Sōka Gakkai', *Japanese Religions*, vol.17, no.2, pp.167–75.

Bethel, D.M. (ed.) (1989) *Education for Creative Living: Ideas and Proposals of Tsunesaburo Makiguchi*, trans. A. Birnbaum, Iowa State University Press.

Bocking, B. (1980) 'Reflections on Sōka Gakkai', *Scottish Journal of Religious Studies*, vol.1, no.2, pp.38–54.

Bocking, B. (1993) 'Is nothing sacred? The Protestant ethos and the spirit of Buddhism', *Journal of Oriental Studies*, vol.5.

Bocking, B. (1994) 'Of priests, protests and Protestant Buddhists: the case of Soka Gakkai International', in P. Clarke and J. Somers (eds) *Japanese New Religions in the West*, Folkestone: Japan Library, pp.118–32.

Bouma, G., Smith, W. and Vasi, S. (2000) 'Japanese religion in Australia: Mahikara and Zen in a multicultural society', in P. Clarke (ed.), pp.74–112.

Causton, R. (1994) 'The Soka Gakkai in Europe', *UK Express*, no.278, August, pp.9–13.

Causton, R. (1995) *The Buddha in Daily Life*, London: Rider.

Chappell, D.W. (2000) 'Socially inclusive Buddhists in America', in D. Machacek and B. Wilson (eds), pp.299–325.

Clarke, P. (2000a) 'Buddhist humanism and Catholic culture in Brazil', in D. Machacek and B. Wilson (eds), pp.326–48.

Clarke, P. (ed.) (2000b) *Japanese New Religions in Global Perspective*, London: Curzon.

Clarke, P. (2000c) '"Success" and "failure": Japanese new religions abroad', in P. Clarke (ed.), pp.272–311.

Dator, J. (1969) *Sōka Gakkai: Builders of the Third Civilization*, Seattle and London: University of Washington Press.

Dumoulin, H. (1976) 'Buddhism in modern Japan', in H. Dumoulin and J. Maraldo (eds) *Buddhism in the Modern World*, London: Collier Macmillan, pp.215–76.

Hammond, P. and Machacek, D. (1999) *Soka Gakkai in America: Accommodation and Conversion*, Oxford: Oxford University Press.

Herbert, D. (ed.) (2001) *Religion and Social Transformations*, Aldershot: Ashgate/Milton Keynes: The Open University.

Hurst, J. (1998) 'Nichiren Shōshū and Soka Gakkai in America: the pioneer spirit', in C.S. Prebish and K.K. Tanaka (eds), pp.79–97.

Hurst, J. (2000) 'A Buddhist reformation in the twentieth century: causes and implications of the conflict between the Soka Gakkai and the Nichiren Shoshu priesthood', in D. Machacek and B. Wilson (eds), pp.67–96.

Hurvitz, L. (trans.) (1976) *Scripture of the Lotus Blossom of the Fine Dharma* (The Lotus Sūtra), translated from the Chinese of Kumārujīva, New York and Guildford, Surrey: Columbia University Press.

Ionescu, S. (2000) 'Adapt or perish: the story of Soka Gakkai in Germany', in P. Clarke (ed.), pp.182–97.

Machacek, D. and Wilson, B. (eds) (2000) *Global Citizens: The Soka Gakkai Buddhist Movement in the World*, Oxford: Oxford University Press.

Macioti, M.I. (2000) 'Buddhism in action: case studies from Italy', in D. Machacek and B. Wilson (eds), pp.375–401.

Métraux, D. (1993) 'The dispute between the Sōka Gakkai and the Nichiren Shōshū priesthood: a lay revolution against a conservative clergy', *Japanese Journal of Religious Studies*, vol.19, no.4, pp.325–36.

Métraux, D. (1996) 'The Soka Gakkai: Buddhism and the creation of a harmonious and peaceful society', in C. Queen and S. King (eds) *Engaged Buddhism: Buddhist Liberation Movements in Asia*, New York: SUNY, pp.365–400.

Métraux, D. (2000) 'The changing role of the Komeito in Japanese politics in the 1990s', in D. Machacek and B. Wilson (eds), pp.128–52.

Murata, K. (1969) *Japan's New Buddhism: An Objective Account of Soka Gakkai*, New York and Tokyo: Weatherhill.

Nattier, J. (1998) 'Who is a Buddhist? Charting the landscape of Buddhist America', in C.S. Prebish and K.K. Tanaka (eds), pp.183–95.

Nichiren, Gosho Translation Committee (eds) (1979) *The Major Writings of Nichiren Daishonin*, Volume 1, Tokyo: Nichiren Shoshu International Centre.

Okubo, M. (1991) 'The acceptance of Nichiren Shōshū Sōka Gakkai in Mexico', *Japanese Journal of Religious Studies*, vol.18, nos2–3, pp.189–211.

Pearson J. (ed.) (2002) *Belief Beyond Boundaries*, Aldershot: Ashgate/Milton Keynes: The Open University.

Prebish, C.S. and Tanaka, K.K. (eds) (1998) *The Faces of Buddhism in America*, Berkeley and Los Angeles: University of California Press.

Resplica Rodd, L. (ed.) (1980) *Nichren: Selected Writings*, Hawaii: University of Hawaii.

Reader, I. and Tanabe, G. (1998) *Practically Religious*, University of Hawaii.

Robertson, R. (1992) *Globalization: Social Theory and Global Culture*, London: Sage.

Samuel, R. (comp.) (1995) 'Dick Causton: an appreciation', *UK Express*, no.285, March, pp.21–3.

Shimazono, S. (1991) 'The expansion of Japan's new religions into foreign cultures', *Japanese Journal of Religious Studies*, vol.18, nos2–3, pp.105–32.

Shupe, A. (1984) 'Militancy and accommodation in the third civilization: the case of Japan's Soka Gakkai movement', in J. Hadden and A. Shupe (eds) *Prophetic Religions and Politics: Religion and the Political Order*, New York: Paragon House, pp.235–53.

Sinha, S. (1994) 'Returning to my roots', *UK Express*, no.277, July, pp.36–7.

Stone, J. (1994) 'Rebuking the enemies of the *Lotus*: Nichirenist exclusivism in historical perspective', *Japanese Journal of Religious Studies*, vol.21, nos2–3, pp.231–59.

Tamaru, N. (2000) 'Soka Gakkai in historical perspective', in D. Machacek and B. Wilson (eds), pp.15–41.

Waterhouse, H. (1997) *Buddhism in Bath: Authority and Adaptation*, Leeds: University of Leeds, Department of Theology and Religious Studies.

Wilson, B. and Dobbelaere, K. (1994) *A Time to Chant: The Sōka Gakkai Buddhists in Britain*, Oxford: Clarendon Press.

Yampolsky, P. (ed.) (1990) *Selected Writings of Nichiren*, New York: Columbia University Press.

Web site

Soka Gakkai in the USA (www.sgi-usa.org/aboutsgi-usa)

CHAPTER 3

Invitation and enculturation: the dissemination and development of Islam in contemporary societies

SOPHIE GILLIAT-RAY

Introduction

Throughout the history and development of the Muslim world, the religion of Islam has absorbed many different languages, cultures and customs, yet retained a common culture of its own that is both global and Islamic (Figure 3.1). This chapter will be exploring some of the means by which Islam has become a transnational, transcultural faith, with followers in most, if not all, of the countries of the world. Through an exploration of the early days of Islam and its global expansion into a community with an estimated one billion followers today (Esposito, 2000), we can begin to appreciate the myriad and often overlapping factors that have led to its growth and influence in the contemporary era. Migration and travel, trade and commerce, and conversion following missionary activity are just some of the reasons why Muslims proudly claim to be part of a global faith community, known as the ***ummah***. Following a short historical survey, the focus in what follows will be upon the modern development of the Muslim community in those countries both within and outside what is regarded as the heartland of the Muslim world, namely Saudi Arabia and the wider Middle East region. We shall be considering the role of Islamic movements and the key thinkers who have inspired both

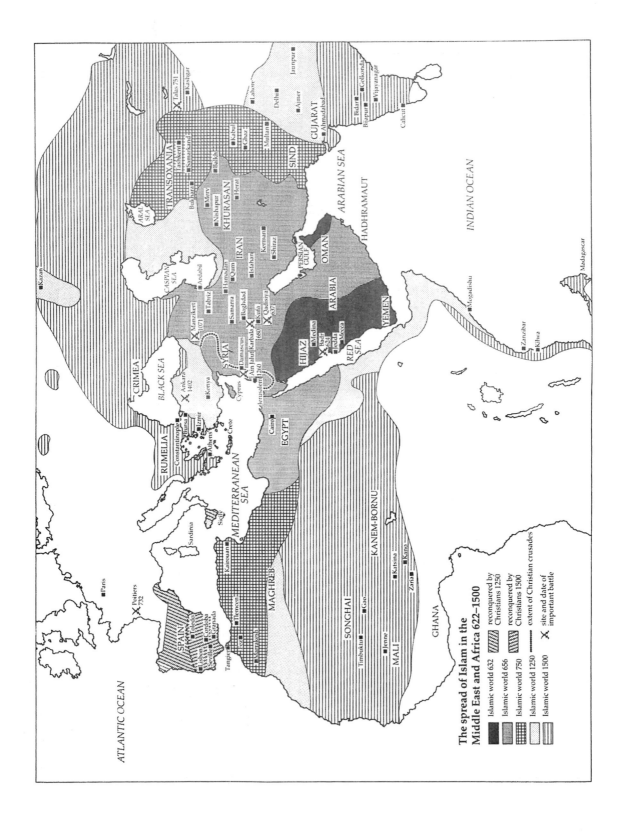

The spread of Islam in the
Middle East and Africa 622–1500

Islamic world 632   reconquered by
Islamic world 656   Christians 1250
Islamic world 750   reconquered by
Islamic world 1250   Christians 1500
Islamic world 1500   ▬▬▬ extent of Christian crusades
                       ✗ site and date of
                         important battle

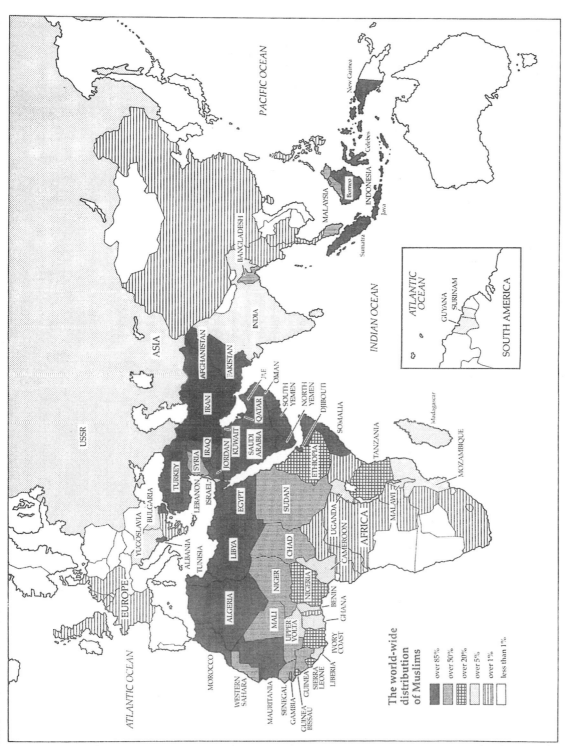

Figure 3.1 Maps showing the spread of Islam. Adapted from Malise Ruthven, *Islam in the World*, Penguin Books, London, 1991, maps 1 and 5. (Note that the map showing the world-wide distribution of Muslims does not include a significant Muslim population in the USA, estimated in 2000 at eight million, which would be in the 1–5 per cent range of the total American population (Rashid, 2000).)

Muslims and non-Muslims to look afresh at the message of Islam. The rapidity of global travel and communication in our modern world has enabled the easy migration of ideas and people, and these influences must also shape our appreciation of Islam as a global faith tradition. Of course, each of these points of focus has been the subject of numerous specialist studies, so this chapter will simply try to capture the essence of Islam's historical significance and, more especially, its contemporary development and growth.

The emergence and development of the Muslim world

Scholars of Islamic history have questioned whether or not the Prophet Muhammad (570–632) intended to establish a world-encompassing faith that might supersede Judaism and Christianity in the Arabian region. Larry Poston contends that 'his original aim appears to have rather been the establishment of a succinctly Arab brand of monotheism, as indicated by his many references to the Qur'an as an *Arab* book' (Poston, 1992, p.12).[1] Certainly, Muhammad did not believe he was bringing a new religion; rather, he was calling upon the people of **Mecca** to heed the same essential message that had been brought by other prophets to countless generations before them, namely the indivisible unity of God (***tawhid***). He was calling people to accept what is regarded in Islam as the 'natural' religion to which humankind is most inherently disposed, the ***din al-fitra***, based on the principle that monotheism is an innate human orientation. Poston goes on to suggest that gradually, and much later on, the idea of greater religious reform in the Middle East region might have occurred to Muhammad, at least partial evidence for this being texts in the **Qur'an** that indicate a 'change in attitude with respect to Jews and Christians over the course of time' (Poston, 1992, p.12).[2]

Whatever Muhammad's original intentions, his followers had a much more single-minded vision and determination to spread the teachings and political influence of Islam, and the Prophet himself lived long enough to see most of Arabia converted to his message. His own reputation as a leader and statesman was a significant factor in

---

[1] Poston refers here to ***surahs*** 19:97, 26:192, 39:28–9, 41:44, 42:5 and 43:2.

[2] *Surah*s 29:45–7, 10:94, 3:113–15 and 3:199 are cited by Poston as contrasting with the tone of other verses, such as 9:29, 3:19, 5:57 and 3:85.

the expansion of the new Muslim territories. Envoys sent by the Prophet to neighbouring tribes and rulers often encountered a willingness to enter into alliance with the new Muslim presence and dominance in Mecca. Through a combination of diplomacy (primarily) and force (rarely), Muhammad was able to unite the multi-tribal society of Arabia into a vast empire that brought social and political order to the region for the first time. John Esposito acknowledges that the Muslim armies were 'formidable conquerors and effective rulers' but they were also 'builders rather than destroyers' (Esposito, 1988, p.39), and the expansion of Muslim rule came about through largely peaceful means. Not surprisingly, Islam's first 'missionaries' saw the successful expansion of the Islamic world as a miraculous validation of God's guidance, and this served to reinforce the confidence of the early Muslim community.

As with Muhammad's original intentions, the precise means by which Islam came to dominate the region are not entirely straight-forward. It is commonly assumed that conversion to Islam was forced, under the threat of death. However, recent scholarship has emphasized that this legendary assumption that Islam was spread 'by the sword' (Esposito, 1988; Turner, 2000) is profoundly mistaken. Instead, political domination by the Arabs, to some extent through warfare, was one means of establishing (although not necessarily intentionally), the conditions for the eventual creation of a Muslim environment and ambience. Via a process of circumspect **Islamization,** the early Muslims were concerned to establish the kind of institutions and social infrastructure that might eventually lead to the gradual conversion of the people, in their own time. Thus, the expansion of the early Muslim community was not solely or entirely motivated by religious conviction; there was also a political and, later, a trade motivation. Once new Muslim garrison towns were firmly established, the flourishing commerce that took place among the Muslims and non-Muslims opened the way for the gradual conversion and acculturation of local non-Muslim communities to the Islamic way of life.

So, the early expansion of Muslim territories did not meet with the kind of resistance that the threat of swords and bloodshed suggests. Poston writes that 'the early *mujahidun* [those fighting for the cause of Islam] had encountered disgruntled and often persecuted adherents of non-Muslim religious traditions, and these persons were not averse to submitting to a tolerant and protective ruling authority' (Poston, 1992, p.23). Evidence for this also comes from another quarter. Ali Issa Othman, a Palestinian sociologist, claims that:

... the spread of Islam was military. There is a tendency to apologise for this and we should not. It is one of the injunctions of the Qur'an that you must fight for the spreading of Islam. [But] after the fighting was over – not just in theory but historically – the conquered people were not vanquished in the usual sense of the word. They became equal with the conquerors, if they accepted the idea of Islam, or if they were already 'People of the Book' like the Christians and the Jews, who were not supposed to become Muslims. For several centuries the conquered Christians remained Christians. Then for one reason or another – whether convenience or not – most of them gradually became Muslims. But they were not compelled to do so.

(Waddy, 1990, p.102)

Due to their status as protected 'People of the Book' (***dhimmis***) and upon payment of a special poll tax (*jizya* tax), Jews and Christians were protected religious minorities in the new Muslim lands. Qur'anic verses supported their right to religious freedom (*surah* 2:256) and some degree of autonomy.

Under the leadership of 'Umar, the second of the **Rightly Guided Caliphs** to assume leadership after the death of the Prophet, the Muslim community expanded to encompass much of what is now Syria, Palestine, Jordan, Lebanon, Iraq, Egypt and Iran. Later, under the third Caliph, 'Uthman, territorial expansion took place in North Africa, and within 100 years of the death of the Prophet, the 'word of his successors was law from south-western Europe, through north Africa into western and central Asia – an extent unmatched by even the Roman empire at its zenith' (Turner, 2000, p.23). Over the following centuries, consolidation and centralization of power in the new Muslim territories was the focus for activity, rather than the securing of further gains.

Beyond the frontiers of those territories conquered during the early history of Islam, Muslim traders often played a significant role in the expansion of Islam, particularly in sub-Saharan Africa and south-east Asia (Voll, 1991, p.211). These merchants were usually accompanied by men who were, in some senses, full-time religious 'professionals' (Levtzion, 1979, p.17). Through the provision of religious services to the trading caravans and newly established commercial centres, these 'professionals' ushered in a new phase in the expansion of Islam 'in which adaptation and contextualization of Islamic precepts took place in the course of proselytization efforts' (Poston, 1992, p.17). However, it was **Sufi** mystics who, from about the eighth century onwards, were the most successful in advancing the cause of Islam outside the new Islamic heartlands (Poston, 1992). Theirs was a populist appeal, as a result of their emphasis upon the transformation not so much of social structures, but of the individual human heart and mind. The later formation of Sufi orders (**tariqa**s), from about the twelfth to the fourteenth centuries, provided a more organized framework to this particular expansion of the Muslim world.

If the strategic emphasis was upon consolidation up to the end of the classical period of Islamic history, approximately 1250, the Islamic world was unsuccessful in initiating a new phase of expansion to follow it. Invasion by the Mongols[3] meant the loss of previously captured territory, but also a redrawing of the Muslim map in both a westerly and an easterly direction. The abode of Islam, the **dar-al-Islam**, now included the Anatolian peninsula (now the Asian part of Turkey), and later this new Turkik power base provided the geographical vantage point for territorial expansion into eastern and central Europe (Colour Plate 12). Similarly, later descendents of Ghengis Khan (1162–1227), who had themselves embraced Islam, successfully established a new Islamic Mogul Empire in the Indian subcontinent. However, the universalist outlook that some of the Mogul rulers, particularly Akbar (1556–1605), had towards religious diversity weakened the missionary ethos of early Islam. Faced with new historical circumstances in the eighteenth and nineteenth centuries, especially rapid developments taking place in western Europe, the Muslim world had to adopt a more defensive rather than offensive strategy if it was to retain control of those territories gained during its early expansion.

Since then, the growth of Islam has largely come about through the migration of Muslims into western Europe and the Americas, and, with this, the conversion of individuals from indigenous populations has taken place. There are no statistics that give any indication of the numbers involved, but the growth in activity associated with 'new Muslims' suggests that converts are an important element in the growth of Muslim communities in the West.[4] In these contexts, a simultaneous process of enculturation by Muslims, and invitation to Islam directed towards non-Muslims, is evident, in many ways resembling an historical pattern first begun by the early Muslim community, although of course in a new and profoundly different context.

Before we turn to examine the modern development of Islam in contemporary societies, we need briefly to consider what gives

[3] Nomad tribes of the Asian Steppes north of China who became a nation under the leadership of Ghengis Khan.

[4] For example, the 'New Muslims Project' organized by the Islamic Foundation in Leicester, UK, has a programme of national events, regional meetings and a newsletter. This project has developed an active profile over the past five years.

theological underpinning to the obligation that all Muslims have 'to call' or 'to invite' others to the way of Islam, Muslim and non-Muslim alike, whether through word, action or example. This entails an examination of the term *da'wah*, and its use both in the Qur'an and in modern Islamic literature.

Invitation (*da'wah*) in Islam: Qur'anic and contemporary understanding

Like the word **jihad**, often simply translated as 'holy war', the term **da'wah,** is commonly given only a rudimentary translation as 'mission', especially directed towards non-Muslims. However, both the words *jihad* and *da'wah* carry a wide range of nuances that are often lost or misunderstood during the process of translation from Arabic to English. For example, *jihad* is more correctly understood as 'struggle', with interior effort to bring correspondence between one's heart and mind and the will of God as the greatest form of *jihad* (as opposed to external 'struggle' for the sake of Islam which may or may not include military defence of the faith). Similarly, *da'wah* also carries a meaning that is somehow less assertive towards others than the oversimplistic translation 'mission' can imply. Manazir Ahsan suggests that the word *da'wah* has been 'so used, misused and abused by Muslim and non-Muslim writers and polemicists that in the maze of discussion and counter-discussion, it has lost many of the dimensions of its true meaning' (Ahsan, 1989, p.13).

Da'wah is best understood as 'calling' or 'inviting', 'invocation' or 'appeal'. We should not therefore be surprised to find the word used in relation to prayer in the Qur'an: 'When My servants ask thee about Me, I am indeed close by and answer the prayer [*da'wah*] of everyone when they pray to me' (*surah* 2:186). Likewise, each 'servant' is enjoined to respond to the call or *da'wah* of God. Thus, a distinctive theme underpinning the concept of *da'wah* in the Qur'an is the reciprocal process, whereby believers call upon God in prayer, and then in turn respond to God's summons upon them. A related duty of Muslims is to take heed of 'the call' of God's agents of *da'wah*, known as **da'i**, whether they be Prophets or simply committed exemplars or scholars of the faith. The **Sunnah** (example) of the Prophet Muhammad himself provides a blueprint for the principles by which *da'wah* is to be understood and practised; indeed, the record of the Prophet's words and deeds can be regarded as a kind of 'textbook' of *da'wah*.

The word *da'wah* carries connotations that are individual and collective; people respond to the message of Islam in their own right, but the community formed as a result, the *ummah*, likewise has an obligation in terms of 'calling to the good, enjoining what is right, forbidding what is wrong' (*surah* 3:104). In this sense, *da'wah* is an activity of the entire community, with implications for both the macro and micro levels of society. Fadlullah Wilmot is emphatic in his concern that *da'wah* should address the many needs of human society. Since Islam is concerned with all the facets of life, the spiritual, the social, the familial, the economic, the political, the educational, the environmental and so on, so too *da'wah* must address the needs of society at all of these levels (Wilmot, 1989). The idea of *da'wah* as external mission directed towards non-Muslims must therefore be understood as just one element of a complex scope of meanings associated with the expansion and dissemination of Islam.[5]

The doctrinal and scriptural ideals of a faith tradition and its lived realities do not always correspond. The vocal and strident voices of some contemporary Islamic activists bear little relation to the etiquette of *da'wah* implicit in the Qur'an. The contrast between the two becomes evident when the much-cited *surah* 16:125 is quoted: 'Call [or invite] to the way of your Lord with wisdom and beautiful preaching and dispute with them in the better manner'. Inherent in this verse is the principle that *da'wah* must be a non-coercive activity, and that the unconvinced should be left alone (*surah*s 5:108; 3:176–7; 47:32). One of the most eminent Muslim scholars to write about *da'wah* in the modern period, Ismail Raji al-Faruqi (1921–86), stressed that for the Muslim, when trying to persuade others of the truth of Islam:

> ... the example of his own life, his commitment to the values he professes, his engagement, constitute his final argument. From this it follows that the societal order desired by Islam is one where men are free to present and argue their religious causes with one another. It is a kind of academic seminary on a large scale where he who knows better is free to tell and to convince, and the others are free to listen and be convinced. Islam puts its trust in man's relational power to discriminate between the true and the false.
>
> (al-Faruqi, 1996, p.284)

[5] Writing in the *Oxford Encyclopaedia of the Modern Islamic World* (Esposito, 1995), Paul E. Walker notes that 'there is little, if any, literature specifically on Qur'anic concepts of *da'wah* in English, in part because it is seldom considered as a separate theme in Qur'anic studies' (Walker, 1995, pp.343–6). He does, however, refer readers to a range of texts that deal with the idea of *da'wah* as a proselytizing activity, at least some of which are cited in this chapter.

M. Ali Kettani stresses that *da'wah* work must be ethical; there should be respect between the caller and the called, free exchange of ideas, and absence of self-interest on the part of the caller. Only when there is regard for the views of the other can *da'wah* be legitimately regarded as an act of worship (*ibadah*) (Kettani, 1990, p.228).

Like Christianity, Islam is a faith which 'is directed outward and seeks to expand its boundaries in both a quantitative and qualitative sense' (Poston, 1992, p. 3). Al-Faruqi wrote unashamedly that, for him, 'no religion can avoid mission if it has any intellectual backbone ... to deny mission is to deny the need to demand the agreement of others to what is being claimed to be the truth by the religion' (Siddiqui, 1999, p.15). In this sense, Islam is clearly a missionary tradition, but the process of bringing people into the faith through *da'wah* is not the coercive activity that the word 'mission' can sometimes suggest. At least part of the reason for this is that it is a concept also directed towards Muslims themselves. It is worth citing al-Faruqi at some length on this point:

> *Da'wah* in Islam has never been thought of as exclusively addressed to the non-Muslims. It is as much intended for the benefit of Muslims as of non-Muslims ... All men stand under the obligation to actualize the divine pattern in space and time. This task is never complete for any individual. The Muslim is supposedly the person who, having accepted the burden, has set himself on the road of actualization. The non-Muslim still has to accept the charge. Hence, *da'wah* is necessarily addressed to both, to the Muslim to press forward towards actualization and to the non-Muslim to join the ranks of those who make the pursuit of God's pattern supreme.
>
> (al-Faruqi, 1996, p.284)

At its heart, *da'wah* is 'primarily inner-directed ... it is essentially a means by which an individual Muslim ensures the vibrancy of her or his iman [faith]' (Abedin, 1989, p.46). This suggests that it is not simply an activity of a professional group, but incumbent upon all individual Muslims. Each has a responsibility to exemplify through his or her words and actions the teachings of Islam for the benefit of all humankind, Muslim and non-Muslim alike. However, those with knowledge and wisdom carry perhaps the greatest burden of responsibility in this regard. The next section of this chapter will be concerned with the efforts of the those thinkers and Islamic movements which have placed the Islamization of their own societies at the centre of their *da'wah* activities. As a preliminary to this survey, it is worthwhile considering the range of meanings that the term *da'wah* now carries in modern Islamic literature, both scholarly and popular.

If there is any observable trend, outreach and mission towards non-Muslims to convert to Islam has perhaps become the dominant sense in which the term *da'wah* is now used, particularly in popular literature associated with figures such as Ahmed Deedat (Zebiri, 1997).[6] However, 'political orientation, interiorization, institutional organisation, and social-welfare concerns' (Masud, 1995, p.350) are also linked with the word *da'wah*, particularly as it is used by contemporary Islamic movements concerned with the Islamization of their own societies. Social welfare as a dimension of *da'wah* is a fairly recent concern of Islamic movements, and to some extent a response to the humanitarian work of Christian missionaries (Masud, 1995). Kate Zebiri has also observed that, increasingly, Muslims are beginning to regard inter-faith dialogue as part of *da'wah* (Zebiri, 1997), although this of course raises a number of theological questions about the precise relationship between the two. But in a religiously diverse global society, where different faith traditions are in close proximity to each other, dialogue has begun to occupy an increasingly prominent place on the agenda of many faith communities, including the Islamic, both within and outside the Muslim world. These encounters, both formal and informal, rarely include an explicitly 'missionary' element; the focus tends to be upon simply the promotion of better understanding between traditions. But, as we have seen, the breadth of meaning contained within the term *da'wah* allows dialogue with non-Muslims *without* a missionary motive, conducted simply for the purpose of increasing comprehension of Islam, to be considered as a legitimate element of *da'wah* activity.[7] Indeed, many of the leaders of contemporary Islamic movements are actively involved in inter-faith dialogue, especially with Jews and Christians (Davis, 1997).

As we might expect, the range of media used to disseminate the message of Islam today is diverse in both quality and content (Figure 3.2). Books, newspapers, audio, video, pamphlets and, increasingly, the Internet provide opportunities to hear and read sermons and speeches, recitations of the Qur'an, commentaries on the sources of Islam, and to enjoy **halal** (Islamically acceptable/

[6] Deedat is a South African Muslim who has travelled extensively promoting the message of Islam, particularly among Christians. He has taken part in numerous television debates with well-known Christian evangelists from America, and his knowledge of both Islam and Christianity is largely self-taught rather than academically grounded.

[7] Muhammad Khalid Masud (1995) cites Anwar al-Jindi's *New Horizons for Islamic Mission in the Western World* (1987) in which he states that *da'wah* is not only a defensive response to western challenges, but also a necessary non-missionary means of educating non-Muslims about Islam.

Figure 3.2 An Islamic information desk, Stuttgart, Germany. © TRIP/B. Turner.

permitted) entertainment. Not surprisingly, making the Qur'an available on the Internet has been regarded by some organizations as an important priority and obligation in terms of *da'wah* (Bunt, 2000). Similarly, Islamic movements have used the Internet as a means of disseminating their theological vision and ideology; more philosophical or mystically orientated voices are harder to locate.

Da'wah and modern Islamic movements

With an appreciation of the breadth of meaning implicit in the word *da'wah*, in this section we shall turn to focus upon the formation and activities of a number of international Islamic organizations, particularly those founded in the twentieth century. Indeed, *da'wah* did not take on an organized, institutionalized character until the beginning of the last century, around 1915; prior to this period, and for much of the history of Islam, the dissemination of Islam was largely carried out informally, by individuals. Many modern Islamic movements have made *da'wah* a defining characteristic of their *raison d'être*, and many were formed in response to colonialism and, later, the perceived negative influence of western modernity on Islamic values, thought and lifestyles. Emerging within traditionally Muslim societies in the Indian subcontinent and the Middle East, initially their focus was Islamization of their own societies and with it the encouragement of lax or non-practising Muslims. The emergence of these movements in territories that, historically, were part of the early expansion of Islam following military conquest indicates that different patterns in the dissemination of a faith tradition can occur within the same society, but in response to very different historical and social realities. Also, where *da'wah* (especially among non-Muslims) and conversion to Islam followed some time *after* the establishment of a Muslim presence in an area, in modern times, the institutionalization of *da'wah* in international organizations has made the call to Islam a much more prominent dimension of both the non-Muslim invitation to Islam and the encouragement of Muslims themselves.

In recent times, particularly in response to the growth of Muslim communities in Europe and the Americas, the efforts of Islamic movements have increasingly (but by no means exclusively) turned to the conversion of non-Muslims in these western settings, and the encouragement of Muslims in minority contexts to engage in *da'wah* and to promote Islam. Inevitably, improved means of communication and travel have meant that there is an increasing international dimension to the work of many movements. Similarly, the greater possibilities and perceived need for training of Islamic workers for the specific task of *da'wah* has led to the establishment of a number of universities (e.g. in Medina in 1961) and university departments (e.g. the *Da'wah* Academy established by the International Islamic University in Islamabad in 1985) solely concerned to equip future *da'i* for effective mission work.

The number of movements currently in existence necessitates some degree of focus upon those with perhaps the strongest international profile and particularly multi-dimensional understandings of *da'wah* (e.g. towards Muslims, non-Muslims, humanitarian relief work etc.), as opposed to those that base their work upon a single issue or campaign (e.g. printing and distribution of missionary literature).[8] There are also other movements that seek to promote

---

[8] There is an extensive amount of literature currently available which profiles various Islamic movements in more depth, including those within **Shi'a** Islam (e.g. Esposito (1983); Ruthven (1991); Davis (1997)). Rather than repeat already accessible material, the 'profiles' in this chapter are intended simply to provide short summaries of the foundations and activities of the most high-profile movements, particularly in relation to their *da'wah* work.

Islam among a particular section of a population, such as the work of the 'Nation of Islam' among Afro-Americans in the USA, but there is no space to discuss these here.[9] Also absent from the survey that follows are those Islamic movements which have turned Islam into a solely political ideology – what we might call '**Islamism**' – promoted by Islamists who have sometimes used violent means to try to bring their own societies back to a pristine form of Islam. Although they are likely to regard their efforts as a form of *da'wah*, the names of some of these groups suggest that their activities are more closely allied to the term *jihad* or struggle. Before concentrating the discussion on some of the most high-profile and active *da'wah* movements, we need to consider the general social and historical background against which they were created.

First, Christian missionary work in various parts of the Muslim world was especially active from the late seventeenth century until the beginning of the twentieth century, particularly in countries under colonial rule. As a means of resisting this presence and perceived threat, a stronger sense of Muslim solidarity and identity was created, and, with it, a number of *da'wah* organizations. *Da'wah* also began to take on an increasingly politicized character:

> ... since the obvious point of difference between the colonialists and the indigenous population was generally religion, the struggle against colonial rule was defined as *da'wah* to seek independence from non-Muslim rule and to establish or restore dar al-Islam ... This *da'wah* helped to popularise political movements because it provided a broader base for developing national identity in countries of ethnic and linguistic diversity.
>
> (Masud, 1995, p.350)

Masud goes on to outline two quite opposite outcomes of this increasingly politicized *da'wah* activity. On the one hand, it fostered a growing sense of transnationalism, and a sense of all Muslims belonging to one worldwide community of faith, the *ummah*. On the other hand, there was a reinforcement of the concept of the nation state. Those Islamic movements calling for the Islamization of their own societies were implicitly recognizing the idea of distinctive geographic and political boundaries. This was later strengthened all the more in those countries whose governments made *da'wah* part of state ideology, such as in Egypt under Gamal Abdel Nasser in the 1960s.

---

[9] See, for example, Tinaz (1996) for a comprehensive survey of the movement including a detailed bibliography.

Secondly, following the demise of colonial rule, the perception of a different kind of 'western' threat emerged in the minds of a number of Muslim thinkers, who subsequently went on to form Islamic movements:

> Although most of the Islamic world had thrown off the colonial yoke of Europe by the mid-twentieth century, for many Muslims the whole process of decolonialization appeared to be little more than a shambolic façade: a cosmetic exercise to lull the Muslim masses into a false sense of security.
>
> (Turner, 2000, p.93)

The influence of what were regarded as characteristically western ideologies, namely secularism and materialism, not to mention Orientalism, was seen to be impacting on their own Muslim societies. Keen to reverse these apparent trends and the threats they posed to the major institutions of society, the movements formed as a response were primarily concerned to awaken the religious identity of Muslims themselves. In this context, the dissemination of Islam was 'the call to become a member of the only righteous Islamic community within the Muslim *ummah*' (Schulze, 1995, p.349), and the Qur'anic verse 'Let there arise out of you a band of people inviting to all that is good' (*surah* 3:104) gave inspiration and theological backing to these new collectivities of resistance.

But what has sustained these movements since their formation, especially since some of the historical and social conditions that led to their creation have now passed? A detailed response to this question could be the basis for an entirely separate discussion, but a few points can nevertheless be made. Rapid modernization of many Islamic societies has led to the creation of a large gulf between rich and poor, migration from rural to urban areas has been commonplace, and there is now increasing awareness, due to travel and communications, of globalization. Each of these has thrown up new internal and external challenges, thus presenting *da'wah* movements concerned for the development and expansion of Islam with a continued *raison d'être*. Furthermore, many Muslims now live in minority contexts in the West, and the attention of some Islamic movements has turned to the support and invigoration of Muslims in these settings, as well as to the conversion of non-Muslims.

Esposito has also observed that, since the 1990s and across the diversity of their forms, Islamic movements now participate to a much greater degree in the mainstream social and political systems of the societies in which they are based (Esposito, 2000). Although isolated extremists are still present, activist organizations are now more visible in the institutions of society, and they contribute more actively to the provision of health, education and publishing. Their understanding of *da'wah* has thus enlarged to make humanitarian action a more significant element of their work. A common assumption underpinning many of the movements is that although they may be based in societies largely composed of Muslims, these societies are not truly Islamic. Some parts of society may conform to the principles of Islam, but many others do not; it is this situation that many of the movements are struggling to change, although their definitions of an 'Islamic society' are not always consistent (Voll, 1991). As part of a general struggle in which many of the larger movements are united, their connections with each other are often strong, and a regular exchange of ideas takes place at international conferences and through publications. Also common to many of the movements is their ability to sustain and develop their activities long after the deaths of their original founders.

Although the political situations in their own countries may differ, Islamic movements are often united by a common fear of western influence upon Muslims, whether they be in majority or minority contexts. They are at pains to emphasize a difference between westernization and modernity, and in this sense they correspond with Eisenstadt's (2000) analysis of those global religious movements more generally that:

> ... deny the monopoly or hegemony of Western modernity, and the acceptance of the Western modern cultural programme as the epitome of modernity. This highly confrontational attitude to the West, or rather to what is conceived as 'Western', is in these movements closely related to their attempts to appropriate modernity and the global system on their own non-Western, often anti-Western, modern assumptions.

(Eisenstadt, 2000, p.6)

Reinhard Schulze (1995) argues that Islamic *da'wah* organizations working for the dissemination of Islam have taken three principal forms: (a) state organizations, such as the Islamic University in Medina; (b) state-sponsored transnational organizations, of which the Muslim World League is a good example; and (c) non-governmental organizations, such as the Muslim Brotherhood (Ikhwan al-Muslimin), Jama'at-i-Islami (The Islamic Society) and Tablighi Jama'at (Propagation Society). Since it is the latter two 'forms' which have tended to have the most significant international profile, especially among Muslims in minority western contexts, the brief survey that follows will concentrate upon these. Also, it is these movements (although particularly those with a non-governmental structure), that have often been the most enduring and 'successful' in their work.

Unlike the state-sponsored organizations, they have often been able to develop a much clearer, independent programme and agenda of activities, usually free from political interference. State-sponsored transnational movements, initially hampered by internal diversity and conflict, gained greater significance and profile in their *da'wah* work from the 1970s onwards, 'when Islamic politics were becoming a major expression of political and cultural struggle' (Schulze, 1995, p.347). However, with the simultaneous foundation in 1972 of the Saudi-sponsored World Assembly of Muslim Youth (WAMY) and the Libyan-backed Islamic Call Society, it is clear that 'the concept of *da'wah* was now also applied to the propagation of specific ideological and theological currents that legitimated Saudi and Libyan rule' (Schulze, 1995, p.347). By now, most of the wealthier Islamic states have their own *da'wah* organizations, and there is a significant degree of 'competition' between the various movements, vying with each other in terms of authenticity, legitimacy and 'success' in regenerating Muslim societies (al 'Alwani, 1996).

The Muslim Brotherhood was established in Egypt in 1928 by a schoolteacher, Hasan al-Banna (1906–49).[10] Initially formed as a youth group, with an emphasis on a revival of moral standards, it took on a party political character in 1939 with the clear intention of ridding the Muslim world of foreign influences and the creation of an Islamic government in Egypt. Al-Banna viewed *da'wah* in terms of concentric circles, beginning with self and radiating out through home, society, country, government, *ummah* and world (Masud, 1995, p.352). The relationship between the government and the Brotherhood was often one of suspicion and tension; al-Banna himself was assassinated in 1949, and in 1954 the movement was banned in Egypt. It is still forbidden to form a political party. However, government opposition only served to increase popular support, and branches of the movement now exist across the world; chapters exist in most capital cities, including London. According to Joyce Davis:

> ... today it is generally considered to be a moderate group led by men long past their prime but who still are devoted to reforming their societies and governments. If once they had been prone to violence in the name of Allah, the ageing process long ago forced the group's senior members to abandon that path in favor of working inside the system for a political voice.
>
> (Davis, 1997, p.xvi)

---

[10] See also Ruthven (1991) for more details about the Muslim Brotherhood.

This perception of an 'ageing' organization contrasts strongly with an alternative view of the Muslim Brotherhood coming from within contemporary Egypt itself. Interviews carried out with activists within the movement in the 1990s not only indicated strong support for the Brotherhood among educated youth (especially students), but also a deliberate effort to create a new generation of younger leaders, sympathetic to the Brotherhood's aims, who might exert an influence upon, and work within, Egypt's professional associations (Wickham, 1997). In trying to reconcile these divergent perceptions of the generational profile of the Muslim Brotherhood, it is possible to infer that the particular sense of energy and youth within the Brotherhood in Egypt has perhaps not been reproduced where the movement exists in diaspora Muslim communities, especially those dominated by Muslims from outside the Arab world. For example, activist Muslim youth in the UK have tended to align themselves with organizations other than the Muslim Brotherhood; these include Young Muslims UK and the Islamic Society of Britain to name but two. Many of them are specifically orientated towards the interests of British Muslim youth and many derive their inspiration from movements active in Pakistan, such as Jama'at-i-Islami (Jacobson, 1998). In many ways this is to be expected, given the 'success' of Jama'at-i-Islami in forming new organizations with a specific British focus (at least compared with the Muslim Brotherhood), the proportion of the UK's Muslim community with origins in the Indian subcontinent, and, as a consequence, the likely inability of many young British Muslims to be fluent modern standard Arabic speakers – the probable common language of the Brotherhood.

Jama'at-i-Islami came into being in 1941 under the leadership of Mawlana Mawdudi,[11] arguably one of the most significant religious thinkers of the twentieth century (Adams, 1983). Esposito credits Mawdudi as a 'trailblazer of contemporary Islamic revivalism' and a man whose 'ideas and methods have been studied and emulated from the Sudan to Indonesia' (Esposito, 1992, p.120). Mawdudi was the movement's leader until failing health forced him to step down in 1972, but his influence upon the movement remains strong and its present senior leadership remembers and reveres his vision and charisma. The Islamic Society was created with the aim of establishing an ideological, political and social movement to make Islam a vibrant force in Pakistan. Mawdudi was concerned about the dominant influence of the West upon developing Muslim societies, and, more particularly, the emergence of modern nationalism as a

[11] For a more in-depth discussion about Mawdudi and the history of Jama'at-i-Islami until the early 1980s, see Adams (1983).

threat to the universalism of the Pan-Islamic ideal. However, as an educated man familiar with, although critical of, modern western thought, Mawdudi was not looking simply to the past for solutions to the problems of the time. Rather, he was concerned to draw upon and apply Islamic sources to address the realities of legal change, the need for educational reform and ideas of government. Through his prolific writings he argued that modernization had to be rooted in Islamic revelation and he sought to synthesize the first principles of Islam with the necessity of modern technology, communications and institutional development. His vision of the Islamization of society would be achieved through social revolution rather than violent political action; employment of western scientific and technological development, but with a critical distance from the values in which they were embedded; revelation rather than secularist reasoning.

After Mawdudi's move to Pakistan from India in 1948, the party voiced ongoing opposition to the government and made repeated calls for the implementation of Islamic law (**shari'ah**). Like the Brotherhood, the relationship of Jama'at-i-Islami with government was often stormy. For example, Mawdudi was accused of inciting religious riots in the 1950s, principally in his opposition to the involvement of members of the **Ahmadiyah** Muslim sect in the Pakistani government. Their removal was for him the only way towards the establishment of a 'true' Islamic state. Unlike the Muslim Brotherhood, which sought a large popularist membership, Jama'at-i-Islami was (and still is) more concerned with the training of an élite of committed, well-educated leaders, mostly drawn from the middle and lower middle classes. In 1994, only 8300 men and women were regarded as true *muttafiq*: those meeting the highest criteria for membership (Davis, 1997), based on their piety, commitment to social and political activism, and knowledge of Islam. At its headquarters on the Multan Road near Lahore, the movement houses a hospital, offices, visitor accommodation, research facilities, a mosque and a library. The Pakistan Islamic Front, established in 1993, is the political wing of the movement, but it has so far failed to attract the kind of voter support necessary to become more than a voice of opposition, although a significant one.[12]

Tablighi Jama'at was founded by the Indian Sufi Maulana Muhammad Ilyas (1885–1944), with a strong emphasis on the

[12] For a discussion about the movement's use of the Internet and for the site address, see Bunt (2000). His observation that for Jama'at-i-Islami 'a website is now an effective medium for promoting an interpretation of Islam to a wide audience and is more cost-effective than other media forms' is particularly interesting to note. He adds 'Cyber Islamic Environments represent economy of *da'wa*' (Bunt, 2000, p.79).

regeneration of Muslims living either in minority contexts or on the margins of majority settings. The word *tabligh* can be translated as 'propagation ... it is an extension in space and time ... it is the act of branching out' (Mawlana, 1996, p.116). This gives us some understanding of the kind of activity that defines the movement: 'the ecological terrain of *tabligh* in an Islamic community emphasises intrapersonal–interpersonal communication over impersonal types, social communication over atomistic communication, and intercultural communication over nationalism' (Mawlana, 1996, p.116). The movement's annual three-day conference held at Raiwind near Lahore attracts around one million preachers from across the Muslim world.[13] The gathering has been taking place in October or November each year since 1949, and encourages *da'i* to practise Islam within their own families, communities and societies, while simultaneously spreading the message of Islam to non-believers. Many of those associated with Tablighi Jama'at carry out their missionary work on a voluntary basis, and the success of the movement in part derives from its Sufi orientation and independence from a political regime (Colour Plate 13).

The Muslim World League came into existence in Saudi Arabia in May 1962 and included *da'wah* as part of is covenant in order to 'unify and to spread the Muslims' word' (Schulze, 1995). Between 1957 and 1967, the Saudis recognized that through *da'wah* work they could broaden their interests, politically and culturally, by 'promulgating the word of God, promoting the message of Islam and bringing the Moslems back to the orbit of Islam' (Bashmil, 1962, p.92). To this end, volunteers undertook *da'wah* work in Africa and south-east Asia in 1973, and in 1975 the Muslim World League hosted an international *da'wah* conference in Mecca. One of the outcomes of the meeting was the re-emphasizing of the role of mosques in disseminating the message of Islam, and later that year a new organization called the World Council of Mosques was established. In 1981, humanitarian relief work in Muslim communities affected by natural disaster or poverty was integrated into the *da'wah* work of the movement. In terms of scale, in 1985, the Muslim World League had

---

[13] While conducting fieldwork in the Punjab during the Autumn of 1993, I attended the final day of the Tablighi Jama'at annual conference prior to the dispersal of the *da'i* across the globe. Inevitably, the large majority of the estimated one million participants were male, and the traffic jam created as the enthused delegates left the open-air meeting was considerable! This experience provided an eye-witness perspective on a contemporary *da'wah* movement and rare exposure to the kind of atmosphere generated when one million *da'i* are roused to the task of *da'wah*. The event received substantial coverage in the Pakistani daily broadsheet newspaper *The News* the following day (15 November 1993).

only 1000 workers under contract, thus making the movement considerably smaller than Tablighi Jama'at and Jama'at-i-Islami.

Adnan Khalil Pasha regards the:

> ... status and means of *dawa* [as] an indication of the health and vibrancy of Muslim civilization, its ability to keep pace with the challenge of history and express itself as a total way of life, harnessing and utilizing all the potential of the time according to its timeless ethic.
>
> (Pasha, 1989, p.1)

The implication of this observation is that we can learn much about Muslims and Islam in the contemporary world by critically evaluating how *da'wah* is undertaken and the problems by which it is beset. This is a subject that has exercised a number of Muslim and non-Muslim writers. A common theme to emerge in some of their observations is the failure of Islamic movements to devise a balance in practice between their own ideologies, civil society and the states in which they are based. For example, Mawdudi, like many thinkers behind Islamic movements, was more concerned with the theological, ideological and philosophical basis for the development of Islam than with the practical business of reforming social structures for the implementation of his ideas (Adams, 1983). Those movements which make exclusive claims to represent 'true' Islam provide a fertile ground for factionalism and hypocrisy, and, like most social movements, Islamic groups have to contend with their fair share of corruption and dogmatism (Davis, 1997). By making such claims, they often 'lose sight of the comprehensive totality of the Qur'an and its methodology, thus losing the opportunity to relate to reality and control the inevitable changes in time and circumstances as the Qur'an behoves' (al 'Alwani, 1996, p.11). Furthermore, few movements have given serious consideration to how to manage societies of ethnic, linguistic and cultural diversity. These are just some of the challenges that face movements working to disseminate Islam in the modern world.

The Qur'an was revealed to the Prophet Muhammad over a period of 23 years, suggesting that the process of adopting Islam, individually or collectively, will be a gradual process of personal or social change. Travel and communication, historically a much slower process, had the advantage of allowing the incremental adaptation of societies to the message and practice of Islam, while also preserving their own distinctive cultures. However, within a context of modernity, where the migration of people and ideas happens at a much faster pace, *da'wah* workers have often struggled to communicate their message (especially among non-Muslims in the West) in a language and style that is appropriate to a global, international context and culture. Recognizing this, some Islamic movements have established networks in local communities – relying upon the involvement of people familiar with the mores of the indigenous population – with a view to not only the sustenance of Muslims living in minority contexts, but also the conversion of local people. James Piscatori notes that many religious movements have become 'so self-consciously organised and extensive that they cannot be contained within national borders ... [and they have become] "deterritorialised"' (Piscatori, 2000, p.78). In the global culture of today, religious identifications are being reorganized and becoming more geographically dispersed. Movements engaged in *da'wah* are part of this process.

A good example of this is the Islamic Foundation near Leicester in the UK (Figure 3.3). This institution has its roots in Jama'at-i-Islami, and most of its past directors, such as Khurrum Murad and Khurshid Ahmad, were at some point closely associated with the movement's founder, Mawlana Mawdudi, but they also held positions of responsibility within Jama'at-i-Islami in Pakistan (Ahmad is still an **ameer** or leader of the movement). Even now, ties with the movement and with Pakistan remain strong, but the Foundation has scope for the development of its own agendas and priorities, many of which reflect the needs and interests of the estimated one million

Figure 3.3 The Islamic Foundation, Markfield, near Leicester. Photo: John Wolffe.

Muslims now living in the UK. Many of the staff at the Foundation are British. A significant element of its work is the dissemination of awareness about Islam in the wider UK society, through conferences, publications and regional networks. Mawdudi encouraged the movement to establish networks in the West, believing this to be essential for the development of international amity and world peace. Moreover, even prior to his death in 1979, Mawdudi was pained by the lack of understanding about Islam in the West, and saw the work of institutions such as the Islamic Foundation as an important step on the way to reversing hostility towards Islam. For himself, Ahmad saw the West as 'in need of Islam's moral influence' (Davis, 1997, p.237); he felt that '*da'wa* should not be confined to the Middle East' (Davis, 1997, p.237). While Director of the Islamic Foundation between 1973 and 1978, he was charged by Jama'at-i-Islami with spreading the Islamic message in Europe.

Contemporary Muslim settlement in non-Muslim societies

Throughout history, Muslims have found themselves in minority situations, but an estimated one-third of the *ummah* now lives in a non-Muslim society (Kettani, 1979, p.5). A number of concepts, some of which are derived from the Qur'an, have been utilized as a means of responding to, and, to some extent, justifying this situation. Some of the key terms are **hijra** (migration), *jihad* (struggle) and *da'wah* (invitation) (Voll, 1991, p.209). However, the distinction between the 'abode of Islam' (*dar al-Islam*) and the 'abode of unbelief' (**dar al-kufr**) – concepts developed by the '*ulema* (religious scholars) during the first three centuries of Islam (Ramadan, 1999) – have become increasingly blurred over time. For example, Mawdudi stressed that *no* society could be rightly regarded as truly Islamic, thus making the spread of Islam through *da'wah* incumbent upon all Muslims regardless of their location (Mawdudi, 1977, pp.17–21). However, the *dar al-Islam* – where Muslims might live according to the *shari'ah* – is strictly speaking the natural and only rightful 'home' of Muslims, and migration from this domain is justified only in special circumstances and for a temporary period. There is no explicit guidance in the Qur'an as to how Muslims should live in the minority context, placing a significant challenge before Muslim minority communities seeking to live according to Islamic law in the West. The only circumstances in which a Muslim might theologically justify travel outside the *dar al-Islam* are in search of knowledge or training, or to

KING ALFRED'S COLLEGE
LIBRARY

take part in diplomatic missions, tourism or commerce. Similarly, those who find themselves for any reason unable to observe Islam within the *dar al-kufr* are required to move to an Islamic society. Given the clear distinctions between these two domains of belief and unbelief, how has understanding about them evolved over time, particularly in relation to the migration and permanent settlement of Muslims to the West in the modern period?

Following the subjugation of Muslim lands during the colonial period, the idea of the superiority of the *dar al-Islam* was weakened. In addition, the scientific progress and material advances taking place in the West during the twentieth century opened Muslims to the idea that the West was not the 'dangerous, uncertain and annoying' (Nyang and Ahmad, 1985, p.277) place that they had long thought it to be. Furthermore, the political regimes in many Muslim countries following decolonialization were sometimes turbulent and repressive; western nations in many ways offered greater freedom and rights than the *dar al-Islam* itself. Some Muslim immigrants utilized the concept of *jihad* to 'justify' their settlement outside the Islamic world. For them, the 'struggle' involved the need and the obligation to affirm Islam in a non-Muslim setting, striving for righteousness, and finding means to serve God in every possible way, especially in what might be difficult circumstances. Taking this one step further, al-Faruqi regarded this sense of mission and struggle as a special kind of *hijra* to the West, rather than away from it. He was calling for active *da'wah* outside the *dar al-Islam*, urging Muslims living in minority contexts to see themselves as ambassadors of Islam, bringing the tradition to the West. He was suggesting that 'if the early Muslims could transform the non-Islamic society of Arabia, contemporary Muslims should be able to transform the society to which they have come' (Voll, 1991, p.212). His vision provided Muslims living in the West with a sense of mission, enabling them to take up a new self-identity as missionaries rather than immigrants. More recently, the Islamic scholar Tariq Ramadan has criticized a dualistic vision of the world, divided between *dar al-Islam* and *dar al-kufr* (Ramadan, 1999). He argues that:

> ... in a world that has become a village, where populations are in constant flux and within which we are witnessing a process of increased complexity regarding financial and political power as well as a diversification in strategic alliances and spheres of influence, it is impossible to stick to an old binary vision of reality.
>
> (Ramadan, 1999, p.127)

Even a third concept, ***dar al-'ahd*** (abode of treaty) does not provide a way out of the impasse. Ramadan is at pains to emphasize the fact that none of these concepts originated in the Qur'an or *Sunnah*, and only a return to these primary sources and the recognition of Islam's suitability for all times and places (**'alamiyya al-Islam**) will enable the Islamic world to address the realities of the diverse environments in which Muslims now live.[14]

The motives of those who decided to migrate to the West in the post-colonial period differed, with factors such as class, ethnicity and gender influencing who migrated and for what purposes. Although this is a generalization, the educated middle classes were more likely to be motivated by Islamic principles (such as *da'wah* among non-Muslims) or the seeking of further education, whereas those with less wealth and status saw possible economic or political advantage (Eikelman and Piscatori, 1990). Sometimes these motives were combined, and in some cases the original motivation changed following migration or settlement for a period of time. A good example of this was migration to the UK after the Second World War. Through a process of 'chain migration', single men from former colonial countries came to the UK, attracted by the economic prospects in towns and cities enjoying a boom in manufacturing and industry. Initially, much of their hard-earned wealth was sent home to their families, and they intended to stay for only a short period of time. However, with the arrival of women and children to join their menfolk in the UK, the intention of returning to their villages and towns of origin gradually receded. They saw a better life for their families by continuing to stay in the UK, with the educational opportunities for their children a significant part of their almost unconscious decision to remain in the UK (Colour Plate 14). Thus, a largely economic motivation for temporarily moving out of a Muslim society changed over the course of time; the benefits in terms of health, education and general standard of living gradually led to permanent settlement outside of the 'abode of Islam'. The third generation, those twice removed from the migration experience, now have a definite sense of the UK as their 'home' (Jacobson, 1998), and they form part of a cohort of youth committed to the development of a new British Muslim identity. Unlike their parents and grandparents, many young British Muslims do not exhibit the kind of isolationism or introverted fear of 'contamination' by the rest of society that was typical among the first generation of migrants.

---

[14] Ramadan is not the only scholar calling for an end to a view of the world as divided into immutable regions of war, peace/Islam or treaty. See, for example, al 'Alwani (1998).

Over the course of time, migrant communities began to establish the kinds of infrastructure that would support the religious and social needs of future generations. Schools and **madrasab**s, shops (especially for the supply of *halal* foodstuffs (Figure 3.4), mosques (Figure 3.5) and Islamic institutions, newspapers and magazines, and social facilities were created. Minarets and domes now punctuate the skylines of many western cities, and Muslims are playing an increasing role in the civil society of many American and European states. The pathway towards institutional completeness is well under way. However, attention is now turning to the more complex task of securing the recognition of Muslim identity in public and political life. Muslims in the UK, for example, are pressing the claim that their religious needs, lifestyles and values must shape their interaction with public institutions, such as prisons, hospitals or higher education (Beckford and Gilliat, 1998; Gilliat-Ray, 2000). This amounts to the demand for 'some degree of Islamicization of the civic' (Modood, 1998, p.387), and the efforts behind it reflect yet another dimension of the spread of Islam in contemporary society.

Scholars with expertise on the Muslim minority situation have observed that the 'successful' development of a new Muslim community outside the *dar al-Islam* often depends upon a number of factors (Kettani, 1979). The quality of the 'founding fathers' in

Figure 3.4 Halal butchers, Finsbury Park, London. Photo: Paul Smith.

Figure 3.5 Mosque, Finsbury Park, London. Photo: Paul Smith.

terms of their commitment to Islam, their education and the status they are able to achieve in the wider society are all significant. The kind of society to which they migrate also plays some role in their capacity either to spread the message of Islam or to form institutions for the sustenance of their own religious identity. For example, many Muslims in the UK hold UK passports and have access to rights associated with full citizenship. Muslims in other parts of Europe do not fare so well, and their status as 'guestworkers' (as is the case for many Turks in Germany) leaves less scope for participating fully in civil society (Figure 3.6). Kettani also suggests that maintaining

Figure 3.6 A Muslim woman worker, Stuttgart, Germany. © TRIP/B. Turner.

contact with the rest of the *ummah* is another important dimension affecting the capacity of Muslim minorities to sustain and/or propagate their faith; in this regard, the annual pilgrimage to Mecca, the ***hajj***, plays a major role in strengthening ties. Finally, the degree to which Muslims in a minority context can achieve some degree of unity, despite their inevitable ethnic, linguistic, cultural or sectarian diversity, appears to be significant in enabling the community to secure the recognition of Muslim religious identity and needs with public bodies.

One of the outcomes of Muslim settlement in minority contexts, especially the West, has been the opportunity to present the message of Islam to non-Muslims at many different levels. In the UK, this has been achieved through branches of international Islamic movements (such as the Tabligh Jama'at and Jama'at-i-Islami),[15] specialist *da'wah* organizations (such as the Islamic Propagation Centre International, a distribution outlet for material by *da'i* like Deedat), interpersonal contact, academic conferences and more general Muslim institutions, such as mosques. Studies of conversion indicate that friendship with a Muslim seems to figure as a significant point of departure for

[15] For an account of the work of the Tabligh Jama'at in Bradford, and the UK Islamic Mission (which is itself strongly connected to Jama'at-i-Islami), see Lewis (1994).

exploring Islam in more depth, although conversion itself tends to be motivated by other factors, such as the simplicity of the faith, its perceived rationality, its emphasis on universal equality, the lack of a priesthood and the scope of Islam (Poston, 1991, p.164). Some Muslim thinkers associated with international Islamic movements have given special consideration to the role that Muslims in minority contexts might play in spreading the message of Islam among non-Muslims. Publications such as *Da'wah Among Non-Muslims in the West* by Khurrum Murad (1986) were both a critique of Muslim efforts so far (Murad regarded these as inadequate and ineffective), and an encouragement to make improvements. Recognizing that other priorities and the limitations of poverty have often impeded the efforts of the early Muslim migrants, Murad called upon Muslims to close the gap between the realities and the ideals of *da'wah*.

Islamic movements, globalization and localization

At this point, the preceding survey of some of the most significant international Islamic movements both within and outside the Muslim world, as well as the growth of Muslim populations in Europe, requires critical analysis set against the background of large-scale social transformation and, in particular, recent processes of globalization. Muslims throughout the world now find themselves part of a global system in which a powerful defining 'centre' largely associated with the USA and the western world defines and asserts domination over 'others'. By locating itself as the normative political and economic centre, defining what counts as democratic, creative, rational and advanced, whatever and whoever is regarded as 'other' is thereby defined as inferior. As noted above, Islamic movements are engaged in a struggle to disentangle the realities and benefits of globalization and modernity from the packaging of westernization, while Muslims communities, especially in the West, are trying to find ways of creating distinctive local identities while being part of a transnational *ummah*. Muslims the world over are caught between simultaneous processes of homogenization and hegemonization, and a struggle to reconcile the dilemmas thrown up by the westernization of the Muslim world in the first half of the twentieth century and the Islamization of the West through migration in the second half of the twentieth century. Some Islamic scholars see the Muslim presence in the West as a critical force, first for resisting cultural homogenization (see, for example, Mazrui, 1998), and secondly for producing credible intellectual responses to issues of globalization from the reserve of Muslim professionals and academics now residing in the West. Unlike the founders of the Islamic movements surveyed in this chapter, many of whom wrote in Urdu or Arabic, the new generation of leaders and thinkers are likely to reflect the multicultural world in which they live by writing in several languages, one of which is almost certain to be English. But whether they manage to reflect on the problems of globalization with any intellectual rigour remains to be seen, and some observers remain sceptical:

> The failure of this Muslim community [in the West] to grasp the central problems surrounding its presence in a non-Islamic, though religiously tolerant environment, reflects the deep social and psychological anguish suffered by Muslims in a Western milieu. The Muslim community is in an ideal position to reflect from within, so to speak, on the nature of globalisation and guide the [rest of the] Muslim world in understanding the hazards created by neo-liberalism and the new forces of the market. It seems to me that it is now time to invent a novel Islamic manner of thinking that responds creatively to the rigorous rules of critical philosophical and ethical thinking. No thinking can probe the problematic of globalisation unless it is totally abreast of recent trends in critical theory, economic and social thought, their implications for religious thought in the Muslim world and the West, and the ethical response that contemporary Islamic thought must present to assert its vitality and relevance.
>
> (Abu-Rabi', 1998, p.17)

However, there are alternative voices within the Muslim world as to the rightful track on this intellectual path, and some have observed a selling out to 'western' patterns of discourse. Literature with titles such as 'Islam and democracy' or 'Islam and women's rights' is regarded by some as a 'sad surrender' (Khan, 1998, p.89) of Islamic values, which fails to serve the real interests of Muslims:

> Rather than understanding the present from the explicit interests of Islam and the *ummah* and then articulating reform and development strategies to enhance Muslim interests, Muslim intellectuals are caught up in the powerful discourses of the West and modernity, discourses that serve only the interests of the West and secular humanism. Even when Muslims defend Islam against Western discourses, in reality they are legitimizing the West and modernity by treating it as a standard against which all things must be measured.
>
> (Khan, 1998, p.89)

While the very nature of the intellectual challenge facing Muslim scholars remains so contested, critical reflection on the identity and

Figure 3.7 Turks demonstrate in Trafalgar Square, London against alleged atrocities committed towards Muslims in Bulgaria. © TRIP/TRIP.

role of Islam and Muslim communities in our global world appears to be a task for future generations.

A number of challenges face those trying to create local identities as British-Muslims, American-Muslims or, indeed, any other variation of hyphenated Muslim identity within a global structure. There is an inherent vulnerability in trying to define the self and to construct new ideas of 'belonging' in a world of constant change. For Muslim minorities in the West, there is a delicate balance to be struck between asserting membership of the *ummah* – defined as 'other' by the US-dominated global 'centre' – while also seeking recognition of Islamic identity and needs in local settings. International conflicts and crises involving Muslims, such as the Gulf War, the Rushdie affair, Bosnia and Kosovo, to name but a few, test the loyalties and interests of Muslim localities (Figure 3.7).[16] There is also the problem for multicultural Muslim communities in the diaspora as to how to agree on the meaning and practice of Islam on 'foreign' soil. Schools of thought and law that were previously separated by vast geographical distances are now brought together and contested by different ethnic

[16] For an interesting case study of this 'testing' process in the British context and in relation to the Gulf War, see Werbner (1994).

and cultural groups within Muslim minority communities. Establishing what counts as essential and what can be regarded as peripheral or simply a cultural dimension of Muslim practice has exercised many new European Muslim communities. These challenges also interplay in a dynamic relationship with 'home' societies, the countries of original migration. As Michael Fischer and Mehdi Abedi note, Muslim societies and diaspora communities 'mirror each other at acute or oblique angles, mutually affecting each other's representations, setting off mutating variations' (Fischer and Abedi, 1990, p.255). Islamic movements are one force among several that sustain connections at each end of the migratory chain; they are therefore an essential part of the global–local dynamic in which Muslims find themselves.

As well as the global–local dynamic between Muslims in majority and minority contexts, the societies to which Muslims have migrated have not been unaffected by their gradual 'Islamization'; the identity of local Muslim communities is therefore also framed in relation to the response of these societies. The estimated 20 million Muslims now present in Europe, not to mention the approximately six million strong Muslim community in the USA (Mazrui, 1998), is challenging the foundations and structures of western claims to pluralism, tolerance and religious freedom: 'For over a century the West has defined itself as antithetical to a negatively conceptualized Islam ... [b]ut now this "despised other" has become a noticeable part of the "self"' (Khan, 1998, p.98).

In the UK as well as in France (and not surprisingly in either case), debates centred around education have provided a stage upon which a process of mutual renegotiation and re-evaluation has been played out. In the UK, the eventually successful campaign for voluntary-aided Muslim schools tested local and national government ideas of multiculturalism, while in France, the ***affaire du foulard*** tested French ideas of *laïque* (the secular separation of church and state) and provided a catalyst for change in many aspects of the French educational system (Davie, 2000). In each case, Muslims themselves were engaged in a complex political process and an assessment of their own self-identity as British-Muslims or French-Muslims, while the identities of the UK and France were also being simultaneously refashioned in the light of these processes.

Conclusion

Islam is widely regarded as one of the fastest-growing world religions today (Turner, 2000), but the expansion of the *ummah* is not so much geographic or territorial, but rather qualitative and quantitative. The movement of Muslims around the world and the political significance of Islam have led to the immediate visibility and recognition of Islamic vocabulary and lifestyles across the globe. At the same time, Muslims themselves have become increasingly aware of their own heritage and identity. They are unashamed of what Islam has to offer, especially when seen against the background of perceived moral laxity and secularism in the West. The resurgence of Islamic identity in Muslim nations and in minority contexts is now well-documented. Conversion, not of wholesale societies, but of individuals who become attracted to the beliefs and practices of Islam, has been the subject of a number of scholarly investigations (e.g. Poston, 1992; Kose, 1995). And now Muslims, like everyone else, are part of the high-tech information era and they are actively using it to promote Islam. This has raised *ummah*-consciousness, but has also led to the virtual expansion of the Muslim world through a new 'electronic *ummah*' (Bunt, 2000, p.36). New 'virtual' communities are also being created, some of which are particularly associated with Sufism. The resulting 'cyber*tariqa*s' provide a transgeographic meeting point for individuals who may never gather physically, while the electronic *ummah* more generally reflects communities of disparate individuals struggling to find a new cultural space and identity (Bryson-Richardson, 1999). 'Cyber Islamic environments provide indicators of what it means to be a "Muslim" in Britain' (Bunt, 1999, p.353), as well as scope for the anonymous promotion of 'deviant' identities or alternative viewpoints. There is considerable potential for important future research that explores the effect of the Internet on the development of existing Muslim groups, as well as the growth of Islam through the creation of new cybercommunities. As more of the Islamic world comes online, surfers will be able to survey the sheer diversity of the Muslim world and observe the effect of unregulated challenges to traditional voices of authority and authenticity.

Islam now has a place in a global environment delineated from a single geographic or social reference point. The collapse of time-measured spatial boundaries is leading to a re-imagination of community and social relations, and the Muslim world in all its diversity is an actor in this new environment. Muslim use of the new technologies of communication is a powerful reminder of the capacity of Islam to be disseminated via a wide range of media and in contexts that would have been unimaginable at the time of the Prophet Muhammad.

Glossary

N.B. Many Islamic/Arabic terms have a variety of spellings when translated into English.

affaire du foulard a sequence of episodes and events that began in 1989, when three Muslim schoolgirls were sent home from a school in France for wearing the *hijab* or headscarf.

Ahmadiyah a Muslim 'sect' founded by Mirza Ghulam Ahmad Qadiyani (1835–1908). Many Muslims do not accept the Islamic identity of Ahmadiyah members on account of their deviance from a number of central tenets of Islam.

'alamiyya al-Islam the application/suitability of Islam for all times and places.

ameer literally, 'commander'. Honorific title.

da'i an individual involved in *da'wah* or the spread of Islam.

dar al-'ahd the abode of treaty.

dar al-Islam the geographical 'abode of Islam', that is, Muslim territory.

dar al-kufr the abode of 'unbelief'.

da'wah the call to Islam.

dhimmis protected religious minority groups, the 'People of the Book', that is, Jews and Christians.

din al-fitra Islam as the 'natural' religion of humankind, the latter being predisposed towards monotheism.

hajj the annual pilgrimage to **Mecca**.

halal that which is permitted/lawful.

hijra migration. Refers to the migration of the Prophet Muhammad from **Mecca** to Yathrib (later known as Medina) at the end of September 622. The year of the *hijra* became the first year of the Islamic calendar.

Islamism an activist political ideology based on Islamic principles.

Islamization the process of bringing thought and practice in line with Islamic teaching.

jihad struggle in the cause of Islam, the greater of which is personal inner struggle, the lesser of which is outer struggle or warfare.

*madrasah*s places of study and learning.

Mecca the birthplace in Saudi Arabia of the Prophet Muhammad.

Qur'an literally, 'the recitation'. The Holy Qur'an is believed by Muslims to be the final revelation of God (Allah) to humankind.

Rightly Guided Caliphs the first four leaders of the Muslim community following the death of the Prophet Muhammad. They were: Abu Bakr, 'Umar, 'Uthman and 'Ali. All four were close companions of the Prophet during his lifetime, and ruled according to His example and the guidance of the **Qur'an**. After them, leadership took the form of a hereditary monarchy which differed markedly from the example of both the Prophet and the Rightly Guided Caliphs.

shari'ah literally, the path or way to water, that is, the way to sustenance, and the path to be followed in Muslim life and living. The *shari'ah*, the canonical law of Islam, is derived from the **Qur'an** and the **Sunnah**. There are four principal schools of Islamic law.

Shi'a a branch of Islam, itself internally diverse, which represents approximately 10 per cent of the Muslim world. Sunni and Shi'a Muslims agree on the fundamentals of belief, but differ on the concept of successorship to the Prophet. Thus, the difference is largely historical and political, rather than doctrinal.

Sufi Muslims who seek a direct and close personal encounter with God (Allah), usually through mysticism and mystical practices.

Sunnah the example of the Prophet Muhammad. This constitutes one of the sources of Islam, along with the **Qur'an** and the *shari'ah*.

*surah*s chapters in the **Qur'an**.

*tariqa*s different 'schools' or orders of **Sufi** thought and practice.

tawhid the indivisible Oneness of God (Allah), a central tenet of Islam.

ummah community/nation. Often refers to the worldwide community of Muslims.

References

Abedin, S. (1989) 'Dawa and dialogue', in M.W. Davies and A.K. Pasha (eds), pp.42–57.

Abu-Rabi', I.M. (1998) 'Globalization: a contemporary Islamic response?', *American Journal of Islamic Social Sciences*, vol.15, no.3, pp.15–44.

Adams, C. (1983) 'Mawdudi and the Islamic state', in J. Esposito (ed.) *Voices of Resurgent Islam*, New York: Oxford University Press, pp.99–133.

Ahsan, M. (1989) 'Dawa and its significance for the future', in M.W. Davies and A.K. Pasha (eds), pp.13–21.

Al 'Alwani, T.J. (1996) *Missing Dimensions in Contemporary Islamic Movements*, Occasional Paper no.9, London: International Institute of Islamic Thought.

Al 'Alwani, T.J. (1998) Editorial, *American Journal of Islamic Social Sciences*, special issue on Globalization, vol.15, no.3, p.vii.

Bashmil, M.A. (1962) *Nationalism in Islam*, Beirut.

Beckford, J. and Gilliat, S. (1998) *Religion in Prison: Equal Rites in a Multifaith Society*, Cambridge: Cambridge University Press.

Bryson-Richardson, M. (1999) 'Cybertariqas: Sufism in the diaspora, identity and virtual community', *Islamica*, vol.3, no.1, pp.71–8.

Bunt, G. (1999) '*islam@britain.net*: "British Muslim" identities in cyberspace', *Islam and Christian–Muslim Relations*, vol.10, no.3, pp.353–62.

Bunt, G. (2000) *Virtually Islamic: Computer-mediated Communication and Cyber Islamic Environments*, Cardiff: University of Wales Press.

Davie, G. (2000) *Religion in Modern Europe: A Memory Mutates*, Oxford: Oxford University Press.

Davies, M.W. and Pasha, A.K. (eds) (1989) *Beyond Frontiers: Islam and Contemporary Needs*, London: Mansell.

Davis, J. (1997) *Between Jihad and Salaam: Profiles in Islam*, New York: St Martin's Griffin.

Eikelman, D. and Piscatori, J. (1990) 'Social theory in the study of Muslim societies', in D. Eikelman and J. Piscatori (eds) *Muslim Travellers: Pilgrimage, Migration and the Religious Imagination*, London: Routledge, pp.3–29.

Eisenstadt, S.N. (2000) 'The resurgence of religious movements in processes of globalisation – beyond end of history or clash of civilisations', *MOST Journal on Multicultural Societies*, vol.2, no.1 (http://www.unesco.org/most/vl2n1eis.htm).

Esposito, J. (ed.) (1983) *Voices of Resurgent Islam*, Oxford: Oxford University Press.

Esposito, J. (1988) *Islam: The Straight Path,* Oxford: Oxford University Press.

Esposito, J. (1992) *The Islamic Threat: Myth or Reality?* Oxford: Oxford University Press.

Esposito, J. (ed.) (1995) *The Oxford Encyclopaedia of the Modern Islamic World*, Oxford: Oxford University Press.

Esposito, J. (2000) 'Political Islam and global order', in J. Esposito and M. Watson (eds), pp.119–30.

Esposito, J. and Watson, M. (eds) (2000) *Religion and Global Order*, Cardiff: University of Wales Press.

al-Faruqi, I.R. (1996) 'On the nature of Islamic *da'wah*', in D.A. Pittman, R.L.F. Habito and T. Muck (eds) *Ministry and Theology in Global Perspective*, Grand Rapids, Michigan: Eerdmans, pp.283–91.

Fischer, M.J. and Abedi, M. (1990) *Debating Muslims: Cultural Dialogues in Postmodernity and Tradition*, Madison: University of Wisconsin Press.

Gilliat-Ray, S. (2000) *Religion in Higher Education: The Politics of the Multi-faith Campus*, Aldershot: Ashgate.

Jacobson, J. (1998) *Islam in Transition: Religion and Identity among British Pakistani Youth*, London: Routledge.

al-Jindi, A. (1987) *New Horizons for Islamic Mission in the Western World*, Beirut.

Kettani, M. Ali (1979) *The Muslim Minorities*, Leicester: The Islamic Foundation.

Kettani, M. Ali (1990) 'Muslims in non-Muslim societies: challenges and opportunities', *Journal Institute of Muslim Minority Affairs*, vol.11, no.2, pp.226–33.

Khan, M.A. (1998) 'Constructing identity in "glocal" politics', *American Journal of Islamic Social Sciences*, vol.15, no.3, pp.81–106.

Kose, A. (1995) 'Native British converts to Islam: who are they? Why do they convert?', *American Journal of Islamic Social Sciences*, vol.12, no.3, pp.347–59.

Levtzion, N. (1979) 'Towards a comparative study of Islamization', in N. Levtzion (ed). *Conversion to Islam*, New York: Holmes & Meier.

Lewis, P. (1994) *Islamic Britain: Religion, Politics and Identity among British Muslims*, London: I.B. Tauris.

Masud, M. (1995) 'Modern usage [of the word *da'wah*]', in J. Esposito (ed.), pp.350–3.

Mawdudi, Mawlana S. Abul A'la (1977) *The Process of Islamic Revolution*, Lahore: Islamic Publications.

Mawlana, H. (1996) *Global Communication in Transition*, London: Sage.

Mazrui, A.A. (1998) 'Globalization, Islam, and the West: between homogenization and hegemonization', *American Journal of Islamic Social Sciences*, vol.15, no.3, pp.1–13.

Modood, T. (1998) 'Anti-essentialism, multiculturalism and the "recognition" of religious groups', *Journal of Political Philosophy*, vol.6, no.4, pp.378–99.

Murad, K. (1986) *Da'wah Among Non-Muslims in the West*, Leicester: The Islamic Foundation.

Nyang, S. and Ahmad, M. (1985) 'The Muslim intellectual émigré in the United States', *Islamic Culture*, July, pp.277–8.

Pasha, A. K. (1989) 'Introduction', in M.W. Davies and A.K. Pasha (eds), pp.1–11.

Piscatori, J. (2000) 'Religious transnationalism and global order, with particular consideration of Islam', in J. Esposito and M. Watson (eds), pp.66–99.

Poston, L. (1991) 'Becoming a Muslim in the Christian West: a profile of conversion to a minority religion', in *Journal Institute of Muslim Minority Affairs*, vol.12, no.1, pp.159–69.

Poston, L. (1992) *Islamic da'wah in the West*, Oxford: Oxford University Press.

Ramadan, T. (1999) *To be a European Muslim*, Leicester: Islamic Foundation.

Rashid, S. (2000) 'Divergent perspectives on Islam in America', *Journal of Muslim Minority Affairs*, vol.20, no.1, April, pp.75–90.

Ruthven, M. (1991) *Islam in the World*, London: Penguin.

Schulze, R. (1995) 'Institutionalization [of *da'wah*]', in J. Esposito (ed.), pp.346–50.

Siddiqui, A. (1999) 'Ismail Raji al-Faruqi: from '*Urubah* to ummatic concerns', in *American Journal of Islamic Social Sciences*, vol.16, no.3, pp.1–26.

Tinaz, N. (1996) 'The nation of Islam: historical evolution and transformation of the movement', *Journal – Institute of Muslim Minority Affairs*, vol.16, no.2, pp.193–211.

Turner, C. (2000) *The Muslim World*, Stroud: Sutton.

Voll, J. (1991) 'Islamic issues for Muslims in the United States', in Y. Haddad (ed.) *The Muslims of American*, New York: Oxford University Press, pp.205–15.

Waddy, C. (1990) *The Muslim Mind*, London: Grosvenor.

Walker, P. (1995) '*Da'wah*: Qur'anic concepts', in J. Esposito (ed.), pp.343–6.

Werbner, P. (1994) 'Diaspora and millennium: British Pakistani global–local fabulations of the Gulf War', in H. Donnan and A. Ahmed (eds) *Islam, Globalization and Postmodernity*, London: Routledge, pp.213–34.

Wickham, C. (1997) 'Islamic mobilization and political change: the Islamist trend in Egypt's professional associations', in J. Beinin and J. Stork (eds) *Political Islam: Essays from Middle East Report*, California: University of California Press, pp.120–35.

Wilmot, F. (1989) 'Dawa: a practical approach', in M.W. Davies and A.K. Pasha (eds), pp.22–41.

Zebiri, K. (1997) *Muslims and Christians Face to Face*, Oxford: Oneworld.

PART
TWO

Thoroughly modern: sociological reflections on the Charismatic movement*

ANDREW WALKER

Introduction

When the 'Marches For Jesus' began in our cities in 1989 it was said by some of the organizers that marching on the streets was a way of 'shifting the demonic atmosphere': they believed that cities and regions of the world could be controlled by 'territorial spirits'. Indeed, these days, demonic infestations, which are legion, seem to be bound up with well known and much sought after exorcists: Bill Subritzky from New Zealand, Derek Prince from the United States, Peter Horrobin from Lancashire, and the Revd Arbuthnot from the London Healing Mission, are just some of the people who have a 'special ministry' in the realm of unclean spirits.[1] Such beliefs and practices might seem evidence enough that the Charismatic movement is pre-modern, a throwback to a primitive or animistic religion – to an era, as Rudolf Bultmann would have put it, when it was only possible to believe in such things before the advent of wireless and electric light.[2]

* This text first appeared in *Charismatic Christianity: Sociological Perspectives*, ed. Stephen Hunt, Malcolm Hamilton and Tony Walter, Basingstoke and London: Macmillan, 1997, pp.17–42.

[1] See S. Hunt, 'Giving the Devil More than His Due: Some Problems with the Deliverance Ministry' in A. Walker and L. Osborn (eds) *Harmful Religion: studies in religious abuse* (SPCK forthcoming).

[2] R. Bultmann, 'New Testament and Mythology' in H. W. Bartsch (ed.), *Kerygma and Myth* (London: SPCK, 1955), p.5.

And it is not just a question of demons: oil miraculously appearing on hands at Kensington City Temple, London, it has been rumoured (a feature of the American healing movement of the 1940s), roaring and laughing at the height of the 'Toronto Blessing' of the 1990s, and that mainstay of classical Pentecostalism, *glossolalia* – all these phenomena seem to inhabit a cultural universe beyond the ken of modernity. So one might be tempted to think that such religious supernaturalism in the modern world is culturally misplaced. To read the religious supernaturalism as primitive, however, is not only usually reductionist in intent but it is also empirically indiscriminate: if Charismatic religion is a throwback then what are we to make of *The X Files*, alternative medicine, crystals and star gazing, the late modern fascination with the weird and the unexplained, the replacement, we might say, of 'mere Christianity' with the merely strange? We might want to offer the rationalistic or aesthetic judgement that these things are bizarre or bewildering – even a form of pre-millennial tension or post-modern fragmentation – but hardly, I would have thought, be satisfied with the epithet 'pre-modern'.

Perhaps we would be on surer sociological ground if we were to reserve judgement on the pre-modern or primitive status of Charismatic phenomena and note that they appear to be firmly fixed to those religious movements that can be seen to be not so much pre-modern as anti-modern. Following Troeltsch and Weber's classic division into church [having a positive view of the outside world] and sect [rejecting the outside world] there have been few sociologists[3] who have not viewed Pentecostalism and its many Charismatic mutations as 'culturally denying' in some sense and thus resistant to modernity. In Niebuhr's seminal *Christ and Culture*, for example, it is quite clear that all things Pentecostal would fit his rubric of 'Christ Against Culture'.[4] Admittedly, theologian John Howard Yoder and sociologist Bryan Wilson would prefer the notion of 'conversionist' to describe the sectarian nature of Charismatic groups, but like Neibuhr and Troeltsch before them they too accept that such sects are still essentially resistant movements to the modern world; certainly not institutional and symbolic carriers of modernity.[5]

---

[3] A. Walker, 'Fundamentalism and Modernity: the Restoration Movement in Britain', *Studies in Religious Fundamentalism*, ed. L. Caplan (London: Macmillan, 1988).

[4] R. H. Neibuhr, *Christ and Culture* (London: Faber & Faber, 1952).

[5] See J. H. Yoder, 'A People in the World: Theological Interpretation' in *The Concept of the Believer's Church*, ed. H. L. Garrett, Jr. (Scottdale, PA: Herald Press, 1969), pp.252–83 and B. Wilson, *Sects And Society* (Greenwood: Press, 1978).

A proper case could be made that some expressions of Charis-matic religiosity cannot be classified by sectarian notions of conversionism,[6] but in this chapter I prefer not to become embroiled in typological issues but rather to argue that Charismatic Christianity is neither essentially pre-modern nor anti-modern. On the contrary, I shall argue, it has embraced modernity either begrudgingly (making Pentecostalism reluctantly modern) or with enthusiasm (with the result that Pentecostal religion can be called thoroughly modern). Such a revisionist historiography seems apposite as we near the end of the century for we can now look back on 100 years of Pentecostal and neo-Pentecostal religion. I do not wish to assert that there are no world-denying elements in Charismatic Christianity, nor no anti-modern aspects to such movements – especially when second adventist hopes are high – but more plausibly to argue that Charismatic Christianity is more modern than not.

Revivalism is itself a modern phenomenon

Pentecostalism, and its Charismatic outcrops, is the twentieth century's most successful embodiment of revivalism. Revivalism itself came into being at the dawn of the Enlightenment and thus can be properly classified as a modern phenomenon. I have argued elsewhere that the literary culture that developed with the invention of printing in the late fifteenth century facilitated not only critical rationality but also individualism and pietism.[7] The Age of Reason was also the age of revivals. Both John Wesley and Jonathan Edwards [see above, page 16], born in 1703, were admirers of science. Edwards may have been a high Puritan but he was considerably influenced by John Locke and Isaac Newton [both leading Enlightenment thinkers].

The Methodist revival in Europe and the First Great Awakening [the first phase of the Evangelical movement in the USA] in New England have to be seen, in my opinion, as part of the cultural shift from feudalism to capitalism. In the United States in particular the revivals ensured the successful transmission of Protestant religion from feudalism into the modern era but they also sounded the death knell for the already crumbling Puritan covenant of 1620. To see the eighteenth century revivals as the cultural carriers of modernity may

[6] The Renewal movement, for example, resides in the historic churches and can hardly be said to have majored on revival.

[7] A. Walker, *Telling The Story: gospel mission and culture* (London: SPCK, 1996), pp.61–74.

seem a strange idea because we tend to think of them in opposition to the Enlightenment preoccupation with rationality, deism and unitarianism. Or again we may be reminded that Gotthold Lessing characterized the Enlightenment as a 'big ugly ditch' that halted historic Christianity in its path.

But the early revivals were not opposed to critical rationality, individualism and progressivism in themselves. Jonathan Edwards, for example, may be remembered for his frightening sermons on God's wrath and eternal perdition but he also provided a thoroughly modern psychological account of the revivals and his own wife's religious experiences.[8] Perhaps the most convincing evidence of the modernizing tendencies of early revivalism comes from Jon Butler's revisionist accounts of the American Awakenings (especially the Second Awakening at the advent of the nineteenth century) where he demonstrates that the passion and piety of the revivals also fuelled the progressivist vision of the American dream. The Puritan vision of the 'city set upon the hill' settled down to a dream of a decent and respectable life in the new Republic. When revivalistic fervour cooled it left a strong residue of ascetic Protestantism, with its commitment to literacy and hard work, and in time provided a ladder of social mobility.[9]

The early revivals had unintended consequences not least because their emphasis on experience and the self was not only thoroughly modern in itself but was also conducive both to the religious freedom of the Republic and to the pietistic but theologically non-specific 'civil religion' of middle America.[10] More obviously revivals were themselves aided both by the technology and the principles of modernity. Not only is this the case with the appropriation of firstly the telegraph and later the phonograph for the more routinized revivals and urban missions of the nineteenth century, but it is also the case that revivalists came to see their campaigns in terms of pragmatic techniques. This assertion does not hold for The First Awakening or the 1801 Cane Ridge revival in Kentucky: the first revivals were too new, spontaneous and unexpected to be honed into a technique. But the assertion does hold for Finney's great revivals of the early years of

[8] J. Edwards, *Religious Affections*, ed. J. Smith (New Haven: Yale University Press, 1979, 2 vols).

[9] J. Butler, *Awash in a Sea of Faith: Christianizing the American People*. Studies In Cultural History (Cambridge, MA: Harvard, 1990). See also N. Hatch, *The Democratization of American Christianity* (New Haven, CT: Yale University Press, 1989).

[10] See R. N. Bellah, 'Civil Religion in America', *Beyond Belief: Essays on Religion in a Post-Traditional World* (New York: Harper & Row, 1970), pp.168–89.

the nineteenth century. As he says in his *Lectures On Revival*: 'A revival is not a miracle, or dependent on a miracle, in any sense. It is purely philosophical results of the right use of constituted means as much as any other effect produced by the application of means.'[11]

Henceforth American Camp Meetings, holiness gatherings, revivalistic campaigns became formatted and routinized: nightly meetings, demotic preaching and singing, altar calls, 'anxious benches' [on which those concerned about their spiritual state would be encouraged to sit]. To this was later added mass publicity, showmanship and most important of all business acumen. George Thomas goes so far as to say that nineteenth century revivalism was isomorphic with the rise of early forms of modernity.[12]

The early revivals, then, contributed to the advancement of modernity because they provided a value matrix conducive to the ascetic Protestantism of early capitalism. The enthusiasm, freedom, individualism and moral values of the revivals entered the mainstream of American society: revivals helped reinforce the work ethic and the expressivism so dear to the heart of nineteenth century America. They also provided a legitimate context for public emotion which in time became transferred to the secular contexts of baseball, football and politics. Vestiges of early revivalism remain in American religious life today through the legacy of sacred songs, vernacular preaching, special conventions and visiting speakers. The long term and lasting effects of the revivals, however, have not been the continuation of an evangelical Camp Meeting tradition but the establishment of numerous denominations and established sects, the contribution to civic life through the building of hospitals and universities, and the provision through education and self-help of a ladder of social mobility from the working class to the middle class.

The thesis that classic revivalism was both a contributor to the modernizing process and in turn adapted to the modernizing process seems less contentious if we contrast these revivals with the millennialism of early Charismatic religion. Pentecostals were convinced that the end of the world was imminent, whereas a proper modern confidence characterized the great revivals – of Wesley, Whitfield, Edwards and Finney. Certainly these founding modern evangelists could see Lessing's ditch as an obstacle in their path but they were convinced that they could jump across it and ride on into a hopeful future. For them there was hope in the future, for

---

[11] Quoted in J. Seel's 'Modernity and Evangelicals: American Evangelicalism as a Global Case Study' in P. Sampson, V. Samuel and C. Sugden (eds), *Faith and Modernity* (Oxford: Regnum Books, 1994), p.293.

[12] ibid. p.293.

there was to be a future. In short, modernity was a challenge but it was not a catastrophe which heralded the end of time as it did for Pentecostals.

It is interesting to compare the optimism of the late eighteenth century/early nineteenth century American revivals with the outbreak of Irvingism[13] in London in the 1820s. Irving can properly be seen as the 'morning star' of Pentecostalism[14] and is certainly the most interesting precursor of twentieth century charismatic Christianity. For our purposes in this chapter what is interesting about Irving is not the outbreak of tongues in Regent Square in October 1830, nor even the establishment of 12 apostles in the wake of his ministry. For us what is striking is that Irving, the Albury circle of which he was a part, and their prophetic journal, *The Morning Watch*, were all convinced that the French Revolution signalled not only the end of an age but the end of time. Irving believed that modernity was essentially evil and was to be resisted: the role of the saints was to endure the coming crisis until the eagerly awaited, and soon to be expected, Rapture.

Irving, unlike Edwards and Wesley, was deeply romantic. Attached to Coleridge and an upholder of feudal traditions, Irving had no place in his worldview for the future. The only future for modern culture was its eventual destruction. The immediate future of the Church was to be snatched from the world like a brand from the burning coals.[15]

The American counterpart to this eschatology of disaster began in New York State in the 1820s with the Church of the Latter Day Saints (they too were tongue-speakers in the early days) and it continued with William Miller in the 1830s. Despite the failure of Miller's predictions, modern day millenialism entered the American bloodstream like a foreign body opposed to the health and progress of the cultural organism. We not only think of the Christadelphians, Seventh Day Adventists, and Jehovah's Witnesses, but also of an abiding fascination with the final things by the ever-growing evangelical movements from the 1860s onwards. Consequently the optimism of the First and Second Great Awakenings, of early

[13] Edward Irving (1792–1834) was a Church of Scotland minister in London. In the early 1830s, there was an outbreak at his church of phenomena such as prophecy and speaking in tongues, which would later be labelled 'Charismatic' or 'Pentecostal'. In this and subsequent footnotes, square brackets around the superscript number in the text indicate a note added by the editor of this volume.

[14] See D. Allen, *The Unfailing Stream: A Charismatic Church History in Outline* (Tonbridge: Sovereign Word, 1994), chap. 6.

[15] See A. Walker, *Restoring The Kingdom: the radical Christianity of the house church movement* (London: Hodder & Stoughton, 1985), chap. 11.

American revivalism, was dampened by pessimistic rumblings fuelled by the many holiness movements that emerged from the Camp Meetings and disaffected Methodism. In time America was to become the homeland of modern millenialism under the enormous influence of Schofield's theories of Dispensations outlined in the Bible that bears his name and which was first published in 1909.[16]

Pentecostalism as twentieth century revivalism

There are a number of reasons why Pentecostalism can be seen as anti-modern in contradistinction to the modernizing tendencies of the early revivals. First, from the early days of Charles Parham at Kansas in the 1890s and Pastor Seymour in Azusa Street in Los Angeles from the first decade of the twentieth century, the manifestations of tongues, prophecy, exorcisms and so on, led to almost universal condemnation by what Irving used to mockingly call 'the religious world'. The jerks and barks of Cane Ridge were outlandish enough for many mainline Christians, but claims that the charismata of the New Testament had been restored to the modern world of science and steam trains seemed preposterous.

Second, the fact that such 'signs and wonders' were appearing among black and white uneducated people was considered to be evidence of their lack of plausibility. The fact that early Pentecostalism was a religion of the dispossessed has been exaggerated[17] but it is true that the majority of the early Pentecostals were working class. For Marxists, as for Anderson years later, Pentecostal experience was an example of 'false consciousness':[18] economically deprived working men and women were turning their backs on the

---

[16] It is not without irony that Schofield learned his millennial theories from the writings of John Nelson Darby one of the founders of the Brethren movement which through its own prophetic conferences at Powerscourt in Ireland were feeding off the same adventist theories as Irving and the Morning Watch. Mark Patterson, a doctoral student at King's College, London, thinks that it might be established that Darby's dispensationalism actually led back to the Albury group and possibly Irving himself.

[17] In Britain, for example, leadership initially came from the upper class Revd Boddy in Sunderland. The so-called 'Cambridge Seven' which included Cecil Polhill were from aristocratic backgrounds. Polhill, it could be argued, helped bankroll the Pentecostal movement and certainly kept Boddy's influential journal, *Confidence*, alive.

[18] R. M. Anderson, *Vision of the Disinherited: The Making of American Pentecostalism* (Oxford: OUP, 1980).

promise of progress through revolutionary struggle and were being hoodwinked by immediate emotional satisfaction on the one hand ('the Baptism of the Spirit') and a false earthly utopia on the other hand (the literal thousand year reign of Christ and the saints).

And this leads us to the third, and in the light of our earlier section on revivals, the most important reason why Pentecostalism has been understood to be against modernity. The new revivalism was 'birthed', to use Charismatic nomenclature, in adventist hope. Pentecostal revival was itself seen by its members as a sign of the end-time. Following Parham, many of them also initially believed that the tongues were the evangelistic means whereby the whole world could receive the good news of the gospel.[19] So early Pentecostalism adopted a conversionist modus operandi because it thought that the time was short, the fields already 'white unto harvest', and that revival – spearheaded by the miracle of tongues – would sweep millions into the kingdom of God as the precursor to the end of the world.

The revivalistic fervour predicated upon Charismatic experience and millennial excitation led either to a hostile stance to the world or an indifferent attitude to civic responsibility and the lure of modern progress. Pentecostals were certainly not right-wing in their early days but rather apolitical and culturally denying.

The antagonistic attitude of the other churches to Pentecostals also facilitated the Pentecostal rejection of both the established churches and the secular world. In this respect at least, when coupled with adventist fervour, classical Pentecostalism was, unlike the earlier revivals, initially anti-modern. However, like those revivals, Pentecostalism, over time, became at the very least an unwitting symbolic carrier of modernity as well as falling prey to the secularizing tendencies of the modern world. Its modernizing tendencies, however, vary between classical and neo-Pentecostalism on the one hand and between the First and Third Worlds on the other hand. Before we proceed to demonstrate this there is one obvious, and much cited, objection to the claim that Charismatic religion is thoroughly modern. This objection is to insist that Pentecostalism is, on the contrary, thoroughly fundamentalist and thus anti-modernist. I believe, at best, that this argument is a red herring, but because of its plausible appeal and widespread acceptance I will deal with it now in the form of an excursus.

---

[19] There was a confusion among Pentecostals between the glossolalia of St Paul in his letter to the Corinthians (1 Cor. 12, 13, 14) – the normative experience of Pentecostal tongues – with the xenoglossy of Acts 2 when according to St Luke's account people in Jerusalem could hear the disciples speak in their own natural languages.

Pentecostalism as fundamentalism

Many of the early Pentecostals were pleased to boast of their fundamentalist allegiance. Official support was widespread for the *Fundamentals* published between 1912 and 1916 by leading conservatives from the Princeton School of Theology and their allies. Words like 'inerrant' and 'fundamentalist' appeared in many a Pentecostal confession of faith. In Great Britain only a few years ago the magazine of the Elim Church bore the legend on its front page that it was 'Pentecostal, Evangelical, Fundamental'.

There are, however, a number of problems in identifying Pentecostals with fundamentalists. The most obvious one is to show that the second generation of Pentecostals, both renewalist and independents, are not wedded to a fundamentalist epistemology. This is clearly so for many Anglican and Catholic renewalists but it can also be said to be the case for 'new church' leaders like Roger Forster of Ichthus and Gerald Coates of Pioneer.[20] Furthermore it could not unreasonably be said that the recent and brief history of the Toronto Blessing demonstrates that Biblical fidelity is not paramount for the new generation of Charismatics; it is difficult to see how, for example, one could ground the Toronto Blessing in Biblical narrative or scriptural proof texts.[21]

It might seem that this argument is sleight of hand as neo-Pentecostals are only distant cousins to their classic brethren. This objection is epistemologically quite strong – neo-Pentecostals are not typically wedded to holiness traditions as classical Pentecostals are – but it is phenomenologically weak: modern Charismatics and Pentecostals are much the same. Admittedly, renewalists are gentrified Pentecostalists but they are not a different genus, and the sociological distinctions we might have made, even ten years ago, between classical and neo-Pentecostal are now difficult to sustain in the light of new Charismatic alignments and the syncretistic tendencies of late Pentecostalism.[22] These days classical Pentecostals feed off the independent or so-called 'new churches' who feed off renewalists who in turn feed off classical Pentecostals. If you visit Kensington Temple in London, for example, it may formally be Elim

[20] See G. Coates, *Divided We Stand* (Eastbourne: Kingsway, 1986).

[21] In one of the most innovative and intelligent defences of the Toronto experience, Patrick Dixon prefers science and history, rather than Biblical exposition, to make his case. See his *Signs of Revival* (Eastbourne: Kingsway, 1994).

[22] Class distinctions still count. Renewalists are still primarily middle class; whereas Pentecostals are still primarily working class and lower middle class.

Pentecostal but it is awash with the methodologies of John Wimber and Rodney Howard Browne, Morris Cerullo, and the indomitable style of its own Colin Dye. Despite its virtually white leadership Kensington Temple also reflects the earlier Camp Meeting style of its large Afro-Caribbean membership.

Alternatively you can visit St Andrew's, Chorleywood, and be introduced to Anglican renewals, with its Wimber clinics, Toronto swooning, and whiffs of Pentecostal holiness prophecy via visits from some of the Kansas City Prophets (who themselves hark back to the healing revivals of North America in the 1940s under the controversial William Branham).

But if we were to accept the sleight of hand argument we would still have to contend with Don Dayton's revisionist history of American classical Pentecostalism in which he contends that Pentecostalism is certainly pietist and rooted in holiness traditions but it is only incidentally fundamentalist.[23] Fundamentalism was in the air before Pentecostalism came into being. To assert your evangelical legitimacy in the early part of the twentieth century you had to sport your fundamentalist credentials. And Pentecostals craved legitimacy among their evangelical peers even if they were indifferent to everyone else. Fundamentalism, in other words, acted as a useful legitimation for a movement that wanted to demonstrate that it was faithful to New Testament Christianity.

Dayton's revisionism is particularly compelling if we look at the more extreme developments of Pentecostalism, for Charismatic Christianity has not always been tied to orthodox belief despite the fundamentalist label. Oneness Pentecostalism, for example, which developed soon after the revivals of Azusa Street in Los Angeles, was heretical in its understanding of God and refused to use the Trinitarian formula for baptism.[24] Again if we turn to the Christology of William Branham in the 1940s we find something more akin to Arianism[25] than the orthodoxy of the Nicene Constantinopolitan creed.[26] And it is clear that if Charles Hodge of Princeton, or

---

[23] D. Dayton, *Theological Roots of Pentecostalism* (Grand Rapids, MI: Zondervan, 1987).

[24] This was not, as is often thought, because they were anti-Trinitarian but because they were Sabellian and hence denied the unique and distinct persons of the Godhead in favour of a threefold modalistic presentation of a monistic God.

[25] Christian heresy derived from the Libyan theologian Arius (d.336), in which the subordination of Christ to God the Father is stressed.

[26] Branham not only had trouble with defining Jesus as truly God but he also was tainted, in the eyes of many Pentecostals, because of his association with Oneness theology.

B. B. Warfield, the intellectual architects of fundamentalism, were to investigate the hermeneutics of say Kenneth Hagin and Kenneth Copeland of the Faith Movement they would turn in their graves.[27] Indeed in many ways the Pentecostal revivals by their very volatile nature have been a challenge to the scholastic rationalism of the fundamentalist movement. Pentecostals have certainly been Bible lovers but they have also been moved by the Spirit, spoken prophetic words and received new revelations.[28]

Ironically if we were to take issue with Dayton and see (to use a pre-modern analogy) Pentecostalism as essentially rather than accidentally fundamentalist then this would actually strengthen our argument that Pentecostalism is modern. This is so because fundamentalism, despite its resistance to modern thought, is itself, modernist. The Princeton theologians in the last quarter of the nineteenth century were convinced that the new higher criticism that was emerging from the German Liberal School of Theology, of Ritschl, Harnack *et al.,* when coupled with the evolutionary theories of Charles Darwin, posed serious threats to the truth claims of historic Christianity. In particular it was felt that redactive criticism and the like called into question the reliability of the Biblical record.

In this respect fundamentalism was part of the religious resistance movement to modernism at the end of the nineteenth century. Rome resisted through Vatican I[29] and the papal dogmas, Protestantism through fundamentalism. Fundamentalism, however, unlike Vatican I was thoroughly modern in method and intent. Nineteenth century philosophers and scientists were looking for rational foundations of reality, so some conservative theologians felt it wise to do the same as part of an apologetically aimed strategy against modernism. The Princeton school alighted on a foundation which they believed

---

[27] See T. Smail, A. Walker and N. Wright, 'Revelation Knowledge and Knowledge of Revelation: The Faith Movement and the Question of Heresy', *Journal of Pentecostal Theology*, vol.5, 1994, pp.57–77.

[28] Curiously modernist Harvey Cox has come to see Pentecostalism in a more positive light precisely because of its experiential nature. See his *Fire From Heaven: Pentecostalism, Spirituality, and the Reshaping of Religion in the Twenty-first Century* (New York: Addison-Wesley, 1994). I think Cox is projecting twentieth century self-expressionism into, what I think will be, an altogether different future. See my conclusion in this chapter.

[29] The First Vatican Council of 1870, an assembly of all Roman Catholic bishops, called by Pope Pius IX.

would rationally shore-up the truth claims of Christianity.[30] To paraphrase a well known fundamentalist book: Christianity is true because the Bible tells us so. And the Bible can be trusted, so the argument went, because God Who is Truth has revealed Himself as truth in the sacred text. The Bible by virtue of this fact is *ipso facto* both the vehicle and the locus of truth.

The sting in the tail for what was an essentially rational epistemology raised to the status of religious dogma is, that as the Bible, as God's book, is true, it can never contradict itself: the Bible is no longer merely 'infallible' to use a well seasoned Reformation word, it is also 'inerrant'. In practice, however, the notion of inerrancy is problematic because this new foundation of truth (unknown in dogmatic form by the Fathers or the Reformers) had to deal with the tricky problem of textual contradictions which appear to be legion. Furthermore many, but not all, of the early fundamentalists recast the first two chapters of the book of Genesis as scientific accounts of the creation of the world so that the Bible was now set up in opposition to biological science as well as German theology.

The high tide of fundamentalist scholarship passed with the First World War where in many evangelical and Pentecostal circles it became ensnared with dispensationalist theories of prophecy. It also became increasingly sectarian and in time even anti-intellectual. After the debacle of the Scopes monkey trial [see above, page 19] in America in 1925 fundamentalism became an object of ridicule in most theological circles and despite its resurgence in the 1980s through tele-evangelism it is now in retreat in many American evangelical seminaries.[31]

This does not alter the fact that early fundamentalism was a rational, not to say modern(ist), attempt to underpin the truth of the Bible by a tendentious theory of the inspiration of scripture. Nevertheless fundamentalism, by virtue of its Biblicism, succeeded in constraining and controlling Pentecostal theology and practice: it kept the new enthusiasm within the evangelical fold and curbed its volatile excesses by an insistence on Biblical fidelity.

[30] A. Noll, comp. & ed., *The Princeton Theology 1812–1921: Scripture, Science, and the Theological Method from Archibald Alexander to Benjamin Beckeridge Warfield* (Grand Rapids, MI: Baker Book House, 1983).

[31] Notably Fuller seminary in California.

The modern tendencies of normative classical Pentecostalism

If we grant that classical Pentecostalism was anti-modern in its revivalistic days we do so simply because it was adventist and quite literally 'other worldly'. Over time, however, as the routinization of charisma set in Pentecostalism trod the well worn path of American nineteenth century urban missions with all their pragmatic tendencies and replete with the latest modern technologies. On the one hand, Pentecostals, unlike Methodists and Anglicans, have not adopted a modern scriptural hermeneutic nor acceded to Enlightenment doctrines of progress and critical rationality. On the other hand, Pentecostals have been open to modern technologies, advertising and management techniques. Their commitment to demotic hymnody – no doubt in order to subvert popular culture – has meant in effect that they have been far more at home with mass media and consumer culture than many of their mainline counterparts.

Furthermore, the fact that the Pentecostals of the twentieth century have not been perceived to have joined the societal mainstream as obviously as Methodists did in the nineteenth century is partially a question of their anti-worldly ideology but also partly a question of a slower assimilation of modern values. Pentecostals, in the First World at least, have been reluctant modernizers and have become thoroughly modern by a slow process of cultural osmosis rather than through ideological acceptance of the modern world. In Great Britain, for example, before the First World War, Bible Colleges were originally eschewed as unnecessary for spirit-filled Christians. By the 1920s, however, the Elim Pentecostal Church had established a Bible College therefore ensuring the professionalization of its pastors and hence contributing to the gradual modernization of the church. This process has taken some 40 years to come to fruition. Today, the Elim Bible College has become Regent's Theological College complete with a director for studies with an earned Ph.D., an undergraduate BA and a new MA course. The Assemblies of God College at Mattersey Hall in the North East of England has a similar story to tell.

It is David Martin's recent studies, however, that provide the most convincing evidence of the modernizing tendencies of Pentecostalism.[32] For if Pentecostals have been a little slow off the mark in diving into the modern stream in Europe and North America, the opposite can be said of South America. Pentecostalism is the fastest

---

[32] D. Martin, *Tongues of Fire: The Explosion of Protestantism in Latin America* (Oxford: Basil Blackwell, 1990).

growing Christian religion in the Third World and in some Central and South American countries Pentecostals already number some 40 million which is approximately one in ten of the population.

To be a Pentecostal in South America is to be a modern in capitalist guise. Pentecostal leaders are not only Spirit-led but also entrepreneurs and small businessmen. 'The Evangelical poor,' on the other hand, says Martin, 'have adopted a discipline of life: no drink or drugs, no fiesta, but hard work, careful budgeting, honesty, family integrity, and discipline in the home. According to social workers their children may well perform above average at school.'[33] Despite the neo-Marxist rhetoric of Catholic liberation theology, Catholicism has not been a successful agency of modernity in South America, but Pentecostalism would appear to be so. This is not just because Marxism is losing out all over the world to free enterprise, but because in South America Marxist Catholics are clearly outnumbered by the many traditional Catholics who support the feudal structures of the traditional landowners. Pentecostals, by contrast, are for free expression, free enterprise, democracy, hard work, individualism and the Holy Ghost. They are thoroughly modern but with 'signs following'.

At the very least upholders of the view that Pentecostalism is anti-modern will have to, in the light of the empirical evidence, revise their thesis to say that Pentecostalism might be said to be reluctantly modern in the First World of advanced industrial societies, but in the Third World Pentecostalism would appear to be at least as significant a modernizing agency as Methodism was in Britain and North America in the eighteenth and nineteenth centuries.

Classical Pentecostalism since Azusa Street has always been an amalgam of ancient and modern – 'a traditional service in the modern manner' as the advertising slogan goes. A feature of my own studies among the so-called house churches or new churches, who are hybrids of classical and neo-Pentecostalism, is that rational and economic goals are often set and adhered to in a sensible manner but these would often be buttressed by Charismatic reinforcements. Bryn Jones of Covenant ministries, for example, offered a perfectly rational argument to me as to why he had pioneered new churches along the west coast of Scotland, England and Wales, but also offered the insight that 'we had a prophecy about that'.[34] Gerald Coates of Pioneer is a very successful Christian leader in Britain, well organized,

---

[33] D. Martin, 'Latin America Pentecost' *Leading Light*, vol.3/1, Summer 1996, p.13.

[34] Interview at Church House, Bradford with Bryn Jones on 28 June 1989.

hi-tech, pragmatic and modern, but he also takes notice of dreams, prophecies, promptings.[35]

(How many secular business agencies, we wonder, take advantage of New Age methodologies to improve their performance indicators?[36] Such activities are surely typical of late or post-modernity rather than indices of anti-modern sentiment.)

To suggest that classical Pentecostalism is at the least reluctantly modern and at the most thoroughly modern is not so much to point to its use of modern tunes, new technologies and secular business techniques – though these are not without significance – but to register the fact that Pentecostalism has ministered to the poor and the disinherited in a culturally appropriate manner and in so doing has initiated them into the working processes and value systems of modernity. In short, Pentecostalism for the working classes has been a continuation of the ascetic Protestantism of Puritanism and the revivals of the Great Awakenings. It has provided modest but real social mobility for working class families in Europe and North America and a fast-track modernizing programme for many in the Third World. Even if we want to apply a Marxist perspective to the phenomenon of Pentecostalism (which we mentioned earlier) and criticize it in terms of religious opium and 'false consciousness' this is not to deny its modernizing tendencies but rather to discredit its revolutionary potential.

From classical Pentecostalism to Charismatic Christianity

It is surely no coincidence that when Pentecostalism was transformed from its working class style to its middle class one we had moved from early to late modernity: an era that with the advent of consumerism in the 1950s saw the demise of ascetic individualism and the rise of hedonistic individualism.[37] When in the 1960s middle class members of mainline churches claimed the 'Baptism in the

[35] In interview with Gerald Coates, op. cit., he told me of a woman's dream about a new direction in his life where he began to dress differently and change his hair style. While dashing off to the airport to meet an important contact he suddenly realized his blazer and new haircut were just as in her dream.

[36] *The Sunday Times* reported on 22 September 1996 in its financial section that the European Bank had programmed astrological configurations as part of its financial forecasting.

[37] See D. Bell, *The Cultural Contradiction of Capitalism* (London: Heinemann, 1976).

Spirit' as their own, classical Pentecostalism found itself with what was initially perceived to be a rival in the revivalist stakes.[38] This new, or neo-Pentecostalism, was not only different in terms of social status and organization but also in tone.

We noticed it first in the name used to tag the new enthusiasm. The specialist and non-threatening adjective 'Charismatic' replaced the proper noun Pentecostal. This was affixed to the altogether more restrained and non-evangelistic badge of belonging known as 'Renewal'. To be in the Charismatic Renewal was to be still a committed Anglican or Catholic, Baptist or Presbyterian. A renewalist was for praise and sanctity, a devotee of religious experience, but he or she was not a revivalist. Those in the Renewal found themselves in ever larger circles, and in increasingly successful ventures, but they moved together, with each other: they did not evangelize the unchurched in any systematic way as the Pentecostalists had done in the flush of the revivals.

Gradually as the Renewal grew tendentious Pentecostal doctrines were dropped, such as the two-stage experience of conversion and Spirit baptism (which was inherited in part from the holiness days of belief in the 'second blessing' of sanctification). Charismatics during the late 1960s underwent what I earlier called a process of gentrification: they sported bishops and canons from the Church of England among their number, nuns and priests from Rome, and even a cardinal from Belgium. Theological literature of a scholarly fashion flowed from the pens of Charismatic apologists.[39] They also attracted pop stars in their orbit such as Sir Cliff Richard, and even for a time captured Bob Dylan who gravitated for a season to a Vineyard church in California.

To be a Charismatic, then, was phenomenologically identical to being a Pentecostal but culturally redefined by class, taste and the late modern preoccupation with therapy and self-fulfilment. Chorus singing, clapping and dancing were incorporated into the new enthusiasm but Charismatics preferred their own tunes and songs – more middle of the road rock and modern anthem than Redemption

---

[38] See W. T. H. Richards, *Pentecost is Dynamite* (Lakeland: Cox & Wyman, 1972).

[39] Most notably from Roman Catholics. For example, D. L. Gelpi, SJ, *Pentecostalism: a Theological Viewpoint* (USA: Paulist Press, 1971).

Hymnal and Moody and Sankey [Victorian revivalists].[40] They maintained interest in physical healings but moved deeper into a realm of inner healings. People in the Renewal were in touch with themselves as well as with God. As the Hobbesian and hedonistic individual replaced ascetic individualism in the larger culture so the Renewal reflected these changes in its style of worship and experientially driven theology. If Pentecostals in the First World were reluctantly modern in their early days, renewalists were thoroughly modern from the start.

The 1960s was a revolution of experience – sexual and chemical – and in some quarters this revolution was seen as counter-cultural. The Charismatic movement in the churches reflected the idealism, the heightened experience, and the hedonism of this counter-culture even though ideologically they were opposed to each other. Within a few years the Renewal also folded back into classical Pentecostalism. Songs, ministries and styles began to cross over the classical/neo-Pentecostal divide. Oral Roberts, for example, during his successful reign as a tele-evangelist from the late 1970s to the mid 1980s became a Methodist. Like those other Pentecostalists, Jimmy and Tammy Bakker (unlike Jimmy Swaggert), he dropped the strident fundamentalism and evangelistic fervour of his earlier days in favour of a folksy, cosy approach.

Tele-evangelism itself reflected the narcissistic streak of American hedonism. Christianity was repackaged so that increasingly there was little emphasis on asceticism – what you could do for God – towards self-gratification – what God could do for you. Steve Bruce superbly captures this mood change.

> The broad road is the pursuit of self-fulfilment, self-satisfaction, and self-esteem. The 'power of positive thinking', roundly criticised by conservative Protestants for its 'this worldly' orientation when it was presented by Norman Vincent Peale in the 1950s, now informs most religious television. This is less of a change for Robert Schuller (like

---

[40] In Martyn Percy's unpublished paper, 'Sweet Rapture: Subliminal Eroticism In Contemporary Charismatic Worship' he demonstrates that by the time of Wimber (1980s) the jolly refrains of classical Pentecostalism, such as 'In my heart there rings a melody', or 'Since Jesus came into my heart' had been replaced by romantic and intimate songs. This theme continues to the present time. For example:

I will be yours, you will be mine
Together in eternity
Our hearts of love will be entwined
Together in eternity, forever in eternity.

(Brian Doerkse, 1994, in song book, *Isn't He/Eternity: Intimate Songs of Praise and Worship*, Anaheim: VMI Publishing, 1995).

Peale a Reformed Church minister and a man who has never claimed to be a fundamentalist) than it is for Oral Roberts, Jim Bakker, or Kenneth Copeland, but the ghastly punning title of Schuller's *The Be Happy Attitudes* will stand as a sign of the orientation of most televangelism.[41]

Not only tele-evangelists got in this groove. Writing in the 1980s James Davison Hunter demonstrated that evangelicals generally, and Charismatics in particular, were borrowing heavily from secular therapeutic models and looking for life-enhancing satisfaction. Here are some of the typical titles Hunter selected from the Christian bookshelves:

- *Transformed Temperaments*
- *Defeating Despair and Depression*
- *God's Key to Health and Happiness*
- *Feeling Good about Feeling Bad*
- *How to Become a Happy Christian*
- *How to Become Your Own Best Self*[42]

Neo-Pentecostals, independents and Charismatic realignments in late modernity[43]

If by neo-Pentecostalism we mean specifically the Charismatic Renewal Movement in the mainline denominations then I think we have to say that it existed in a pure form for only a very few years – say from 1965 to 1980. The 1970s was the decade of its greatest influence when barely a major denomination had not been flooded with the new songs, the excitement and the renewal of religious commitment. Looking back it was the Kansas City Conference of 1977 that stands out as the Woodstock of Charismatic ecumenical experience. At Kansas the Renewal seemed at its most joyous and least strident. Final and formal worldwide recognition for the Renewal came in 1980 at Bossey in Switzerland when the World Council of Churches held its one and only consultation on the

---

[41] S. Bruce, *Pray TV: Televangelism in America* (London: Routledge, 1990), p.237.

[42] J. Davison Hunter, *American Evangelicalism: Conservative Religion and the Quandary of Modernity* (New Brunswick, NJ: Rutgers University Press, 1983).

[43] By late modernity I am signalling consumer capitalism rather than affirming a Marxist theory of capitalist development.

movement.[44] By the time I wrote 'A new light for the churches' for the Agenda page of *The Guardian* newspaper on 24 November 1980 the Renewal was already waning.

Writing now over 15 years later I think that although the Renewal was analytically distinct from classical Pentecostalism – not least because it was middle class and non-denominational – I now think that it was never a totally distinct phenomenon; it was never exclusively middle class or totally free from sectarianism.[45] Neither did it totally free itself from Pentecostal theology and practices. Fr Peter Hocken has demonstrated that a number of independent movements, classical streams and new renewal groups not only overlapped but intertwined in Great Britain from at least the 1960s.[46] Men from classical Pentecostal backgrounds, such as David du Plessis from the Assemblies of God and Cecil Cousens from the Apostolic Church, had considerable influence on the theology and belief systems of the burgeoning Renewal. Maverick groups, such as the North American healing movement of the 1940s and the 'Latter Rain' movement of Canada in the 1950s provided numerous personnel who found their way into the Renewal in one way or another.

From the late 1970s until the present time what we have seen since the heyday of the Renewal is the emergence of numerous independent ministries, maverick organizations, new networks of churches, parachurch groups. These new movements did not destroy the Renewal movement but they did rival it, then penetrate it, and eventually alter its nature. In the 1980s, for example, by far the most significant Charismatic growth in Great Britain came from the so-called Restorationist house churches. These were certainly not renewalist for they taught a radical separationist doctrine and condemned the historical churches as moribund. With their commitment to apostolic and prophetic leadership, and their 'shepherding' or discipleship doctrines, these independent churches were in effect a threat both to the Renewal and to classical Pentecostalism. Restorationism was not a new version of classical Pentecostalism as I mistakenly thought in 1985: it was a syncretistic amalgam of classical, renewalist and independent streams.[47]

---

[44] I was at the consultation representing the British Council of Churches with Professor James Dunn and the Revd Michael Harper.

[45] See my concept of the 'sectarian implant' in 'Harmful Religion', *Leading Light: Christian Faith And Contemporary Culture*. vol.2/3, Autumn 1995, pp.5–7.

[46] P. Hocken, *Streams of Renewal: Origins and Early Development of the Charismatic Movement in Great Britain* (Exeter: Paternoster Press, 1986).

[47] See my *Restoring The Kingdom*, op. cit.

Restorationists were like renewalists in terms of their middle class affiliation and their emphasis on experience and new songs. They were also similar to classical Pentecostalists in two respects: they were more enthusiastic about evangelism than the renewalists, and they regrouped themselves into enclaves that were sociologically sectarian in character. It could also be said of Restorationists that they were a throwback to Irving and the Catholic Apostolic Church (CAC) of the 1830s.[48] Like the CAC, Restorationists initially thought that their movement in itself heralded the end of time. In this sense they were millennial and one might have expected them to be anti-modern. However, unlike both Irving and early Pentecostalism, Restorationists were optimistic about the future and were committed to the establishment of a powerful Church before the thousand year reign of Christ.[49] This 'eschatology of victory' led them to be optimistic about the future, and by the early 1980s their business acumen and organizational flair lent them a thoroughly modern air.

By the mid 1980s, however, strange things began to happen. As Bryan Wilson put it to me at All Souls, Oxford, religious changes were taking place at a bewildering pace in the late twentieth century.[50] This speeding-up process meant that Christian religious formations were coming and going, starting and stopping, with the speed we associate with New Religious Movements. Restorationism in a ten-year period, for example, underwent the kind of growth, changes, splits, and realignments, that took Elim and the Assemblies of God 60 years to undergo.

With the advent of niche marketing, video and audio tape sales, rapid movement from country to country, and the beginning of information technology, Charismatic Christianity went into overdrive in the late 1980s. The Evangelical Alliance persuaded most of the house churches, now being called 'new churches', to join them. The family oriented Spring Harvest celebrations became a catch-all Charismatic supermarket where classical Pentecostals, renewalists, independents and non-Charismatic evangelicals came together. In 1993 some 80,000 people attended Spring Harvest.

Meanwhile a Californian Charismatic, John Wimber, made considerable impact in Britain from 1984 onwards. Initially popular with Anglican renewalists through his connection with the late Canon David Watson, Wimber soon appealed to the new churches too. Terry

---

[48] Not least in their espousal of apostles and prophets.

[49] It was envisaged that powerful Christian communities and businesses would flourish.

[50] A. Walker, *Restoring The Kingdom*, op. cit. (1988 edn) p.333.

Virgo, Restorationist apostle of New Frontiers in Hove, became a close friend. Wimber majored on spectacular 'slaying in the Spirit', and wherever he went there was, as Nigel Wright put it, the smell of cordite.[51] Wimber was controlling but Californian in style not strident in the Bible-Belt tradition.[52] Wimber prefigured what was to come in the 1990s in the form of Benny Hinn's spectacular ministry and the mayhem of the Toronto Blessing.[53]

Following Wimber's success many of the Restorationists 'loosened up' and began to work with people that they had earlier eschewed. Gerald Coates, for example, apostolic leader of Pioneer in Cobham, Surrey, went on to become a national church leader working with the ecumenical Youth With A Mission (YWAM) and Roger Forster of Ichthus in South London to establish the Marches For Jesus as a world-wide phenomenon by 1994.

If this were not enough the classical Pentecostals began to make a comeback. Elim and Assemblies of God recovered from the raiding parties made on their fellowships by Restorationists. Kensington City Temple in London (Elim) probably has the largest church membership in Great Britain. Their leading pastor, Colin Dye, now has one of the highest profiles of any Charismatic leader in England.

In the 1990s, however, British Pentecostals appear virtually indistinguishable from renewalists and independent Charismatics in terms of hymnody and practices. All these groups, regardless of social class or denominational affiliation, cross over in terms of their songs, video ministries, paperback tales of the miraculous, favourite gurus and so on. They are all open to penetration from overseas ministries: Kenneth Copeland, John Wimber, Morris Cerullo, Derek Prince from America; Rodney Howard Browne and Reinhart Bonnke from South Africa; and Bill Subritzky and John Smith from New Zealand. All have been blown over by the Toronto Blessing.[54]

The last two decades have seen Charismatics riding a roller coaster of excitement that to the sober outsider seems almost, at times, like a frenzy. There seem to have been more demons, more outlandish

---

[51] A phrase he frequently used in a lecture series on the Charismatic movement organized by the C. S. Lewis Centre in the early 1990s entitled 'The love of power and the power of love'.

[52] See M. Percy's *Words, Wonders and Power* (London: SPCK, 1996).

[53] For a less than enthusiastic view see C. F. Porter and P. Richter, *The Toronto Blessing – Or is It?* (London: DLT, 1995). cf. D. Roberts, *The Toronto Blessing* (Eastbourne: Kingsway, 1994).

[54] This probably does not hold for the remnant of British Catholic renewalists. The rise of the Evangelical Alliance and the numerous independent Protestant groups has not been conducive to Catholic sentiments.

experiences, a greater thirst for new things, than ever classical Pentecostalism knew. We cannot put this down to millenialism even though a literal millennium approaches and may yet make its impact in terms of adventist excitation. Neither can we talk of revivalism being the cause of such excitement in the sense of church growth resulting from evangelization. Charismatic growth has resulted primarily through recycling Christians from one denomination to another, or renewing pockets of established denominations and sects.

Perhaps we cannot altogether account for these directional changes (given their multi-causal nature), but we can usefully attempt to characterize them. The argument of this chapter has been that the Charismatic movement has followed the same contours of secular modernity from its early to its late phase: it has in fact been for the spirit of the age rather than against it. It has perhaps, in David Harvey's understanding of late capitalism, capitulated to the consumer and experiential hedonism of late modernity and become commodified and corrupted.[55] It has arrived, at the dawn of the new millennium, as no longer reluctantly or thoroughly modern but ultra- or hyper-modern.

The hyper-modern status of the Charismatic movement is highlighted by the so-called 'Toronto Blessing' from 1994 to the present time. Whether the laughing experience has come in Toronto fashion, complete with growls and jerks, or in the Rodney Howard Browne guise – no animal noises but gales of uncontrollable laughter – Toronto has become a watershed in Charismatic experience. Toronto has not yet been shown to be the prelude to a nineteenth century style religious awakening like Finney in America or a twentieth century style revival like Roberts in Wales. So what has it been? Sociologically, at least, it seems clear, that it has been a craze.[56]

Toronto is phenomenologically similar to some of the lesser known aspects of Wesley's and Edwards' revivals and some of the excesses more usually associated with the New Age human potential movement. On the other hand it has not been typical of classical Pentecostalism: falling like ninepins, guffawing and gasping, uncontrollable crying and laughing, are not unknown in the older revivals but they were untypical or epiphenomenal. Powerful preaching, the

---

[55] D. Harvey, *The Condition of Postmodernity: An Enquiry Into the Origins of Cultural Change* (Oxford: Basil Blackwell, 1989).

[56] John Moore adopted this category from Smelser's typology of changing collective behaviour to investigate Catholic renewal in the 1960s. See his 'The Catholic Pentecostal Movement' in M. Hill (ed.) *Sociological Year-book of Religion, 6*, (London: SCM, 1963).

gifts of the Spirit of 1 Cor. 12, chorus singing and conversion were their hallmarks. Classical Pentecostalism could certainly be said to have been thaumaturgical but Toronto has developed a style, inherited from Wimber, that we might call theanthropic therapy. This is reflected in the emphasis by Toronto enthusiasts on God visiting his people, blessing them, playing with them, releasing them and refreshing them.

Indeed for many touched by Toronto it has been impossible to interpret it with the theological tools to hand. In a way Toronto has been an abyss of primordial experience – a disintegration of liturgical and Biblical norms. Many who looked into the abyss have abandoned Charismatic affiliations altogether. Peter Fenwick, for example, respected elder statesman from the Sheffield House Church, sees Toronto as Pentecostalism gone mad. Others, such as Clifford Hill, sociologist and prophet, see the whole thing as an omen of disaster. Former enthusiasts for Toronto, such as Holy Trinity Brompton, are now concentrating on *Alpha* courses as God's direction for the future.[57] John Wimber has disowned Toronto and excommunicated John Arnott, pastor of the Toronto Vineyard Church. Some people, somewhere, are still falling over, giggling, and feeling blessed, but the momentum of the movement is passing. The craze, like modernity, seems to be fading with a final gasp.[58]

But in many ways Toronto can be seen as the logical outcome of recent Charismatic developments. Over the last ten years Charismatic Christianity has drunk deeply at the well of modern cultural forms: the 'clinics' of John Wimber; the concern with inner healing; the endless in-house entertainment of conference, convention and celebration – for all the world like a spiritual equivalent of the rave culture. No longer restrained by fundamentalist edicts, or the mainline theology of writers like Anglican Tom Smail and Catholic Steve Clark,[59] Charismatic Christianity increasingly appears fey and orphic.[60]

[57] *Alpha* is a course of Christian initiation, not dissimilar to the early Church catechumenate but with the expectation that it will lead on to personal conversion and perhaps the Baptism in the Spirt.

[58] This seems to have led to two reactions; either waiting for the next big wave of revival, or realizing that Toronto is a bridge too far and retreating into a more 'business as usual' (normative) Pentecostalism.

[59] See T. Smail, *The Giving Gift* (London: DLT, 1995) and S. B. Clark, *Redeemer* (Ann Arbor, MI: Servant Press, 1992).

[60] One of the themes of Harold Bloom in his *The American Religion: The Emergence of the Post Christian Nation* (New York: Simon & Schuster, 1992).

When all is said and done as we near the end of the twentieth century the defining theologian of the Charismatic movement will turn out not to be a Jonathan Edwards, a Charles Hodge, or even a Charles Parham: they were all too constrained within the bounds of historic orthodoxy. The theological father of the movement will turn out to be none other than the father of modern liberal theology, Friedrich Schleiermacher, who in rebelling against German rationalism and classical theology arrived at a religion of feeling and God consciousness which he managed to meld with the pietism of his Moravian background. Charismatic Christians have not formally followed Schleiermacher for he is associated with liberalism but they have unwittingly followed his direction because of their growing tendency to allow experience to become the touchstone of orthodoxy.[61] This touchstone is not a return to New Testament Christianity, as is believed, but a thoroughly late-modern concern with the self and its satisfaction.

Pentecostalism rushed into the twentieth century like a hurricane at Azusa Street, Los Angeles, in 1906. Perhaps it finally blew itself out at Toronto Airport in 1994. Azusa Street acted as a beacon to enthusiasts from many countries: pastors and church leaders came to see the revival for themselves and through them the Pentecostal blessing was diffused and distributed throughout the world. Toronto has repeated history in this respect but because of air travel and the Internet the diffusion has been far quicker – perhaps too quick to have a lasting effect. Churches take time to build up and establish themselves, but Toronto may have been merely a new experience in a dying modern world that treasures novelty for its own sake and craves signs and wonders as its daily fare.[62]

[61] Such a generalization probably does not hold across the board. I doubt if this is a fair assessment of Anglican Renewal Ministries, for example, nor the ecumenical movement associated with Fr Michael Harper and the Sword And The Spirit communities. And although this trend can be seen in many new churches it would be a distortion to say it is an accurate characterization of Ichthus communities and all those within the Pioneer network of churches.

[62] Although Professor William Abraham of Southern Methodist University and Dr Graham MacFarlane of London Bible College (both excellent scholars and men whose judgement I value) feel that Toronto, although a mixed blessing, has more to recommend it than I can see for the moment.

Conclusion

Neo-Pentecostalism has been more thoroughly modern than its classical counterpart but also more open to the cultural obsessions of late-modernity. I believe that classical Pentecostalism has on the whole been modern in a positive sense though more obviously so in South America and South Korea than in Europe and North America. At the very least Pentecostalism throughout the world has not only provided meaning and succour to its adherents but it has also equipped many of them with the values of ascetic Protestantism so useful to the modern enterprise, and so essential for social mobility in a capitalist economy.

Conversely, with the possible exception of the early Renewal movement, neo-Pentecostalism has overstressed self-experience and what Jung Ha Kim has called 'supply side spirituality'.[63] As modernity has waned this concern with the self and commodity religion has run the risk of becoming an indulgence if not a sinking into decadence. Arguably this decadence has infiltrated classical Pentecostalism, unleashing the narcissistic and irrational forces that were latently there but mostly kept under control.[64] But because of the pluralistic nature of late-modernity the inevitable syncretistic strands of a religion of experience have become increasingly volatile. Far from seeing Pentecostalism rushing into the new century with the force of the old I believe that it will be buffeted by theological confusion and social fragmentation.

If we follow Zygmunt Bauman[65] instead of Harvey and see the modern world not as decaying but as fading – in transition to a post-modernity – we must ask whether Charismatic Christianity is well equipped to survive in the future. Post-modernism not only eschews the metanarrative of rational discourse but it also distrusts the lordship of the self and inner experience. If the world emerges like Foucault's landscape, where reality is seen as a discursive achievement and the certainty of universal truths are denied, what will

[63] Supply side spirituality like supply side economics is a feature of an abundant or affluent ideology. A demand-side spirituality would be more concerned with the fight for justice and deliverance associated with the poor. See J. H. Kim, 'Sources Outside of Europe' in P. Van Ness (ed.) *Spirituality And The Secular Quest*, World Spirituality Series (London: SCM Press, 1996), p.63.

[64] Nowhere is this more obvious, in my opinion, than in the recent fascination with demons. See my chapter 'The Devil you Think You Know' in T. Smail, A. Walker and N. Wright, *Charismatic Renewal: The Search for a Theology* (SPCK new edn 1995, pp.86–105).

[65] See, for example, his *Intimations of Postmodernity* (London: Routledge, 1992).

Charismatic utterances mean? It mattered not in modernity if tongues were interpreted as babblings because they were seen to release or realize the self. But with the self on hold what will glossolalia come to signify? On the day of Pentecost xenoglossy was seen as a reversal of Babel – a time when charismata as gifts from God indicated His presence. Real presence – any wager on transcendence – as George Steiner has shown[66] is a problem in post-modern understanding. Given such a linguistic turn will xenoglossy and glossolalia[67] be a return to a new Babel where tongues will be seen as meaningless noise – a sign of absence – of the *deus absconditus* [departed God]?

We should, however, be careful not to confuse post-modernism as intellectual fashion with a genuine cultural shift to a post-modernity. 'Perhaps' I wrote recently, '... postmodernism is not the ideology of the future, of the Internet, mass culture and cultural pluralism. Instead it is the language of limbo; the go-between gossip of transition; the discourse of leave-taking, travelling from modernity to the not yet.'[68] If post-modernity turns out to be a new cultural era we can expect that it will share as many continuities with the past as discontinuities so there is no doubt that Pentecostalism will survive in the future. In the Third World, for some time to come, it will no doubt continue to be thoroughly modern. But in the post-industrial societies a different religiosity is likely to abound. It will be one that will not repudiate the past. Nor will future religion always be wanting God to be doing a 'new thing' which late-modern Charismatics have craved. A post-modern religion will certainly look for a 'form of life' and a narrative of belonging but it will not trust experience to be at the heart of things. It will be one that will open up to other living traditions. It will be one that will value story over feeling, narrative over experience, icon over text, prophecy over tongues.

In fact such a religion is happening right now under the nose of the Charismatic movement. Like a phoenix from the ashes the alternative

---

[66] G. Steiner, *Real Presences: Is There Anything In What We Say?* (London: Faber & Faber, 1989).

[67] Notwithstanding my earlier distinction between tongues as natural languages and ecstatic utterances, they are both treated in the New Testament as post-Pentecostal experiences.

[68] A. Walker, *Telling the Story*, op. cit. p.180.

liturgical movement is emerging from 'happy clappy Bappy' land, as the Revd Nick Mercer calls it,[69] and is merging with Celtic spirituality, Taize[70] chants, Eastern Orthodoxy, Reformed Theology, Charismatic happenings. Such a syncretistic mix may or may not end up Christian, as the Nine O' Clock Service[71] forewarns, but then neither will it any more be modern.

[69] Former vice-principal of London Bible College and now an Anglican priest in the liberal Catholic tradition.

[70] Taizé is a Roman Catholic community in central France, which is a magnet for pilgrimage, especially for young people, and the source of distinctive, simple worship chants in contemporary language.

[71] Under the leadership of the Revd Chris Brain, the Nine O'Clock Service moved from Wimber neo-Pentecostalism to Matthew Fox neo-Paganism. See R. Howard, *The Rise And Fall of the Nine O'Clock Service* (London: Mowbrays, 1996).

American Evangelicalism embattled*

CHRISTIAN SMITH

[M]odern American evangelicalism enjoys a religious vitality –
measured sociologically – that surpasses every other major Christian
tradition in the country. Whether gauged by belief orthodoxy,
salience of faith, robustness of belief, church attendance, participation in social and religious mission, or membership recruitment
and retention, the conclusion is the same: American evangelicalism is
thriving. [...] [A] variety of sociological theories [...] offer to explain
differences in religious strength in an effort to see which might best
interpret evangelicalism's strength. Some [are] more satisfactory than
others. Still, [...] none of the existing theories [are] entirely adequate
for explaining evangelicalism's vitality. We therefore [propose] an
alternative theoretical approach, which we call the subcultural
identity theory. It maintains, essentially, that religions can survive
and thrive in pluralistic, modern society by situating themselves in
subcultures that offer morally orienting collective identities which
provide their adherents meaning and belonging. Furthermore, our
theory suggests, in a pluralistic society, those religious traditions will
be stronger which better possess and utilize the cultural tools needed
to create both clear distinction from and significant engagement and
tension with other relevant outgroups.

This chapter uses the subcultural identity theory of religious
strength to interpret evangelicalism's striking religious vitality,
relative to fundamentalist and, especially, mainline and liberal
Protestantism. So as not to belabor what is already well known, we
begin by simply acknowledging the fact – without spending words to
document it – that evangelicalism has constructed for itself a
distinctive religious subculture. We also simply recognize that this
subculture sustains a distinctive Christian collective identity which

*This text first appeared in *American Evangelicalism Embattled and Thriving*,
Christian Smith, with Michael Emerson, Sally Gallagher, Paul Kennedy and David
Sikkink, Chicago and London: University of Chicago Press, 1998, pp.120–53.

serves as a primary source of individual identity, if not as a master status, for those who believe and participate in the subculture. Anyone familiar with evangelicalism is aware of these points. In other words, we will not primarily concern ourselves here with applying or evaluating the subcultural identity theory of religious *persistence*. Rather, we concentrate on employing the subcultural identity theory of religious *strength* to interpret evangelical vitality. Our analysis below suggests that evangelicalism utilizes its culturally pluralistic environment to socially construct subcultural distinction, engagement, and tension between itself and relevant out-groups and that this builds religious strength. Evangelicalism, we contend, flourishes on difference, engagement, tension, conflict, and threat. [...]

[E]vangelicalism's conspicuous vitality is not the result of any protective social, demographic, or geographical distance from, or fundamental accommodation to secular modernity. Rather, its strength results from the combination of its socially constructed cultural distinction vis-à-vis a vigorous sociocultural engagement with pluralistic modernity.

Constructing distinction, engagement, and conflict

Distinction, engagement, and conflict vis-à-vis outsiders constitutes a crucial element of what we might call the "cultural DNA" of American evangelicalism. The evangelical tradition's entire history, theology, and self-identity presupposes and reflects strong cultural boundaries with nonevangelicals; a zealous burden to convert and transform the world outside of itself; and a keen perception of external threats and crises seen as menacing what it views to be true, good, and valuable. These, we maintain, go a long way toward explaining evangelicalism's thriving.

Viewed in historical context, one can go to virtually any point in American evangelical history – but particularly beginning with the latter third of the nineteenth century – and readily detect in its elite discourse a sense of crisis, conflict, or threat. In all cases, the perception of crisis serves to invigorate and mobilize evangelical vitality rather than to undermine or disintegrate it. Examples, beginning with the Puritan jeremiads (Bercovitch 1978) and running through to the present day, are innumerable. [...]

American evangelical elite discourse charged with a similar sense of engagement and apprehension can readily be found in almost any historical time period. After reading enough of these narratives, one begins to develop the distinct sense that evangelicalism actually feeds upon such engagement, tension, and crisis for its own vitality.

But concern with difference, engagement, conflict, and threat is not limited to evangelical elites. Ordinary evangelicals socially construct reality using the cultural tools of the very same tradition, though in perhaps less intellectualized or entrepreneurial ways. Here we examine in greater detail some of the more prominent features of distinction, engagement, and conflict embedded in the evangelical subcultural worldview, features which help constitute the core sensibilities of the preponderance of ordinary contemporary evangelicals.

A sense of strong boundaries with the non-evangelical world

Evangelicals operate with a very strong sense of boundaries that distinguish themselves from non-Christians and from nonevangelical Christians. Evangelicals know who and what they are and are not. They possess clear symbolic borders that define the frontiers beyond which one is not an evangelical. The implicit distinction between "us" and "them" is omnipresent in evangelical thought and speech, so much so that it does not often in fact draw to itself much attention. Yet it subtly and profoundly shapes evangelical consciousness and discourse. No good evangelical operates without this distinction in their cultural toolkit.

Consequently, evangelicals would never accept the minimizing or erasing of distinction between the Christian and non-Christian [recommended by] some mainline and liberal Protestants. [...] Indeed, when evangelicals use the word "Christian," most likely they are instinctively meaning *evangelical* Christian – or some approximation thereof; such as "real," "born again," or "genuine" Christian, as they might alternatively say. Generally, all of the others, including liberal and mainline Protestants, Roman Catholics, Jehovah's Witnesses, Mormons, and various participants in what some evangelicals call "cultural Christianity" are spoken of as Christian only as a broad religious classification (as opposed to Muslims or secularists, for example). But they are usually not what evangelicals are talking about when they say "Christian" in ordinary parlance. For well-known boundaries distinguish, in their own minds, evangelicals as the real or most faithful kind of Christians from all of the rest. Not that evangelicals are overtly conceited or imperious about it. To the contrary, so pervasive and natural are these identity borders that mark the evangelical identity from others that few of the evangelicals we interviewed seemed even aware of their operation.

Evangelical boundaries with other types of Christians are most often drawn using the all-important symbolic markers of a "personal relationship" with Jesus Christ and obedience to the authority of the Bible. Those lacking the former or disavowing the latter are seen as out of proper identity-bounds. For example, this evangelical Anabaptist man explained, "Being an evangelical, I guess, separates me from the average person that would go to a Protestant church that may not personally have a personal relationship or personal commitment to Christ. The word evangelical to me emphasizes that there is a personal faith, which you may not find in a mainline denomination." Alternatively, this Baptist woman stated, "In terms of liberals, I wouldn't identify myself with someone who doesn't recognize Jesus as the son of God, as both divine and human, or with those who don't see Scripture as the basis of authority." This evangelical Presbyterian man elaborated the point this way:

> There is a distinction between what I would call mainstream Christianity – many of the larger mainline denominations – and an evangelical church. One of those distinctions would be that evangelicals try to maintain a biblical worldview following the inerrant Scriptures. But other churches sometimes ordain clergy who are clearly practising what the Scripture calls sin, and have no remorse or intention of stopping. First thing I look for in a church is their stand on Scripture. Do they see scripture as God's word? Does the preaching follow that principle?

In these ways, evangelicals draw powerful distinctions between themselves and Christian "others."

Evangelicals also maintain a clear sense of the difference between "Christians" (themselves) and "the world." Evangelicals do not spend a lot of time talking about what is "worldly," mostly because such discourse has been characteristic of separatistic fundamentalism, and evangelicals want to maintain strong boundaries between themselves and such fundamentalists. However, evangelicals are keenly aware that something out there – "the world" – exists, that they stand in opposition to that something, and that they have an obligation to interact with it redemptively. Actually, "aware" may be an overstatement, for distinction with the world is something more consistently lived and breathed by evangelicals, than consciously contemplated. However, its very unassuming nature makes this difference all the more powerful. Evangelicals may not always contemplate their distinction from the world, but they consistently feel it in lived experience. Confused mainliners and liberals may puzzle the question, "Huh? What do you mean 'the world?' This is the world. We are the world." But evangelicals are not confused. They know that out there is an "other" that is fundamentally not who or what they are.

Distinction from "the world" weaves in and through all evangelical talk. While explaining how she has had to sacrifice the acceptance of her own parents and siblings and financial security for being a Christian, this Bible Fellowship woman concluded, "But we are very strong in saying '*we're us.*' We use that with the kids, too, when they want to imitate the world and do things or have things or go places they can't – and we have to say we don't operate according to other people's standards, we operate according to our own." This Baptist man shared: "There are a lot of pressures that we as Christians feel in society because of the values the world espouses today. Look at the pressure to go to the movies that are riddled with sex and unbearable language – that creates real problems and pressures for Christians." And this woman who recently helped to found a nondenominational Charismatic church concluded her discussion about the spiritual dangers of wealth and intellectual pride with the observation, "There are so many things in the world that could become a stumbling block to us, but Jesus forewarns us not to let those things become our god." Evangelicals rarely speak of "the world" as something to escape; rather almost always as something to be present in and engaged with, but not mastered by. [...]

A sense of possessing the ultimate truth

For many moderns, not to mention postmodernists, the idea of Truth with a capital "T" has become problematic. The belief that there exists objectively an unchanging foundation or standard that applies to everyone simply feels too narrow, too absolutist, too old-fashioned to maintain comfortably. Not so for evangelicals. American evangelicals believe not only that an unchanging and universal Truth exists, but – more audaciously, perhaps – that *they* are the ones who know it because God has revealed it to them. On this basis, the Carl Henries[1] of the world speak of the "fixed truths and shared values," which they know and hold, as the only solution to society's problems.

Most of those we interviewed simply presumed knowledge of the Truth. In a discussion of politics, for example, this man from a Holiness church mentioned as an aside, "I find that a lot more non-Christians are not principled because they don't have a foundation for truth, everything is relative." However, some, such as this Pentecostal

---

[1] Carl Henry is described earlier in the chapter as 'one of the leading lights of the modern evangelical movement'.

woman, argued the point more explicitly: "Do you just make up your own rules and as long as they seem okay to you then they're fine? No, there are essential truths that apply to all of humanity, because we were all created by God, and his truth is truth." She continued:

> Relativism is a problem, where everyone does their own thing and makes up their own rules and there are no absolute truths or values, and that it is thought anti-intellectual to believe otherwise. Christians need to be equipped to have answers to that, to learn, to study the issues, to know God's word, to be bold and speak out and not be intimidated, and impact the culture. Because we have the truth.

When asked how Christians ought to relate to believers of other religions, this Christian and Missionary Alliance man said, "We should speak the truth. There is only one standard, only one God, and one true path. These people will eventually come to the truth because it is the truth." And to the same question, this Holiness woman stated, "We as Christians have to understand that we have the answer. At the same time, that really offends people when you say you have the only way. We just need to let the truth speak for itself." In fact, most evangelicals are not particularly arrogant or triumphantistic about their belief in knowing the ultimate Truth. For evangelicals, it is merely a basic, if wondrous, fact of life that they have received the Truth. What our interviews revealed about evangelicals' beliefs about knowing the Truth, our survey data substantiate: in table [1], we see that evangelicals, compared with all other groups, are by far most likely, for example, to believe in the existence of absolute, unchanging standards as the basis for morals.

Epistemological and moral relativism leave everyone in the same condition – deprived of absolute foundations – and so tend to highlight commonality. But the belief in having come to understand the ultimate Truth necessarily creates distinction between those who know and believe and those who do not. The most extreme expression of this distinction is the traditional Calvinist doctrine of double predestination: some are chosen for heaven, and some for hell. But most evangelicals operate with a much less predetermined, though not a less surely believed and experienced, distinction between the children of light and the children of darkness. And this boundary, this identity distinction, is not seen as merely theological, but as spiritual and, ultimately, eternal.

A sense of practical moral superiority

Evangelicals also believe that their practical way of life, their morality, their functional standards – which are seen as deriving directly from the ultimate Truth they understand – simply "work" better than anybody else's. On this point, evangelicals are pragmatists. They believe God has created reality in a certain way and that those whose moral practices violate that reality will unavoidably suffer frustration, malfunction, and, ultimately, spiritual death. To use a typically evangelical type of illustration, it is like driving on the highway: those who observe the rules of the road get where they want to go; those who do not get into accidents. This woman from a nondenominational church said it plainly, "I feel sad about things today, because I believe so strongly that a faith in Jesus as Lord and adherence to a Christian lifestyle is the best and healthiest state to be in. And I think that some of our social problems arise from a cultural drift away from a Christian norm in the past two or three decades." Or as this Charismatic woman remarked, "Sure Christians have answers to today's social problems. Go to the Bible and get your answer. Most definitely."

Table [1] illustrates the consequences of this view. Evangelicals are much more likely than any other group to believe that Christian morality should be the law of the land, even though not all Americans are Christians. Conversely, evangelicals are the least likely to agree that people should be able to choose their own moralities, even if they are not Christian moralities. And when it comes to the concrete issue of moral instruction in public schools, evangelicals – even if only a minority – are the most likely to believe that schools should teach distinctively Christian morals. Most of the reasoning behind these attitudes is not a craving for cultural dominance, but a sincere belief that everyone would simply be better off following God's ways. This woman from a nondenominational church, for example, explained, "Based on certain absolutes in the Word of God, there are ways that people can function and live that resolve a lot of things. If you are really giving yourself to loving your neighbor as yourself; it's going to be real unlikely that you are going to pull a pistol out of your pocket to resolve a dispute." This man from an independent Charismatic church spelled out that logic in greater detail:

> The Bible offers the solution. Talking about abortion and teen pregnancy, if you save yourself for marriage, you won't have teen pregnancy. Then your abortion rate is going to drop. You apply Thou Shalt Not Kill to your life, then you aren't going to have people out here murdering and killing. The solution is for people to live up to the morality that God has laid out in the Bible.

[...]

Not all evangelicals are this optimistic. Some more readily admit that Christianity may not have all the answers. Yet, even in the speech

Table [1]: Beliefs about Morals and Values, by Tradition (percent)

	Evangelicals	Fundamentalists	Mainline	Liberals	Catholics	Nonreligious
Believe morals should be based on absolute, unchanging standards	75	65	55	34	37	15
Christian morality should be the law of the land, even though not all Americans are Christians	62	58	45	34	23	10
People have the right to live by their own moralities, even if they are not Christian moralities	59	64	64	75	77	–
Which morals should be taught in public schools?						
Christian morals	19	17	9	9	9	1
General morals	52	49	61	59	67	61
Teach morals at home	30	34	30	32	24	38
How different should Christians' values and lifestyles be from the rest of American society?						
Very different	74	61	46	32	–	–
Somewhat different	17	23	29	32	–	–
A little different	3	5	5	10	–	–
Not different	6	11	20	27	–	–
N	(430)	(389)	(576)	(431)	(114)	(60)

Note: Chi-square for all figures is significant at the .0000 level.

of these more doubtful evangelicals, like this Presbyterian woman, a sense of practical moral superiority remains evident:

> I don't think we are ever going to be able to answer all the social problems we have in today's world. To think that we can is egotistical. I think that the difference between us and a secular social worker is maybe we have 75 percent success and they have 25 percent success. Because we can show people Jesus. I don't think there is any other answer than that. A changed life is the only way to change this world.

This believed moral superiority has the important consequence for evangelical consciousness of creating a distinction between those seen as trying to live godly lives and those who are not similarly committed. On the one hand are Christians living as God intended people to live. On the other hand are the indifferent, the rebellious, the promiscuous, the selfish, the backsliders. It is very important to recognize here, however, that what evangelicals generally view as superior is not their own behavior, per se – which would constitute "works-righteousness," a serious evangelical sin – but the moral standards themselves that God has established. For this reason, despite the not infrequent appearance of a rather arrogant moral posture, evangelicals are not particularly morally pompous people. They simply believe that, practically speaking, the way God calls people to live is good for everybody, whether humans like it or not. Hence, even when evangelicals admit to moral failure themselves – which they readily do – the distinction in their consciousness between the narrow road that leads to life and the broad road that leads to destruction remains intact. What matters then is simply that they, by God's grace, get themselves back on the narrow road. But the distinction between the two roads is never blurred.

A sense of lifestyle and value distinctiveness

Evangelicals see themselves as living an aberrant way of life from that of the surrounding world. If evangelicals ever viewed themselves as belonging to the cultural mainstream, they do not much think so any longer. Rather, evangelicals see themselves as embracing traditional, common-sense values in a broader culture that has abandoned them in pursuit of narcissistic, licentious, and self-destructive values and lifestyles (see Wacker 1984). On television, in schools, on the news, and at work, evangelicals see and hear a set of values and lifestyle commitments that feel to them fundamentally alien and inhospitable. Thus, evangelicals, like this Baptist man, are increasingly becoming aware of themselves as peculiar, as different, as strangers in their own land: "Strong, Bible-believing evangelical and fundamentalist

Christians are in the minority in this society. There has to be some standards, but I certainly don't think our society any longer has the Bible as a standard. I feel constantly under attack through the media and through the workplace." Similarly, this woman who attends an independent "seeker-church" said, "We're almost a persecuted group, to some extent. The apostles all lived in the same kind of society, a small group within a larger secular society. That's the same position we Christians are in." Likewise, this woman who attends a Covenant church remarked:

> I work in a public university environment which is very secular. I only know one or two other Christians there. And the perception of people in the university environment is that Christians are radicals and nonthinkers. And so I do feel very different. But I also feel like, "I'm not the way you characterize me."

Having rejected the fundamentalist strategic option of isolationist separation, however, evangelicals feel compelled to struggle to remain involved with and relevant to the emerging mainstream American culture. But they do so keenly aware of their difference from it. Hence, according to the results in table [1], evangelicals, far and above those of any other Protestant tradition, including fundamentalists, believe that Christians' values and lifestyles should be very different from the rest of American society. This self-consciousness about difference shone through in our interviews in a variety of ways. Some, like this Lutheran woman, characterized a Christian's distinctiveness as a matter of commitment and selflessness in relationships:

> I can tell Christians from non-Christians real clearly. The best example comes from my experiences with friends who are non-Christians, who end up in divorce court over small problems. Instead of working it through as a family, they say, "I'm leaving." So the biggest thing I find is that non-Christians are more "me"-oriented than "we"-oriented.

Others, like this Pentecostal woman, focus more on trying to please God by obeying God's will:

> You know we're in the world, but we're not supposed to participate in things that are of the world. When I used to be a thief, I didn't desire the things of God. But now I desire to walk with him, to please him. I don't drink, I don't pollute my body, I don't sleep around. Because that's what the Bible says. You know what I mean?

And still others, such as this Charismatic woman, pointed more to subjective attitudes and emotions she thinks should set Christians apart:

> It's a peacefulness. People in this world are very confused, tense, stressed out, and looking for peace. You can have money, a family, everything, but if you don't have peace, you are not going to be capable of structuring your life in this world. But I know people who have given themselves to Jesus Christ and have found peace. You know, the stress of the world doesn't bother them.

But however evangelicals construct difference from the world, most affirm it as a good sign, believing that faithful Christians will naturally be different from non-Christians. As this man who attends a nondenominational Bible church said, "When I go to work in a secular environment, I feel that I don't fit in. Which is the way it should be." In yet another way, then, evangelicals' lifestyle and value distinctiveness creates significant distinction, engagement, and even conflict – in their own minds, at least – between themselves and outsiders.

A sense of evangelistic and social mission

[An] influential presence in the evangelical subculture [is] an "evangelical burden" of responsibility to evangelize the world and ameliorate its social and political needs. [...] [E]vangelicals generally view no sphere or activity of life as outside of God's redemptive plan. As this Baptist woman remarked, "We need to love in the midst of all this hate and be strong in our convictions and ethics and morals and laws based on the Bible. They should show through our lives. Everything down to taxes or business dealings or kids in school, whatever – the world should be able to see it." Again, our survey evidence confirms this view. Table [2] shows that, comparatively speaking, evangelicals are extraordinarily likely to believe that religion is not a private matter but that it appropriately belongs as a voice in public debates over social and political issues (also see Regnerus and Smith 1998). And in their social activism, evangelicals are, among Protestant groups, the most prepared to exert an influence in a way that they know may cause tension and conflict. Furthermore, according to table [2], evangelicals are the least likely to try hard not to offend other people with their Christian views. Altogether, we see evangelicalism as a tradition firmly committed to a vigorous evangelistic and social mission.

This construction of determined social responsibility toward the outside world works, again, to create distinction between the agents and the recipients of the work of evangelical mission. The very structure of thought, evident in this Presbyterian woman's statement, clearly differentiates the missionaries from the missionized – when

Table [2]: Beliefs about Cultural Engagement, by Tradition (percent)

	Evangelicals	Fundamentalists	Mainline	Liberals	Catholics	Nonreligious
Religion is a private matter that should be kept out of public debates over social and political issues	25	33	48	61	62	84
Christians need to try to change society using ways they know may cause conflict or set people against each other	37	31	28	23	–	–
Tries hard not to offend people with their Christian views[a]	67	76	72	75	–	–
N	(430)	(389)	(576)	(431)	(114)	(60)

Note: Chi-square for all figures is significant at the .0000 level, except [a]prob. = .082.

"mission" is directed toward the "unchurched" – the ones who have something to give from those perceived as needing to receive:

> Sometimes I get really excited because I think we have a lot to offer people in a broken world. I know I do. From battered women in my neighborhood, to searching college students I work with, to musicians I play with. God has created us for people who are searching for truth. It's exciting to think I'm out there, even though it's really a difficult place to be. Being a Christian isn't an easy thing and I don't know the easy answers. And I have some very close friendships with people who have completely different belief systems. Sometimes it's really hard to connect with them. But it's important.

Organized evangelical ministries designed for "outreach" work are not frequently distinguished by a strong sense of humble reciprocity with those ministered to, although individual evangelicals in ministry often may be so. More typically, an "us" and "them" mentality prevails, often along with a certain un-self-critical paternalism.

But the evangelical burden creates more than distinction. It prompts evangelicals to work hard to spread their faith. To start with, many evangelicals view themselves as constantly on-stage, being scrutinized, so that they must always be a good "witness." For example, after describing in detail ways that Christians should work to be different from the world in order to influence it, this Congregational man concluded, "A lifestyle that is first of all plugged into God and then into our society can make a difference in ways we don't even notice. People will be watching." Specifically, this Congregational man advocated:

> Humility. Being really sacrificial, especially with our time. Setting aside our materialism and living simpler lifestyles. Those things really go against the grain of what the world out there is seeking. I think they look to people who are really noticeably different by their choice of words, the way they live, their lifestyle, what kinds of things they think of. And prayer, setting aside time for intercessory prayer for others, allowing God to change us so that when we get out there we have a different quality of spirit that is apparent to others. We can be more patient, have a greater love, show a lot more self-control when we pray, when the Word of God penetrates our souls. Otherwise we will be out there acting exactly like everybody else, and we wouldn't make a difference.

[...]

Many, such as this Baptist man, who was raised by an alcoholic single mother, strongly advocate not only setting good examples, but also direct evangelization:

> Christians need to share their faith in Jesus Christ in direct testimony without being embarrassed. I always look for the opportunity to share

something about my faith in Christ. I spent nine years doing real estate training for about 4,500 people. I always shared my testimony in one course module that was on positive, upbeat thinking, called "The Winning Attitude." I was able to share my past and how, through a personal relationship with Jesus Christ, my life and attitude have been changed.

The evangelical burden also drives evangelicals beyond personal evangelism to engage society at many levels to try to exert a positive Christian influence. The evangelical vision of engaged orthodoxy fosters a sense of involvement with, challenge from, and struggle on behalf of the outside world. There are friends and colleagues to influence, new ministries and programs to establish, the afflicted to be fed and comforted, and political offices to be filled with wise and godly leaders. All of this requires attention, mobilization, involvement, and persistence. This Baptist man's sense of calling to ministry in the public schools, for example, is archetypical of the evangelical mentality about active cultural engagement:

> We have consistently held that our children should be in public schools. If Christians want public schools to be the way they want them, then Christian children have to be there. I know full well my children are going to receive viewpoints and lifestyles that are clearly in opposition to what my family and I believe. But if we aren't there to present an alternative, people are not going to choose that alternative. In a way, it is a mini-mission field.

This statement exemplifies well the earnest and widespread evangelical sense of personal responsibility for the state of the world, evangelicals' keen awareness of their differences from the world, and their firm commitment nonetheless to engage the world to try to transform it. Below we will suggest that evangelicalism actually benefits from this engagement with what it views as an oppositional-but-needy world, as much or more as it thinks the world benefits from it. For now we need simply to observe that this "evangelical burden" has the practical consequence of continually exposing evangelicals to and involving them with their surrounding culture and society. Far from remaining distant or sheltered from modernity, evangelicals have earnestly embraced the idea of engaged orthodoxy and engrossed themselves in debate with, involvement in, and attempts at the reform of modern institutions and culture. Evangelicals really are, as they might say, "out there, where things are happening."

A sense of displaced heritage

Widespread among evangelicals is the belief that America was founded as a Christian nation, that America is now turning its back on its Judeo-Christian roots, that mainstream institutions are becoming increasingly anti-Christian, and that as a consequence America is in a state of moral and social degeneration. The view of this Baptist man is typical:

> America was founded on Christian principles. Some of our founding fathers were maybe immoral in some of their lifestyles, but they as a whole founded our nation on "one nation under God." They believed in a supreme being, in God Almighty, and they wanted our nation to espouse those values and beliefs. They put it into our Constitution, the Declaration of Independence, and on the currency. They made it an indelible imprint on our society.

And what about today? He continues, "Today it's shaky. Our nation is on the edge and falling from the true meaning of being a Christian nation. I think it's foundation is being eroded from way down deep." [...] This Charismatic evangelical woman concurs:

> America started really turning away from Christianity back when Darwinism and evolution came in. Then they took the Bible out of the schools, and ever since it seems like America has gone downhill. There used to be higher family values, higher morals, whereas today, you know, anything goes! Even twenty to thirty years ago it was quite different. It is gradually getting worse and worse and worse.

According to table [3], evangelicals, more than any other major Christian tradition, subscribe to this general view. Particularly striking are evangelicals' perceptions of hostility from the mass media, public schools, and feminism. In all cases, evangelicals are between one-third to almost three times more likely to view them as hostile to their own values and morals than are mainliners, liberals, Roman Catholics, and nonreligious Americans. Clearly, very many evangelical Christians are feeling displaced, marginalized, and denigrated in important sectors of the world they occupy. This nondenominational woman, for example, observed, "I think Christians are stereotyped and often dismissed as not having much intellectual capacity, if they adhere to a strong Christian viewpoint. I see it on your basic sitcom, you know? In the media, the entertainment industry, and journalism, Christians are almost always characterized in a negative way." [...]

For evangelicals, there is bitter irony in this. For in the view of many, it was precisely America's open commitment to its Judeo-Christian heritage that explains its prosperity and freedom. America is thought to have become great because it was founded on Christian

Table [3]: Beliefs about Cultural Displacement, by Tradition (percent)

	Evangelicals	Fundamentalists	Mainline	Liberals	Catholics	Nonreligious
America was founded as a Christian nation	92	84	90	72	79	60
Christian values are under serious attack today	92	88	82	65	—	—
View as hostile to own values and morals						
Mass media	76	72	57	46	47	42
Feminists	66	56	38	25	34	24
Public schools	57	52	35	29	23	20
We are seeing the breakdown of American society today	95	95	90	88	87	71
N	(430)	(389)	(576)	(431)	(114)	(60)

Note: Chi-square for all figures is significant at the .001 level.

principles, recognized God's laws, and fostered a Christian-based culture. But then, at the height of its wealth and power, the nation God blessed turned its back on God and displaced from their rightful place the carriers of the heritage to which it owes its success. From this perspective, America's shift to a post-Christian or, for some, anti-Christian culture reflects an ingratitude toward Christianity and ignorance of the workings of history. Nevertheless, few evangelicals express personal resentment about their perceived displacement. Most simply report feelings of sadness, disappointment, and frustration for and about America.

What makes the displacement of their heritage especially difficult for evangelicals, however, is their commitment to engaged orthodoxy, which means they may not simply withdraw and sulk in subcultural isolation. Instead, evangelicals feel compelled to remain involved in society, to engage the culture, to be "salt and light" to the world, and to transform it for Christ. Yet this puts evangelicalism in the position, essentially, of a spurned lover: evangelicals are forever passionately pursuing a culture which increasingly disregards and mistreats them. But the more they are spurned, the more evangelicals believe they need to pursue and influence the culture. Employing even the language of a troubled romantic relationship, this Baptist man maintains, "I think it would take something fairly catastrophic for America to be slapped in the face and realize that our nation has gone away from God, and if they would come back, things would get better." Pursuing a rejecting culture is a difficult task for evangelicals, but one to which they nevertheless appear fully committed.

A sense of second-class citizenship

One consistent theme we heard from the evangelicals we interviewed was their perception of a double-standard in American public discourse that discriminates against Christians. Time and again we heard evangelicals observe that every racial, ethnic, religious, political, and ideological perspective existing is given fair time and a fair hearing, *except* the Christian perspective. Instead, Christians' views are seen as routinely slighted, whether subtly or blatantly. And this feels like unfair discrimination, an unacknowledged infringement of freedom of speech. According to this Charismatic woman, "Schools have completely removed anything that has to do with Christianity or God or the Bible or any of that. And then they will let in books like *Heather Has Two Mommies*, real secular and anti-moral books." A few evangelicals, like this Presbyterian woman, said they thought some Christians may be partly to blame for creating prejudice against Christians as a whole: "I think many in mainstream society have been wounded by fundamentalist and some evangelical Christians who are not willing to love, who are judgmental. And they carry those wounds and act the same way, judgmental and isolationist." But most evangelicals thought it was simply unjustified discrimination for no good reason.

For some, perhaps many, evangelicals, this creates the feeling of being demoted to second-class citizenship, of being suppressed by a selectively liberal mainstream that lives in denial of that suppression. Many, such as this nondenominational woman, a certified public school teacher herself, see a double-standard in public schools, "Some teachers think it is inappropriate to explain at Easter time that people known as Christians believe in Jesus' resurrection – but they don't have any problem spending a month on Native American spirituality. Christianity is sometimes penalized because it was once the norm, but now is not. It is seen as something not to be addressed in any way in public schools." [...] According to this Presbyterian man:

> The state is involved in almost every facet of society, but with extreme interpretations of separation of church and state, the church is left out. I see it as a discrimination or bias. Even something like Americorp, the national service program, its regulations are written so that volunteers can't volunteer in any program with "sectarian bias." So other volunteerism is being subsidized, but Christian volunteerism is left out. Values are being tilted against Christians, in the name of neutrality.

[...]

A few respond with resentment and anger, but most simply feel frustrated and disappointed. What bothers evangelicals about this is not so much the element of personal offence but the duplicity of a culture which professes openness to all views and the concern that America has gotten so far off-track that it positively discriminates against Christians. According to this Baptist man:

> It frustrates and annoys me probably more tha[n] anything. It sometimes angers me, depending on a situation. I may become very frustrated over it, feeling like I want to react strongly and dogmatically. But I feel like I have to be careful in what I say. It does sometimes anger me when I see some of the news reporting on some issues – abortion, homosexuality, free sex. Those things disgust and frustrate me. I have a sense of, what really can be done to stem the tide?

Naturally, this perceived prejudice merely serves to heighten evangelicals' boundaries with the outside world, alienation from mainstream culture, and sense of displacement from their rightful

American heritage. The distinction, engagement, and conflict are only intensified.

(For some) a sense of menacing external threats

Finally, at the farthest extreme of cultural tension and conflict, some, but certainly not all, evangelicals see external threats even more menacing than a displaced heritage and demotion to second-class citizenship. More than a few evangelicals are concerned by what they believe are increasingly powerful, organized groups in America with clearly anti-Christian agendas. To be sure, some evangelicals express tremendous self-confidence and see no particular conspiracy set on undermining Christianity. However, other evangelicals do discern rumblings of what they fear could become a frightful future. And yet others, a definite minority, are convinced that the barbarians are already now battering down the gates.[2]

Some, such as this Baptist man, tend to view the issue in terms of social movements and politics: "Yes, I see groups that are hostile to Christianity, absolutely. The whole homosexual movement is extremely anti-Christian, and very hostile towards anybody who would espouse a Christian view. I think the pro-choice movement is extremely hostile towards Christians and Christian values, because they see their freedom of choice limited by the Christian belief that says life has meaning and value. So they are very strongly against Christian groups." Others – particularly Pentecostals, it seemed to us

---

[2] George Marsden (1980) has suggested that analytical leverage may be gained by thinking about early twentieth-century fundamentalism as functioning as an ethnic group. Interestingly, the subcultural-identity dynamics described above find similar expression in the experience of ethnic minorities in the context of less-than-hospitable majorities. First-generation immigrants, new minorities in a new country, for example, tend to strengthen their sense of ethnic identities (for a classic statement, see Hansen 1952). From the evangelical perspective, perhaps the closest ethnic analogy is with native Americans, who once "owned" North America, but who were invaded and marginalized by an alien culture and displaced from their own land. Interestingly, Cornell (1988) has shown that a "supra-tribal" consciousness and identity-movement – closely analogous to modern evangelic-alism's trans-denominational religious movement – first emerged in the 1950s, when the United States federal government began a "termination policy" that threatened to dismantle completely the reservation system, the last refuge of autonomous Indian life. That was precisely when astute native Americans first really began to think of themselves more as pan-tribal "Indians" than as members of disconnected, local tribes, as "Menominees" or "Cherokees." It took exactly such an external threat to mobilize a collective Indian identity and resources to counter the threat. The parallel with the evangelical experience is striking.

– like this Pentecostal woman, spoke more in terms of a spiritual battle between good and evil forces:

> I think there's a radical atheistic part out there, or your homosexuals, and the rest of them. As far as I know, those are the devil's people. I know they are. But they can be saved. Certainly, some are trying to turn America away from its Christian heritage. Certain radicals. Hey, we are in a battle here, you know, and the devil has his people. The Bible says it. "You are of your father, the devil," Jesus told somebody once. I'm talking about homosexual groups and atheist groups and the very liberal. We are in a spiritual battle on this earth. I see them as hostile and opposed to Christianity. And they try their best to get their laws passed. I am absolutely opposed to their beliefs, although I pray for them. Because they are just deceived by the devil, they don't know. Like I once was. I didn't know.

Throughout this interview, it was clear that many of this particular woman's views – which included conspiratorial theories about the Illuminati – were strongly influenced by Pat Robertson and his television program, *The 700 Club*. Yet others, such as this Presbyterian man, cast the battle more in terms of clashing ideologies and worldviews:

> There are two opposing views, a Christian worldview and a secular worldview. And one is going to be crowded out and denied their freedom to live by the standards they hold to. They might say "well just leave us alone," but the thing is they won't leave the Christian community alone. They are impinging on us. There is a war going on, and when you're in warfare, you battle to take ground, not just hold it. They're not just trying to hold ground, they are trying to take ground, which is our right to live in a Christian society. There are a lot of people that would deny us any rights. They aren't passive, they are active.

Summary

In these and other ways, modern American evangelicalism illustrates and corroborates the basic principles undergirding the subcultural identity theory of religion. Evangelicalism appears, indeed, to construct and maintain its collective identity largely by its members drawing symbolic boundaries that create distinction between themselves and relevant outgroups. It also appears that evangelicalism strategically renegotiates its collective religious identity by reformulating the way its constructed orthodoxy engages the changing sociocultural environment it confronts. For example, issues which in previous decades animated evangelical sensibilities – antimodernism, anticommunism, anti-Catholicism, sabbatarianism –

have been gradually supplanted by new, more culturally "relevant" issues: moral relativism, social decay, homosexual rights, etc. Yet, in this process of "accommodation," evangelicals appear no more or less cognitively contaminated or ideologically compromised – judged on their own terms – than they were in previous decades.

Modern American evangelicals are also clearly able to establish strong religious identities and commitments in the face of the inescapable modern fact that each individual can and often must choose their own religion. Evangelicals are aware of alternatives to their own version of faith; indeed they are aware that many others think differently from and even critically of them. Yet, this does very little to undermine their own beliefs and commitments. This evangelical self-confidence appears related to the evangelicals' ability to define their values and norms and to positively evaluate their identities and actions in relation to reference groups of other Christians with similar values of evangelical engagement with the "world"; indeed, the perceived dissimilar and antagonistic outgroups of nonevangelical Christians and non-Christians seem capable of serving evangelicals as negative reference groups. Evangelicals, in other words, have fashioned for themselves a very effective "sacred umbrella" under which to live. It is apparent that modern pluralism facilitates for evangelicalism conditions that promote the formation of a strong religious subculture, which sustains a self-perceived semi-"deviant" identity. Likewise, tension and conflict between evangelicals and relevant outgroups appear positively to strengthen evangelical identity, solidarity, resources mobilization, and membership retention. Finally these rapid sociocultural changes and the accompanying relativism that typify modernity clearly seem to increase for evangelicals the appeal of their own faith, which satisfies for them the felt needs and desires for stability, assurance, and truth – needs which modernity intensifies. Overall, the subcultural identity theory appears to render a fitting interpretation of modern American evangelicalism.

One caveat

We have emphasized here the distinction, engagement, and conflict that evangelicals construct in their relations with the outside world because we believe they provide an important key to understanding evangelical religious vitality. But we do not wish to leave the impression that evangelicals are essentially or primarily a defensive, frightened, wounded lot. With different purposes in mind, we could have highlighted much different elements of their stories.

We could have emphasized the contentment, openness, self-assurance, and joy that is also evident in evangelicals. We could have told of evangelicals who love rock-and-roll and opera, who have risen to positions of power in public universities, who operate in the world with warmth and amiability and broad-mindedness. The reality, of course, is complex and paradoxical. And all analytical interpretations actively frame and therefore necessarily simplify. Still, we think that the interpretation here is both descriptively accurate and analytically helpful. We only need to remember that to underscore certain real features of a movement or subculture for analytical reasons is not to tell all possible stories. It is simply to draw attention to one set of crucial factors that helps to answer one, specific question – ours being: what explains the vitality of contemporary American evangelicalism?

References

Bercovitch, Sacvan. 1978. *The American Jeremiad*. Madison: University of Wisconsin Press.

Cornell, Stephen, 1988. *The Return of the Native: American Indian Political Resurgence*. New York: Oxford University Press.

Hansen, Marcus L. 1952. "The Third Generation in America." *Commentary* 14: 492–500.

Marsden, George. 1980. *Fundamentalism and American Culture: The Shaping of Twentieth-Century Evangelicalism, 1870–1925*. New York: Oxford University Press.

Regnerus, Mark, and Christian Smith. 1998. "Selective Deprivatization among American Religious Traditions: The Reversal of the Great Reversal." *Social Forces* (forthcoming).

Wacker, Grant. 1984. "Speaking of Norman Rockwell: Popular Evangelicalism in Contemporary America." In *The Evangelical Tradition in America*, edited by Leonard Sweet, pp. 289–315. Macon, GA: Mercer University Press.

The explosion of Protestantism in Latin America*

DAVID MARTIN

The Latin American heirs of the Iberian empires have suffered cumulative political and economic defeat at the hands of the North American heirs of the British empire. To point this out is not in any way to detract from the greatness or richness of Hispanic civilization, nor is it to endorse yet another covert version of the 'Whig interpretation of history' tricked out with the vulgarities of Manifest Destiny. It is only to note an obvious and extremely important fact about the impact of contrasting cultural templates. There are 'crucial events' in the history of most, perhaps all, societies, which set the general tenor of their future and either circumscribe their options or open out their potentials. These are the donations of history, givens which point towards relatively persistent outcomes.[1]

The general tenor of North American political history was set by the cumulative and largely unreversed impact of the English Civil War from 1642 to 1660 and the 'Glorious Revolution' of 1688–9, which the American Revolution of 1774–83 then continued and considerably extended. In the economic field the tenor of North America also derived from Britain. The industrial revolution began in mid-eighteenth century Britain and was quickly picked up and later dramatically extended in the United States. Indeed, the United States developed a complete set of crucial processes which were initiated in the British Isles: political democracy, industrialism – and religious pluralism. To these should be added, as Claudio Veliz has argued, the

*This text first appeared in *Tongues of Fire: The Explosion of Protestantism in Latin America*, David Martin, Oxford: Basil Blackwell, 1990, pp.271–95.

[1] Seymour Martin Lipset, *Revolution and Counterrevolution* (London: Heinemann, 1969), ch. 1.

special impact of the English language and the English common law.[2] The importance of English language and law lies in the way they loosely accumulate rather than respond to centralized definition and control.

By contrast the tenor and texture of Latin American societies lacked all these elements. Even where parliamentary democracy was quite early established it eventually turned out to lack stability or staying power; religion remained a Catholic monopoly, and industrialism achieved only a partial or patchy penetration.

Such dramatically different historic profiles deriving on the one hand from the south-west European seaboard, and on the other hand from the north-west European seaboard, focused initially on religious difference. Whatever the subsequent salience of that religious difference, there have been continuous eruptions of geopolitical rivalry for four centuries. The rivalry intensified as an independent United States enthusiastically shouldered the imperial burden on its own account and either annexed parts of what Latins regarded as their historic patrimony or subjected Central and South American nations to preponderant economic power.

That is the long-term historical context within which the current overflow of evangelical religion from North to South America takes place. It is, moreover, the framework within which many Latin Americans still choose to see it, whether they happen to be old-style Catholic nationalists or intellectuals of the left. Accompanying the prolonged economic and political defeats and expropriations comes a cultural invasion spearheaded by religion. It is not necessary to endorse the nationalist or Marxist (or Marxist-nationalist) case to recognize the relevance of this rivalrous *longue durée* [rivalry extended over a long period of time]. In any case, the prevalence of the nationalist view is one of the facts of the current situation, providing an almost obligatory definition of Protestantism as the religious version of economic dependency or the religious guise of an alien, not to say inferior, culture. Latin Americans do not respond sympathetically to the kind of sentiment enunciated by President Bush in his acceptance speech at the Republican Convention in August 1988: 'We have whipped the world with our culture.'

But where exactly in the historic incubators of north-west Europe was the evangelical religion now crossing over from North to South America first generated? Where was this rich and potent trouble hatched? The answer is that the voluntarism [voluntary, independent religious activity, contrasting with the state-run churches that were

---

[2] Claudio Veliz, Personal Communication. Cf Claudio Veliz, 'A world made in England', *Quadrant* 187, Vol. XXVII, No. 3, March 1983, pp. 8–19.

then the norm] came about as part of the thrust of Calvinist reform in England, which also almost simultaneously crossed the Atlantic as one element in the founding culture(s) of British North America. Channels of religious independence (and sometimes also of religious 'enthusiasm') were dug on both sides of the Atlantic. These channels were to remain countercultural in England and to become the core of the future culture of America. Of course, the dissenting and fragmented mode stood a better chance of becoming central to America because it was supplemented by rival ethnic groups, especially in the middle colonies.

The establishment of voluntarism in both cultures is a familiar cliché, but however familiar it needs once again to be underlined as a world-historical event breaking up the age old unity of faith and community, church and state. Insofar as Britain and the USA have developed in somewhat different ways the difference turns to a discernible degree on the partial retention of the overarching framework in Britain and its collapse in British North America and the United States. The same goes for an associated phenomenon: the partial retention of the aristocratic ethos in England and its collapse in America.[3]

Another common element generated in the two versions of English social and religious culture was a religious election to political destiny, which offered a path through the wilderness and an entry into lands of promise. As in the matter of voluntarism so also in the matter of special political providence, the nascent culture of North America expanded and elaborated on its English original. John Milton [leading seventeenth-century English poet] was its most eloquent spokesman.[4] Political messianism passed from the English 'to the American strand', and entered into the founding myths and charters of 1776. Though the notion of providence still continued to help forward British expansion for three further centuries, it was never the *raison d'être* of national existence as it was in the United States. Part of the ontological security and confidence experienced by American evangelical missionaries in Latin America had its roots in this conception of special providence and in its partial mutation into the notion of progress. In this way messianic aspirations originally generated by seventeenth century England were able to pierce the ingrained superiorities of *Hispanidad* [the Spanish empire].

[3] Martin J. Wiener, *English Culture and the Decline of the Industrial Spirit, 1850–1980* (Cambridge: Cambridge University Press, 1981).

[4] Richard W. Pointer, 'Freedom, truth and American thought 1760–1810' in Ronald A. Wells and Thomas A. Askew, *Liberty and Law* (Grand Rapids, Mich.: Eerdmans, 1987), pp. 25–42.

The final shared Anglo-American incubation came about when eighteenth century revivalism poured along the channels of voluntary and independent religion dug more than a century before by classic Calvinist dissent. The roots of this revivalism are diverse. One major source was German Pietism, the small pious cells of intense and personal faith created by Spener[5] and his successors and by the Moravian fraternity. The evangelical revival in England combined influences from Pietism and from the Moravians, with movements for the reform of manners and reminiscences of high church piety, and these mingled and contended with a modified Calvinism. In British North America the Great Awakening(s) owed a great deal to a modified Calvinism, but much of the power generated by the Awakening(s) eventually flowed in a Methodist direction. The important point is that the channels of religious deviance were dramatically widened in both societies, creating a major channel of alternative religiosity in Britain and creating the main channel of religiosity in the United States.

What flowed in those channels was a voluntary, lay, participatory and enthusiastic faith. As on the mainland of continental Europe the groups it created might be quietist or activist, for or against established power, but the cultural logic of its forms was active, participatory, fissile, egalitarian and enthusiastic. In short, it represented an autonomous mobilization of mass-consciousness, transforming and energizing individual persons, and bringing about myriads of competitive voluntary networks for sharing and for mutual support. These networks might encompass such diverse activities as choral singing or inventing volleyball and basketball in the YMCA.

To put it in a[nother] way [...]: the prototypes of Pentecostal and evangelical religion now went into full cultural reproduction, ready for eventual transportation across the Rio Grande [the river that marks the frontier between the USA and Mexico]. That transportation would have to wait for some while until the same breakdown of overarching monopoly which occurred in seventeenth-century English culture on either side of the Atlantic occurred also in Latin America.

Whatever debate there may be about the details and the precise influences and sequences operating, there is little doubt that the initial creation of a voluntary, participatory and enthusiastic form of faith in England, and its realization in America, was the first and enormous step in the process of differentiation of spheres, whereby religion came increasingly to exercise its influence at the level of culture – and in discrete voluntary associations. The power of religion

[5] Philipp Jakob Spener (1635–1705), whose book *Pia Desideria* (1675) was a seminal influence on Pietists.

operated above all through its assumptions concerning the potency of individual initiative and concerning the centrality of personal experience and experiment, and from the political assonances of its organizational style. It offered the active popular supports or, minimally, the passive cultural residues above which small 'enlightened' elites might erect revolutionary structures.

It also acquired a dynamic adaptability which prevented the great cities of America becoming centres of secularity as they did in Europe and Britain. Because America lacked the association of *a* major religious institution with a class culture or cultures it was able to engender religious forms which could adapt to and reverse the anomic conditions of the city.[6] *Religion did not have to cope with a combination of anomic personal chaos and class alienation. To have reversed or at least nullified a major secularizing tendency in this way suggests that tendency is contingent on certain circumstances, not a necessary aspect of universal processes. The reversal is important because the adaptations have been passed on to the varieties of Pentecostal and evangelical religion now expanding (for example) in the megacities of São Paulo and Seoul.*

[...]

The Americanization of Latin American religion?

Before this question can be properly addressed it is necessary to recapitulate and to step back to survey the whole social panorama. In Latin America, religion and the social fabric have been woven together as one, at the level of the state and the level of the local community, so that for over three centuries the continent was shut off from outside religious influence. What is now occurring is the rapid acceleration of a process of break-up which began anything from seventy to one hundred and forty years ago. This same process occurred almost four centuries ago in English cultures on both sides of the Atlantic, and it proceeded by relatively easy accretions of free social space. In Latin America today it proceeds with great speed and considerable violence.

In the technical language of sociology Latin American society is undergoing the differentiation which occurred much earlier and more slowly in 'Anglo' society. This process would have occurred independently of the earlier influence of Britain or the later influence of the United States, though, of course, those countries provided

---

[6] Rodney Stark and Roger Finke, 'Religious economies and sacred canopies: religious mobilization in American cities, 1906', *American Sociological Review* 53 (March 1988), pp. 41–9.

models for the protagonists of change, and by reason of their power and progress brought Latin America within the scope of their cultural radiation.

However the opening up of free space through the process of differentiation is always problematic. In the Catholic (or Latin) societies of southern Europe the monopolistic nature of Catholicism has inhibited differentiation and has tended to give rise to rival secular monopolies under the aegis of the state, some of them promoted by radical liberals, some by communists. These monopolies have mirrored Catholicism in their comprehensiveness, and there has been a war between the old and new kinds of monopoly lasting from 1789 to 1960. Even in northern Europe, the comprehensive national churches have given rise to centralized secular structures and pervasive ideologies. Social Democracy in Scandinavia is (or has been) comprehensive in its scope. In Britain, of course, there was a long tradition of religious voluntarism and an accepted area of free space, but the state church did after all remain in place and subsequent structures of communication and education like the BBC, have mirrored its comprehensiveness.

Wherever religious monopolies had historically been powerful in Europe there were persistent movements of comprehensive reintegration, especially in times of strain, some of the left, some of the right, some violently opposed to religion, some combined with it.

In general the patterns most characteristic of southern Latin Europe were replicated in Latin America, in particular movements of radical secularism, of radical populism and clero-fascism [fascist movements linked to the clergy]. Britain and America remained relatively free of these movements, though not entirely so, especially in the 1930s.[7]

Thus the creation of free space was by no means the inevitable result of differentiation and of the break-up of age-old monopolies exercised by state religion. On the contrary, more often some form of reintegration was quite likely, under the comprehensive aegis of secular ideology, or else society would be distracted by struggles between the old religious monopoly and the hegemonic ambitions of the new. However, these reintegrations or struggles did not occur where religious voluntarism had been most firmly established and the monopoly and/or the power of the centre most extensively undermined. Indeed, the extensive propagation of *voluntaristic* evangelical Christianity and such reintegrations or struggles were

---

[7] Cf. Michael Billig, *Fascists* (London and New York: Harcourt Brace Jovanovich, 1978); David J. O'Brien, *American Catholics and Social Reform* [chapter 7 on Father Coughlin] (New York: Oxford University Press, 1968).

mutually incompatible. Continental Europe and Latin America remained impervious to this kind of Christianity and the Anglo-cultures of the North Atlantic remained impervious to the reintegrations and the struggles. A free, voluntaristic evangelical Protestantism is creature and creator of free social space.

If this analysis holds then it is possible to re-state what is currently happening in Latin America and then to approach the vexed and vexatious problem of Americanization. In Latin America, as in Latin Europe, the spirals of repulsion between militant secularism and Catholicism are unwinding, but in Latin America this disengagement takes place after a shorter period of struggle. Only in one or two quite small countries – Uruguay for example – has militant secularism under the aegis of the state gained control. In many countries, above all perhaps Brazil, the church has been weakened by radical governments (and/or by long periods of co-option) but the culture itself has not been secularized. However much the church has been weakened, religious understandings remain pervasive. Indeed, Brazilian culture retains a complete and free-floating atmosphere of 'spiritism'.

Now, at precisely this juncture Latin American societies have been exposed to the economic power and cultural radiation of the United States at the height of its world ascendancy. This cultural radiation includes the voluntaristic evangelical religion central to the original emergence and to the continuance of the United States. *This means that two patterns of secularization once mutually exclusive have crossed to bring about a distinctive new pattern.* In Europe the north-western pattern of Britain and the south-western pattern of Spain remained distinct; in the Americas they have mixed together. The confluence is as dramatic and revolutionary as it is unexpected. In the earlier phases of North and South American contact, it looked as if evangelical religion would simply remain as a minor element alongside other militantly anti-Catholic movements, whether political or religious. It took a minor role alongside freemasonry, positivism, and the 'societies of thought', and in general it seemed that Latin America would be as impervious to evangelical penetration as continental Europe has been.[8] That turns out not to be the case. *As the sacred canopy in Latin America is rent and the all-encompassing system cracks, evangelical Christianity pours in and by its own autonomous native power creates free social space.*

[8] Rosa del Carmen Bruno-Jofre, *Methodist Education in Peru: Social Gospel, Politics and American Ideological and Economic Penetration 1888–1930* (Waterloo, Ont.: Wilfred Laurier University Press, 1988).

Perhaps the process under examination can be rephrased in a simpler form. Suppose an 'advanced' socio-religious system to exist, as does the United States, representing a state of radical disarticulation. The adjacent civilization of Latin America is strongly articulated, and as that articulation collapses it is convulsed by violence. What then travels across from the United States as contribution to and consequence of that crisis is precisely the kind of powerful but fragmented and competitive religiosity bound up in the very emergence of 'Anglo' civilization. It will enter into the open spaces, simultaneously enlarging them and operating as a potent competitor within them. Given that it is a disarticulated form of faith, it cannot re-form the old monopoly in a new unified Protestant format, but is able to fructify solely at the cultural level.

However, so violent are the convulsions within the old monopolistic system, that it tries to recover lost unities either under the aegis of secular radicalism, as has been the case over long periods in Uruguay, or, as is more usual, under the aegis of a bureaucratic military dictatorship. Or both, including both together. The former is resistant to evangelical penetration; the latter may tolerate evangelical religion since it initiates change solely at the cultural level, and otherwise seeks to avoid being drawn into the polarities of political violence. Thus a faith originating in a radically disarticulated system can find itself located as a silent pillar of a rearticulated system, contingent precisely because of those radical origins. Nevertheless, its contingent and temporary political role is quite contrary to its cultural logic, and it is the long-term operation of that logic which will have to be expounded as this argument develops further.

Clearly, in the *special* sense just outlined, the influence of the United States is immense. Indeed, its influence is the precondition of the local empowerment since the fragmentation and the disarticulation inherent in American religion both imply autonomy. But the religious influence is only one aspect of a broader influence, economic, political and cultural. The religious traffic moves alongside the economic traffic, sometimes with the religious slightly ahead of the economic, and sometimes vice versa; sometimes in cooperation, occasionally in antagonism. The two kinds of traffic will have a family likeness: perhaps similar economic and political assumptions, certainly similar ideas, ideals, language, techniques, know-how and forms of communication and self-presentation. Yet none of this flow from North to South in any way depends on the specifically religious bridge, even though the religious bridge provides a definite reinforcement. The sign and symbol of this reinforcement may be the US-style supermarket at one end of the boulevard and the US-style church at the other end.

It is important to realize that Americanization is by no means limited to the expansion of evangelical Christianity. After all charismatic Catholicism began in North America. Again, the ordinary priesthood of the Latin American Church is partly drawn from abroad, and many of the partisans of liberation theology [a movement in theology that seeks to combine Catholic teaching with Marxist-inspired social radicalism] are from the USA. The business-like styles of promotion and organization found among evangelicals are also being adopted by the Catholic Church. Catholicism in Latin America is developing a committed active membership and entering into the religious competition with all the means of communication available to it. These are partly processes which belong to the autonomous development of South America, but they are speeded up and reinforced by the cultural traffic entering from the United States. You can attend mass in Rio and find yourself singing an offertory hymn to the tune of the Battle Hymn of the Republic!

So the Americanization that enters Latin America as one aspect of the incoming religious traffic reflects the reality of US cultural power in general. While the organs of nationalist opinion naturally and understandably inveigh against this, millions of simple folk simply want a share in the sources of US power whatever they may be. To put it in such a way is to make the transfer of power appear too direct and unmediated, but there are without doubt images of power behind the evangelical incursion. The aspiration for a better life, broadly understood, in terms of moral standards, economic prosperity, personal dignity, and health of body and mind, has some kind of US attachment, even though people simultaneously recognize that the United States is morally chaotic. Some commentators develop the theme of Americanization much further, and see evangelicals as really in the business of making Anglos out of Latins, in outward appearance and vesture as well as in inward disposition. If that is true of any group it is true of the Mormons.

The Latin Americanization of American religion?

There is no precise measure of the extent of North Americanization through evangelical faith, but it is important to stress the extent of the reverse process: the Latin Americanization of Protestantism. What historic Protestantism has lacked and still lacks is precisely the capacity to 'go native'. The first important instance of 'inculturation' occurred at the beginning of the century through the revival which brought about the Methodist Pentecostal Church of Chile. This has been the elusive goal sought by enlightened missionary endeavour over centuries, from the time of the controversy over Chinese rites, but the cost may well be less enlightenment, at least as understood by Europeans and North Americans. The total autonomy of Pentecostalism is part and parcel of its immersion in Latin American culture, and of its successful propagation by persons of roughly the same educational level as the apostles. The autocratic leadership and the partial retention of patronage networks is the other side of being a 'popular' movement in the Latin American context. To say that Pentecostalism reproduces some of the characteristics of *caudillismo* (authoritarian leadership) and of 'patriarchal relations' on the hacienda is to say that it lies close to the social roots. This is not in any way peculiar to Protestantism. Indeed, it is the incapacity of Protestantism hitherto to cross cultural divides and 'go native' that has historically given the edge to Catholicism or led to separatist native churches as in Africa. In all movements of religious conversion and change there is a dialectic of external influence and local adaptation. If local adaptation is insufficiently radical then conversions will be slow, though it must be said that the small community thus created may eventually be sustained and identified precisely by its distinctiveness.

The potent combination of external influence and radical local adaptation found in Pentecostalism is related to another characteristic source of power: the union of the very old and very modern. For example, it brings together the ancient layers of spiritism, in black Africa and indeed almost everywhere, with a modern sense of the union of psyche and soma. It brings together the ancient notion of illness as located in the community with the modern concept of community medicine. It unites the ancient layers of solidarity with the kinds of expansive organizational principles recommended by specialists in church growth. And the Pentecostal preference for stories, for gesture and oratory, belongs simultaneously to pre-literate and to post-literate society. Pentecostalism retains the participation found in the fiesta and unites that to a spiritual version of the contemporary encounter group.

Critical paths

Through what conduits, then, does evangelical religion most easily pass into the culture of Latin America? In the past, as already emphasized, it entered as a minor motif alongside other anti-catholic elements and was most influential through its welfare and educational agencies. Its path was eased wherever the Catholic Church was already weakened by state control or governmental antagonism and wherever people were mobile or had acquired a modicum of economic and social independence.

Nowadays, of course, the number of conduits has considerably increased and they carry vastly greater numbers of people. Protestantism may in one context gain attention and adherence among those who are at the margins of subsistence and are threatened by the advance of a market economy and the depredations of local caciques. In another context Protestantism may acquire a base among small independent producers who need to band together and who are determined to assert themselves, in particular by bypassing the Ladino middle-man. Everywhere it offers a network of mutual support which may include a variety of services: groups for female interaction and for training in some skill, a source of information and communication, access to helpful contacts, a brotherhood within which to initiate economic cooperation, reliable friends to help out at home while you are away, and other friends to offer you a second home. Often the converts are those who are already ill-at-ease in their customary roles and who have begun to move out into a wider world. They see in Protestantism a new milieu in which to take an active and independent part. For such people it provides an escalator for yet further movement, and a belief corresponding to their raised aspirations.

A major conduit for evangelical expansion is provided among minority ethnic groups who have either been passed over by Catholicism or suffered too much repressive attention. The smaller ethnic groups and tribes generally exist in the remoter forest and mountain regions, and evangelization is for them a dangerous introduction to the wider world, including the wider national community. Evangelization opens up these groups and quite often offers some modest protection against the more corrosive effects of modernity and internal colonialism. Depending on circumstances, missions may lead either to cultural and linguistic revitalization or to fragmentation and collapse. On occasion pastors and local visionaries become leaders in cultural defence and act as political go-betweens. Certainly these small groups are going to be brought within the scope and impact of modern communications, whether or not their initial contact takes place through missionaries rather than through traders and prospectors. They are not going to be kept in isolation just because they are needed for theses in anthropology.

So far as the larger ethnic groupings are concerned their openness to Protestantism depends on the depth of Catholic coverage currently provided, and on how far people perceive the priest as offering genuine personal concern and continuous local involvement. It also depends on how far Catholicism has been associated with distant and foreign overlordship, as in Peru, or even with massive repression. Once alienation of this kind exists whole tribes or villages may collectively decide to adopt a non-Catholic faith. Effectively they opt to reconstitute themselves as a new society, and with that total reorientation they may perhaps acquire a hospital, or a school, or other communal facilities.

By far the largest conduit for evangelical Protestantism is provided by the massive movement of people from countryside or hacienda to the mega-city. The new society now emerging in Latin America has to do with movement, and evangelicals constitute a *movement*. Evangelical Christianity is a dramatic migration of the spirit matching and accompanying a dramatic migration of bodies. In undertaking this migration, people become 'independent' not at all by building up modest securities but by the reverse: by the loss of all the ties that bind, whether these be familial, communal or ecclesial. Pentecostalism in particular renews these ties in an atmosphere of hope and anticipation rather than of despair. It provides a new cell taking over from scarred and broken tissue. Above all it renews the innermost cell of the family, and protects the woman from the ravages of male desertion and violence. A new faith is able to implant new disciplines, re-order priorities, counter corruption and destructive machismo, and reverse the indifferent and injurious hierarchies of the outside world. Within the enclosed haven of faith a fraternity can be instituted under firm leadership, which provides for release, for mutuality and warmth, and for the practice of new roles.

In this way millions of people are absorbed within a protective social capsule where they acquire new concepts of self and new models of initiative and voluntary organization. Even if they eventually leave the capsule they still carry the imprint of these possibilities, these concepts and these models with them. Thus the template of culture undergoes a process of constant revision by the passage of people through an alternative society – as well as by the emulation of that alternative which is forced upon the Catholic Church itself. *Influence consists not only in what X does but in what X forces Y to do.*

The crucial characteristic of evangelical Christianity in the vast urban agglomerations of Latin America is self-government. People are able to devise their own social world for themselves. And as these worlds expand numerically they gain a sense of latent power, which above all becomes manifest as they come together in vast public gatherings. The growing network of chapels represents a walkout from society as presently constituted. The evangelical believer is one who has symbolically repudiated what previously held him in place, vertically and horizontally. He cannot overturn the actual structures and is, in any case, committed to non-violence, but he can emigrate from the ecclesiastical symbol of its all-inclusive claims: Catholicism. This occurs even if Catholicism itself has in fact engaged in a parallel migration. He can reject the fiesta and *compadres* ['mates'] in favour of his own charismatic feast and the solidarity of the evangelical brotherhood. Pentecostalism is his very *own* fiesta.

Such a fundamental shift of social location generates a very hostile psychic charge. In the countryside, for example, the new convert comes to feel that the old therapeutic techniques are powerless and the traditional Christo-pagan practices dirty and contaminating. His – or her – adoption of a new life means drinking pure and 'living water'. In the city the new convert protects his new orientation by the erection of boundaries and the acceptance of visible 'markers' which set him off as someone under new and different disciplines. And he has to be seen to obey those disciplines both by the believers and by his ordinary peers if he is not to be dismissed as a hypocrite.

This negative charge associated with social departure is matched by a counter-charge designed to extrude and exact costs. With the first arrival of evangelical Christianity in a given area the response will often be violence or extrusion or dismissal from employment. The old system and the new mutually repel each other and reinforce their boundaries, even though this repulsion may tail off with time. (Indeed, a relaxation of attitudes on the Catholic side has been known to cause serious disorientation to Protestant converts.)

In these circumstances, it is not surprising that the evangelical groups, more particularly the Pentecostal ones, often restrict their reforms to the interior of the group. The achievement of radical changes in behaviour and the reversal of the hierarchies and priorities obtaining in the outside world can only be achieved in a protected environment. In any case, people without any global theory of society cannot easily extrapolate from their own situation to the complexities, compromises, and contingent twists and turns of political action. This is not to say they do not recognize the corruption of the system and the unworthiness of many of their political leaders. On the contrary, they are all too deeply aware that the political realm is deeply resistant to moralization, especially under Latin American conditions. In any case, the kind of voluntary organization represented by evangelical Christianity is contrasted with the Catholic Church precisely by its incapacity to promulgate the kind of norms which are tuned to *specific* conditions of the *whole* society. Its central priority is the recovery of moral densities and solidarities, and the regeneration of hope.

This is the root difference between the evangelical churches, or at any rate most of them, and the Roman Catholic base communities.

The base communities are lay and 'Protestant' in form and style, and likewise concerned with the recovery of moral solidarities, but they are linked to a hierarchically articulated church which still has the intellectual resources, and claims the social remit, to promulgate norms governing whole societies. The Catholic Church is still adjusted to the political realm, which in Latin America is both strength and weakness. The strength arises from the universal scope of Catholic moral concern; the weakness arises from remaining implicated symbolically in the massa perditionis [things under divine condemnation], and sometimes remaining implicated in it in practice, that is contaminated.

As already argued the evangelical groups work upon society by the 'cultural logic' they imprint and exemplify. How then, does this cultural logic operate? How are new potentials in the form of models and images and concepts of the person and of organization stored in the religious capsule, and (maybe) later released into the mainstream of society?

The peaceable operation of cultural logic

Primitive Christianity itself began as a movement active solely at the level of culture, and in this aspect, as in many others, evangelical Christianity represents a return to that primitive condition. The contemporary evangelical in Latin America has walked out of the extant structures and devised an experimental capsule or cell in the interstices of culture. Here he may reinvent himself in an atmosphere of fraternal support and give 'tongue' to his frustrations and aspirations.

This new cell can only survive and maintain its pristine character by peaceability. Peaceability is of the essence, and the poor of Latin America may well feel that up to now political zealotry has only increased their misery. In Latin America there exists a ready-made spiral of violence such that when any group engages in physical aggression it triggers opposite and equal (or more-than-equal) aggression. Apart from the straightforward danger of annihilation, this spiral of aggression and counter-aggression will distort and perhaps reverse the messages carried by the new cell. As among the early Christians, among the monasteries, and among the sects of the radical reformation, peaceability helps ensure that the radical coding inside the cell is preserved intact. The insistence on peaceability, plus protective social devices, like maximum association within the group and minimum association outside it, keep the message alive. That is why monasteries conceived themselves as remote and secret 'gardens of the Lord', and why radical sects regarded themselves as a peculiar people set aside for special purposes. Without such 'peculiarity' no serious revision of consciousness is possible.

The revision of consciousness activated within the Pentecostal or evangelical cell is remarkably thoroughgoing in that it abolishes mediations. All large-scale social organization, religious or political, is based on hierarchy and mediation, and the establishment of lay and unmediated channels of communication is a revolutionary reversal of all social order. However, this reversal itself requires a strict discipline and unequivocal leadership such as is provided by the pastor. Sheep may safely graze only when there are pastors, as well as folds and safe enclosures.

Thus enclosures and pastors constitute the paradoxical precondition of any serious revision of consciousness and social practice. A very large number of the models of change which have gone to make up our modern world were set in position in precisely this way. Women gained authority in the nunnery or the right to prophesy in the sect. Peaceability was nourished in the monastic fraternity and among Quakers and Mennonites. Food reforms were initiated among Swedenborgians and Adventists. The rejection of corporal punishment and the invention of modern schemes of educational reform originated among the Bohemian Brethren. The therapies of shared experience were devised and encouraged among the early Methodists. Religious groupings construct advanced platforms in consciousness, and test their viability in enclosed protected environments. They send out signals about what may be possible, and the wider society in time picks these up. The most powerful signals ever sent out were those which established fraternity, which abolished mediation, and which indicated how social worlds could be constructed not only on ties of blood and natural contiguity but on spiritual affinities voluntarily embraced. These are precisely the signals sent out by Pentecostalism under exemplary images: the last being the first, the lame walking, the bedevilled restored to their right mind – and the dumb singing or finding their 'tongues'.

Of course, if it is argued that culture is an impotent creature of structure then all such revisions of consciousness and innovations of practice are signals which will never be picked up and translated. However, the reverse may be true. Inductions into new worlds and socialization in symbolic reversals may in time become diffused to whole populations. The latent may be made manifest and the limited free space devised by religion may be suddenly enlarged as it was in the Civil Rights Movement led by Martin Luther King [among blacks in the USA in the 1950s and 1960s]. A mutation in self-consciousness in the religious sphere, or skills in public address and in organization, may be transferred to any other sphere whatsoever. They may be transferred to whole movements, or alternatively they may be carried by individuals. They are protean in their potentials.

[...]

Secularization and the global perspective

Clearly this startling and unanticipated development in Latin America, now spreading to the Eastern Pacific rim and Africa, is part of much wider global changes. The first of these is a world-wide growth of religious conservatism in Judaism, and in Islam, as well as in Christianity. A balance once supposed to be tipping automatically towards liberalism is now tipping the other way.

Quite what the parallel developments in Islam and Judaism portend is much disputed. Some see it as a reaction to external pressure and a reflex of fear leading to an attempt to recover 'mechanical solidarity'. Others see it, at least in the Islamic version, as a modernization and a radical mobilization carried out inside a conservative frame. It is significant that Catholicism also tried to create a militant fortress mentality in the mid-nineteenth century, and that it came nearest to success where it was implicated in the struggles of repressed nations. It may be that Islam stands a better chance of strengthening its 'fortress', given that it has received warnings earlier in the process of disintegration and is implicated in nationalistic struggles in many societies from Algeria to Malaya.

Whatever may be the case with multiple religious monopolies like Catholicism and Islam, or even a single and weak 'monopoly' such as orthodox Judaism in Israel, the success of evangelicalism depends rather on the *reverse* process, that is on the break-up of monopolies and the restriction of religious influence to the realm of culture. This is absolutely crucial: whatever the surface similarities of conservative versions of all three monotheistic faiths, developments in Latin America run quite counter to those in the Middle East. Evangelical religion represents an advanced form of social differentiation and can operate best where hitherto monopolistic systems are disintegrating. Once the monopolies begin to crack and to lose contact with the core structures of society, evangelical Christianity can emerge to compete within the sphere of culture. There it can stand in for what were once the local territorial units of solidarity, re-forming them in an active, mobile and voluntary format. In this way it counters chaos and restores moral densities. There is no chance it will become a substitute established church, though it may create a widely shared ethos for some oppressed ethnic group. This dramatic restriction to the cultural sphere is, of course, one aspect of secularization, but whether this means that religion has finally ceased to be socially significant depends, as suggested above, on whether culture is regarded as impotent and dependent. If culture is regarded as without serious influence then religion is indeed marginalized beyond recovery and can be dismissed as just one leisure-time activity among others.

Theories of secularization indicate how religion, and specifically Christianity, relinquishes (and/or is deprived of) its hold on the central structures of power. It ceases to be the symbolic keystone in mechanical solidarity and is released from the centripetal pull which aligns it with elite interests and explicit party attachments. Theories of secularization also specify a complementary process whereby the state takes over and develops all kinds of organizations and functions, especially in education and social welfare, which were previously under religious aegis. This advance of the omnicompetent state is associated with the growth of professions whose interests come to lie in the extension of state action, and with the propagation of ideologies which define the religious contribution as irrelevant to the efficient running of society. As Bryan Wilson has argued, a net of rational bureaucratic regulation can supplant the moral densities, the conscientious sensitivities and the commitments once generated by communities of faith.[9]

The question then becomes whether this process is contingent, i.e. dependent on specific circumstances, notably those which have obtained in Europe, or is a necessary and inevitable part of social development.[10] Clearly if the latter is the case then a certain estimate of the significance and future of the phenomena discussed in this book follows. It is simply that temporary efflorescence of voluntary religiosity which accompanies a stage in industrialization and/or urbanization. As Methodism flourished during just such a period in Britain so Pentecostalism flourishes today in Latin America. The

---

[9] Bryan R. Wilson, 'Secularization: the inherited model' in Phillip E. Hammond (ed.), *The Sacred in a Secular Age* (Berkeley and Los Angeles: University of California Press, 1985), pp. 9–20, and 'The Functions of Religion: a Reappraisal', *Religion* 18, June 1988, pp. 199–216.

[10] Cf. David Alfred Martin, *A General Theory of Secularization* (Oxford: Blackwell, 1978). [...] [This] chapter fill[s] in a gap in my previous work relating to the modification in Latin America of the 'Latin' pattern of secularization. For a treatment of the general situation of Roman Catholicism cf. David Alfred Martin, 'Introductory essay' in Thomas Gannon (ed.), *Catholicism in Transition* (London: Macmillan, 1988), pp. 3–35.

problematic stemming from Halévy[11] applies to them both as parallel moments in a story which will end as they shrivel at the cold touch of rationalization and the omnicompetent state.

This may, of course, be the case. But there is the alternative view based on the notion that the European experience is contingent and fails to provide the universal paradigm to which all other societies must in time approximate. According to that alternative view the effect of establishment and religious monopoly such as existed in Europe has been to inhibit the adaptability of religion to social change, above all to the industrial city. However, the North American paradigm seems to show that once religion is no longer a matter of a relation of a particular body to the elite and to the state, religion adapts quite successfully to a changing world. In all the *proper* senses of the word it becomes popular.[12] Indeed, it shows itself endlessly inventive and actually succeeds in assuaging the anomie and combatting the chaos of the megacity.

It may well be that the inventiveness displayed in North America has now been transferred to Latin America and the cycle of spirals derived from Europe thereby slowed or halted, even maybe reversed. If that is so, then secularization as understood in the European context is a particular kind of episode. If there is a universal element to it, that is restricted to the shift from structural location to cultural influence discussed earlier. Should that restricted and episodic view of secularization turn out to be correct then the crossing of the 'Anglo' and Hispanic patterns currently observed in Latin America is not a repeat performance of a sequence already played through and played out in Britain, but a new moment with new possibilities.

The matter can be put another way. The Protestant experience in Britain exhibited a religious efflorescence at the time of industrialization and urbanization that tailed away into ineffectiveness. The Latin experience in Southern Europe exhibited spirals of repulsion between the Catholic ghetto and the forces of militant secularism. In both, religion eventually receded as the state advanced. But in North America the factors which eventually curtailed the religious efflorescence in Britain did not obtain, and a new pattern emerged of immense expansive power. It is that North American pattern which has now become admixed with the Latin

---

[11] Élie Halévy, an early twentieth-century French historian, argued that the Methodist movement 'saved' Britain from political revolution insofar as it eased the social tensions consequent upon early industrialization and urbanization.

[12] There is also useful material in Reginald Bibby and Merlin Brinkerhoff, 'Circulation of the Saints in South America', *Journal for the Scientific Study of Religion* 24 (1985), pp. 39–55.

cultures of South America. In those cultures it so happens that certain characteristic spirals of antagonism over religion are now rapidly weakening. The long shadow of 1789 [the French Revolution] disappears and a new moment arrives in which a sizeable sector of mainstream religion rejects its old alliances on the right. It follows that as the spirals of antagonism weaken and as there is a strong admixture of the kind of religion originally generated in North America, the old tendencies may well be nullified. Should that be so then the 'tongues of fire' may not so easily sputter out.

The Soka Gakkai in Southeast Asia*

DANIEL MÉTRAUX

SGI claims a following of 800,000 to 900,000 in Asia. Its initial growth in Southeast Asia started in ethnic Chinese communities in Hong Kong and Thailand[1] in the early 1960s, and spread to Chinese communities in Malaysia, Singapore, and elsewhere by the mid-1960s. Today ethnic Chinese constitute an overwhelming majority of SGI members in Malaysia, Singapore, and Hong Kong. There is also a minority ethnic Indian membership and a scattering of other Asian and Western members.

Shimazono's thesis[2] concerning the appeal of Japan's new religions to upwardly mobile urbanites also applies quite well to

*This text first appeared in *Global Citizens: The Soka Gakkai Buddhist Movement in the World*, ed. David Machacek and Bryan Wilson, Oxford: Oxford University Press, 2000, pp.404–29.

[1] There are many Thai members as well, especially in less urban and more rural areas. Interviews with three Thai members in Japan in Nov. 1998 indicate that except for the fact that SGI has a lower percentage of ethnic Chinese members than in other countries studied in this chapter, its basic characteristics are very similar to SGI elsewhere in Southeast Asia. Most members grew up as Buddhists and regard SGI as a reaffirmation of their Buddhahood. They appreciate SGI because of its focus on the needs and desires of the individual and because Nichiren Buddhism in their opinion not only provides a clear explanation of why they suffer, but also provides a clear path to greater happiness, personal transformation, and satisfaction in life. SGI in Thailand is very community-oriented and has excellent ties with the government.

[2] The Tokyo University professor Susumu Shimazono's thesis is referred to earlier in this chapter:

One of the common characteristics of the New Religions is their response to strongly felt needs of individuals in their daily lives, their solutions to discord in interpersonal relations, their practical teaching that offers concrete solutions for carrying on a stable social life, and their provision, to individuals who have been cut off from traditional communities, of a place where congenial company and a spirit of mutual support can be found. As capitalistic industrialization and urbanization advance, large numbers of individuals are thrown into new living environments, thus producing conditions that require spiritual support for the individual. ... Japanese religions are abundantly equipped with cultural resources that answer the needs of just these people in treading the path towards the urban middle class. ("Expansion of Japan's New Religions," *Japanese Journal of Religious Studies*, 18/2–3 (1991), 116.)

younger SGI members in Malaysia, Singapore, and Hong Kong. Career-oriented SGI members in these countries maintained that SGI's emphasis on individual responsibility and initiative, together with the organization's ability to provide them with a strong sense of optimism, happiness, and a meaningful "extended family," were things which made membership in the organization very appealing. Another key factor in SGI's success in many Asian states, however, is that as a strong Buddhist movement it represents one of the largest and most traditional of Japan's schools of Buddhism. Most Asian countries have strong Buddhist traditions of their own and almost half of SGI members surveyed indicated that their families were Buddhist and that they had actively practiced some form of Buddhism in the past, usually as children. Many SGI members suggested that when they joined SGI, they felt that they had found a deeper and more relevant form of Buddhism. They had not left their Buddhist tradition; rather, they had found an enhanced version of it.

Why should a Japanese-based Buddhist movement be so successful among ethnic Chinese in Malaysia, Singapore, and Hong Kong? Memories of Japanese World War II military atrocities against Chinese in each of these areas remain very vivid, especially among the elderly. Still, SGI has won broad official and public acceptance in these countries, and most SGI members indicated that they had only rarely received criticism from friends and relatives when they joined. There are apparently several reasons for this ready acceptance. The Soka Gakkai strongly opposed the war effort, and its leaders at the time – Tsunesaburo Makiguchi and Josei Toda – were imprisoned when they refused to cooperate with government authorities. The Soka Gakkai also has a long and genuine record of friendship with cultural, educational, and political leaders in the People's Republic of China. SGI's Buddhist identity, however, is the most important factor.

SGI's success in Southeast Asia may thus be attributed to a combination of factors: its ability to provide members with a strong Buddhist foundation in their lives and its appeal to individuals living in rapidly urbanizing and industrializing societies. Interviews with members indicated that they had experienced a strong spiritual vacuum before joining SGI and that their membership had helped them to fill this void. Every member expressed satisfaction with their new lives and alleged that a positive transformation of personality was the source of their increased happiness.

The keys to this transformation are the twin concepts of karma and responsibility for one's own actions. SGI leaders stress that Buddhism is not for those people who like to be told how to order their lives, who look constantly for guidance from an outside authority, whether in the form of a priest, scripture, or ritual. Throughout the Gakkai's teaching, along with the insistence on a balanced life and common sense, there is a stated obligation for each person to think things out for himself, to make up his own mind and to make his own decisions. The doctrine of karma requires each believer to be responsible for his own salvation.

No matter how bad things have been in the past, the SGI faithful see a bright future *in this lifetime* for those who demonstrate strong faith, work hard for their own career development, demonstrate compassion, and offer a helping hand to others. People who are convinced that they can wipe away the burdens of the past and improve their lot in life will take positive action to upgrade their existence and will take risks for success in a free enterprise economy. A pioneer female member in Hong Kong exclaimed:

> Becoming a Soka Gakkai member was like emerging out of a cold dark tunnel into the bright sunshine. I had been a prisoner of my past, but then I joined a loving family whose members genuinely enjoy taking care of each other. Trivial matters that used to worry us about our own lives pale into significance compared to the problems facing society as a whole.

SGI works hard to make members feel comfortable with its Buddhism. For example, the Singapore Soka Association (SSA) reports that a number of older members left the movement in the early 1990s when Soka Gakkai broke with the Nichiren Shoshu priesthood. Older ethnic Chinese Buddhists in Singapore had always maintained close relationships with Buddhist priests and temples and were not entirely comfortable when SGI broke its ties with the priesthood. Some of these older members returned to the Soka Gakkai in 1997 when it opened a modern temple and brought in a "reformed" Nichiren priest from Japan who is a strong supporter of the Soka Gakkai.[3]

Local chapters are fully organized, financed, and led by local nationals. They receive publications, doctrinal documents, and

---

[3] The priest, Yuhan Watanabe, is a 40-year-old graduate of Soka University whose parents are Soka Gakkai members. He had received training as a Nichiren Shoshu priest before breaking with the sect when it expelled the Soka Gakkai in the early 1990s. Watanabe reports that some conservative Singapore members were offended by the fact that Nichiren Shoshu priests often married and had large families. Watanabe is single and was hired in Singapore on the condition that he will remain celibate. Watanabe criticizes the traditional Nichiren Shoshu priesthood because it allegedly places itself "above" the people, insisting that priests alone have the power to alter people's karmas. He asserts that priests are in every respect equal in status with the lay believer and that the role of the priest is to assist the lay believer in strengthening his faith. Watanabe left Nichiren Shoshu and joined a small group of "reformed priests" willing to work together with Soka Gakkai.

writings by and about Daisaku Ikeda, but little else. An SGI leader in Hong Kong stated proudly, "We are a Hong Kong-based Buddhist organization serving Hong Kong people. We work very independently of Tokyo.... The key links between us and Tokyo are our faith in Nichiren Daishonin's Buddhism and our deep respect for Daisaku Ikeda. We finance all of our own operations."

Profile of SGI members in Malaysia, Singapore, and Hong Kong

Although each SGI organization has its own distinct characteristics, there are significant similarities in membership. Extensive surveys conducted by me among SGI members in Malaysia, Singapore, and Hong Kong reveal a Soka Gakkai the membership of which is at the same time quite stable yet changing rapidly. It is stable in that followers have always been almost entirely ethnically Chinese (about 98 percent in each of these countries), but it is changing in that the movement, initially consisting of not very well-educated adult females, is becoming increasingly young and well educated with an even distribution of male and female members. The founding members of SGI in Southeast Asia were overwhelmingly older women; there were very few young members. A rapid jump in youth membership in the 1970s came as a result of the willingness of children to follow their parents into the organization, and their presence attracted other young members recruited from among their peers. Today, SGI membership in Asia has become quite young; most are in their twenties, thirties, or very early forties. They are virtually all high school graduates, and most have attended some college. A large percentage of members in Malaysia and, to a lesser extent, in Singapore have done graduate work as well. While many older members were housewives or involved in some form of small business or traditional occupations such as teaching, younger members are more likely still to be students or have professional careers in business, high tech, accounting, and teaching.

There is every indication that most members were satisfied with their lives before joining SGI. Only about a third report having been decidedly unhappy. Indeed, members of all age groups in Asia also report highly optimistic worldviews. Over 98 percent of members felt that both the short-term and long-term future of the world looked very bright and that the Soka Gakkai, with its programs fostering "peace, education, and culture," was a "precious vehicle" for peace.

There were, however, a few active members with more cynical perspectives. They speculate that the world outside their movement had become so corrupt that not even Nichiren Daishonin's Buddhism could ultimately save the world. One youth division member even called Daisaku Ikeda a "sincere idealist" who "meant well," but whose peace proposals were out of place in a "Machiavellian" world.

Questions concerning religious activity and concerns about religion before joining SGI indicated strong differences between Malaysian and Singapore members on the one hand, and Hong Kong members on the other. A majority of Singapore and Malaysian members followed their parents' beliefs and practices in traditional Taoism and Buddhism, while a large majority of Hong Kong members were previously "free thinkers" – people without any active religious beliefs.

Motivation for membership

Respondents in all three countries (N = 305) were asked to write brief essays explaining their motivations for joining SGI. This approach has the advantage of providing believers with an opportunity to express themselves freely rather than forcing them to choose from preselected categories. The disadvantage, of course, is the large number of varying responses. Still, most of the essayists provided two or more factors that brought them into the Soka Gakkai movement. Table [1] gives the most frequently mentioned circumstances.

The most noteworthy statistic is the number of believers who joined because of family relations. The leading source of conversions is within individual families. A middle-aged mother in Hong Kong, for instance, joined because she was distressed over her husband's acute illness and the financial panic that ensued once her husband's paycheck disappeared. The husband recovered, and credited his wife's new religion with this "miracle." Able to resume work, he joined immediately, and the couple's three children, the wife's parents, and the husband's two brothers and one sister also joined. Thus, the typical pattern is for the new faithful to convert members of their immediate families, while the children, when they reach their mid-teen years, convince some of their own peers to join.

The survey and interviews indicate that people who joined on their own often spoke of problems related to health, human relations, occupation, and anxiety ("peace of mind") that led them to Soka Gakkai. Family health problems were more numerous than personal illness, but both were quite often accompanied by financial problems and, not surprisingly, these circumstances often led to family stress.

Table [1] Reasons for joining SGI

Reason	Number
Parents, family members already belonged to SGI	96
Family illness	38
Personal illness	33
No direction in life	29
Poor personal, family finances	27
Disharmony in family	24
Relative cured of illness	21
Searching for meaning in life	21

The few people who wrote that they were searching for a new religion when they joined SGI were a distinct minority.

Benefits of SGI membership

Respondents to the survey of SGI members in Southeast Asia were also asked what benefits they had derived from their faith and membership in the organization. The respondents could check off as many items as they pleased from the list in Table [2].

Table [2] Benefits of membership

Benefit	Number
Improved health	117
Better financial situation	156
Happiness, more confidence	221
Hope for the future	210
Happier family	100

Respondents were also asked to provide essay responses concerning their benefits. The following four responses are representative:

> It is very easy to explain the benefits of SGI membership. I have cut down on BAD CAUSES and instead channel my resources (time, energy, and money) for one GOOD cause: HAPPINESS of my family, friends, people in my town and country, and the world. These changes are reflected in my daily life. No more night-life, no more drinking, no more movies or TV. Instead, more time with my family, building friendships with others, helping others to improve themselves, reading more, being less stressed in daily life. I am happier because I know that I am the cause of what I am and what I am not. I can be what I want to be. (40-year-old male businessman in Malaysia)
>
> My kidney problem became so severe that my doctor advised against marriage and bearing children, but when I joined the Soka Gakkai and

started chanting there was rapid improvement in my condition. I married happily, gave birth to two children, and am still healthy. I am happy because my practice gives me the life force to sustain a healthy constitution even though my kidney problem still exists.

Buddhism also taught me not to be an escapist, but to face all of my problems squarely and to overcome them happily. It also taught me not to depend on outside stimuli to be happy. Happiness must be found from within. My family life is also happy because I really do not attach myself to love, but instead thrive on compassion and the love generated spontaneously from the love of a harmonious family. (30-year-old female office worker in Hong Kong)

I was once a stubborn and argumentative person, but after studying Nichiren Daishonin's writings, I came to understand my weaknesses and decided to improve. I give much of my time and resources for the benefit of others. Life has much more meaning now. My husband's once severe health problems have also improved.

This Buddhism gives me the courage and wisdom to face the realities of life. Although life is always changing, we must work hard to bring happiness to others. Life is meant to be enjoyed – materialism cannot guarantee our happiness. It all depends on our hearts to feel joy, but that joy depends on how much we do for others. In the past I had no goals in life. I never thought about value or human potential, but having joined in SGI activities, I now understand that each one of us has unlimited potential. SGI activities have shown us the courage and care needed to live. (40-year-old female in Singapore)

I am happier. My family members are all very happy and harmonious. Everyone in the family is very happy, positive, and possesses a strong life force. They possess the Buddha's wisdom to overcome all obstacles. That is what we call absolute happiness, not relative happiness. (A general contractor in Hong Kong)

While roughly half of the SGI members surveyed said that membership had brought them better health, fewer financial worries, and improved family relations, an overwhelming majority felt that they have undergone a deep positive transformation that had made them happier and more confident as individuals. There was constant reference to their belief that they were no longer lonely, that they could enjoy the benefits of a genuinely caring extended family. There was a feeling that they had a greater degree of control over their own lives, that they had been empowered with the ability to maximize their own potential.

Devotion to the movement also implies financial support. Members give generously not only to support day-to-day activities, but also to special fundraising campaigns to build large community centers. Malaysian SGI leaders reported, for example, that when they formulated plans for a new community center and inaugurated fundraising drives, the response had always been rapid and strong. A successful ethnic Chinese businessman and Soka Gakkai Malaysia (SGM) leader in Kuala Lumpur explained: "I have profound happiness through Nichiren Daishonin's Buddhism. My business career has also prospered since my entire family joined SGM. It is a Chinese custom to enthusiastically support an organization that has brought one so much good fortune."

Nurturing and leadership

SGI thrives as a voluntary association, many of the leaders and active members of which volunteer considerable amounts of their free time to the welfare of the organization and its members. The concept that the Soka Gakkai in Southeast Asia is every member's extended family is very real. The heart of the movement is a system of nurturing, where each member is, in essence, responsible for the health and welfare of other members.

The role of an SGI leader at any level is to provide and organize care for a group of members. The leader is supposed to nurture the member, encourage study, and chant with and for him, but making home visits, attending study meetings, and involvement in activities takes up much of one's free time. The leader must keep in constant touch with members, and if she or he sees any hint of trouble, the member will almost certainly receive a phone call or, more commonly, a home visit. One leader stated that on average she made up to three or four home visits each week. The same leader recalled how she had helped a family suffering from financial stress, another household in which a housewife was receiving physical and mental abuse from a violent husband, and a mother whose child had just developed cancer. A member who had been in the hospital for a difficult operation reported that many members visited him to boost his spirits and to chant together with him before the day of the operation.

The care and devotion that a troubled member receives is very personal. An important objective is to let the person know that he is not alone, that he does not have to face a difficult situation without the devotion and support of other members. A leader in Hong Kong reported how she had just visited a fellow member who had suffered considerable verbal and physical abuse from her husband, a successful businessman who was suddenly doing badly during an economic recession. She had several children, no money, very little education, and no place to escape. She felt trapped and isolated. Her SGI comrade's main initial task was to be a good listener, reassuring her that her many friends in the Soka Gakkai sympathized with her plight and would do anything possible to boost her morale:

> A group of fellow members went to her house and chanted with her before the family *Gohonzon*. Later I reminded her of the karmic law of cause and effect and that it was up to her to change the family karma for the better. She seemed to gain strength and resolve through her chanting and the encouragement we gave her. Her husband was so deeply moved by her strength and tenacity that he joined her in chanting. His anger seemed to subside, and gradually he apologized to her for his former conduct and became a kinder person.

Qualifications for leadership include strong spiritual commitment and genuine or "spontaneous" devotion to the movement – and especially to the welfare of other members. A leader should also have experienced success in his career, and his family should manifest well-being. Malaysian leaders said that their husbands or wives have to adapt themselves to these circumstances as part of their commitment to the Soka Gakkai movement. When both parents are leaders, older children must look after themselves and their younger siblings, or accept or receive care from grandparents or other family members.

A lengthy discussion with a group of twelve Malaysian women leaders indicated that they were out five or six evenings a week and all day Sunday. As a group they estimated that they spent up to 80 percent of their free time in SGI-related activities. There was little time for non-SGI-related activities such as longer vacations, visits to restaurants, or even downtime with other family members. They insisted that SGI was their life work and source of enjoyment, and that their family lives had actually improved because many, if not all, family members had dedicated their lives to the movement and had found great joy in their ability to help others.

Other SGI leaders indicated, however, that while there were many individual SGI leaders and members who devoted most of their free time to the movement, such time-intensive commitments were not the norm. Leaders throughout the movement work long hours to further the movement and assist other members, but they are also expected to spend quality time with their families, get adequate rest, and to pursue other hobbies and activities.

The large amounts of time and devotion expected of an SGI member and leader, however, may cause problems for future generations of SGI leaders. Some younger leaders clearly must devote fewer hours to the movement because of tremendous time commitments at work and a desire for some quality time with their families. While there is clearly a core of young leaders and members who make extraordinary efforts to further the cause, Bon Chai Ong, general director of the SSA, openly chided a large gathering of youth leaders in July 1998 for an attendance rate at SSA meetings of only 32 percent over a recent period. An SSA youth leader confided that it had taken an inordinate amount of time to find about ninety-six youth members to take part in the 1998 national youth festival celebrations. A youth leader in Hong Kong confessed that youth today have to work so many long hours at school or for a company that they have very little time or energy for SGI events: "Members such as myself deeply care about the future of SGI, but we have professional careers that simply wear us out. There is no such thing as the forty-hour work week here – especially during the current recession. Our faith is strong, but we must manage our time very carefully."

Despite the problem of free time, it does appear that the average member in Southeast Asia devotes more of his time to SGI than his counterparts in North America. A key factor is that chapters in the West tend to be much smaller and thus offer far fewer activities for members. SGI community centers in Asia are humming all day seven days a week, but SGI culture centers in such places as Toronto and Montreal are generally quiet during the day.

Education and "cultural activities"

Soka Gakkai organizations throughout the world perform a variety of activities to promote "Peace, Education, and Culture." The Gakkai is an "engaged" Buddhist movement that seeks to influence major social institutions with "Buddhist values." Education, for example, is important not only for the teaching of basic facts or concepts, but also for inculcating in students a sense of tolerance, compassion, and respect for the dignity of life. Peace activities include exhibitions to remind citizens of the horrors of war, and events to bring together people of different cultures and backgrounds to establish common bonds. Cultural activities include a wide variety of activities from music and dance groups to garden clubs to help members find greater enjoyment in the movement, to establish friendship among members, to study and practice the faith together, and to deepen a sense of commitment to the organization.[4]

The SGI organizations in Hong Kong, Malaysia, and Singapore have built large and very successful kindergartens for the children of

[4] Cultural groups in the SSA are organized by the various divisions. For example, the men's division choir and drum groups; the women's division dance and choir groups; the young men's division brass band, lion dance, choir, and calisthenics groups; the young women's division fife and drum corps, choir, and dance groups. The SSA Chinese orchestra and the symphonic band comprise members from all divisions. These cultural groups perform at certain SSA activities and cultural shows. Since 1975 SSA has staged many cultural shows. Besides these, the groups are occasionally invited by other organizations to perform.

both members and others in the community.[5] The schools are housed in modern, spacious, and colorful buildings that create an ambience to delight the minds of the students. Classes are small, teachers are well trained and benevolent, and students appear to be delighted to be where they are. When asked how education in a Soka Gakkai school system differs from other schools in her country, a teacher at the Soka kindergarten in Malaysia described SGI's view of "humanistic education":

> Every child in Malaysia learns reading, writing, math, science, and other subjects in school to help them earn a living. But these same schools are often lacking in their ability to teach youngsters about daily life in society – how to deal with anger, how to reconcile conflicts, how to breathe, smile, and get along. We offer a revolutionary approach to education. Our "humanistic education" focuses on training students in the art of living in peace and harmony. Our students learn about courtesy, compassion – it is perhaps even more important for a child of 5 to learn how to play and share with other 5 year olds than it is for him to pass a test in math. But, as it turns out, our children go on to do very well in primary and secondary school.

Religious life

The Soka Gakkai, however, is specifically a religious movement, so it is hardly surprising that worship and Buddhist practice occupy most of the time and attention of Southeast Asian SGI members. Members pray at home in front of a Buddhist altar (*butsudan*) for a period of time every morning and night. Each community center has a room or – in the case of Singapore – a temple where members and visitors can drop in for a period of chanting with other members.

Discussion and dialogue meetings (*zadankai*) are held regularly at members' homes or, in the case of Hong Kong, at Soka Gakkai community centers, where friends and relatives come together on a regular basis to study Buddhist philosophy, discuss problems in their daily lives, and enjoy each other's company. Members often bring nonmember guests to acquaint them with the movement and teachings.[6]

I attended a number of discussion meetings in Malaysia and Hong Kong. The typical Malaysian *zadankai* was a congenial gathering of members. Approximately fifty residents of a middle-class

---

[5] Children of nonmembers outnumber children of members in Malaysia and Hong Kong.

[6] Bringing nonmember guests to meetings and activities is the most common form of proselytization.

neighborhood gathered in the spacious family room of a member. It was a noticeably relaxed family affair. Most of those in attendance were young or middle-aged couples and their children, but there were also a representative sampling of older women and men and a larger number of teenagers and young adults. Parents with children too young to leave at home brought them to the host's home. While the meeting progressed, small children ran back and forth from the kitchen to their parents. It was a congenial, warm atmosphere.

The meeting opened with the entire group chanting in unison before the host's *butsudan*. Members then rose to sing two rousing Soka Gakkai songs, which seemed to put the group into a joyful mood. There followed the reading and discussion of a passage of the sacred writings of Nichiren as well as a reflective essay on the reading composed by SGI president Daisaku Ikeda. Two members provided testimonials in which they told how the "Daishonin's Buddhism" had brought joy and health to their lives. The meeting ended with another song and a brief period of chanting. Friends gathered into small groups for a few moments of small talk before taking their leave.

These meetings are central to the activities of SGI members worldwide. The purpose of the *zadankai* is to cultivate a feeling of solidarity and harmony among local members and to provide a time when they can socialize and pray together and hear about each other's triumphs, hardships, and concerns. A Singapore member aptly described these meetings as a "wonderful form of group therapy." It is also a time when local SGI members and leaders can discuss issues facing SGI and make announcements about forthcoming events.

SGI–community relations in Southeast Asia

Since their inception in the 1960s SGI organizations in Southeast Asia have worked hard to build strong ties with their communities and local and national governments. SGI leaders continually stress that Buddhism emphasizes both personal gain and service for the benefit of society, the nation, and the world. SGI sponsors publicly visible programs in each of these countries with the hope of playing a meaningful role in community and national events, and building a solid relationship with the outside world. It is also apparent that local and national governments and communities surrounding SGI community centers generally have a positive view of SGI. An important factor in this development is that each of the three national SGI organizations consists of, and is led by, local nationals with a strong accommodating stance. Each SGI organization is very independent of Tokyo.

The SSA performs regularly in annual national New Year's Day and in National Day parades and in biannual Singapore youth festivals. There are also highly effective community programs, including one that brings elderly citizens for a month-long "course" designed to help them make the transition into retirement. Participants, most of whom are not SGI members, declared that the SSA program had helped them build new and quite active social lives.

The SGI organizations in Malaysia and Hong Kong are equally involved in local and national activities: Hong Kong SGI members played a highly visible role in ceremonies marking Hong Kong's 1997 return to Chinese rule, and over 5,000 Malaysian members performed in the opening and closing ceremonies of the September 1998 Commonwealth Games in Kuala Lumpur.

The following sections portray the close relationship between SGI organizations in Southeast Asia and their respective communities and governments. In 1999 SGI had approximately 20,000 members in Singapore and 40,000 to 50,000 followers each in Malaysia and Hong Kong.

The Singapore Soka Association: a patriotic civic organization

Patriotism and national service are important themes in all Southeast Asian SGI organizations, especially in Singapore. Singapore today is both an immigrant society and a Chinese city state. When Great Britain acquired the island in 1819, Singapore had a population of several hundred Malays living in small simple fishing villages, but by the year 2000 it had become a thriving nation of about 3 million citizens with the highest per capita income in Asia outside of Japan. There is a significant Indian minority population and a much smaller Malay community, but political, commercial, and cultural power are in the hands of the ethnic Chinese majority.

One of the major themes in Singapore history since World War II has been the effort to create a distinct Singapore identity. What does it mean to be a Singaporean? How can the dominant Chinese cultural heritage be transformed into a distinctly Singaporean culture? How can minority populations be successfully incorporated into this new culture? How can a small, predominantly ethnically Chinese city state learn to get along with much more populous but less prosperous Malay Muslim neighbors in Malaysia and Indonesia?

SSA responds by emphasizing its role as a patriotic organization working to enhance Singaporean nationhood. A 1996 SSA publication emphasized this point, describing the role SSA played in making that year's National Day parade a success despite terrible weather conditions at the National Stadium:

> Despite the overwhelming obstacles, the spirit to persevere, to give one's best and succeed for our nation, for the people of Singapore prevailed. Driven by the sense of mission, 520 performers and another 235 working behind the scenes displayed the kind of pioneering spirit and resolve that our forefathers possessed to build the nation we proudly call, Singapore. Their valiant struggle was based on resolute faith and a harmonious unity that was imbued with the spirit of mutual care and support.[7]

The Singaporean government in turn has praised SSA for its service to the nation. The prime minister made the following observations when he attended the opening ceremony of the new Soka culture center in January 1993:

> We have made a conscious effort to separate religion from politics. Religious leaders in Singapore understand why we have the Religious Harmony Act. Many, like the Singapore Soka Association, have contributed to better national understanding, over and above their usual religious teachings: I congratulate the Singapore Soka Association for its consistent efforts in promoting social, cultural, and educational activities for the benefit of all Singaporeans.

This identification with both community and nation has helped SGI place itself as an acceptable – even positive – force in every Asian society it has entered. SGI's native membership, its hard work to foster good relations in local communities, and its active participation in national events in Malaysia, Hong Kong, and Singapore indicate that SGI organizations in Asia ironically have achieved a degree of national acceptance never found in Japan despite the organization's Japanese origins.

Soka Gakkai Malaysia: Chinese Buddhists in an Islamic nation

The key social factors in Malaysia are ethnic division and a delicate balance among ethnic groups that is needed to form a united nation. There are more than sixty ethnic or culturally differentiated groups

[7] Eternal Aurora (Sept. 1996), 27.

among Malaysia's population of about 20 million, but the most critical population division is between Bumiputera and non-Bumiputera people. The Bumiputeras are those with cultural affinities indigenous to Peninsular and Bornean Malaysia and the surrounding region. Malays constitute the main Bumiputera group and account for around 55 percent of Malaysia's population. Non-Bumiputeras are people whose cultural origins lie outside Malaysia – principally people of Chinese and Indian descent. Chinese constitute about 32 percent of Malaysia's population and Indians about 8 percent.

Malaysia is anything but a "melting pot." Each of the major cultural groups maintains its own linguistic and cultural traditions even today. Thus, ethnic Chinese still communicate among themselves in one of several Chinese dialects and have their own Chinese newspapers, although most Chinese Malaysians also speak Malay and English. Ethnic Indians maintain their own traditional communities as well, and Malays have their own distinct cultural identities. One can walk down any street in Malaysia and quickly find Hindu and Buddhist temples blending with mosques.

The ethnic division of Malaysia was strengthened by economic stereotyping during the British colonial era, which extended from the mid-nineteenth to the mid-twentieth centuries. Chinese dominated such areas as finance, transportation, construction, small-scale industry, and retail trading. Upper-class Malays entered professional careers in law and government, while ordinary Malays worked as rice farmers and fishermen. Most Indians labored on rubber estates.

Terrible racial riots in May 1969 led to the conclusion by all parties that each cultural group must learn tolerance and must work together for the salvation of the nation. Malay and Chinese leaders saw the need to tackle vigorously the economic and social disparities that had fueled racial antagonism. Measures were adopted to facilitate quality universal education, and to encourage the participation of all ethnic groups in the rapidly modernizing economy. Wealthy Chinese had to agree to considerable government control over business, and favoritism shown to Malays in such areas as education and employment. Malays in turn learned to be more tolerant of Chinese participation in the economic and political life of the nation. The result is that all of Malaysia's ethnic groups have gained significantly from the nation's rapid economic growth of the 1980s and 1990s.

Religion, however, is still a critical issue in Malaysian society. With government patronage, Malaysia is a much more insistently Islamic society than it was even a generation ago. The entire Malay population is Islamic, and it is very much against the law for any person to even attempt to convert a Moslem to another faith. Most of the Chinese in Malaysia are either Taoists or Buddhists. Some are

Christians and a small percentage follows Islam. A vast majority of the Indians are Hindus, although a few embrace other faiths including Islam, Sikhism, Buddhism, and Christianity.

Although there is a tiny Indian membership in SGM, the membership is essentially Chinese. The fact that ethnic Chinese introduced the SGI movement to other Chinese and that Malays are forbidden by law to convert to Buddhism has meant that SGM has remained a Chinese-based religious and civic organization. Malaysian constitutional guarantees of religious freedom mean that SGM members can practice their faith without fear of government interference as long as SGM makes no attempt to win converts from the Malay majority. The survival of the Malaysian nation, however, depends on more than just simple tolerance. Wherever one goes in Malaysia, there is a deliberate effort by many groups to work together for the benefit of the whole country, and SGM is an active partner in this process. An SGM leader stated emphatically that while SGM projects itself as a social organization "based on the life philosophy of Nichiren Daishonin, we respect the cultures, customs, traditions and religious practices of other groups."

There is a long history of SGM members learning cultural dances of other ethnic groups and inviting non-Chinese individuals and organizations to participate in SGM cultural events. SGM has been invited to perform at various functions organized by the government or government agencies at the district, state, and national levels including National Day celebrations, state ruler birthday celebrations, and multinational sports events. The SGM Soka kindergarten has also hired two Malay teachers to teach their language to the mainly Chinese group of students.

SGM thrives not only because of the many benefits members feel that they derive from Nichiren Buddhism, but because it is also a cooperative and patriotic civic group that participates in important local and national activities, strongly respects the cultures, customs, and religious practices of other ethnic groups, and, perhaps most importantly, respects laws forbidding the attempted conversion of Malays. This respect, and its contributions to the welfare of other cultures, has led to SGM's general acceptance in Malaysian society.

SGI-Hong Kong and the Chinese community

Unlike Singapore and Malaysia, both full-fledged nations with distinct characters, Hong Kong is a political entity in search of its identity. The

British have left, and the Chinese government is maintaining a very low profile, so to a certain extent the people of Hong Kong have the city to themselves, but when I asked them of which nation they considered themselves citizens, I got confused, startled looks and blank stares. "Although we are proud to once again be together with China, we identify ourselves with Hong Kong."

SGI-Hong Kong (SGI-HG) faces some of the same problems as the city itself. It lacks the characteristic patriotic demeanor of Singapore and even Malaysia, but there is a sense of civic pride. SGI-HG identifies itself with Hong Kong and specifies that a crucial goal is the enrichment of the lives of Hong Kong people, but it is more inwardly directed than other Asian SGI groups. More of its cultural events seem to be for its own members than for outsiders. Although SGI-HG played an important role in the July 1997 celebrations marking the return of Hong Kong to China as well as other important local civic events, a younger SGI leader noted: "We are in fact comparatively little involved in community affairs. We need to play a more visible role in public events."

SGI-HG has experienced explosive growth in Hong Kong since the 1960s. Since 1961, when President Ikeda inaugurated the first district of eight members, Hong Kong has developed into an organization consisting of eleven community headquarters, fifty-three chapters, and 40,000 members. Ten of the headquarters serve a Chinese membership that demographically resembles Hong Kong as a whole. SGI-HG's headquarters #10 serves as an umbrella organization for non-Chinese members. Meetings are held in a variety of languages including English, Tagalog, and Korean.

SGI-HG makes no attempt to extend its organization and proselytization into mainland China despite the proximity of the People's Republic. The Japanese Soka Gakkai has carefully built up a long-term relationship with various Chinese political and cultural leaders and institutions over four decades. There is a strong desire to refrain from any activity that might jeopardize these relations by running afoul of Chinese laws forbidding proselytization on Chinese soil by nonresident Chinese or foreigners.

SGI-HG is also unique because a few of its leaders are also foreign. General Director Kong Sau Lee is a Japanese national who has helped to lead the organization since the mid-1960s, and several other members of the SGI-HG staff are also Japanese. Several Chinese SGI-HG staffers attended university in Japan (primarily Soka University) and speak fluent Japanese. President Ikeda has made more than twenty official visits to Hong Kong, whereas he has visited Singapore only twice and Malaysia only once. Although SGI-HG is in an overall sense a very Chinese and Hong Kong-based organization, its ties with the Soka Gakkai in Japan are extraordinarily close.

There are notable socioeconomic differences between Hong Kong members and those in Singapore and Malaysia. The Singapore and Malaysian members are generally better educated, hold better jobs, and have higher incomes than their counterparts in Hong Kong. The SGI in Malaysia in particular has attracted a number of extraordinarily wealthy members. SGI-HG has its share of wealthy leaders and members, but one cannot compare them to Malaysia.

When SGI-HG got its start in the early 1960s, members were mostly middle-class proprietors of shops and small company proprietors. Vigorous propagation activities succeeded in building a strong membership base in the poorer sections of Hong Kong, including many who lived their lives on boats in the harbor. The living conditions of members improved dramatically in the 1970s and 1980s, but there is still a high percentage of middle-aged and older women members who have received very little education. Indeed, older women members outnumber their male counterparts by a ratio of about three to one. Younger members, on the other hand, are far better educated, have rising career prospects, and have a much stronger male–female ratio.

Of the three organizations, SGI-HG most nearly fits the image of a religious organization that attracts alienated people living in an urban industrial environment. A majority of members had no strong religious background and lacked a sense of direction or confidence before they joined SGI-HG. Their strong dedication to the movement, their current happiness with their lives, and their renewed optimism and confidence indicate that SGI-HG plays a constructive role in the Hong Kong community.

Soka Gakkai International Indian minority

The SGI organizations in Malaysia, Singapore, and Hong Kong are overwhelmingly Chinese, but there are several hundred Indian members in each organization. Most are the children or grand-children of Hindu Indian immigrants from southern India who arrived in Southeast Asia earlier this century. SGI Indian members in Asia were typically brought up within the social caste and Hindu traditions of their parents, but became dissatisfied with the role of religion in their lives until they found Nichiren Buddhism.

Indian members in Singapore and Malaysia have their own chapters within both SGI organizations, where they meet with other Indians and converse in their own languages. This cultural–linguistic division of membership, which is quite common among SGI organizations worldwide, is said not to be seen as discrimination against minority members or as a way of segregating them from the mainstream. Indeed, various scholars have found that one of the most noteworthy aspects of SGI is the excellent relationship that exists among people from different races, cultures, and linguistic groups worldwide within each organization. Indeed, the creation of separate units for minority members is strictly voluntary and largely for the convenience of members. When anglophone members meet in Quebec or Tamil-speaking Indians gather in Penang (Malaysia), they can converse in their own language and relate to other people from their own culture. Multicultural meetings where translators are continually at work are slow and cumbersome. An Indian not fluent in Chinese would feel isolated in a Chinese-only meeting but would benefit from hearing testimonials and lessons in Tamil. He might also feel more comfortable discussing personal problems with people from his own culture. On the other hand, members from different cultural backgrounds do meet frequently at larger cultural activities and study or prayer meetings.

I held a long discussion with a Singapore-born descendent of Indian immigrants, who plays an important role in SSA. He was a 43-year-old manager in a construction company and father of two young children. His father was a devout Hindu, and his son had strong religious interests since youth. He recounts going to a local temple, where he would ask religious authorities to explain the causes of certain events and was told that what happens is always the will of god. Since Hinduism failed to provide a rational explanation for hardships in his and his family's life, he left the religion and became a skeptic and "free thinker." He went on to describe the attraction of SGI for him:

> I eventually found a copy of the SGI publication *Seikyo Times* where I read that suffering is caused by karma and that we are responsible for our own actions. Indians traditionally believe that good fortune comes as a result of their own actions while bad luck is the "will of the gods." But if you realize that you are fully responsible for your conduct, you can create an entirely new life for yourself and your family.
>
> Nichiren Daishonin's Buddhism teaches us compassion for others and helps us find happiness here and now. SGI encourages each of us to foster our own cultures while gaining respect for others. All Nichiren Buddhists are equals and even though we are a minority, we never

experience any form of discrimination. Singapore is a nation built on the compatibility of different cultures, and SGI is a living model of what our nation must develop.

Because we all have inherent Buddha-nature, we can overcome our suffering and help others overcome theirs. We bring happiness to others and in so doing enrich our own lives.

Another Indian member in Penang made these comments:

Nichiren's Buddhism strengthens our own community, but also helps us to bridge the gap to the Chinese community. When I realized that my destiny in life was entirely in my own hands, I became free to develop my own career and to help other people find their own happiness.

Many younger Indians, like their ethnic Chinese counterparts in Southeast Asia, have found their traditional cultural life including the caste system to be irrelevant in a modern urban capitalist environment. They are attracted to a new religion which closes the gap between different cultures and encourages them to work hard to develop not only their own lives, but also those of their friends and family members.

Conclusion

SGI organizations flourish in Asia because, to their members, they represent a form of extended family. There is extensive caring and concern for fellow members. There is also a genuine sense of warmth and kindness – a sharing of all the ups and downs of the lives of all members – and a spirit of joy and warmth. One sees a sense of purpose and hope, a certainty that they live in a good world, which, despite all of its problems, can become better. There is a strong desire for peace and harmony and a realization that even the most difficult problems can be solved for the best. SGI members are happy and successful; they feel full of confidence and manifest a sense of optimism.

The Soka Gakkai has also succeeded in Southeast Asia because, in a context of rapid socioeconomic change, many people have felt a need for new religious inspiration. Many of Japan's new religions thrived because they satisfied the spiritual needs of people living in the midst of postwar Japan's urbanization and industrialization. When a number of these religions expanded to Southeast Asia in the mid to late 1960s, they encountered people likewise experiencing socioeconomic change.

Professor Bryan Wilson has noted:

> Nichiren Buddhism is a strongly individualistic religious orientation: one takes responsibility for oneself, and chanting has a powerful, albeit not exclusive, role in self-transformation. Realizing one's true identity, transcending one's karma, coming to terms with reality by using the *Gohonzon* as a mirror of one's own individuality – all of these central preoccupations reflect the extent to which Nichiren Buddhism focuses on self-improvement and self-help.[8]

This sense of an individualistic orientation and responsibility for oneself is ideally suited for younger upwardly mobile members of Southeast Asia's increasingly educated and professional emerging middle class.

The Soka Gakkai has succeeded in Asia also because it provides members with a new extended family. Ethnic Chinese are traditionally family-oriented, but many younger members of the new middle class have moved away from their traditional families and now live alone or as part of their own nuclear families. Nevertheless, a number of members interviewed by me expressed a strong need for "family" and proudly stated that SGI had become their new family.

The Buddhist background of many members made it easier for them to accept a movement that is itself Buddhist. Virtually all members interviewed stated that their strong desire for some degree of religious practice and/or spirituality in their lives made the Soka Gakkai attractive to them once they came in contact with the organization and its members. The fact that many of them had Buddhist backgrounds and that the Soka Gakkai is itself a Buddhist movement made SGI inherently more attractive than Christianity or other "foreign" faiths. Religious and racial tolerance in Singapore, Malaysia, and Hong Kong permits new faiths a chance to develop strong local roots.

Beyond these considerations lies a further contributing factor in SGI's success in these countries – virtually all SGI leaders are natives who have strong ties with the local community. Their willingness to work closely with local leaders and with the government enhances their prestige and facilitates their endeavor.

---

[8] Bryan Wilson and Karel Dobbelaere, *A Time to Chant: The Soka Gakkai Buddhists in Britain* (Oxford: Clarendon Press, 1994), 186–7.

Tablighi Jamaat and the Deobandi mosques in Britain*

JOHN KING

Tablighi Jamaat is an internationally proselytising and preaching movement, dedicated to reaffirming the basic principles of Islam and to drawing back into the fold of the religion Muslims who may have strayed. At the same time, the preaching is intended to confirm and to strengthen the faith of the Tablighi missionaries themselves. Tabligh is professedly a non-political organisation, and because it operates entirely within the Muslim community, it is relatively invisible to outsiders.

Tabligh is influential, but within the South Asian context of its origin, its influence is limited to certain sections of the Muslim community. As this chapter demonstrates, it is especially linked with the Deobandi school of Islam. Nevertheless, Tabligh appears to have discovered a mission to the wider world where its influence is not so constricted, and it is attracting increasing attention among Muslims throughout Europe.

Tabligh's founder, Muhammad Ilyas, lived in India from 1885 to 1944. He studied at the Islamic university at Deoband, with which his family had been connected, and was a Deobandi *'alim* (religious scholar). He also became a Sheikh of the Sabiriyah branch of the Chishtiyah Sufi order, and the practices of Tabligh draw to some extent on Sufi ideas. Ilyas's own preferred title for his movement was Tahrik-i-Iman, in Urdu 'The Faith Movement'.

In this chapter I describe the origins of Tablighi Jamaat and its relationship with the Deobandi expression of the Muslim faith. I make some conjectures about the nature of its vitality as a world

*This text first appeared in *Islam in Europe: The Politics of Religion and Community*, ed. Steven Vertovec and Ceri Peach, Basingstoke, London and New York: Macmillan, 1997, pp.129–46.

movement and as a means by which Islam is transmitted both geographically and from one generation to another. I will also describe the reasons for the limitation of Tabligh to the Deobandi community in the context of South Asian Islam, in India and Pakistan, as well as in Britain and round the world. Tabligh's apparent success among another population, Maghrebi Muslims of North African origin, will also be explored.

Global scope is of the essence of Tabligh. According to the most comprehensive study of Tabligh in English (Haq, 1972), by the early 1970s the movement had spread from India to thirty-four countries throughout the Indian subcontinent, in Arab territories, as well as across Africa and in South-east Asia. Toward the end of the 1980s, it was estimated to have reached ninety countries (Kepel, 1987), including Muslim minorities in the United States, Canada and Trinidad.

The British presence of Tabligh is now very well established, with a national structure whose centre is at the Markazi Mosque and its associated *madrasa* (school) at Dewsbury, sometimes known as the Dar ul-Uloum, whose official title is Jamiat Talimul Islam. Tabligh is also well represented today in other European countries, especially France (cf. Kepel, 1987) and Belgium (Dassetto, 1988a, b). In these francophone countries Tabligh is often called '*Foi et Pratique*' ['Faith and Practice']. British Tabligh members have mentioned to me the presence of Tabligh in Spain and the Netherlands. It appears that the spread of Tabligh in Europe follows the spread of Moroccan communities across Europe while Jørgen Nielsen (1992, p.19) remarks that it is particularly strong in Algeria.

Tablighis are of course nothing if not adventurous, and on an anecdotal level I should record that I have met or been told about British-based Tabligh members who have undertaken the preaching missions, known as *gush* in Urdu or *khuruj* in Arabic, as far afield in Europe as the former East Germany, the former Czechoslovakia and Hungary. These more far-flung excursions involve personal intrepidity on the part of those who undertake them, as they are well aware that they will appear exotic to customs and immigration officials in the countries they visit, and that their mission to contact and visit with Muslims they may encounter in the countries through which they pass may well not be successful.

The fact that such missions are undertaken at all indicates two underlying and, to some extent, contradictory features of the Tabligh movement. The first is that the motivation of the members of Tablighi Jamaat is powerful and they are driven by a profoundly serious faith, so that they are more than willing to encounter the difficulties inherent in missionary work in unfamiliar countries in order to fulfil the obligations they have willingly undertaken. The second is that to Muslims who are in any case part of a world-wide network of contacts and influences, such excursions appear more parochial and easier to undertake than might be supposed by Western observers.

The core theme of my research regarded the manifestation of Tabligh in Britain and its relationship to the world movement, including the surprising connection between Tabligh in Britain and in Morocco – a connection which reflects much about the movement's flexibility and adaptability. There are continuing contacts between British Tabligh and Morocco, with senior students from Morocco among the students and visitors at the *madrasa* and also younger Moroccan pupils at the *madrasa*, mainly from Moroccan families living in France. The implication is that the version of Muslim solidarity expressed through and engendered by Tabligh is capable of transcending not only profound cultural and linguistic differences but also internal divisions within the learned tradition of the Muslim community, since North Africans follow the Maliki madhhab [branch or school] of Islamic law while the Indian tradition is Hanafi. I describe below ways in which this transmission of the Tablighi idea takes place across cultural divides within the Islamic world.

Whatever the reason for the appeal of Tabligh, a vital feature of the movement is that it is in a very real sense a cosmopolitan phenomenon. To take the case of a Moroccan pupil in Dewsbury, whose mother tongue may be French or Moroccan Arabic or both: he will be coping with classical Arabic and Urdu, the language of instruction at Dewsbury, while he will hear both Gujarati and English spoken around him. According to informants, English is not infrequently the language adopted for international communication by meetings of Tablighi Muslims of varying national, linguistic and ethnic origins. Meanwhile, informants encountered during the course of my own research into the Tabligh movement included Gujarati Muslims from Cape Town in South Africa and from Zambia, as well as Keralese Muslims from Southern India, resident now in Birmingham, Leeds and Dewsbury. All have travelled outside the country since their migration to Britain.

One Tabligh activist of my acquaintance comes originally from Trivandrum, the capital of Kerala in Southern India, where the Muslim community is proud of its ancient origins, which predate the arrival of the Mughals in Northern India and are traceable to the sea trade between Arabia and the Indian coast. He came to Britain as a young man by way of an upbringing in Rangoon, the capital of Burma, where he was sent to live with an uncle after the untimely death of his father. His mother tongue was Malayalam, and he also acquired Burmese, Urdu and English while in Burma, in addition to his reading knowledge of Qur'anic Arabic. In Rangoon he studied for British educational qualifications and came into contact with Tablighi preachers. His commitment to Tabligh flowered after his arrival in Britain, when Pakistani students took him to Tabligh meetings in Dewsbury. In a sense, this man's polycultural and multilinguistic background, and his casual awareness of the wider world, make him a typical and emblematic Tabligh figure.

I should also remark at this stage on the impact made on the researcher by the intense and very real piety and enthusiasm of Tablighis. Activists insist that there is no qualification to become a member of Tabligh and no compulsion on any Muslim to join. But it is their quietly joyful contemplation of God and of the good Muslim life, as well as the opportunity of a context in which to achieve the fulfilment of the Muslim's active duties towards society which draws Muslims into the movement to become members and activists.

Perhaps the movement's strength lies in its concentric structure, with an inner core of full-time workers, and an outer group of enthusiasts who may come and go (Dassetto and Bastenier, 1988), an arrangement which is conducive to the mobilisation of activists.

Tablighis often speak of the quiet satisfaction inherent in a preaching mission, when a group of ten or so Muslims will go to another town, another region, or even another country to preach their faith to their fellow Muslims. Away from familiar surroundings and everyday cares, the talk is all of religious and ethical subjects, with the more experienced leading the discussion of the neophytes, and the preachers themselves will return home refreshed, renewed and gratified.

There is no doubt that as a global movement Tabligh is a success. In these pages I examine some reasons as to why this may be the case. But first I shall look at the origins and nature of the Deobandi Muslim movement in India, which was the soil in which the seed of Tabligh first germinated, and in which it flourishes today, to the exclusion of other areas of South Indian Islam.

The Deobandi dimension of Tabligh

Jørgen Nielsen refers to Tabligh as 'the active pietism of the Deobandi movement' (1992, p.133). The link between Tabligh and the Deobandi interpretation of Islam is historical and arises directly out of the circumstances of Tabligh's establishment. It is still a close and intimate relationship in Britain, as well as in other places where the Muslim population is of South Asian origin. In other countries where the movement has gained a foothold, but where the Muslim population is not of South Asian origin or descent, the link between Tabligh and the Deobandi interpretation of Islam is not of central significance.

Within the context of South Asian populations, however, the connection is of considerable importance and limits the way Tabligh spreads and operates, because of the basic division within South Asian Islam between the Deobandi school and the Barelvi schools, to one or other of which most (but by no means all) South Asian Muslims belong. Asked by non-Muslims about the distinction between them, both Deobandis and Barelvis will play down the differences and stress that the most important fact is that both are Muslims. There is much justification for this attitude, especially as the purpose of inquiries by outsiders may be precisely to discern lines of separation in a Muslim community which would rather regard itself as unified.

Nevertheless, it must be admitted that there is a very real intellectual and emotional distinction between Deobandis and Barelvis. Though both are Sunni, and both interpret Islamic law following the Hanafi school of Islamic jurisprudence, Deobandi and Barelvi populations differ markedly in their approach to Islam, and their difference is sometimes expressed as mutual distaste which can sometimes take a strong form (Alavi, 1988).

This potential or real antagonism gives rise to the paradox that within the South Asian community, inside which Tabligh originated, the movement is limited to the Deobandi section, while outside, in the Muslim world as a whole, its appeal is more universal and less limited to a particular segment of the Muslim population.

The division between Deobandi and Barelvi communities is familiar to those who have studied Islam in its South Asian or British context, but is less well known to those whose contact with Muslims lies more with populations of North African or Turkish origins. Francis Robinson (1988) has described the situation in Britain in the context of its South Asian background. The historical circumstances of the development of the Deobandi school help to throw some light on the way Tabligh is structured today.

The Deobandi movement came into existence in India in the mid-nineteenth century, and takes its name from the site of the movement's great Islamic university, the Dar ul-Uloum at Deoband in Uttar Pradesh, in India, now widely viewed as the Islamic world's second great university after Al-Azhar in Cairo. The university at Deoband was founded in 1867. In its origins, the movement was linked with the resistance against the British colonial domination of India which began to gather pace during the 1840s.

Khurshid Aziz has pointed out that most British observers at the time of what was known in Britain as the Indian Mutiny and in India as the First Indian War of Independence, in 1857, believed that Muslims were the prime opponents of the British in India (Aziz, 1962). Muslims certainly took up arms against the British with enthusiasm (Mortimer, 1982). In any case, in the aftermath of the struggle of 1857–8, Muslims in India sought ways to intensify the practise of their faith in a more private way, while a lasting antagonism between the Muslims and the colonial authority took root. The reaction of Deoband was to look for a pure and austere form of Islam suitable for the private practice of the faith, derived from Islam's basic texts and the interpretations of the Hanafi jurists (Metcalf, 1982).

Deoband's great rival, the Barelvi movement, also originated in the latter half of the nineteenth century, and took shape under the leadership of Sheikh Ahmad Raza Khan. It is important to understand the nature of its opposition to Deoband. Though it was similar in its origins, as a movement which sought to organize the popular expression of Islam it drew on a different clientele, and took a different theological direction (Robinson, 1988; Alavi, 1988). Named after the town of Bareilly, also in Uttar Pradesh, the Barelvi school embraced Islam as it was found in the India of its day.

As distinct from the Deobandi school, Barelvi Islam is quite explicitly a popular expression of the faith. It is linked to the cult of *pirs*, or saints who are believed to have the power of intercession with God and to be able to bring about cures and other favourable outcomes. In addition, festivals are celebrated, including the celebration of the birth dates of saints – especially of the great twelfth-century Sufi saint Abd al-Qadir al-Jilani, the eponymous founder of the Qadiriyya Sufi order which in the Indian sub-continent is found particularly in the Punjab and in Sind. Much personal devotion is offered to the Prophet Muhammad, and this of course is an explanation why it was the Barelvi community in particular which took the lead in attacking the British writer Salman Rushdie, whose work was interpreted by them as an assault on the Prophet's private life [...].

Barelvi mosques in Britain sometimes refer to themselves as 'Sufi', but though the *ulama* (trained religious scholars) associated with these mosques may well be practising members of Sufi orders, it is perhaps misleading to see this as their principal point of distinction from the Deobandi mosques. Deobandis may also be members of Sufi brotherhoods (Metcalf, 1982, pp.157–64): indeed, one of the leading founders of the university at Deoband, Maulana Muhammad Qasim Nanautawi, was a leading sheikh of the Chishtiya [a Sufi

Order]. But the principal difference between the two schools is in their style of devotion, in which the Deobandis are as plain and austere as the Barelvis are ornate and enthusiastic.

Hamza Alavi's (1988, pp.81–4) work on ethnicity and ideology in Pakistan underscores the point that the Deobandi/Barelvi distinction is crucial to an understanding of South Asian society; by implication, this point is significant by way of approaching South Asian social patterns as they are transplanted to Britain. 'Deobandis and Barelvis differ in every respect,' Alavi initially observes, 'by virtue of their different doctrinal positions, the different classes (and regions) amongst whom they have influence and their different political stances.' He goes on to stress the doctrinal difference which gives rise to antagonism between the two groups:

> In contrast to the Deobandi ulama, Barelvis profess a populist Islam, more infused with superstition, and also syncretism, that make up the religious beliefs of the peasantry. The Barelvi version of Islam emphasises belief in miracles and powers of saints and pirs, worship at shrines and the dispensing of amulets and charms, all of which are detested by the Deobandis as un-Islamic. Deobandis and Barelvis detest each other and much sectarian conflict consists of fights between the two.

Alavi also underlines the separate origins and loyalties of the two groups:

> Historically, Deobandis have tended to be mainly urban and from the middle and upper strata of society, whereas Barelvi influence has been mainly in rural areas, with a populist appeal. This has changed somewhat in recent decades, for Barelvi influence has extended to towns and cities. ... Traditionally Barelvi influence has been weaker in the UP [then United Provinces, now Uttar Pradesh] ... than in the Punjab and to some degree in Sind. On the other hand the main base of Deobandis was in UP, especially among urban Muslims, who are the muhajirs[1] (refugees from India) in Pakistan.

To this, Alavi adds that Deoband has made inroads among the rural and urbanised Pathans in Pakistan. In addition, I would like to observe that Deoband has also spread among the Gujarati Muslim community who were early converts to Islam through their trading contacts with Arabia, like the South Indian Muslims of Kerala.

The predominance of Barelvi mosques in Britain is therefore a consequence of the mainly Pakistani origin of the South Asian Muslim population in Britain [...]. The constituency of Deoband lies largely

---

[1] *Muhajir*s are migrants or people fleeing from persecution. The word derives from *hijra*, the occasion when the Prophet Muhammad left Mecca for Medina in 622 because conditions in Mecca made it impossible to practise Islam.

with the smaller group of Indian Muslims, or those of Indian origin who may have arrived in Britain by way of a family emigration from India to Africa at an earlier stage, who make up some 168,000 of Britain's total South Asian Muslim community.

None the less, the number of Deobandi mosques is significant, with a clientele composed either of these Indian Muslims, many of them from the Gujarati community, which plays a major part in the Deobandi movement in Britain, or of Pakistani *muhajirs,* descended from migrants who left India for Pakistan at or after the partition of India in 1947, or of other Pakistanis who have attached themselves to Deoband by choice, or of Pathans.

As a local phenomenon, Deoband has strong roots within the Gujarati Muslim community in Britain, but it would be wrong to suppose that the Deobandi movement is in essence linked with Gujarati ethnicity. A list of graduates of Deoband in the Dar ul-Uloum's first century from 1867 to 1967 included only 138 Gujaratis among over seven thousand graduates. But in Britain, Gujaratis do seem to play a major part in both Deoband and Tabligh. The British 'Amir' of Tablighi Jamaat, who with his advisory council controls the mosque and school at Dewsbury, is a Gujarati, for example, and Tablighis I have met socially at Dewsbury spoke as if a strong Gujarati presence there was to be taken for granted. One key informant for the present study, who is the head of the mosque committee at a leading Deobandi mosque in Birmingham, is also Gujarati.

The particular nature of the Gujarati community in Britain and its significance in the international context deserves some attention. Gujaratis are prominent among Asians abroad because of their role as a merchant community which has spread round the world from its Indian base. Alavi remarks that the Gujarati trading community adopted Islam at the time of its early contacts with Arab traders. Gujarati merchants have spread throughout India, and then into Asia and Africa, and now into Europe and the Americas. They have taken Islam with them, and their habits as travellers and their international family and business links have naturally led them to be attracted to the similar spreading network represented by Tabligh, and to be ideally able to serve Tabligh's purposes at the same time as their own business interests.

Structurally, then, Deoband and Tabligh coexist, feeding and reinforcing each other. The Deobandi mosques form the static framework of a system which also involves Tablighi Jamaat as a mobile element. The Deobandi mosques provide a haven for Tablighi preachers and other travellers engaged in *khuruj,* while they also encourage their own members to leave their local areas in order to preach, either for short periods, or for spells of months or even years which may involve foreign travel, to India or to other Muslim countries, or to countries with minority Muslim populations. The following section describes some of the attraction of Tabligh, the way it recruits its activists and the way they work.

The wider appeal of Tabligh

So far, we have looked at the Tablighi Jamaat within the South Asian context and as part of the way the Deobandi community functions. One set of important features which remains to be explained is the movement's wider appeal and the way in which it has spread to be a world-wide phenomenon, the mechanisms of which also relate to its success within the Deobandi community itself. The way in which Tabligh is transmitted internationally is clearly one key to this question.

Tabligh has found four major means of dissemination. These are: the pilgrimage to Mecca; the network of Indian merchants in Asia, Africa and Britain; the immigration of workers to Western countries; and the Deobandi connection (Gaboriau, 1986). The last three of these relate essentially to the Deobandi link and to the development of Tabligh within the Deobandi community. However, the pilgrimage to Mecca, and pious journeys to Mecca by Muslims at other times of the year, seem certain to have been a means of transmission. The founder of Tabligh, Mawlana Muhammad Ilyas, himself made the pilgrimage twice in his lifetime. Contacts between Muslims of different nationalities and ethnic origins in Mecca have always been a fruitful channel for the world-wide dissemination of Muslim ideas. In more modern circumstances Tabligh members take every advantage of travels undertaken either for the specific purpose of preaching or for any other purpose, business, family or social, to pursue their religious aims. But if there have been, and are increasingly in an age of migration and rapid travel, many opportunities for Tablighis to work, the question remains, what is it that has made a success of Tabligh as a missionary movement outside its community of origin?

The answer seems to lie in the style of Tablighi proselytisation, which both motivates activists to spread their faith abroad as far as possible and appeals in different ways to the recipient audience. The activities of Tabligh follow closely the prescription of the movement's founder, Muhammad Ilyas, who was also a Deobandi 'alim. He began his own personal mission, which in due course developed into Tablighi Jamaat, because he was overcome by the urge to bring the truth of Islam as he saw it to the ignorant nominal Muslims by whom he was surrounded in North India, and to teach them the real nature of the faith. His practice was based on the ways of the Prophet Muhammad himself, as Ilyas understood them.

Ilyas set out principles, which include emphases on: (1) the centrality of the *kalimah*, the statement that there is no God but God and Muhammad is the prophet of God, which must be understood as well as enunciated; (2) the importance of prayer, whose inner purpose is to help the believer to refrain from sinful or base actions; (3) correct behaviour towards fellow Muslims, whoever they may be, in pursuit of which one must be prepared to sacrifice one's own rights; (4) the ideal that every Muslim must undertake each action with the primary aim of pleasing God, and with only the secondary aim of improving himself; and (5) the view that every Muslim must be prepared to take part personally in preaching expeditions, and in the endeavour to spread an understanding of the true faith within the community. To these positive principles is added the negative rule that Muslims should refrain from wasting their time in superfluous talk and action, and should of course refrain from sinful acts. These are all Sufi principles.

Towards the end of his life, Ilyas became more specific about the ways in which preaching, teaching and *khuruj* should be undertaken – including an emphasis on *zikr* 'remembrance', (repetition of divine names or religous formulae) and on learning and knowledge, or *ilm*. Haq (1972, p.145) points out that:

> Ilyas regarded learning and *zikr* as the two wheels of the carriage of his work, and said that knowledge without *zikr* led people into darkness and gloom, while *zikr* without learning placed temptations before them and caused dissension. He felt that without knowledge and *zikr* his movement would lose its spiritual character and become materialistic.

Why should this movement – begun in India in the 1920s – have such a strong appeal in modern circumstances and in diverse countries and circumstances? Gilles Kepel suggested a mechanism which would explain the appeal of Islam in migrant populations outside their country of origin and beyond the *dar-ul-Islam* or realm of Islam (personal communication; [...]). This lies in the migrant's search for identity, and applies with perhaps even more force to the children of Muslim migrants who may have the right to, or have acquired, a European citizenship. An Algerian, for example, will find increasingly as his period of residence in France or elsewhere in Europe lengthens, that he is cut off from his own original country whose experience he has not shared. At the same time, his French neighbours make it clear to him that he cannot regard himself as

French, whatever the legalities of his situation may be. The attraction of Islam is obvious: it serves as a constant source of identity available to a person who has lost his national orientation.

A parallel but separate attraction applies to some Muslim inhabitants of Islamic countries (that is to say, countries where Islam is the religion of the majority and may be the official religion). Many such countries are in the process of economic transformation which has created new and marked economic distinctions and has imposed materialist criteria of success. In this case, as Majid Tehranian (1992) has suggested, poverty itself becomes identified as deviancy within the society, and the poor will turn to the alternative value system which is at hand – Islam – which seems to belong to them more than the imported standards and criteria do, thereby giving value to their lives.

Tabligh, whose philosophy encourages its adherents to travel ever more widely and to take advantage of all forms of contact to spread the faith of Islam, is ideally suited to satisfy these contexts and developments. The reason is that it is simple and broadly democratic, and offers instant progress for the newly recruited believer. The neophyte is urged from the beginning to take part. From his first profession of the *kalimah* and his embarkation on a programme of prayer and *zikr*, the newcomer is ready to take part in a junior capacity in preaching excursions himself. At the most basic level, the appeal of Tabligh is such that it tells the new recruit there is something he can do immediately to serve the organisation, while more sophisticated understanding may come later.

Like some other organisations, Tabligh uses the concept of service within the group both to bind the loyalty of its members and to give them satisfaction. Short periods away from home in the company of other Tabligh members serve to deepen the loyalty and commitment of members. Because of the 'concentric' organisation, where an inner group of full-time Tabligh personnel is surrounded by an outer ring of more experienced members and an outermost circle of more loosely attached collaborators, there is always both a level within the organisation where a member can feel comfortable and another activist who is known to him to whom he can turn for advice.

Here I would like to return to the question of what Tablighis, following Sufi tradition, call *zikr*, and its significance and its role in Tabligh's activities. The word literally means 'remembrance' in Arabic, or even, as Haq (1972, p.201) suggests, 'commemoration'. Its adoption from Sufi orders was quite deliberate, Haq (1972, p.62) suggests: 'Bearing in mind the long sufi tradition among Muslims in India, Ilyas inaugurated a religious movement which aimed at reviving spiritual devotion by emphasising Sufi practices which he adopted for his work with certain changes.'

According to Metcalf (1982), the founders of the university at Deoband were mainly Chishti sheikhs. Muhammad Ilyas himself enrolled some of his more enthusiastic disciples into the Chishtiyah order, but believed that some aspects of Sufism were important for all his followers. Of these *zikr* was central. The actual practice of *zikr* consists of repeating either silently or aloud a prescribed number of times a prayer, or a name of God, or the *kalimah*. This must be done a certain number of times each day, and silent *zikr* can also be performed. In the Sufi context it often involves rhythmic chanting, but Deobandi and Tablighi practice is, I gather, more restrained.

It is this centrality of Sufi practice, the Sufi nature of Ilyas's rules and prohibitions, and *zikr* in particular which has no doubt provided the link between Tablighi and the Muslims of North Africa. Sufi orders (the *tariqat)* are a central part of North African Muslim experience, and particularly in the rural and popular contexts. A proselytising movement which works partially through the Sufi orders, and which relies in any case on some aspects of Sufi practice even for its non-initiated members, is in possession of an important key to influence in North Africa. In addition, the Chishtiyah order, with which Tabligh is linked, takes a very ecumenical view of other orders, and does not shrink from absorbing Qadiri, or Naqshbandi practices, or ideas from other orders.

As to the actual dates of transmission, Tabligh seems to have been limited to the Indian subcontinent during the lifetime of Muhammad Ilyas, but to have begun to expand in the 1950s. According to my own informants, the first Tabligh groups came to Britain in 1956. Tabligh appear to have begun to make its major move into other parts of Europe in the 1960s. For example, although a first Tabligh mission to France in 1962 failed, by 1968 the organisation was effectively established in that country (Kepel, 1987, pp.190–1). A final conjecture may be made about the way in which the movement spreads, in connection with the reason for its activists efforts in Europe rather than the mechanisms of their success, if we suppose that the urge to travel outside the English-speaking world and to find new fields for conversion may spring from a sense of frustration at the movement's limitation within the English and Urdu speaking sphere.

Conclusion: Tablighi Jamaat, Muslim modernity and cosmopolitanism

It is easy for outside observers to see an organisation such as Tabligh as seeking to reimpose the discipline of a mythical past, or leading to communal separatism or seclusion. Indeed, Muslim society is regarded as 'backward' by Western commentators who fail to interpret what they see. Such observers not infrequently order their perceptions in the light of what they refer to as Islamic 'fundamentalism'. But 'fundamentalism' is basically a Western concept, rather than a Muslim one. It is a way in which Western observers of Islam can categorise and link Muslim organisations which may in practice have little in common with each other, an example of what Edward Said (1981) calls a 'coercive label'.

The idea of 'fundamentalism' is connected with the notion that Islamic activists are backward-looking, and that their way of thinking is in some sense medieval and opposed to Western ways of organising society, which are here taken to be axiomatically the most favourable to social and human development. There is much here to argue with, but I will content myself with a critical appraisal of the notion that Islam itself is backward looking, and argue that organisations such as Tabligh are essentially innovative and pioneering rather than retrogressive.

On the one hand, there are some senses in which Tabligh is the kind of organisation which might be described from a Western point of view as 'fundamentalist', or, as the French put it, 'intégriste'. The movement demands that Muslims with whom it comes into contact should reinstate Islam as the central element in their lives, and that Islam should provide the criteria according to which they structure their lives. It also makes it clear that it is impossible for a Muslim to pick and choose about which parts of Islam will fit into his life: it is all or nothing. On the other hand, the notion of 'fundamentalism' is itself controversial from the Muslim perspective. Muslims will explain that they are not adding anything to Islam, or carrying out their observances in any special way. Many Muslims will make the point that what is described, mainly in the West, as 'fundamentalism' is nothing more nor less than wholehearted Islam.

There is a clear sense in which Tabligh is non-'fundamentalist', since it is concerned only with religion in the private sphere; it is non-political. Contemporary organisations in Muslim countries identified by the West as 'fundamentalist' in general tend to have political ambitions – particularly in the present post-Iranian-revolution period. Even within Islamic countries, however, Tabligh does not concern itself with the argument that Islam should provide the framework of political life (although it did, after initial reluctance, support the foundation of the state of Pakistan). Meanwhile, Tablighis adopt the orthodox Muslim view that outside Islamic countries Muslims are under a political obligation to live as responsible citizens of the society in which they find themselves.

But whether or not Tabligh can be meaningfully said to be 'fundamentalist', a more important question arises about how 'fundamentalist' movements – that is to say, pious, militant, or political Islamic movements – are seen by the outside world. A common Western view of Islamic 'fundamentalists' is that they are harking back to the past, and want a return to some mythical state of Islamic society, or adherence to some set of rules which has formerly been accepted. Quite to the contrary, however, I believe phenomena such as Tablighi Jamaat, whether or not they are seen as 'fundamentalist', should be regarded as thoroughly modern.

Tablighis do not call for a return to some former version of Islamic society, but rather attempt to construct something new and in tune with contemporary needs. It can be argued that no social organisation has been truly Islamic since the earliest days of the state constructed and left behind by the Prophet Muhammad in Arabia. Modern 'fundamentalists' do refer to that as an ideal, but realise that their enterprise must be concerned with the construction of a new and different form of social organisation.

The body of Islamic tradition and jurisprudence to which they refer was constructed in the times which followed Muhammad's early society, and the later polities in Muslim countries were in many senses not Islamic. Organisations such as Tabligh are responding to changing circumstances with a flexible approach to the organisation of an Islamic society, not rejecting anything from the past, but applying it and adapting it in new ways. The flexibility of Islam is something which many informants have stressed.

Furthermore, Tabligh is not an inward looking organisation which sees its aim as the production of an isolated and withdrawn society. It is often held that notions such as 'the Muslim community' are misleading and inappropriate when used in the British or other European contexts, because the Muslim populations of Europe come from diverse sources and do not constitute a single group. Tabligh's aim, however, is to weld different groups together, and to produce a Muslim society which is not only Islamic and modern but also cosmopolitan.

The style of Tabligh, from the days of its founder Muhammad Ilyas, confirms this view. Initiating neophytes into his Sufi order, Ilyas claimed to welcome them simultaneously into the four orders locally prevalent in north India: the Qadiriya, the Naqshbandiya and the Suhrawardiya as well as his own Chishtiyah. And in the context of the schools of Islamic law, he tried to reconcile the teaching of his own Hanafi school with the interpretations and judgements of the other schools.

Modern followers of the founder take a similar view. The chairman of a mosque committee in Birmingham deplored and played down the distinction between Deobandi and Barelvi Islam, and emphasised the underlying importance of Islam's basic principles on which everyone agrees. The Amir at Dewsbury disclaimed the idea that the interpretations of any particular religious school took precedence in the teaching at his *madrasa*. Though regretfully admitting that, in the words of one informant, 'we go where we are welcome', Tablighis have a clear vision of a single Islam of mutually supportive and understanding believers, and do not look inward to particular communities.

Tablighis are proud of the international extent of their movement, recall fondly their own travels, and draw attention to the diverse membership of the organisation. My impression is that they see Tabligh's destiny as the framework on which a global Islamic society can be built. The non-political nature of their movement and their stated intention of good relations with the civil and political structures of the non-Muslim societies in which many of them live is also an indication of another aspect of their cosmopolitan ambition. The Islamic society they aim to construct will be an essentially new phenomenon.

References

Alavi, H. (1988) 'Pakistan and Islam: Ethnicity and Ideology', in F. Halliday and H. Alvi (eds), *State and Ideology in the Middle East and Pakistan* (Basingstoke: Macmillan).

Aziz, K. K. (1962) *Britain and Muslim India* (London: Heinemann).

Dassetto, F. (1988a) 'Le Tabligh en Belgique'. *Sybidi Papers*, No. 2 (Louvain La Neuve: Academia).

Dassetto, F. (1988b) 'The Tabligh Organisation in Belgium', in T. Gerholm and Y. Georg Litman (eds), *The New Islamic Presence in Europe* (London: Mansell).

Dassetto, F. and A. Bastenier (1988) *Europa: nuova frontiera dell'Islam* (Roma: Edizioni Lavoro).

Gaboriau, M. (1986) 'What is Tablighi Jamaat? Preliminary Thoughts about a New Strategy of Adaptation to a Minority Situation' (unpublished manuscript).

Haq, M. Anwarul (1972) *The Faith Movement of Mawlana Muhammad Ilyas* (London: Allen & Unwin).

Kepel, G. (1987) *Les banlieues de l'Islam* (Paris: Seuil).

Metcalf, B. (1982) *Islamic Revival in British India: Deoband 1860–1900* (Princeton, NJ: Princeton University Press).

Mortimer, E. (1982) *Faith and Power: The Politics of Islam* (London: Faber).

Nielsen, J. (1992) *Muslims in Western Europe* (Edinburgh: Edinburgh University Press).

Robinson, F. (1988) 'Varieties of South Asian Islam', University of Warwick Research Papers, No.8 (Coventry: Centre for Research in Ethnic Relations).

Said, E. (1981) *Covering Islam* (London: Routledge).

Tehranian, M. (1992) 'Interview with Malise Ruthven', *Sunday*, BBC Radio 4, 28 March.

Translatability in Islam and in Christianity in Africa: a thematic approach*

LAMIN SANNEH

Introduction

Religious expansion in Africa of Islam and of Christianity has raised intriguing comparative questions on the nature and character of Muslim and Christian communities on the continent. In several parts of West Africa – what the Arabic sources call *bilād al-sūdān* [the land of the blacks] – Islam is at least a thousand years old, whereas in the same areas Christianity is barely a hundred. This chronological disparity overlaps another disparity, that of attitudes toward indigenization. For Islam, in spite of its venerable longevity, vernacular languages were considered unsuitable for adoption as a scriptural and canonical medium, while Christianity adopted these languages as necessary and sufficient channels of biblical revelation and worship. This indigenous disparity far outranks its chronological counterpart in social effects and it primes the temper of reform sensibilities in the two traditions (Sanneh 1989b). Muslim reform in Africa tended to pit the hackles of nontranslatability against sluggish local accommodation, sometimes with thrones and empires at stake. Christian reform, by contrast, constituted the vernacular into a principle of renewal and national pride, usually one with non-African standards at stake. Throughout their spread and expansion in Africa,

* This text first appeared in *Religion in Africa: Experience and Expression*, ed. Thomas D. Blakely, Walter E.A. van Beck, Dennis L. Thomson, with the assistance of Linda Hunter Adams, Merrill E. Oates, Monograph series of the David M. Kennedy Center for International Studies at Brigham Young University, London: James Currey, 1994, pp.23–45.

Islam and Christianity have reiterated their contrasting and distinctive forms.

In Christian reform, Africans have utilized the vernacular both for self-understanding and for appropriating Christian religion, whereas Muslim reform achieved the equally remarkable goal of alienating the vernacular by applying the progressive pressure of the nontranslatable Qur'ān. This contrast has major implications for how we view mission and vernacular pluralism in the two religions, as well as for the nature and purpose of conversion. And it is in the context of this contrast that I would like especially to examine the issues of religious "reform", "renewal", and "revival".

The Islamic paradigm

It is important to spell out the contrasting conditions before considering detailed local contexts for the principle of translatability. Muslims ascribe to Arabic the status of a revealed language, for it is the medium in which the Qur'ān, the sacred scripture of Islam, was revealed. In several passages the Qur'ān bears testimony to its own Arabic uniqueness, what the authorities call its *i'jāz*, or "inimitable eloquence" (Qur'ān x:38–39; xi:l–2, 16; xvi:104–105; xxviii:49; xxxix:24, 29; xli:41–42; xliii:1–3). The author of the Qur'ān, who is God, thus came to be associated with its speech, so that the very sounds of the language are believed to originate in heaven (see Guillaume 1962:74; Gibb 1974 [1963]:36–37). Consequently, Muslims have instituted the sacred Arabic as the language of canonical devotions. Given the lay character of Islam, these canonical devotions have brought the sacred Arabic to the ears of the ordinary believer, although normally only religious specialists understand this language in any satisfactory fashion (von Grunebaum 1962:37–59).

The active participation of lay Muslims in the ritual acts of worship [*ṣalāt*], fasting [*ṣawm*] and, less frequently, the pilgrimage [*ḥajj*] to Mecca means that Arabic phrases, however imperfectly understood, remain on the lips of believers wherever and whoever they happen to be. Even in thinly or unevenly Islamized areas, the changes in perspective arising from use of the sacred Arabic provide the impetus for reforming local practice, rather than yielding to indigenous forms.

An intriguing situation arises in which the prestigious and revered status of Arabic acts to disenfranchise the vernacular. Mother-tongue speakers find themselves in the anomalous position of their languages being considered profane [*'ajamī*] for the decisive acts of the religious code, a consideration that bears little relationship to one's fluency in the Arabic. In fact, both the expert Arabist and the illiterate convert share a common veneration for the sacred language: the expertise of the one is the standard toward which the other aspires.

The success of Islam as a missionary religion is founded on the perpetuation of the sacred Arabic. As the religion arrived among the preponderantly non-Arab populations, its double blade gleamed with the pointedness of faith in one God and acceptance of the primacy of the sacred Arabic. In this situation it was often difficult to say which blade cut deeper, for often non-Muslim populations appropriated Qur'ānic phrases long before they converted to Islam. There is in fact an old tradition of non-Muslims venerating the sacred script. For example, the "Veil of St. Anne" is kept in a fifteenth-century bottle in the church of Apt, in the south of France. It turns out that the "holy" relic has an Arabic inscription containing the *Shahādah*, the Muslim creed, as well as the names of the Fāṭimid Caliph, al-Mustaʻlī (reigned 1094–1101) and his prime minister, Afḍal, with an indication that the textile was woven in Egypt in 1096–1097 (Schacht and Bosworth 1974:298).

The characteristic missionary institution of Islam is the Qur'ān school, where boys and girls are taught to memorize passages in Arabic from the sacred book (Plate [1]). Rote memorization in school, rather than scriptural translation, has been the mode of Islam's expansion through sub-Saharan Africa and elsewhere. It is important to separate this matter from the question of adopting Arabic as the language of administration, business, and education. Sudan is the only black African country where one could say "Islamization" was accompanied by a thorough "Arabization". In the rest of the continent one may speak confidently of "Islamization" being accompanied by the enthronement of the sacred Arabic as the uncompromising standard of religious orthodoxy, even though Muslims have continued to use the vernacular in everyday life.

[...]

It is this phenomenon that I wish to highlight as a contrast to the Christian case. One may argue that one effect of the preeminent, exclusive role of the sacred Arabic has been to discourage general Muslim interest in the languages of non-Muslims. This is not the same as saying that Muslims did not learn other languages, for they did, but that such languages, apart from their practical value, had no status in the Muslim dispensation. African Muslims who have only a nodding acquaintance with mosque Arabic feel proprietorial about it and are unwilling to allow non-Muslims to take responsibility for it. Ordinary Muslims have even in certain instances organized to oppose the teaching of Arabic by non-Muslim Arabic speakers in secondary

Plate [1] Pupils at Qur'ān school in Djenne, Mali, learn to read and write the words of the Qur'ān on their polished wooden boards. The phrases of the sacred Arabic are learned by heart: recitation is important, not translation. Their teacher has jotted down texts on each of their boards and recited them for the students, who then repeat many times what they heard until the text as well as the writing of it are mastered. Robert G. v. Wendel de Joode.

schools. In their eyes the religion of Islam has a right to exercise proprietary control over Arabic, whether it is the Arabic of the Qur'ān or of the marketplace. Conversely, non-Muslims might also resist the introduction of Arabic for fear that Islamic conversion might be demanded as a price. In both cases we have a synthesis of language and religion, and it is surely one of the deeply interesting facts about Islam that in its remarkable missionary expansion it has preserved this synthesis, defying the forces of vernacular usage to carve a prestigious place for the sacred language.

The Christian counterpoint

Christianity in Africa has been characterized by a vigorous vernacular process from the period of the earliest Christians on the continent. Thus, the Coptic church dates its founding to the period coinciding with religious upheavals in Upper Egypt about the middle of the third century A.D. In that upheaval, Coptic villages, long resistant to conversion, embraced the new Christian religion to the point of being prepared to suffer martyrdom in its defense (Eusebius 1984 [1965]: 337ff.). There soon followed, in the late fourth and early fifth centuries, the commencement of a vast and vigorous Coptic literature. This literature later enabled the Copts to long maintain a strong, if at times inhibiting, sense of identity, especially under Muslim Egypt from the seventh century A.D. onward (von Harnack 1905 [v.2]:304–323; Butler:1884). In any case, Coptic translation work marked a genuine advance on the cumbersome hieroglyphic and foreign Greek writing systems of earlier times, which excluded ordinary people. Kenneth Scott Latourette agrees:

> In Egypt it was the successful effort to provide the masses of the population with a literature in the speech of everyday life which halted the exclusive use of the alien Greek for the written page and which stimulated the development of an alphabet which could be quickly and easily learned by the multitude in place of the ancient hieroglyphics which could be the property only of the few. Through this medium Coptic Christian literature came into being, largely the work of monks.

(Latourette 1975:250–251; see also Frend 1984:577)

Similarly, with the introduction of Christianity into Ethiopia, schools were established; and by the middle of the seventh century, most of the translation work into Amharic had been completed, with the Ethiopian Orthodox Church becoming the nerve center of Ethiopian nationalism (Tamrat 1972; Davis 1967:62–69). These and other materials begin to suggest that scriptural translation and similar linguistic efforts are a force in the rise of mother tongue aspirations – an early form of national sentiment. Also in modern Africa, mother-tongue aspirations have sometimes provided an impetus and vehicle for expressions of national sentiment[1] and certainly have been bulwarks in the fight against colonialism and against political, economic, and cultural imperialism. Literacy in the mother tongue has often been – and continues to be – a factor in indigenous renewal and the pluralist dispensation in Africa. And the missionary role in

---

[1] For example, Kiswahili in Tanzania, Kirundi in Burundi, Somali in Somalia, Sesotho in Lusotho.

instituting mother tongues as part of Christianity has thus been important in all of these developments.

By contrast, we are confronted with a reverse picture for Islamic gains in Africa: Muslim orthodoxy holds to the principle of nontranslatability, which made vernacular self-understanding incompatible – this, notwithstanding the fact that Africans were themselves the preponderant agents in the dissemination of the faith and thus presumably free from external pressure to propagate prescriptive Islam. It is within this symmetrical framework that we have to ask about the status of linguistic and cultural pluralism under the decisive rubrics of faith and practice in Islam and in Christianity. An unconventional conclusion awaits our evaluation of the evidence.

Reform, renewal, and revival in the Islamic tradition

When we consider the nature and outcome of renewal movements in Islam and Christianity in Africa, we find a situation considerably affected by the translatability question. In the Islamic tradition the springs of reform and renewal were fed by the perennial premillennial figure who was to appear at the head of every Islamic century to set right the affairs of the people. In African Islam, an important occurrence of such messianic ideas was in the correspondence between the king of Songhay, Askiya al-Ḥājj Muḥammad Ture, and the itinerant North African scholar ʿAbd al-Karīm al-Maghīlī (d. ca. 1505–1506). The Askiya had inquired of al-Maghīlī, who was visiting Songhay in 1502, about the conditions under which religious reform might be necessary, a momentous question whose consequences extended into the nineteenth-century reform movements in other parts of West Africa. It is worth quoting this tradition in full. Al-Maghīlī acquainted the Askiya with the following authoritative opinion regarding reform:

> Thus it is related that at the beginning of every century God sends [people] a scholar who regenerates their religion for them. There is no doubt that the conduct of this scholar in every century in enjoining what is right and forbidding what is wrong, and setting aright [the] people's affairs, establishing justice among them and supporting truth against falsehood and the oppressed against the oppressor, will be in contrast to the conduct of the scholars of his age. For this reason he will be an odd man out among them on account of his being the only man of such pure conduct and on account of the small number of men like him. Then will it be plain and clear that he is one of the reformers [al-muṣliḥūn] and that whoso opposes him and acts hostilely towards him so as to turn people away from him is but one of the miscreants,

because of the saying of the Prophet, may God bless him and grant him peace: "Islam started as an odd man out [*gharīb*] and thus will it end up, so God bless the odd men out". Someone said, "And who are they, O Messenger of God?" He said, "Those who set matters aright in evil times". That is one of the clearest signs of the people of the Reminder [*ahl al-dhikr*] through whom God regenerates for people their religion.

(Hunwick 1985:66–67; Hiskett 1962:584)

In the hands of al-Maghīlī, reform and renewal are complementary. Reform may be more narrowly understood as undoing the harm that results from neglect of the religious code, while renewal may be taken to mean the level at which prescriptive standards are applied after the removal of impediments. The two parts are conjoined in the standard scriptural injunction: *amal bi-ma 'rūf wa nahy 'an al-munkar* [to enjoin good works and restrain from what is disapproved of] (xiii:21–22). "Revival" in the technical sense of religious enthusiasm is discouraged by Muslim religious authorities, for as they see it, the issue is alignment of conduct to make it conform to established prescriptions, not that of seeking the signs of the Spirit. Consequently, the opinions of al-Maghīlī on mixing Islam with African religion carry the mark of a rigorist. He is not satisfied with less than the explicit application of the code; it is not sufficient to imply in conduct acknowledgment of its authority. Thus he spells out what is to be done with those Muslims who also participate in non-Islamic rites. These, he says,

are polytheists [*mushrikūn*] without doubt, because anathematizing [*takfir*], according to the manifest meaning of the Law, is for less than that, and there is no doubt that Holy War against them is better and more meritorious [*afḍal*] than Holy War against unbelievers who do not declare the witness of faith: "There is no god except God; Muḥammad is His Apostle".

(Hiskett 1962:584, translation amended)

[...]

Several factors galvanized the reform impulse in African Islam: the concern with safeguarding the monotheist ideal against the sin of "association" [*shirk*], grievances over the unjust treatment of foreign Muslims in the state, the burdensome nature of levies and imposts, compromises in Muslim behavior and conduct, the threat of the organized state becoming the instrument of a well-coordinated traditional religious life, and the scandal of the nimble-tongued scholars pandering to the esteem of capricious rulers – all this increased the tension. By throwing in the idea of a messianic dispensation almost at hand, al-Maghīlī added an incendiary charge.

Yet the fundamental question has still to be asked: Why should such materials continue to appeal to African Muslims long and far removed from the Islamic heartlands? or, Why, given this distance in time and space, should the Islamic legacy be able to preserve its affinity with the Islam of first-century Arabia? The capacity of Muslims to invoke the ideal past as a model for their own time and place remains one of the most remarkably consistent features of the religion – and that without a "Vatican" or similar universal bureaucratic structure. By what principle, then, do African Muslims act to rescind the authority of indigenous tradition and practice and replace it with the prescriptive force of Islam?

The nontranslatability of Muslim scriptures: the motive force in reform

A few provisional ideas are necessary on what is a large and complicated issue. We should dismiss outright the idea that Muslim opposition is forced by the nature of the inherent corruption and contradiction in indigenous traditions, for that accepts the verdict of a protagonist. Nor should we be content with looking for justifications in structural factors, such as the limitations of traditional political institutions when faced with the demands of a supratribal world of Muslims, foreigners, a cosmopolitan trading community, a literate elite, and the wider orbit of international diplomacy. All those factors are important, but they do not add up to the intense singlemindedness of Muslims cast in vastly different circumstances and time. We have a clue in the impatient outburst of al-Maghīlī regarding what he considered an incriminating defect in the scholars. "One of their characteristics", he charges, "is that they are not Arabic-speaking [*'ajam*]; they understand no Arabic except a little of the speech of the Arabs of their towns, in an incorrect and corrupted fashion, and a great deal of non-Arabic, so that they do not understand the intentions of the scholars" (Hiskett 1962:581).

Writers make relatively little of this complaint, even though it recurs in much of the standard literature. Its force stems from the nontranslatability of the Muslim scriptures, and it is, therefore, able to sweep aside local resistance and make capital of its foreign identity. Those African Muslims who begin their life with the obvious disadvantage of worshiping in a strange and foreign language will sooner or later reach, or be made to reach, the stage where practice, however imperfect, creates proximity – and culpability, as the words of al-Maghīlī prove. Our appreciating this point should help illuminate other areas of Muslim objection. In the sphere of its monotheist tradition, to take one example, Islam is able to act with effective authority because its judgment is enshrined in the material of a nontranslatable Qur'ān, which itself fosters a devotion and veneration bordering on the magical. In the area of worship, the reformers had the advantage of trying only to *reorient* and restrict a wide habit that encompassed worship at many shrines rather than having to invent the habit anew. The instrument of restriction was the mosque, and its responsibility for the prescribed acts of worship. [...]

Although they wrote in the vernacular, the men of the Fulani Muslim caliphate [in northern Algeria in the nineteenth century] looked upon Arabic as the preeminent standard of the religious and political life. Hiskett pinpoints this element in the Muslim reform heritage, saying it was the universal principle that guided the reform movement and inspired the leaders:

> These forces of Islamic ideology served to create in these men a sense of Islamic universalism. That is to say, they had a vision of a single, world-wide Islam, in which the way of life, the way of government and the morality and social behaviour of all individuals were regulated according to the Sharī'a and Sunnah, the Law and Tradition of the Prophet. They were determined that they would tolerate nothing less than this in their own countries. The *jihads* were the practical expression of this determination.
>
> (Hiskett 1984:170–171)

The large stock of vernacular Islamic literature serves only as embellishment on the Arabic motif, and this function has been amply demonstrated in some recent works such as that of Haafkens (1983), who was writing mainly of Adamawa in the present Republic of Cameroon. It is intriguing to reflect on how the Fulani Muslim leaders came to lose most of their own language as the reform impulse strengthened under the caliphate. Thus it was that the headquarters of the reform order was constituted to reflect the ethos of a Middle Eastern Arabic-speaking environment (Hiskett 1975:136).

It must be stressed that accommodating religious functionaries, whom we class under the generic title "clerics", have continued to preside over a vigorous tradition of Islamic practice. For example, Patrick Ryan, in a dissertation at Harvard, has shown how Muslim Yoruba have ingeniously blended Yoruba tradition with their understanding of Islam (Ryan 1978). Certainly at that level a form of translation goes on, and no one who is familiar with Muslim Africa will question that. Ian Lewis for one has argued forcefully for a formulation that includes within mainstream Islam elements normally consigned to the periphery and outside the religious core as marginal or syncretic (Lewis 1983:55–67).

What remains fascinating in so many accounts of Muslim conversion, however, is how people begin their journey by embarking on the path of divination during a time of misfortune, for example, only to arrive at the point where, eventually, the unfamiliar, and for them modest, medium of the sacred Arabic becomes the operative medium of religious truth. Among the Mossi of Burkina Faso, barrenness among non-Muslim women may be treated by the divinatory diagnosis that the would-be children are refusing to be born except as Muslims. The obvious remedy is conversion to Islam. Among the Giriama of Kenya, to take another example, people falling ill are diagnosed as having been possessed by Muslim spirits for which the cure is, once again, conversion to Islam. In both cases, however, the destination is clear, or soon to be clear, even if the route is arcane. Every Muslim convert, however remotely located, must encounter Islam through the sacred Arabic. It is inconceivable to claim the Muslim name without sooner or later performing at least some of the mandatory five daily prayers. To do that, worshipers are obliged without exception to employ the Arabic of the Qur'ān. I have examined in detail one outstanding historical example of an African Muslim clerical tradition centered in the Jakhanke (or Jahanke) people of Senegambia. This group achieved a major transposition of Islam by repudiating for themselves – but not for others – *jihād*, and other forms of armed militancy, and by cultivating a reputation for political neutrality in which they refuse to hold political office. This pacific clerical tradition has a long history behind it; the accounts speak of its roots going back to the thirteenth century (Sanneh 1989a). Such peaceful dissemination of Islam inevitably implies a high degree of tolerance for mixing, and Jakhanke Islam is no exception. Yet both in the traditions concerning the founder of that clerical tradition as well as in the detailed work of the clerical center, what the Jakhanke themselves refer to as the *majlis*, Mecca remains the unwavering point of religious orientation, reinforced by observance of worship in the *salāt*, the standing reminder of the *ḥajj* pilgrimage obligation, and the use of Arabic in study, teaching and devotion (Sanneh 1976).[2]

[2] For a continuation of this theme into the modern era, see Sanneh 1981a and 1981b; and for how the Arabic theme might work in other situations, see Sanneh 1979.

The comparative Christian example: reform and vernacular renewal

The picture of mission and renewal in Christianity in Africa sharply contrasts with the Islamic one. For example, Henry Venn (d. 1873) – a nineteenth-century missionary statesman who was in close touch with the African situation – clearly saw that for Christianity to be successful, it must encourage national characteristics, for it utilizes the vernacular paradigm to express its message. The vernacular had particularly accompanied the spread and expansion of Christianity. So Venn argued that even if missions had a united view about the primacy of Jesus Christ, it was impossible that "distinctions and defects will vanish. ... But it may be doubted whether, to the last, the Church of Christ will not exhibit marked national characteristics which, in the overruling grace of God will tend to its perfection and glory" (Knight 1880:284, cited in Walls 1981:48; see also Warren 1971:77). The worldwide Christian mission was not, for Venn, the vehicle for propagating the universal values of Western political domination, but rather the commitment to the "national" enterprise of the respective societies affected. Missionaries, he observed, were already "reeds shaken by the wind" of scarcity, and no statistical notion of their work does justice to what they are really about, which is to foster vernacular self-confidence. It is their job, he maintained, "not to supply an European pastorate, but to prepare native pastors, and to endeavour, by divine help, *to fix the spiritual standard in such Churches by securing for them a supply of vernacular Scriptures*" (Warren 1971:119, emphasis added). Thus Venn's formulations came pretty close to expressing the idea that might be considered the flagship of modern missions. As a principle this idea undercuts – whether intentionally or not – the idea of colonialism, at least in its obvious effects on indigenous cultures.

The vernacular principle had explosive consequences in the nineteenth-century mission in the Niger Delta in Nigeria. There, African Christians thought of "reform" in terms of greater indigenization, an orientation that rejects foreign models for the church in Africa. The paradox is that missionaries themselves were the foremost advocates of the vernacular principle, whether or not they intended its manifest implications. Some of the earliest protagonists in the struggle for an indigenous Christianity in Nigeria were local Baptists, and their movement was a by-product of the American Civil War. During that war, American missionaries were withdrawn from the Baptist Mission, leaving the work in the hands of local leaders. When these missionaries returned in the 1870s, they found a church that was self-governing, self-propagating, and self-reliant. After more than a decade of protracted negotiations, the missionaries and their African congregations decided to end their relationship. In March 1888, a group of disaffected Africans broke away to form the Native Baptist Church, taking with them all the great African pioneers of the cause in Nigeria. This secession "ushered in a new era of Christianity among the Yoruba. A spell was broken" (Webster 1964:61). In the meantime, growing restiveness among the Niger Delta churches stemmed from attempts by the [Anglican] Church Missionary Society (C.M.S.) to revise the terms of the Niger Mission, which was founded in 1841, and remove Africans from positions of leadership. Bishop Samuel Ajayi Crowther (ca. 1811–1891), a victim of raids by the Fulani Muslim forces and eventually rescued from the slavery into which his Muslim captors sold him, was the dramatic embodiment of the Niger Delta tensions (Ajayi 1969:206–273). In August 1890, following a difficult committee meeting, Bishop Crowther was dismissed from the Niger Mission to which Venn had appointed him as episcopal leader. A meek and mild man, Crowther continued to counsel conciliation right up to the end. However, his African associates and sympathizers felt he had been betrayed, and many of them – though not including his youngest son, Archdeacon Dandeson Crowther (1844–1938) – decided to strike out independently from the C.M.S. On the anniversary of Bishop Crowther's disassociation, a meeting was convened in Lagos to map out a strategy. A resolution was adopted that became the foundation statement of the United Native African Church (U.N.A.C.). It affirmed

> that Africa is to be evangelized and that foreign agencies at work at the present moment taking into consideration climatic and other influences cannot grasp the situation; resolved that a purely Native African Church be founded for the evangelization and amelioration of our race, to be governed by Africans.

(Webster 1964:68)

In making a conjunction between the Christian religious vocation and indigenous ascendancy, the U.N.A.C. had invoked a powerful theme in an environment primed to exploit it. Both the history of Christian mission and the indigenous aspirations it excited made the call for a "native" church inevitable. "Reform" in Christian Africa has, therefore, rested on the vernacular premise – a contrast to the meaning of "reform" in Muslim Africa. One of the most articulate proponents of Christianity as a vernacular movement was Bishop James Johnson (1836–1917), a long-time colleague of Bishop Crowther and a robust figure of his era. He grasped fully the implications of Christianity adopting the vernacular as an extension of Christian life. He commented that

> Christianity is a religion intended for and is suitable for every Race and Tribe of people of the face of the Globe. Acceptance of it was never intended by its Founder to *denationalize any people and it is indeed its glory that every race of people may profess and practise it and imprint upon it its own native characteristics,* giving it a peculiar type among themselves without its losing anything of its virtue. And why should not there be an African Christianity as there has been a European and an Asiatic Christianity?
>
> (cited in Ayandele 1970:304, emphasis added) [3]

[...]

The vernacular in Christian revival

The vernacular principle was the pulse of the "revival" movements that swept across the Niger Delta and Yorubaland in the first decades of the twentieth century. One of the most spectacular of these movements was the Aladura revival of Yorubaland, which occurred between 1928 and 1930. One of its representative figures was the charismatic Joseph Babalọla. The manner of his preparation and call; his appearance when he first emerged as a prophet; and the stress he placed on the spiritual gifts of prayer, healing, and prophecy (what may be considered the golden charismatic triad) made "revival" a tangible, popular force in local Christianity. One account describes the manner of his call as follows:

> Joseph Ayo Babalọla was born in 1904 at Ilofa, a small town just inside Ilorin Province, Northern Nigeria, where his father was Baba Ẹgbẹ of the C.M.S. He attended various schools in Lagos (where a brother was a schoolteacher) and elsewhere, leaving in 1928 with Standard IV [grade 4] to become a steam-roller driver with the P.W.D. [Public Works Department]. He was working on the Ilesha-Akure road in south-western Ekiti when, in October 1928, his roller stopped working, and a voice called his name three times, and told him to leave his work to go and preach the Gospel. There were three palm leaves stuck to the roller; one was dead and dry, one was turning dry, the third fresh and green with life. Towns which heard his gospel were like the third leaf. He was told to take a bell, and was given the message that prayer and *omi iye*, the "water of life", would cure all sickness; all "medicines" should be destroyed.
>
> (Peel 1968:70)

[3] This is a topic dear also to the heart of Dr. Edward Wilmot Blyden. See his magnum opus, *Christianity, Islam, and the Negro Race* (1967 [1887]:164–168), and his work *African Life and Customs* (1908:62–64, 66).

A little earlier than the dramatic experience of Babalọla, another charismatic figure with Creole roots, Abiodun Akinsowon, an eighteen-year-old girl, experienced a trance on Corpus Christi Day (18 June 1925). Her father, a clergyman of the African Church Movement at Porto Novo, Dahomey (now Benin), summoned the help of one Moses Orimolade, a charismatic leader, who enjoined prayer, asking people in the house to clap and call on the Spirit of God to heal Abiodun. People rushed to the place where Abiodun was, and after the spiritual ministrations, she recovered and subsequently joined Orimolade to found a spiritual society, called then the Seraphim Society, with Holy Michael the Archangel adopted by special vision as Patron or Captain of the Society. In 1927 the name of the society was expanded to Cherubim and Seraphim, an indication that the revival leaders were keeping very high company indeed. "All the major doctrinal and ritual developments were sanctioned by vision. Meetings were held in numerous private houses and parlours, as a widening circle of members became adepts in the spiritual activities which Orimolade and Abiodun had initiated" (Peel 1968:73). One active member confessed, "'Prayer was the object. In our [previous mission-founded] churches with their set services there was not sufficient time for us to develop spiritually. When you do a thing you must reap the benefits; what we were taught in church we do not experience in practice. We Africans are so low in everything, but by prayer we may win everlasting power in God's Kingdom. In a word, practical Christianity'" (Peel 1968:73).

> What brought the Seraphim to people's notice more than anything else were the huge anniversary processions, involving thousands of people arrayed in white robes with special uniforms and adornments for different ranks and sections. A contemporary report describes how Moses Orimolade and "energetic assistant Captain Abiodun" sat together in a go-cart under a canopy very similar to that used at Corpus Christi and inscribed with a motto celebrating the power of the Trinity. Twenty-four elders with stars as ornaments on their clothes and long staffs accompanied them, followed by 3,000 members. They made their way to Balogun Square and as the moon appeared the leader "delivered the usual message of Christ and his love".
>
> (Peel 1968:75)

As the membership rapidly increased, the prayer sessions and processions were backed by a support network of Bible study groups, each under a leader. Orimolade acquired the sobriquet Baba Aladura, the "prince of prayer", while the spiritual elite who formed the backbone of the revivalist intercessory meetings was called the Praying Band, Ẹgbẹ Aladura, so important was that exercise in the entire revival atmosphere. The term *aladura* itself is of Arabic derivation, *al-du'a*, meaning invocatory or supplicatory prayer.

Beginning in July 1930, a series of remarkable occurrences in Aladura circles gave the movement a dramatic lurch forward. The numerous unconnected centers experienced an "outbreak" of revival showers, with spontaneous outpourings of charismatic powers and gifts and dramatic instances of personal conversion. The entire religious landscape in Yorubaland and beyond began to stir with the *sturm und drang* of the Aladura cavalcade. In this spiritual upheaval, St. Michael the Archangel "became an appropriate *Balogun*, or war-chief, leader of the Seraphim in their fight for victory over the forces of Satan" (Peel 1968:149). According to a popular teaching of the Christ Apostolic Church – considered an elite among the charismatic churches – prayer, which is the activating force of revival [*isoji* in Yoruba], is likened to gunpowder; and the Holy Spirit, that terror of the invisible enemy, is regarded as the gun, with the Bible as the ramrod. This is perhaps the closest that Christian revival came to the sphere of the sword of the Muslim reformers, though even here the revival theme made the believer both subject and object, agent and target, of the message. One leading convert, for example, spoke of participating in a "tarrying meeting", waiting for the manifestation of the Holy Spirit, when "there was something like a storm and I see that my tongue is changed; since then, ah! (he laughed) – there is a happiness in my life!" (Peel 1968:146). The "sword of truth", the Muslim *sayfal-ḥaqq*, had for Christian revivalists a recoiling effect, for it identified them as the unerring target. To that extent, translatability was itself a consistent force in transferring authority from the culture of the European missionary translator to that of mother-tongue speakers in Africa, with missionaries sooner or later becoming victims of vernacularization.

Summary

This chapter has looked at the contrasting effects of religious expansion in Muslim and Christian Africa by using historical and religious examples. The emphasis in Christianity on vernacular translation fomented mother-tongue aspirations and thus helped to establish the indigenous context for "reform", "renewal", and "revival". The repudiation of non-African standards for religious appropriation is one dramatic effect of the vernacular translations of the scriptures. Consequently, Christian African pioneers came upon fresh boundaries and new forms of identity in vernacular self-understanding. From the earliest epoch, both Coptic and Ethiopian Christianity encouraged religious translation work, which became the main carrier of the sentiments of cultural autonomy, giving the forms of the religion their distinctive national flavor.

In the modern period an identical vernacular emphasis helped to bring into being the prophet movements in sub-Saharan Africa. The followers of these movements adopted the vernacular to embark on far-reaching innovations in church, ritual, and theology, considerably modifying Western forms of the religion while simultaneously introducing adaptations into local forms. What emerged was a fresh synthesis between a scripturally based religion and a newly envisioned African heritage. In the songs, testimonies, rituals, and polities of these new religious movements we encounter Christianity as it descends, at first unwillingly, but finally with gravity, from its chilly Teutonic rehabilitation, caught in the pulsating rhythms of its tropical vernacular expansion.

This chapter also draws a contrast between the effects of Islamic expansion in the nontranslatable Qur'ān and the pressure it brought upon vernacular resources. From the Arabic of scripture, law, and devotion sprang the roots of religious reform in Muslim Africa, guiding the sentiment and course of religious developments and bringing Muslim Africans much closer to the norms and prescriptions of orthodoxy. With the adoption of the Islamic religious calendar based on the lunar year, reform-minded Muslims appealed to the millennial theme to discredit the process of adaptation among their untutored coreligionists. Thus a messianic figure was designated who at the proper time would come to overturn existing practices and inaugurate the age of virtue and rectitude. Such teachings delegitimized the establishment and focused attention on ideas and agents uncompromised by indigenous identity. The idea of religion as a foreign intrusion was elevated to a prescriptive virtue by an appeal to Islam as *the odd man out*, essentially estranged from indigenous compatibility. The impressive gains of Muslims were threatened more by the breach of this rule than by its observance.

Muslims and Christians in Africa understood "reform" and "renewal" in contrasting ways, and such understandings connected with the religious status they gave to indigenization. Clearly, Islam engaged traditional languages and cultures at a point considerably distant from where Christianity encountered them. For Muslims thus oriented, the vernacular was the obstacle that reform overcame, whereas for their Christian counterparts it constituted the irreplaceable frontier of opportunity. The strength of Islam in making excellent capital out of its Arab character in Africa was the weakness of Christianity when Christianity failed to shed its European forms.

And conversely, the strength of Christianity in making vernacular self-understanding and integrity the principle of religious vitality was Islam's weakness in denying to mother tongues the consecrated status of scriptural legitimacy. In their different ways, Muslim and Christian Africans have lived out the truth of these distinctions, although many Western scholars have tripped up badly by treating the two religions in an inverse symmetry, taking Muslim gains as proof of indigenous originality and Christian gains as the lack thereof. What I have suggested in this chapter is the particularity of religious distinctiveness that absolves neither community from the searching critique involved in making claims destined for indigenous adoption.

References

Ajayi, Jacob F. A. (1969). *Christian Missions in Nigeria, 1841–1891: The Making of a New Elite.* Evanston, Illinois: Northwestern University Press.

Ayandele, Emmanuel Ayankanmi (1970). *Holy Johnson: Pioneer of African Nationalism, 1836–1917.* New York: Humanities Press.

Balogun, Ismā'il A. B, ed. and trans. (1975). *The Life and Works of 'Uthmān dan Fodio.* Lagos: Islamic Publications Bureau.

Blyden, Edward Wilmot (1908). *African Life and Customs.* London: C. H. Phillips.

Blyden, Edward Wilmot (1967 [1887]). *Christianity, Islam and the Negro Race.* Edinburgh: Edinburgh University Press.

Butler, A. J. (1884). *The Ancient Coptic Churches of Egypt.* Oxford: Oxford University Press.

Davis, Asa J. (1967). The Orthodoxy of the Ethiopian Church. *Tarikh* 2(1):62–69 and 458, 459, 455, 470, 472, 474, 478, 481, 482.

Eusebius (1984 [1965]). *History of the Church.* New York: Pengiun.

Frend, W. H. C. (1984). *The Rise of Christianity.* Philadelphia, Fortress Press.

Fūdī, 'Abdallāh B. (1963). *Tazyīn al-Waraqāt.* Mervyn Hiskett, ed. and trans. Ibadan: Ibadan University Press.

Gibb, Hamilton A. R. (1974 [1963]). *Arabic Literature: An Introduction,* 2nd ed. London: Oxford University Press.

Guilluame, Alfred (1962 [1956]). *Islam,* 2nd ed. New York: Penguin.

Haafkens, Johannes (1983). *Les chants musulmans en Peul.* Leiden: E. J. Brill.

Hiskett, Mervyn (1962). An Islamic Tradition of Reform in the Western Sudan from the Sixteenth to the Eighteenth Century. *Bulletin of the School of Oriental and African Studies* 25(3):577–596.

Hiskett, Mervyn, ed. and trans. (1963). *Tazyīn al-Waraqāt*. By ʿAbdallāh B. Fūdī. Ibadan: Ibadan University Press.

Hiskett, Mervyn (1973). *The Sword of Truth: The Life and Times of Shehu Usuman Dan Fodio*. New York: Oxford University Press.

Hiskett, Mervyn (1975). *A History of Hausa Islamic Verse*. London: School of Oriental and African Studies.

Hiskett, Mervyn (1984). *The Development of Islam in West Africa*. New York: Longman.

Hunwick, John (1985). *Sharīʿa in Songhay: The Replies of al-Maghīlī to the Questions of Askia al-Hājj Muhammad*. London: Oxford University Press.

Knight, W. (1880). *The Missionary Secretariat of Henry Venn*. London: Longman, Green.

Latourette, Kenneth Scott (1975). *A History of Christianity*, Volume 1, 2nd ed. New York: Harper & Row.

Lewis, Ian M. (1983). The Past and Present in Islam: The Case of African "Survivals". *Temerios: Studies in Comparative Religion* [Helsinki] 19:55–67.

Ogharaerumi, Mark Onesosan (1986). The Translation of the Bible into Yoruba, Igbo, and Isekiri Languages of Nigeria, with Special Reference to the Contributions of Mother Tongue Speakers. Ph.D. dissertation, University of Aberdeen.

Peel, John D. Y. (1968). *Aladura: A Religious Movement among the Yoruba*. London: Oxford University Press for the International African Institute.

Ryan, Patrick J. (1978). *Imale, Yoruba Participation in the Muslim Tradition: A Study of Clerical Piety*. Missoula, Montana: Scholars Press.

Sanneh, Lamin (1976). The Origins of Clericalism in West African Islam. *Journal of African History* 17(1):49–72.

Sanneh, Lamin (1989a[1979]). *The Jakhanke Muslim Clerics: A Religious and Historical Study of Islam in Senegambia*. Lanham, Maryland: University Press of America.

Sanneh, Lamin (1989b). *Translating the Message: The Missionary Impact on Culture*. Maryknoll, New York: Orbis.

Schacht, Joseph and C. E. Bosworth, eds. (1974). *The Legacy of Islam*, 2nd ed. Oxford: Clarendon.

Tamrat, Taddesse (1972). *Church and State in Ethiopia 1270–1527*. Oxford: Clarendon.

Tasie, Godwin M. (1978). *Christian Missionary Enterprise in the Niger Delta: 1864–1918*. Studies on Religion in Africa 3. Leiden: E. J. Brill.

Von Grunebaum, G. E. (1962). Pluralism in the Islamic World. *Islamic Studies* 1(2):37–59.

Von Harnack, Adolf (1905). *The Mission and Expansion of Christianity in the First Three Centuries*, 2 vols. New York: G. P. Putnam's Sons.

Walls, Andrew F. (1981). The Gospel as the Prisoner and Liberator of Culture. *Faith and Thought* 108(1–2):39–52.

Warren, Max, ed. (1971). *To Apply the Gospel: Selections from the Writings of Henry Venn.* Grand Rapids, Michigan: William B. Eerdman's Publishing Company.

Webster, James (1964). *African Churches among the Yoruba: 1888–1922.* Oxford: Clarendon.

Acknowledgements

Grateful acknowledgement is made to the following sources for permission to reproduce material in this book:

Texts

Walker, A. (1997) 'Thoroughly modern: sociological reflections on the charismatic movement from the end of the twentieth century', in S. Hunt *et al.* (eds) *Charismatic Christianity: Sociological Perspectives*, Palgrave Publishers Ltd. By permission of Macmillan Press Ltd. Selection and editorial matter © Stephen Hunt, Malcolm Halmilton and Tony Walter 1977. Chapters 1–10 © Macmillan Press Ltd 1977.

Smith, C. *et al.* (1998) 'Evangelicalism embattled', *American Evangelicalism Embattled and Thriving*, University of Chicago Press.

Martin, D. (1990) 'The argument summarized and extended', *Tongues of Fire*, Basil Blackwell Ltd.

Métraux, D. (2000) 'The expansion of the Soka Gakkai into Southeast Asia', in D. Machacek *et al.* (eds) *Global Citizens: The Soka Gakkai Buddhist Movement in the World*, Oxford University Press.

King, J. (1977) 'Tablighi Jamaat and the Deobandi mosques in Britain', in S. Vertovec and C. Peach (eds) *Islam in Europe: The Politics of Religion and Community*. By permission of Macmillan Press Ltd. © Macmillan Press Ltd 1977.

Sanneh, L. (1994) 'Translatability in Islam and in Christianity in Africa: a thematic approach', in T.D. Blakely *et al.* (eds) *Religion in Africa: Experience and Expression*, James Currey Publishers, London and Heinemann, Portsmouth, NH, USA.

Every effort has been made to trace all the copyright owners, but if any has been inadvertently overlooked, the publishers will be pleased to make the necessary arrangements at the first opportunity.

Index

KING ALFRED'S COLLEGE
LIBRARY